Conservative Juda...
Our Ancestors to Our Descendants

By Elliot N. Dorff

United Synagogue of Conservative Judaism
Department of Youth Activities

T0068605

UNITED SYNAGOGUE OF CONSERVATIVE JUDAISM
DEPARTMENT OF YOUTH ACTIVITIES

Jules A. Gutin, *Director*
Gila R. Hadani, *Assistant Director*
Ari Y. Goldberg, *Assistant Director for Education*
Marsha B. Goldwasser, *Activities Coordinator*
Nadine R. Greenfield, *Projects Coordinator*
Marc L. Stober, *Publications Coordinator*
Dovi Paritsky, *Central Shaliach*
Yitzchak Jacobsen, *Director, Israel Office*
David Keren, *Nativ Director*

CENTRAL YOUTH COMMISSION

Marshall Baltuch, *Chairman*
Jonathan S. Greenberg, *Education Committee Chairman*

UNITED SYNAGOGUE OF CONSERVATIVE JUDAISM

Alan Ades, *President*
Rabbi Jerome M. Epstein, *Executive Vice-President*

A publication of the National Youth Commission,
United Synagogue of Conservative Judaism
155 Fifth Avenue, New York, New York 10010
Revised Edition, 1996

Manufactured in the United States of America.

Cover photograph courtesy of Rabbi Elliot Dorff
Photo reproduction by Mr. Jules Porter

In memory of my parents

Sol and Anne Dorff

and in honor of Marlynn's parents

Manuel and Barbara Wertheimer

Who were and are among the most informed

and active of Conservative Jews

and the most dedicated and

loving of parents

Rabbi Gamliel, the son of Rabbi Judah, the President, said:...All who exert themselves in the interest of the community should do so for the sake of Heaven, for then the virtue of their ancestors sustains them and the Patriarchs' righteousness will be passed on to their descendants forever... [Avot 2:2]

רבן גמליאל בנו של רבי יהודה הנשיא אומר. . .וכל העוסקים עם הצבור יהיו עוסקים עמהם לשם שמים.
שזכות אבותם מסיעתן וצדקתם עומדת לעד. . .

ACKNOWLEDGMENTS

The editor expresses appreciation to the following publishers who have kindly granted permission to reprint selections from the following material:

THE AMERICAN JEWISH COMMITTEE, New York: *The Condition of Jewish Belief: A Symposium, Compiled by the Editors of Commentary Magazine,* Reprinted by permission; copyright © 1966 by the American Jewish Committee.

THE AMERICAN JEWISH COMMITTEE, New York: *Commentary,* Vol. 102, No. 2 (August 1996).

THE AMERICAN JEWISH CONGRESS AND WORLD JEWISH CONGRESS, New York: *Judaism,* Vol. 26, No. I (Winter 1967).

BEHRMAN HOUSE, INC., PUBLISHERS, New York: *A Jewish Theology,* Louis Jacobs, 1973.

BLOCH PUBLISHING COMPANY, New York: *A Faith for Moderns,* Robert Gordis, 1960.

BEN ZION BOKSER, New York: *Judaism: Profile of a Faith* [The Burning Bush Press, 1963].

THE BURNING BUSH PRESS, New York: *Seminary Addresses and Other Papers,* Solomon Schechter, 1959. Prepared for publication by the National Academy for Adult Jewish Studies of the United Synagogue of America, copyright by the Burning Bush Press. Reprinted by permission.

CENTRAL CONFERENCE OF AMERICAN RABBIS, New York: "Reform Judaism: A Centenary Perspective," June, 1976.

Excerpted with permission of Farrar, Straus & Giroux, Inc. from *God in Search of Man* by Abraham Joshua Heschel, Copyright © 1955 by Abraham Joshua Heschel.

An excerpt from "A Declaration of Conscience" from *The Insecurity of Freedom* by Abraham Joshua Heschel, Copyright © 1964 by Abraham Joshua Heschel. Reprinted with the permission of Farrar, Straus & Giroux, Inc.

THE JEWISH PUBLICATION SOCIETY OF AMERICA, Philadelphia:
Solomon Schechter: A Biography, Norman Bentwich, 1938.
Studies in Judaism, Solomon Schechter, 1958.
The Prophets, Abraham Joshua Heschel, 1962.
The Emergence of Conservative Judaism, Moshe Davis, 1963.

THE JEWISH THEOLOGICAL SEMINARY OF AMERICA, New York: *The Halakhic Process: A Systematic Analysis*, Joel Roth, 1986.

THE JEWISH THEOLOGICAL SEMINARY OF AMERICA, THE RABBINICAL ASSEMBLY, UNITED SYNAGOGUE OF AMERICA, WOMEN'S LEAGUE FOR CONSERVATIVE JUDAISM, FEDERATION OF JEWISH MEN'S CLUBS, New York: *Emet Ve-Emunah: Statement of Principles of Conservative Judaism*, 1988.

THE JEWISH THEOLOGICAL SEMINARY OF AMERICA, THE RABBINICAL ASSEMBLY, UNITED SYNAGOGUE OF AMERICA, New York: *Willing, Learning and Striving: A Course Guide for Teaching Jewish Youth Based on Emet Ve-Emunah*, Steven M. Brown, 1988.

KTAV PUBLISHING HOUSE, INC., New York: *Law and Theology in Judaism*, David Novak,1974 (Series I); 1976 (Series II).

JAKOB J. PETUCHOWSKI, Cincinnati: *Ever Since Sinai* [Scribe Publications, 1961].

Reprinted by permission of THE RABBINICAL ASSEMBLY, New York: *Tradition and Change: The Development of Conservative Judaism*, Mordecai Waxman, ed., 1958.

Reprinted by permission of THE RABBINICAL ASSEMBLY and THE JEWISH THEOLOGICAL SEMINARY OF AMERICA, New York: *Conservative Judaism*, Vol. XXVIII, No. 4 (Summer, 1974); Vol. XXX, No. 1 (Fall, 1975); Vol. XXXI, Nos. 1-2 (Fall-Winter, 1976-1977).

RECONSTRUCTIONIST PRESS, New York: *Questions Jews Ask: Reconstructionist Answers*, Mordecai M. Kaplan, 1956.

THE WESTMINSTER PRESS, Philadelphia:
A New Jewish Theology in the Making, Eugene Borowitz, 1968.
How Can a Jew Speak of faith Today?, Eugene Borowitz, 1969.

WORLD UNION FOR PROGRESSIVE JUDAISM, LTD., New York:
The Rise of Reform Judaism, W. Gunther Plaut, 1963.
The Growth of Reforrn Judaism, W. Gunther Plaut, 1965.

The "Flow Chart of Halakhah," on page 276, was designed by Robert Gamer.

"...*He who repeats something in the name of him who said it brings deliverance to the world...*" (*Avot 6:6*)

‏. . . כל האומר דבר בשם אומרו מביא גאולה לעולם.‏

TABLE OF CONTENTS

Editor's Preface to First Edition..1

Editors Preface to the Revised Edition...2

Preface to First Edition..3

Preface to the Revised Edition..5

Chapter I: First Thoughts About Conservative Judaism..7

Chapter II: The Development and Structure of Conservative Judaism................................9

    A. The Development of Conservative Judaism...9

        1. The Emancipation Brings Freedom and Assimilation..9
        2. Orthodox and Reform Attempts to Combat Assimilation in Europe.....................11
        3. The Pittsburgh Platform, The Russian Immigration,
        and the Emergence of the Conservative Movement
        in the United States..12
        4. The Ideological Stance of Early Conservative Judaism:
        Positive-Historical Judaism and Catholic Israel..17
        5. Conservative Judaism in the Twentieth Century..30
        6. The Builders of the Conservative Movement..39

    B. The Structure of the Conservative Movement..43

        1. The Academic Centers of the Conservative Movement......................................44
        2. The Professional Organizations of the Conservative Movement.........................45
        3. The Lay Organizations of the Conservative Movement......................................45
        4. "Joint Commissions"..47

Chapter III: Jewish Law Within the Conservative Movement..49

    A. The General Approach of Conservative Judaism to Jewish Law:
    Tradition and Change..49

    B. The Historical Development of Jewish Law..53

        1. The Formation and Writing of the Oral Law: 444 B.C.E. - 200 C.E....................53
        Time Line of Jewish Law..54
        2. The Period of the Amora'im and the Talmud: 200 - 500 C.E.............................60
        3. The Periods of the Sabora'im and Geonim: 500 - 1050 C.E.............................62
        4. The Commentators, Posekim, Rishonim, & Synods: 1000 - 1550 C.E................64
        5. The Aharonim: 1550 C.E. - Present..67

    C. Tradition and Change in Rabbinic Literature...69

        1. The Substitution of Interpretation of the Torah for Prophecy.............................69
        2. Retaining Coherence in the Law..77
        3. Affirming the Divine Authority of the Law..85
        4. The Significance of the Law to the Jewish People..91

    D. The Question of Authority: Orthodox, Reform, and
    Four Conservative Theories of Revelation...101

        1. Orthodox..101
        2. Conservative I...104
        3. Conservative II..111
        4. Conservative III...117

    5. Conservative IV (=Reconstructionist Tendency)................................139
    6. Reform..144
  E. Living Jewish Law as a Conservative Jew...151
    1. The Communal Nature of Jewish Law Within the Conservative Movement............152
    2. The Grounds Which the Conservative Movement Recognizes for Changes in Jewish Law..162
    3. Educating and Guiding Conservative Jews in Fulfilling the Mitzvot........165
    4. Making Conservative Judaism Significant in Your Life......................166

Chapter IV: The Beliefs of the Conservative Movement..................................193
  A. The Interaction of Action and Belief..193
  B. The Core of Conservative Beliefs...198
  C. The Types of Theology Within the Conservative Movement....................208
  D. The People Israel..211
  E. Zionism and Israel..215
  F. Judaism as a Religious Civilization...221

Chapter V: Conservative Judaism: Looking Ahead......................................225
  A. Facing the Future: Particular Points to Ponder.................................226
    1. Assimilation..227
    2. Intermarriage...228
    3. Synagogue 2000 and Beyond...230
    4. Jewish Education...232
    5. Men and Women...235
    6. Pluralism Within Our Movement..237
    7. Relating With the Other Movements in Judaism and With Non-Jews.....238
    8. Israel..241
    9. Conservative Jewish Ritual Practice...242
    10. Moral Issues Facing the Conservative Movement.........................247
  B. Envisioning the Future of Conservative Judaism...............................248

Endnotes...253

Appendix I: The Menu of the "Trefah Banquet"..269

Appendix II: The Pittsburgh Platform (1885) - Reform................................270

Appendix III: Charter of The Jewish Theological Seminary of America.........272

Appendix IV: Preamble of the Constitution of the United Synagogue.............273

Appendix V: The Structure of the Mishnah..274

Flow Chart of Halakhah...276

For Further Reading...277

Guide to Hebrew Names for Books of the Bible

Bereshit = Genesis

Shemot = Exodus

Vayikra = Leviticus

Bamidbar = Numbers

Devarim = Deuteronomy

Shoftim = Judges

Melakhim = Kings

Tehillim = Psalms

Mishlei = Proverbs

Shir HaShirim = Song of Songs

Eikhah = Lamentations

Kohelet = Ecclesiastes

EDITOR'S PREFACE TO FIRST EDITION

The choice of Conservative Judaism as the theme of this sourcebook was prompted by necessity. All too many of our members have only a vague understanding -- or often, misunderstanding -- of the Movement. They often think that one "graduates" from one movement in Judaism to another by becoming more "religious." That is not true. As explained through the entire sourcebook, there are essential differences among the movements and the decision to affiliate with any of them should be based on the tenets and philosophies it reflects. The decision to be part of one movement and not another must be based not on how observant one is, but rather on how one is observant.

United Synagogue Youth is especially proud to have Dr. Elliot Dorff as author of this book. He has long combined his scholarship with a concern for educating Jewish youth, and we are fortunate to benefit from his knowledge and devotion. This text has also been enriched by advice from those who read the original manuscript and whom we thank: Jules Gutin, Irving Hellman, Miriam Shapiro, and Rabbis Paul Freedman, Neil Gillman, Marvin Goodman, Robert Gordis, William Horn, Benjamin Z. Kreitman, David Novak and Bernard Raskas.

Finally, in many ways the famous statement of the sage Hillel parallels the need for studying our theme.

If I am not for myself, who will be for me: we, in the Conservative Movement, must be familiar with the development and beliefs of our movement;

But if I am only for myself, what am I: comparisons with other movements are offered only to clarify our own positions, not to minimize the importance of other approaches;

And if not now, when?: with the many challenges and options currently available to our constituency, the continued growth and development of the Conservative Movement demands our turning to this theme, now.

S. G.
Fall 1977

EDITOR'S PREFACE TO THE REVISED EDITION

Shortly before this volume was sent to the printer, the Ratner Center for Conservative Judaism published Conservative Synagogues and Their Members: Highlights of the North American Survey of 1995-96. The statistical results of this survey are certain to be the basis for a great deal of discussion about the strengths and weaknesses of the Conservative Movement. It was reassuring to learn that "most members of Conservative synagogues today have developed a more positive and less apologetic attitude toward [Conservative Judaism]. They are genuinely attracted to Conservatism." Furthermore, 62% of the survey's respondents agreed with the statement that Conservative Jews are obligated to observe halakhah (Jewish law). On the other hand, the survey illustrates numerous areas in which the majority of Conservative Jews do not uphold the practices and philosophies of the Conservative Movement.

How can we come to understand this contradiction? Clearly there is no one unequivocal answer to this question. However, an important starting point is to take an honest and in-depth look at the history and ideology of our Movement.

Since its initial publication almost twenty years ago, Conservative Judaism: Our Ancestors to Our Descendants has become one of the classic works among the myriad books which have been written in an attempt to educate Jews about the Conservative Movement. However, the rapid and significant change within the Conservative Movement since this book's debut has made it a necessity to issue an updated and revised edition.

We are pleased and honored that Rabbi Elliot Dorff agreed to take on the task of revising his work. Readers who are familiar with the initial edition of this sourcebook will note that the revisions go beyond aesthetics. The final two chapters have been rewritten, to represent the new dynamic of the Movement in the 1990's. In addition, significant changes were made in other sections. This new edition takes an open and honest look at the past, present, and future of our Movement, and gives us the tools with which to better understand Conservative Judaism.

Once again, tremendous thanks are due to my wife, Stacy, for all her love and support of the work that I do. In addition, I hope the late night "clicking" of computer keyboard keys was not a disturbance to my daughter, Rina Chana. A peek into her crib was always the perfect cure when my eyes would get drowsy from staring too long at a computer screen.

Ari Y. Goldberg
November 1996

PREFACE TO FIRST EDITION

In some ways, writing this sourcebook was a sheer act of nerve. Conservative Judaism, after all, is a very complex phenomenon. It means many different things to people. How could I presume to tell anyone else how to conceive of it?

And yet, I wrote this. I wrote it because I strongly believe that Conservative Judaism is Judaism at its best, that it is the most historically authentic form of Judaism and that it holds the greatest promise for the future. I wrote it because many people, including a number who have identified with the Conservative Movement all their lives, know very little about it. I wrote it also because we in the Conservative Movement have been all too timid in explaining our position and arguing for it. If we are interpreting Judaism correctly, then let us say so, clearly, intelligently, and passionately!

This is not, however, simply an advertisement for the Movement. It is written with a clear view of the high standards of intellectual honesty that have characterized the Movement from the outset. Consequently, these pages record the problems within the Movement as well as its strengths in hope that a frank and open discussion of them will ultimately lead to solutions. Moreover, I have tried to take careful note of the areas in which there is diversity of opinion among those affiliated with Conservative Judaism, explaining the various positions and the reasons for them. It would be both misleading and counter-productive to pretend that all Conservative Jews agree on everything. We do agree about a great many things, but we disagree about others, and the openness and pluralism of our Movement is one of its greatest strengths.

Rabbi Stephen Garfinkel has been the major architect of this project. It was he who prodded me into undertaking it, and he guided it all along the way. I am sincerely grateful to him for the care, time, and talent that he invested in it. Rabbi Moshe Rothblum convinced me to accept this assignment: it has been an important, instructive, and joyful experience for me, as he predicted – but if you do not like it, blame him! I would also like to thank the readers of all or part of the first draft of this book for their helpful suggestions and kind words, including Dr. Joel Rembaum and especially Dr. Neil Gillman, whose trenchant comments were the occasion for some of the most stimulating philosophic discussions that I have had in a long time. Mrs. Nellie Brunswick, Mrs. Beth Leebolt, and Mrs. Sophie Gross painstakingly typed the manuscript from my incomprehensible scrawl; I would like to thank them and the University of Judaism for making their time available to me. My wife, Marlynn, has been the good source of suggestions and encouragement that she always is. And finally, I would like to thank my teachers at Camp Ramah and the Seminary, who got me interested in Conservative Judaism in the first place and sustained my interest through their intellectual rigor and personal good sense. If this project succeeds in its task, it will be largely due to them.

Elliot N. Dorff
University of Judaism
Los Angeles, California
October 18, 1977

PREFACE TO THE REVISED EDITION

Much has happened within the Conservative Movement in the nineteen years since I wrote the first edition of this book. Women have taken on new roles in synagogue services and governance, they have assumed the responsibilities of leadership in a number of our institutions, and some have been ordained as rabbis. A Commission on the Philosophy of the Conservative Movement was convened between 1985 and 1988, and it produced the first official statement of the philosophy of Conservative Judaism. The United Synagogue of Conservative Judaism and the Rabbinical Assembly have established a Joint Committee on Commitment and Observance, which has created important programs to enhance the level of Jewish practice among Conservative Jews. The United Synagogue of Conservative Judaism has established a Commission on Intermarriage to suggest ways to prevent intermarriage and to respond to it when it does occur. From 1992 to 1994, the Rabbinical Assembly's Commission on Human Sexuality produced its Rabbinic Letter on Intimate Relations, which will probably be the first of a number of rabbinic letters on important social and moral issues so that the philosophy of the Conservative Movement can have direct and explicit effect on concrete issues in our personal and social lives. These are just some of the many new, significant programs which institutions of the Conservative Movement have developed in the intervening years in North and South America, Israel, Europe, and even in the countries of the former Soviet bloc.

While some individuals within the Conservative Movement had already formed the Reconstructionist Rabbinical College in 1968, when I wrote the first edition of this book in 1977, most Reconstructionists at that time still considered themselves to be part of the Conservative Movement; now that is no longer the case. Other individuals within the Movement left its ranks over the issue of ordaining women as rabbis. These defections from the Movement were both painful, but they were small in number and have left the broad center of the Movement more coherent.

In the meantime, the demographics of the Jewish community which the Conservative Movement serves have changed radically. Fully fifty percent of American Jewry and eighty percent of Israeli Jewry are not affiliated with any synagogue, and fifty percent of all marriages involving Jews in North America are intermarriages. Because Jews go to college and graduate school in very high percentages, they commonly postpone marriage and having children until their late twenties or thirties and then suffer from the problems of infertility in far higher percentages than the rest of the population. For that and other reasons, we suffer from low reproductive rates. These factors have required the Conservative Movement to formulate policies on intermarried Jews and their children and to create programs to encourage in-marriage and conversion of non-Jewish spouses of Jews, and the Jewish community as a whole and the Conservative Movement in particular have been challenged to create dynamic, new ways to assure Jewish continuity. In light of its centrist stance and its dual commitment to tradition and modernity, the Conservative Movement is uniquely situated to be a key player in the effort to show Jews the meaningfulness, the intelligence, and the spirituality of Judaism.

It is, then, a remarkably new world in which this second edition is written, for Jewry as a whole and for Conservative Judaism in particular. The history of the Movement now includes new developments, and the institutions of the Conservative Movement have taken on new shapes and sizes. The problems which we face now and the opportunities we have are, in some ways, the same as they were nineteen years ago, but in some ways they have changed substantially in either degree or kind. Through it all, I am convinced that Conservative Judaism remains the most intelligent, mature, personally meaningful, and authentic form of Judaism. It is the one which has the most potential to bring the riches of our heritage to bear on our lives in the present and future so that we can, with the help of Judaism, make our lives meaningful and, indeed, holy.

For this edition, I would like to thank Mr. Ari Goldberg, who suggested writing this revised edition to me in the first place and who has skillfully and gracefully shepherded it through the process of copyediting and publication. I would also like to thank the readers: Jonathan Draluck, Rabbi Jerome M. Epstein, Jonathan S. Greenberg, Jack Gruenberg, Jules A. Gutin, Gila R. Hadani, and Cheryl Magen for their supportive comments and good suggestions; this book is all the better for their careful reading and valuable reactions. I would also like to thank Mr. Jules Porter of Jules Porter Photographers in Los Angeles, a wonderful friend and past international president of the Federation of Jewish Men's Clubs, who found a way to reproduce an old picture of my mother's parents for the cover. (To answer a question I am often asked, no, the people on the cover of the first edition are not my grandparents -- I frankly do not know who they are – but the people on the cover of this edition are indeed my grandparents!) Finally, I would like to thank my wife, Marlynn, the love of my life for these past thirty years, who has contributed immensely to Conservative Judaism through her own work in Jewish education and who has helped me understand many aspects of Conservative Judaism in practice as we have watched it make our lives and those of many others more meaningful, more morally sensitive, more beautiful, and more imbued with a sense of God and the holy.

Elliot N. Dorff
University of Judaism
Los Angeles, California
August, 1996

CHAPTER I:
FIRST THOUGHTS ABOUT CONSERVATIVE JUDAISM

Sometimes it is easier to learn something new if you have never heard about it before. It may be hard to think about something that you have never experienced, but at least then you have not formed any wrong ideas or prejudices which you now have to correct.

ACTIVITY:

Write a 5-7 sentence statement on what it means to be a Conservative Jew. Discuss your answer with a partner, and ask each other questions to clarify the meanings. As you read through this sourcebook, think about how your statement agrees with, or differs from, the material which you are studying.

This sourcebook is about Conservative Judaism. You probably have had considerable experience with Conservative Judaism. All of that experience will help you understand the material that you are about to read. As you read it, you will be able to think about the Conservative synagogues, youth groups, schools, and camps in which you have participated for several examples of how the ideas presented here take concrete form. On the other hand, your experience may make it difficult for you to understand some parts of this sourcebook because you have come to identify Conservative Judaism with the particular experiences that you have already had. The Conservative Movement does have a specific way of thinking about Judaism, but there are many ways in which its approach can be expressed. In fact, part of the goal of this sourcebook is to help you understand why the Conservative institutions do what they do, and to show you how and why other groups affiliated with the Conservative

Movement do things differently. After studying the materials in this sourcebook, you will hopefully understand both the unity and diversity of the Conservative Movement.

In order to begin that process, perhaps it would be good to consider your own experiences with Conservative Judaism and your present understanding of what it stands for. The following questions will help you do that.

QUESTIONS:

1) Do you attend services in a Conservative synagogue? If so, describe them.

    Have you participated in services in more than one Conservative synagogue? Were there any differences? If so, how do you explain them?

    Have you ever attended services at a synagogue of another Movement? What principal differences did you notice?

2) Did you study at a Conservative religious school? If so, what subjects did you study there? Was there anything special about the way they were presented?

    What parts of Judaism do you think the school was trying hardest to teach you? Do you have any idea why it concentrated on those elements rather than others?

    (Note: If you have ever studied at a Reform or an Orthodox school, or if you know anybody who has, it may be helpful to contrast their experience with yours in answering these questions.)

3) Have you been part of a number of USY activities? Have you attended Camp Ramah? In what ways are those experiences similar to, and in what ways were they different from, the experiences you have had in Conservative synagogues and schools?

    How do your youth group and camp experiences broaden your understanding of the nature of Conservative Judaism?

CHAPTER II:
THE DEVELOPMENT AND STRUCTURE OF
CONSERVATIVE JUDAISM

Try to remember the first time that you met one of your friends. How did you get to know him or her? Do you remember your first conversations? If you were doing something together, then you probably talked about that. Or maybe you both knew someone else, and so you talked about how you knew that person. Or perhaps you talked about things that you like to do. In any case, before the friendship continued very far, you probably got to know where your friend lives, who the members of her or his family are, and what they are like. As you got to know your friend better, you probably learned more and more about past events in his or her life as you shared more and more of your own experiences and had new ones together.

Getting to know a movement is much the same thing. You have to learn something about where it comes from, the members of its family, and how it conducts its business. Once you know that, you can begin to ask about its inner life – that is, the ideas that motivate it and give it direction, and the hopes that it has for the future. Consequently in this chapter we will briefly consider how the Conservative Movement came to be and how it functions, and then, in the succeeding chapters, we will turn to the ideas which define it and shape its program for the future.

A. *The Development of Conservative Judaism*

The late Professor Alexander Marx used to say that Jewish history since 1800 is really current events.[1] In a sense he was right because the problems of self-definition and self-understanding that Jews faced then are almost the same as they face now.

1. The Emancipation Brings Freedom and Assimilation

By 1800 C.E. Jews in parts of Western Europe (e. g., France, Holland, and England to a certain extent) had generally been allowed to study at the universities, enter the professions and government, and develop freely as Jews, just as we can today in the Free World. That was a major change from the ghettos and persecutions that characterized Jewish life before that time, and Jews welcomed the changes. In fact, the period of Jewish history from about 1760 C.E. to 1800 C.E. is called "The Emancipation" -- that is, the period in which Jews in central and western European countries were freed from the restrictions which had been placed upon them and became full citizens of the countries in which they lived.

The Emancipation was not an unmixed blessing, however. As Jews took advantage of their new freedoms and opportunities, they increasingly considered themselves not only Jews, but also citizens of Germany, France, or England. This created a new problem for them: how were they to identify both as Jews and as citizens of the modern, secular, Western world since they were no longer permitted to govern themselves by Jewish law? After all, as Jews they were supposed to observe the dietary laws and the Sabbath, but how could they do that if being successful in business required eating at all sorts of restaurants with both Jewish and non-Jewish customers and keeping the business open on Saturday? And how could you become a lawyer or doctor and still remain Jewish if you had to attend classes in law school or medical school on Saturday and other Jewish holy days? Aside from those specific problems, Jews found that non-Jews were willing to do business with them and treat them as equals only if they forgot about their Jewishness (or at least hid it) and acted like any other German, French, or English citizen.

Under these circumstances, many Jews assimilated. They considered it impossible to be both Jews and full citizens of the modern world, and since they were afraid or unwilling to compromise their new freedoms, they abandoned their Jewish identity.

ACTIVITY:

List ways in which your identity as a Jew and your identity as a citizen of the country in which you live may sometimes conflict? (E.g. "the Christmas problem," Friday night sporting events, your allegiance to the State of Israel, etc.)

How did (do) you resolve the problem? How do some of your friends deal with it?

(Do you understand now what Professor Marx meant in saying that the problems that Jews faced in Western Europe in the early 1800s are the same that we face today?)

_____

_____

_____

_____

_____

_____

2. Orthodox and Reform Attempts to Combat Assimilation in Europe

Those who fought against this assimilation in Europe did so in two different ways, called "Reform" and "Neo-Orthodox."

It is important to understand that the Reform Movement did not arise as a reaction to Orthodoxy: it was rather a response to the assimilation resulting from the Emancipation. In trying to capture the hearts and minds of those Jews who were giving up their Jewish identity, the Reformers admitted openly that observing Jewish law made it hard to be both a Jew and a person of the modern world. They went further: they claimed that observing some of the laws was actually harmful because some rituals prevented Jews from creating relationships with non-Jews, and some were intellectually misleading or aesthetically offensive. But if Jews gave up their observance of the ritual laws, they could still maintain their Jewish identity because those laws were not binding anyway, according to the Reformers' interpretation of Jewish history. All post-biblical law was made by human beings who intended it to have authority only during their time period.

Of the laws in the Bible, only the moral norms continued to be binding because the Prophets canceled the authority of the ritual laws, according to the Reform interpretation of their writings. Consequently, to be a Jew you did not have to observe Jewish ritual law, which made life as a Jew in the modern world so difficult. You simply had to go back to the religion of the Prophets (as the Reformers understood them), and that consisted exclusively of morality and belief in God. All developments in Judaism since the prophetic period were temporary adjustments to the times and thus irrelevant to the maintenance of pristine, prophetic Judaism. This would solve the problems that Jews had with the ritual laws, and it also would eliminate the conflict that Jews felt between their Jewish identity and their identity as citizens of the countries in which they lived. There need be no such conflict because Judaism, according to the Reformers, was a religion and not a nationality. Thus, to be a Jew you only had to believe in God and morality, which most modern, intelligent people of the nineteenth century believed in anyway.

A second group, the "Neo-Orthodox," was founded in reaction to the Reform ideology. It was "Orthodox" because it claimed that Jews continued to be obligated to observe all of Jewish law; it was "Neo-Orthodox" (that is, a new form of Orthodoxy) because it claimed that Jews were permitted to learn secular culture and participate in the non-Jewish world. That permission, however, came with a strong condition attached to it: since Western culture was the product of human beings and Judaism was the will of God, Jews should take advantage of their new freedoms only to the extent that they did not conflict with the Torah or disobey God's law.

Human beings dared not change God's law because they would then be putting themselves above God. They would also be endangering the future of Judaism, because as soon as you allow one change to be made, there is no way to prevent other changes, and so eventually Judaism would become unrecognizable and worthless. Moreover, Jews did not need to change Jewish law in order to live in the modern world. In fact, as the Neo-Orthodox saw it, the only reason why so many Jews were assimilating was because they did not know enough about their Judaism. Consequently the major efforts of the Neo-Orthodox to combat assimilation were concentrated in creating schools to teach Judaism to both children and adults. Thus while the Reformers changed the nature of Judaism in order to combat assimilation, the Neo-Orthodox tried to change the nature of Jews.

QUESTIONS:

1)   What was causing the widespread assimilation in Europe of the 1800's according to the Neo-Orthodox understanding of the situation? How, then, did the Neo-Orthodox leaders respond to it? Answer the same questions for the Reformers.

2)   The Orthodox and Reform programs of action were based on different interpretations of where Jewish law came from and what part of it was still binding upon us. Explain their views on those subjects, and show how their positions on those issues influenced their suggestions for action.

3)   List the strengths of the Reform position? The weaknesses? Do the same for the Orthodox approach.

3. The Pittsburgh Platform, The Russian Immigration, and the Emergence of the Conservative Movement in the United States

There were very few Orthodox Jews in the United States before 1880 C.E. since almost all of the Jews living here were Reform in orientation. In fact, in that year only 12 of the 200 synagogues in America identified themselves as something other than Reform.[2]

Two things happened in the years immediately following to alter this picture: the Reform Movement changed, and the number and nature of the American Jewish population changed. As for the first, the Reform Movement took two steps which clarified its position and made

12

it impossible for more moderate reformers to continue their association with that movement. The first of these was the famous (or infamous) "Trefah Banquet." Under Rabbi Isaac Mayer Wise, the dominant figure in the early American Reform Movement, those who wanted to create a distinctly American and liberal form of Judaism had founded the Hebrew Union College in 1875 for the training of rabbis. In 1883 the first class of rabbis was to graduate and a banquet was planned at an exclusive restaurant in Cincinnati, where the school was located. In order not to offend the more traditional members of the group the meal was supposed to be kosher. When clams were served for the first course, the traditionalists immediately stood up and stormed out of the room in protest. Some historians claim that this was not simply a mistake or an oversight, but rather a deliberate attempt by Isaac Mayer Wise to drive the more traditional members out of the Reform camp so that he could more easily form a radical program for the Reform Movement. These historians are supported by the fact that the meal was to include transgressions of virtually all of the laws of kashrut, including the laws prohibiting shell fish and amphibians, meat and fowl that had not been slaughtered or prepared according to Jewish law, and the mixing of milk and meat.[3]*

Whether the violations of Jewish dietary law at that meal were intended or not, there was a second development in the Reform Movement which certainly was intended to emphasize its break from traditional Jewish practice, and this directly led to the formation of an independent Conservative Movement. In 1885 the Reform Movement produced its Pittsburgh Platform, which declared, among other things, that "all such Mosaic and rabbinical laws as regulate diet, priestly purity, and dress, originated in ages and under the influence of ideas altogether foreign to our present mental and spiritual state [and are] apt rather to obstruct then to further modern spiritual elevation," and that "we consider ourselves no longer a nation, but a religious community, and therefore expect neither a return to Palestine nor the restoration of any of the laws concerning the Jewish state."**

The "Trefah banquet" could possibly be excused as an oversight, but the Pittsburgh Platform forced the few non-Reform Jews in the United States of the 1880s to realize exactly how much they disagreed with the direction of the Reform Movement. Consequently they came together to take steps to combat the increasing Reform influence. The group included very traditional Sephardic Jews, led by Rabbi Sabato Morais of Philadelphia and Rabbi H. Pereira Mendes of New York, and it also included Reformers of a more moderate type who disagreed with the Pittsburgh Platform — men like Rabbi Marcus Jastrow of Philadelphia and Rabbi Alexander Kohut of New York.

---

* A copy of the menu for that meal can be found in Appendix I.

**The entire Platform is included in Appendix II.

These rabbis, together with a number of important laymen, succeeded in creating a rabbinical school, called The Jewish Theological Seminary Association, which opened its doors to eight students in 1887. The constitution of the new school declared its goals to be "the preservation in America of the knowledge and practice of historical Judaism, as ordained in the law of Moses and expounded by the Prophets and Sages of Israel in Biblical and Talmudical writings" — a clear reaction to the Reform interpretation of Judaism and Jewish history, which had denied the importance of any developments in Judaism after the period of the Prophets.

The second factor which radically changed the nature of American Judaism was the arrival of a large group of traditional Jews from Eastern Europe. In 1881, when Alexander II began to rule Russia, a series of pogroms broke out against the large Jewish community there. The Russian masses ruthlessly attacked Jews and their property, often with no warning and no clear reason. (Those of you who have read or seen Fiddler on the Roof will remember this.) As you might imagine, this produced absolute terror for the Jews living there, and many left. Since prior to 1923 the United States did not put a limit on the number of those who could enter this country and become citizens, between 1881 and 1923 several million Jews from Russia and other countries in Eastern Europe settled in North America. The religious Jews among them were almost all Orthodox. Thus while there were approximately 250,000 Jews living in the United States in 1880, there were about 3,500,000 in 1920; and while most American Jews were Reform in 1880, the vast majority were Orthodox by 1920.[4]

The leaders of the Jewish community which had been here before the Russian immigration considered the newcomers both an embarrassment and a responsibility: an embarrassment, because their language, mode of dress, and habits were distinctly foreign; a responsibility, because they were, after all, Jews. That meant, negatively, that if these new Jewish immigrants caused problems for American society through unemployment or crime, or even if they were simply disdained for their foreign ways, all Jews, and not just the immigrants, would be tarred with a bad reputation. The Reform Jewish leaders therefore had a vested interest in making sure that the new Jewish immigrants adjusted well to American society. Positively, many of these Reform Jewish leaders sincerely felt a duty to help these parts of their extended family find homes, work, and a new life in America.

These leaders realized, however, that the new immigrants would never accept Reform Judaism. Therefore, they sought to train a group of rabbis who, on the one hand, would be traditional enough in their views and practices to be acceptable to the new immigrants, but who, on the other hand, could speak English well and talk intelligently about general philosophy and history so that they could help to Americanize the new immigrants. That is why Reform bankers, merchants, and lawyers like Jacob H. Schiff, Louis Marshall and Daniel

14

and Simon Guggenheim rescued the Seminary from near bankruptcy in 1901, reorganized it, and brought Solomon Schechter from England to lead it: they wanted to transform the new Orthodox population into modern, Americanized Jews.

The chief goal of the Reform laymen who supported the Seminary in its early years was the Americanization of the new Jewish immigrants. The rabbis who worked to establish the Seminary and who taught there shared that goal, but for them it was not the major one. They wanted primarily to increase the Jewish commitment and knowledge of American Jews. They were convinced, however, that in order to do that, they had to speak about Judaism in the language and style of the United States because only in that way could they convince Jews that being a committed Jew did not conflict with being a full American. Thus, on the one hand, the rabbinic founders of the Seminary were pleased not only by the scholastic achievements of the first eight students, but by the fact that most of them were American-born.[5] Similarly, Solomon Schechter later wrote that three changes were necessary in order to make traditional Judaism attractive to American Jews: sermons delivered in English, order and decorum in the synagogue, and the use of modern methods, especially in the education of children and adults.[6] He even said that "They [the American-born generation] accept all the ancient ideas, but they want modern methods, and this, on the whole, may be the definition of Conservative Judaism."[7]

On the other hand, that same Solomon Schechter was very distressed when he discovered that Americanization of the immigrant was the only goal of the Reform supporters of the Seminary, because for him the maintenance of traditional Judaism was the main objective:

> I must take it out of their minds that I came into this country for the purpose of converting the downtown lower East Side Jew to a more refined species of religion... No consideration... would ever have induced me... [to assume the post of President of the Seminary] had I known that the Seminary was largely meant for a particular section of the community, forming a sort of higher Talmud Torah, having the purpose of reconciling the most unruly element in Jewry and giving it a little religious refinement. It is absolutely impossible that the Institution [the Seminary] should flourish and succeed in its ultimate aims on support coming from those who are not in complete sympathy with it.[8]

It was Schechter's feeling that the immigrants needed "Judaization" more than they needed Americanization because they were quickly shedding their traditions, and Judaization was the goal of the faculty of the Seminary as well. Thus, when the Seminary held opening exercises on January 2, 1887, Alexander Kohut. professor of Talmud, explained the Seminary's purpose this way:

The hope is based upon the assumption that in the new Seminary [in contrast to Hebrew Union College] a different spirit will prevail, different impulses will pervade its teachings and animate its teachers. This spirit shall be that of Conservative Judaism, the conserving Jewish impulse which will create in the pupils of the Seminary the tendency to recognize the dual nature of Judaism and the Law, which unites theory and practice and acknowledges the necessity of observing the Law as well as of studying it.[9]

Despite this conflict between them, the Reform lay leaders and the rabbis on the faculty agreed on the importance of expressing Judaism in an American idiom, and therefore they could and did cooperate in founding and supporting the Seminary through the 1920s. By the 1930s, however, Americanization of the immigrants was no longer a problem, and consequently the Reform lay leaders lost interest. Before that happened they had succeeded in creating a distinctly American movement in Judaism -- so American, in fact, that until the 1950s the Conservative Movement was exclusively confined to the North American continent.

QUESTIONS:

1) "The first institution of the Conservative Movement, the Jewish Theological Seminary Association, was founded by people who were reacting against the beliefs and demands of the Orthodox Movement." True or false?

   If true, why did they begin the process which ended in the development of a whole new movement rather than just adopt a moderate version of Reform Judaism? If false, why did they begin the Conservative Movement? Explain both reasons.

2) When was the Seminary established and who were some of the people involved?

3) Who were some of the people involved in reorganizing the Seminary as The Jewish Theological Seminary of America?

   Which of those were primarily interested in Americanization, and which were primarily interested in Judaization?

4) What kind of "order and decorum in the service" do you suppose Schechter was thinking of?

   Do the Conservative congregations you have attended reflect this order and decorum?

If so, does it enhance your religious experience compared to any other styles you have seen?

Are there limits to the amount of order and decorum that is desirable? For example, should young children be allowed to attend an adult service, since we know that they will want to run around and do what young children do?

5)   Why do you think the Reform rabbinical school was called a college and the Conservative rabbinical school a seminary?

6)   Do you consider Conservative Judaism to be "traditional?"

ACTIVITY:

At the turn of the century, Solomon Schechter wrote about three changes that he felt were necessary in order to make traditional Judaism attractive to American Jews. What three changes would you suggest in order to make Conservative Judaism more attractive today?

1._____

_____

2._____

_____

3._____

_____

---

4. The Ideological Stance of Early Conservative Judaism: Positive-Historical Judaism and Catholic Israel

Some of the rabbinic leaders of the early Seminary (e. g., Henry Pereira Mendes, Bernard Drachman) simply wanted to teach Orthodox Judaism more effectively to American Jews. Others of the founding rabbis (e. g., Marcus Jastrow, Frederick de Sola Mendes) were considerably more liberal but were bothered by the excesses of the Pittsburgh Platform; they wanted to teach a more moderate version of Reform Judaism, one which retained the main elements of Jewish law. Since there were few American Jews in the 1880's who were not Reform, these two groups united in founding the Seminary.

These two groups clearly needed an ideology (that is, an explanation and justification of their position) which could at once unite them and also show how there could be several different approaches to Judaism which could all be legitimate. They found it in the work of Zacharias Frankel, head of The Jewish Theological Seminary of Breslau, Germany, who, together with a number of other European scholars, had developed the *"positive-historical" approach* to Judaism. That approach is *historical* in several senses:

a) Method:

The fundamental doctrine of the historical approach is the claim that if we want to understand Judaism correctly, we must *study it historically*. That is, when we examine Jewish texts, we must use the same intellectual techniques that we would use if we were analyzing the documents of any other group of people. So, for example, in any Jewish writing we must distinguish between the meaning that the author intended (the *"peshat"* פְּשָׁט) and the meaning(s) given the text by the later tradition (the *"derash"* דְּרָשׁ).

Orthodox schools recognize that distinction, but they claim that if you want to know the correct meaning of the biblical text, the divinely intended meaning, you should consult the classical Jewish commentators (e. g., Rashi). The Orthodox use that method because they believe that God revealed both the written text of the Torah and the interpretations God intended at Sinai and that those interpretations were passed down from generation to generation until they were ultimately written down in the Midrash and medieval Jewish commentaries. Consequently, while the words of the text may sometimes seem to mean something different from the traditional interpretations of them, that is of no consequence: the *peshat* is to be seen through the *derash* exclusively, because God's intent was to say what is in the derash.

In contrast, the Conservative Movement and others who use the generally accepted methods of literary analysis would claim that we must understand the text as is. The *derash* may alert us to unusual features of the text which must be investigated, but it is a *later*, and therefore quite possibly *different*, meaning from that contained in the original text. In fact, an important way of learning about Jewish history is to *distinguish* the laws and ideas that appear in the Bible from those that were developed later -- even if the later authorities justified their philosophies and legal decisions by reinterpreting earlier sources in the Bible and Talmud.

To discover the original meaning of a selection from the Bible or Talmud, we must learn the languages, ideas, and practices of the surrounding nations because we must assume that our ancestors, like all other people, were influenced in how they thought and spoke by the people living around them. We also must use the most thorough literary, archaeological, and historical methods that we can in determining the date of a text and the events and ideas in it.

Identifying the original meaning of a text does not mean that the later interpretations are wrong and the original meaning is right: on the contrary, sometimes interpretations of a text are much more interesting, instructive, or historically or legally important than the text itself! But a commitment to using the historical method does mean that you have to *distinguish the levels of meaning* of a text by separating its original meaning from the various ways it was interpreted later.

b) Intellectual Result:

When you study Judaism using historical techniques, you discover that Judaism has been a phenomenon *in history*, influenced and changed by the various people and ideas with which Jews came into contact and the political, social, and economic conditions under which Jews lived. In other words, Judaism has not been the same during all of the years of its existence; on the contrary, its ideas, values, and practices have changed in response to the changing conditions in which Jews found themselves -- just like the religion and culture of every other human group. Putting the same point negatively, Judaism is *not ahistorical*; that is, it is not something which has existed outside of the normal pressures and influences of history. It **has** changed, and you will read about some concrete examples of such changes later on in this sourcebook.

Sometimes the changes that Judaism has experienced took place deliberately and quickly, and sometimes they developed almost unconsciously and slowly. Jews have changed Judaism by adding to its thought or practices, and they have also changed it by modifying or dropping some things. One thing is certain, though: Judaism of today is not the same as the Judaism of a century ago in either America or Europe, and Judaism of a century ago was not the same as that of Maimonides, Rabbi Akiba, or Moses. All of those forms of Judaism differed from each other in significant ways.

That does not mean, however, that Judaism has changed so much from one period to another that there are no connections between our Judaism and that of Moses. The point is, rather, that Judaism has changed *organically* throughout the ages. An "organism" is a living thing. All living things undergo major and continual changes during their lifetimes. Think about yourself: with the exception of your brain cells, not a single cell in your body now was there seven years ago or will be part of you seven years from now. Yet nobody would have difficulty recognizing you as you because the changes occur slowly (from one moment to the next, more than 99% of you remains the same) and they all fit the general pattern of how you looked before. If you were a dark, brown-eyed male a year ago, you did not become a light. blue-eyed female a year later. That kind of radical change does not occur often in nature. and when it does – as, for example, when the caterpillar becomes a butterfly – we say that there has been a "metamorphosis" (a total change) and we generally even call the two forms of the living thing by different names. Most changes in nature, however, occur gradually and follow general patterns that we have seen before in that species, and that is why we can say that you will be the same person ten years from now even if your body, ideas, desires, interests. and friendships will all be quite different then.

The same is true of Judaism and all other living cultures. There may be some significant distinctions between the ways in which Jews think about Judaism and practice it here and now from the ways in which Jews do so elsewhere or did so at various times in the past. We still call our patterns of behavior and thought "Judaism," however, because our form of Judaism has much in common with the various types of Judaism that existed before and that exist elsewhere and because we can trace the gradual process by which Judaism changed in form and even sometimes in content from Moses to our own day.

Alexander Kohut, who in many ways was the clearest spokesperson for the new movement on ideological matters, stated this intellectual result of the historical method this way in 1886:

> Judaism is a consistent whole. The Mosaic, prophetic, talmudic-rabbinic, Judaism is an organic totality...The Judaism of history is a unity, an organic development. May Moses be its head, the prophets its heart, the Rabbis its links: one without the other is a halfness, a wanton mutilation...[10]

In this he was responding to the way in which the Orthodox over-emphasized the place of the Shulhan Arukh, a sixteenth century code of Jewish law, and he was also reacting to the way in which the Reformers stressed the importance of the Prophets to the exclusion of all other times in Jewish history until modernity: for the Conservative, historical approach, each period in Jewish history contributed its part to the ongoing tradition that we know as Judaism. Some periods may have been more productive than others, and we may like some developments more than others, but an objective study of our tradition must consider them all.

c) *Practical Result*:

Moreover, Judaism *should* change from one time and place to another. The simple fact is that the world does not stand still, and consequently all living organisms *must* learn to live under new circumstances if they are going to survive. Judaism is no exception. It not only is "historical" in that it has been influenced and changed in the past by new ideas and practices that Jews developed themselves or learned from others; it must also change in the present and future if it is going to continue to be a part of history, an ongoing concern of a living people.

Once again Kohut expressed the point clearly and strongly:

> The chain of tradition continued unbroken from Moses through Joshua, the Elders, the Prophets and the Men of the Great Synagogue, down to the latest times. On this tradition rests our faith, which Moses first received from God on Sinai. On this foundation rests Mosaic-rabbinical Judaism today; and on this foundation we take our stand...
>
> But you may ask: Shall the fence around the garden, shall reverence be extended around everything that the past hedged in...? "Remember the days of old," said Moses, *and have regard to the changes of each generation* (Devarim 32:7). The teaching of the ancients we must make our starting-point, but we must not lose sight of what is needed in every generation...
>
> And as these elders did, so can – yes, so must we, the later Epigoni [successors] -- do in the exigencies of our own day. If the power to make changes was granted to the Elders, is not the power given equally to us? "But they were giants," we are told, "and we, compared with them, are mere pygmies." Perhaps so; let us not forget, however, that a pygmy on a giant's shoulder can see further than the giant himself.
>
> Let us now revert to the question raised at the outset: Is Judaism definitely closed for all time, or is it capable of and in need of continuous development? I answer both Yes and No. I answer Yes, *because Religion has been given to man*; and as it is the duty of man to grow in perfection as long as he lives, he must modify the forms which yield him religious satisfaction, in accordance with the spirit of the times. I answer No, insofar as it concerns the word of God, which cannot be imperfect...You Israelite, imperfect as you are, strive to perfect yourself in the image of your perfect God. Hold in honor His unchangeable law and let it be your earnest task to put new life into the outward form of our religion.[11]

Similarly, he left no doubts that in matters of belief too we might well differ from our ancestors:

Ought we to maintain two kinds of logic, one for theology and the other for science? I believe decidedly, no! The indubitable results of science can and must agree with the truths of religion, for a religion which cannot bear the light of science or must first soften it through all kinds of lenses is to be classed with the dead. Such a religion could vegetate among the lower classes, lead a sad existence, become sometimes dangerous by fanaticism, but could not exercise a decisive influence upon the development of mankind.

Fortunately the Mosaic religion does not belong to religions that fear the light...There never existed a time or party or sect which required, recommended, or even asserted as admissible, to neglect the use of reasoning...[12]

d) The "Positive" Part of "Positive-historical Judaism:"

This brings us to the other part of the title of the approach which Conservative Judaism adopted. The full name of that approach is "*positive*-historical Judaism."

The "positive" part of that name can have one or two meanings. "Positive" can mean "concerned only with observable, empirical data." In that sense, "positive-historical Judaism" would describe a method of study which analyzes the history, ideas, and practices of Judaism as objectively and dispassionately as possible. That is certainly what is intended by the method of study described above in (a).

But "positive" can also denote enthusiasm, agreement, support and concern, as when we say that a person has "a positive attitude" toward something. That sense is almost exactly the opposite of the one above: the former denotes dispassionate objectivity; the latter refers to passionate involvement.

Whether the original members of the "Positive-Historical School" intended the latter meaning as well is questionable, but it certainly does describe another important element of the way in which the founders of the Conservative Movement planned to use the methods and results of that approach. Specifically, they were deeply interested in taking and promoting a positive attitude toward Judaism, that Jews honor it, hold it dear, and seek to preserve it. We should try to be as dispassionate and objective as possible when we study Judaism for the sake of honesty, but that should not prevent us from being very passionate and actively concerned about its present and future. In fact, the movement is called "The Conservative Movement" because its members seek to *conserve* as much of the Jewish tradition as possible through its work in Jewish law, thought, publications, community matters. and, especially, in Jewish education.

22

e) "Catholic Israel:"

But if the Conservative Movement recognizes changes in Jewish law, how can it at the same time conserve it? The answer lies in making the decision of when, what, and how to change a law a matter for *communal* decision. There is no guarantee that the community or its representatives will be any wiser than an individual, but at least then we will be drawing upon the collective wisdom of the people involved. Moreover, that method has preserved Judaism until now. Furthermore, we really cannot do more than try to make intelligent and necessary changes at the appropriate time with the best judgment we can muster: life does not come with guarantees, especially in important decisions.

Among the early leaders of the Conservative Movement, there were two different programs for gaining communal involvement. Alexander Kohut claimed that legal decisions should be made by the rabbis in each generation. In this he was simply restating the way that most decisions had been made in Jewish law from the time of the Bible onwards, for Judaism always had entrusted the law to those who knew most about it, the rabbis of each generation. The Jewish community never chose its interpreters of the law by a vote of the people or by a calculation of how much land or money a person had, and heredity ceased to be a relevant factor in the appointment of judges shortly after the destruction of the Second Temple. Since Ezra's time, a person who wanted to gain authority in Jewish law first had to *learn* enough to earn the authorization to act as a teacher or judge. From the first century C.E. onwards, those who gained that authorization were called "rabbis," or "teachers," as a sign of their education, and to this day they are the ones who make decisions regarding Jewish law. Kohut would continue that practice:

> Our religious guide is the Torah, the Law of Moses, interpreted and applied in the light of tradition. But inasmuch as individual opinion cannot be valid for the whole community, it behooves individuals and communities to appoint only recognized authorities as teachers; such men, that is to say, as acknowledge belief in authority, and who, at the same time, with comprehension and tact, are willing to consider what may be permitted in view of the exigencies of the times and what may be discarded without changing the nature and character of the foundations of the faith.[13]

There was always another factor that influenced Jewish law, however, and that was the customs of the people. The decisions of the rabbis and the practices of the people were often identical, but sometimes they were not. When that happened the rabbis sometimes attempted to change the practices of the people to fit the law, but sometimes they adjusted the law to fit the customs of the people. In fact, in some cases the customs became so strong that the rabbis claimed that "custom uproots a legal decision."[14] In any case, Jewish law was always a product of an interaction between the rabbis and the rest of the Jewish people. In recognition of that, Solomon Schechter, President of the reorganized Seminary from 1902 to his death in 1915, claimed that Jewish law should be determined by "catholic Israel."

We are used to using the term "catholic" as a proper name referring to the Catholic Church and not as a common adjective describing other things, and so we have to be careful here to avoid misunderstanding. "Catholic" means "the whole of," and thus "catholic Israel" means "the whole of Israel," or "the whole of the Jewish community." That was Schechter's translation of the Hebrew term כְּלָל יִשְׂרָאֵל "Klal Yisrael," and he used it to indicate that decisions in Jewish law should be determined by the practices of the whole community of Israel:

> Another consequence of this conception of Tradition is that it is neither Scripture nor primitive Judaism, but general custom which forms the real rule of practice. Holy Writ as well as history...teaches that the law of Moses was never fully and absolutely put in practice. Liberty was always given to the great teachers of every generation to make modifications and innovations in harmony with the spirit of existing institutions. Hence a return to Mosaism would be illegal, pernicious [destructive], and indeed impossible. The norm [laws] as well as the sanction [authority] of Judaism is the practice actually in vogue. Its consecration is the consecration of general use -- or, in other words, of Catholic Israel.
>
> Since...the interpretation of Scripture or the Secondary Meaning [in addition to what it meant originally] is mainly a product of changing historical influences, it follows that the center of authority is actually removed from the Bible and placed in some *living body*, which, by reason of its being in touch with the ideal aspirations and the religious needs of the age, is best able to determine the nature of the Secondary Meaning. This living body, however, is not represented by any section of the nation, or any corporate priesthood, or Rabbihood, but by the collective conscience of Catholic Israel as embodied in the Universal Synagogue.[15]

In Schechter's time, most Jews were observant, and therefore he could confidently base decisions in Jewish law on the practices of the Jewish community. In our own time, most Jews do not observe Jewish law, and therefore we cannot look to the practices of the *whole* Jewish community to decide issues in Jewish law. If we were to do that, then almost all of the major practices of Judaism would fall by the wayside! Still, the concept of "catholic Israel" makes sense and remains an important part of the process of making decisions in Jewish law if we follow the reinterpretation suggested by Robert Gordis and consider only the practices *of Jews who try to observe Jewish law* in making our decisions.[16] That is certainly the group to whom we refer when we talk about the custom of Jewish communities in the past, and it is that group to whom we must refer today too if we are to understand the interaction between the rabbis and the community, between דִּין *din* (law) and מִנְהָג *minhag* (custom).

Those who are not observant may still be Jews, but their own choice to neglect the laws of Judaism excludes them from consideration when we want to know the *minhag*. It is, of course, regrettable that so many Jews are not observant -- and Conservative Judaism has been increasingly trying to correct that situation -- but Schechter's concept is still crucial for an adequate understanding of Jewish law.

In every age it has been the decisions of the rabbis and the practices of the *observant* Jewish community which together determine the nature of Jewish law and which together make the decisions *communal* decisions. Just as observant communities have had differing interpretations of Jewish thought and practice in times past, so too in the present there may well be several separate understandings of proper Jewish observance among the various communities of observant Jews -- the spectrum within Conservative Jewish practice, the various American Orthodox groups, the various segments of Israeli Orthodox Jews, Sephardic Jews, etc. The original founders of Conservative Judaism hoped to formulate an interpretation of Judaism for the entire American Jewish community, but the historical model of several different communities won out -- and perhaps it is better that way.

The Conservative Movement, then, is new in the historical method that it applies to Judaism and its history, but is traditional in that it maintains much of the tradition from generation to generation and is yet willing to make changes when necessary or desirable. There were other beliefs that the early leaders of Conservative Judaism had, and we shall discuss them in detail in Chapter IV. The concepts of positive-historical Judaism and catholic Israel were the major ideas that brought them together to found a Seminary and ultimately a movement; on other issues they exercised considerable freedom of opinion.

As Schechter said:

> The historical school has never, to my knowledge, offered to the world a theological program of its own. By the nature of its task...it pays but little attention to purely dogmatic questions....As far as we may gather from vague remarks and hints thrown out now and then, its theological position may perhaps be thus defined: -- It is not the mere revealed Bible that is of first importance to the Jew, but the Bible as it repeats itself in history, in other words, as it is interpreted by Tradition.[17]

25

The method and program contained in the notions of positive-historical Judaism and catholic Israel were more than enough, however, to launch the new movement and to give it a distinctive character.

QUESTIONS:

1) *"From the very beginning, the rabbis involved in the Conservative Movement have interpreted and practiced Judaism in a variety of ways."*

    What were the varying positions of the rabbis who worked for the founding of the Seminary? What practical considerations brought them together? How did they explain their cooperation ideologically? That is, what beliefs or attitudes did they hold in common?

2) If a person adopted the method of "positive-historical Judaism" in reading and understanding the Bible, Talmud, and other texts of the Jewish tradition, how would s/he determine the meaning of the text as the original author intended it ("the *peshat*")?

    How would this be different from the way in which an Orthodox person would ascertain the meaning of the text?

    (Hint: How would each of them use traditional interpretations of the text?)

3) In the following, explain *the original meaning of the biblical verse* as an Orthodox Jew would see it and then as a Conservative Jew would see it:

    > *"You shall not boil a kid in its mother's milk."* (Shemot 23:19; 34:26; Devarim14:21)

    > *"In three different verses the law 'You shall not boil a kid in its mother's milk' is written: Once for the purpose of prohibiting the eating [of meat with milk], once to prohibit us from deriving any other benefit [besides eating] from such a mixture, and once to prohibit the boiling [of meat with milk]."* (Mekhilta [= the rabbinic Midrash mostly on the legal sections of Exodus] on Shemot 23:19)

4) The Conservative Movement's method of study, as we have noted, distinguishes between *peshat* and *derash*. In doing so, the Conservative Movement continues a stream of scholarship that began in the Talmud and took on a new form in the Middle

Ages.[18] Specifically, when the Rabbis of the Talmud make the distinction, they mean by *peshat* <u>the accepted meaning of the text within their Jewish community</u>, even if the words of the Bible clearly do not mean what the tradition takes them to mean. Medieval Jewish commentators, though, use linguistic techniques to determine the *peshat*, and they mean by that <u>the meaning of a word or phrase in its literary context</u>. Medieval commentators, however, assume that the entire Bible, and even the Aramaic translations, all come from the same time period. Modern, Conservative scholars would use some of the same linguistic techniques that Medieval scholars used, but they would also use more contemporary methods of literary analysis as well as archaeology, cross-cultural studies, and historical techniques to decipher the original meaning of the text. Conservative scholars would also study and prize the additional meanings which our classical texts took on over the centuries, and they would follow Jewish law as it developed over time and not as it was originally stated in the Torah. Honesty demands, though, that we try to understand the Torah, as Conservative scholars do, <u>in its original setting</u> as well as through the lenses of later generations.

So that you can better understand the difference between these three understandings of the difference between *peshat* and *derash*, consider the following two examples from Rashi (1040-1105), the most popular Jewish interpreter of the Middle Ages, commenting on two biblical passages. In each case, ask yourself these questions:

> a) How, according to Rashi, do the Rabbis of the Talmud interpret the passage?
> b) Why does Rashi think that the Rabbis' interpretation is not the *peshat*?
> c) What does Rashi think that the *peshat* is? How does he arrive at that interpretation?
> d) If you were using the methods of modern, historical scholarship, as the Conservative Movement does, what factors other than the literary ones Rashi uses would you want to know in order to identify the original meaning of the text? Can you imagine evidence from any or all of those sources which would alter your understanding of the meaning of these passages in the Torah from that of either the Rabbis or Rashi?

(Hints: In the passage from Shemot 16, consider what archaeological, historical, or biological sources might tell you about phenomena in the Sinai wilderness as a way of understanding what manna was in the first place and when and how it appears. Do any of these sources help you understand how it might be possible for it to appear

in approximately the same quantity for five days, double the amount on the sixth day, and not at all on the seventh day? Even if that remains a mystery (miracle?), do these sources help you to understand how the Israelites might have been nourished by the manna for forty years?

In the passage from Shemot 23, can you imagine how parallel laws about court procedures in surrounding countries – e.g., Hammurabi's Code, the Hittite laws – might help you understand the Torah's original meaning here? Note that Israelite law may be similar to, or different from, the law in those other codes, but they may still shed light on what the Torah means by what it says.

Note in both passages the way that Rashi uses the literary context of the verses to determine their meaning.)

i) Exodus 16:11-15, 21-22, 26-31:

The Lord spoke to Moses: I have heard the grumbling of the Israelites. Speak to them and say: By evening you shall eat flesh, and in the morning you shall have your fill of bread; and you shall know that I the Lord am your God.

In the evening quail appeared and covered the camp; in the morning there was a fall of dew about the camp. When the fall of dew was lifted, there, over the surface of the wilderness, lay a fine and flaky substance, as fine as the frost on the ground. When the Israelites saw it, they said to one another, "What is it?" – for they did not know what it was. And Moses said to them, "That is the bread which the Lord has given you to eat..."

So they gathered it every morning, each as much as he needed to eat, but when the sun grew hot it would melt. On the sixth day they gathered double the amount of food...(for Moses said) "Six days you shall gather it; on the seventh, the Sabbath, there will be none."

Yet some of the people went out on the seventh day to gather, but they found nothing. And the Lord said to Moses, "How long will you men refuse to follow My commandments and My teachings? Mark that the Lord has given you the Sabbath; therefore He gives you two days' food on the sixth day. Let everyone remain where he is: let no man leave his place on the seventh day." So the people remained inactive on the seventh day.

The house of Israel named it "manna"...

Rashi on Exodus 16:29:

"Let no man leave his place on the seventh day." [According to the Rabbis, this verse establishes] the 2000 cubits of the Sabbath limit [i. e., that it is forbidden to walk more than 2000 cubits about 3000 feet – from your home on the Sabbath] (Mekhilta); but this is not expressly mentioned here because the command relating to the Sabbath limits is only a law that the Scribes enacted. The text itself only speaks about those who gathered the manna [and does not constitute a prohibition regarding the Sabbath for all Jews in all periods of time].

ii) Exodus 23:2:

Do not side with the many to do wrong, and do not give perverse testimony in a dispute by leaning toward the many.

Rashi on Exodus 23:2:

There are many legal interpretations of this verse given by the Sages of Israel, but the wording of the text does not fit in well with them. They derive from here that we must not decide a person's guilt by a preponderance of one judge, and the end of the verse they explained thus: but if there is a majority of two or more judges on the court who declare the defendant guilty, then decide the matter as they declare that he is guilty. The verse, they say, deals with cases involving capital punishment. The middle part of the verse, "do not give perverse testimony in a dispute" (Hebrew reev) they explained as though it were written rav, meaning that one should not give an opinion different from that of the presiding judge of the court, and therefore we ask the youngest judges to express their opinion first...But I think that if you wish to explain the verse so that everything fits in properly, you must interpret it this way: If you see many people making a wrong decision, do not say, "Since they are many, I will do as they do." [And the second part of the verse means that] if the defendant asks you about the [wrong] verdict, do not justify the majority, thereby hiding the truth, but tell him the decision as it should be and let the collar hang around the neck of the majority [that is, if you are outvoted, let the majority bear the responsibility].

5) When you use the historical method, you are, in effect, looking for changes that occurred in Judaism from one period of time to another. Is it just circular reasoning then to declare that there are such changes? In other words, when you use the positive-historical approach, do you actually *discover* changes in Jewish ideas and practices throughout our history, or does your use of the method mean that you are simply *assuming* such changes?

(Hint: when you use the historical method, do you ever discover that no change *has taken place? When do you say that there has been a change, and when do you say that there has not been? Compare this process with what chemists do when they look for changes in something in a test tube.)*

6)   What does the "positive" part of "positive-historical Judaism" mean?

Explain both possibilities. Can you objectively study the Jewish tradition and yet be committed to it? What would a committed Jew have to be careful about in his or her study of Judaism?

7)   Can you think of actual situations in which Conservative Jews have adopted the historical approach and in which other Jews have not?

5. Conservative Judaism in the Twentieth Century

As we have seen, the founders and supporters of the Seminary were interested in spreading a form of Judaism which would be both traditional and modern. Their efforts were directed at the many immigrants from Russia and Eastern Europe who came to the United States between 1880 and 1923. Although the leaders of the Conservative Movement in those early years did manage to make some headway toward their goals, most Jews of that generation were simply not interested. They were working long and hard hours in order to earn a living. Their primary goal was to make it possible for their children not to work so that they could attend school and become "real Americans." They themselves did not have time for that. Many tried to learn English and some American history, but in religious matters they were quite content to transfer the Judaism that they knew in Europe to these shores as well as they were able.

It was the second generation, the children of the immigrants, who took to Conservative Judaism and made it the most popular form of Judaism in America. The young adult Jews of the 1930s, 1940s, and 1950s had completed high school and often college and professional school thanks to their parents' prodding and hard work, and they were intensely interested in succeeding. That included a desire for financial success, a desire which was largely realized as more and more Jews became members of the middle (and even upper) economic classes. But it also included a keen desire to be accepted socially as full-fledged Americans.

In many ways social acceptance was a harder goal to achieve than economic success because many of the Christians in America shared the same anti-Jewish biases that Christians in Europe had had. We Jews tend to gloss over that because it is uncomfortable for us to think about it, but in many areas of the United States and Canada there was crude and public anti-Semitism in the 1930s and 1940s. Father Coughlin's stridently anti-Semitic radio programs were broadcast widely, and the Ku Klux Klan's activities against Jews were much more respected and influential than they are now. (Those of you who read or saw *Give 'Em Hell, Harry* will remember that the only election that former President Harry Truman lost was because he refused to support the Ku Klux Klan.) Even more troublesome for Jews was the quiet but wide-spread anti-Semitism that prevented Jews from attaining high positions in major corporations and banking institutions, that excluded Jews from buying homes in certain areas of town and from membership in elite social clubs, that barred Jews from staying at a number of hotels and resorts, and that produced the quotas of Jews who could be accepted to the universities and professional schools of this land. In many cases these policies were not even a conscious decision; they were simply a "gentleman's agreement." (You may have read the 1947 book or seen the 1953 movie by that name which illustrate that type of anti-Semitism graphically.)

In the face of this, many Jews were trying to blend into the American scene by becoming like white, Anglo-Saxon Protestants ("WASPS") as much as possible because that was the majority culture and Jews were convinced that being like WASPS was the only way that they could fully achieve both their economic and social goals. Jews were strengthened in this by the theory that was popular at the time which pictured America as "a melting pot," in which people from all backgrounds would lose their ties to those backgrounds and melt into one American mold, the white, Anglo-Saxon Protestant mold. As a result, Jews often changed their names and did a number of other things to hide their Jewish origins. Some even converted to Christianity or married non-Jews, but the vast majority did not go that far. Most Jews wanted to maintain their Jewish identity, but they also wanted to identify as Americans. Conservative Judaism, which from the beginning had been designed to combine Judaism and Americanism, served their needs precisely, and so more and more second-generation American Jews joined Conservative synagogues in the 1930s, 1940s, and 1950s, making Conservative Judaism the most common affiliation of American Jews.

The desire to be socially accepted as Americans explains not only the popularity of Conservative Judaism at that time, but also the forms that it took. The accepted practice among Christian Americans in those years was to belong to a church, and so Jews striving to be recognized as Americans in the fullest sense had to have a Jewish equivalent. Consequently, many Jews who knew little about Judaism and had dropped most of its

31

practices nevertheless affiliated with synagogues: it was the socially accepted thing to do. Moreover they wanted synagogues which were similar in form to Protestant churches so that it would be clear to Jew and Christian alike that this was just a Jewish form of an unquestionably American institution, the church. Synagogues therefore were built using the floor plan of churches, in which the people on the platform face the audience (instead of the traditional Jewish arrangement in which the cantor faces the ark with his back to the congregation). Rabbis and cantors put on robes, like Protestant ministers. Decorum (order and quiet) became a major value. In fact, Jews were both amused and embarrassed by the talkative, slightly chaotic services that Orthodox congregations still had; they spoke of the lack of decorum there with disdain and condescension as if their Orthodox coreligionists had not yet left the Stone Age. Since "full" Americans attended American public schools, day schools were considered un-American. As a result, synagogues established religious schools which held classes in the late afternoon hours, and Jewish education became more and more of a part-time thing. In fact, most Reform and many Conservative congregations instituted a Confirmation program – again a borrowing from the Protestant churches – for those who wanted to attend only on Sunday mornings. Some of these forms had been used in other Jewish communities before, but second generation American Jews were not interested in them because of that: they adopted the forms described above because they wanted to become as much like the majority culture as possible.

Rabbis and other Jewish leaders were happy about the fact that Jews were joining synagogues, but they were not at all happy about the increasing non-observance and ignorance of American Jews. They therefore initiated major educational programs. The Jewish Theological Seminary of America established a Teachers Institute as early as 1909 in an effort to supply American teachers for Jewish schools. Also through its Herbert H. Lehman Institute (established in 1951) and its other graduate programs, the Seminary has managed to train native American scholars of Judaica who now teach at the Seminary and more than 100 other American universities – an especially important achievement in light of the total destruction of the European centers of Jewish learning during the Second World War.

In addition, many educational and youth projects were established, such as Leaders Training Fellowship (1946), Camp Ramah (1947), and United Synagogue Youth (1951). The Conservative Movement also founded and nurtured numerous other programs and institutions, many of which are outlined below in "The Structure of the Conservative Movement."

All of these efforts to intensify Jewish education through central organizations were matched on the congregational level by a continually expanding roster of adult education classes, an attempt to set minimum standards for Bar or Bat Mitzvah training, and, especially in recent years, increased educational and social programs for young adults in their teens and twenties. Synagogues have also sponsored Shabbat family dinners in order to teach families how to celebrate Shabbat through direct experience, and they have held retreats and intensive seminars on specific subjects. Rabbis have increasingly used services and the congregational bulletin as opportunities for teaching.

As good as all of that is, it is clearly not enough. The third and fourth generations of American Jews grew up in homes which, by and large, were geared toward becoming full-fledged Americans and not seriously concerned with transmitting Jewish knowledge or commitment. As a result, Jews from their teens to their forties are taking two opposite paths. Some are saying to themselves that since Judaism meant little to their parents, and since they themselves know and care little about it, they will live their lives without much attention to their Jewishness. Some are even actively rejecting Judaism by converting to other faiths, but most members of this group are simply passive about it. They do not go out of their way to deny their Jewishness, but they do not put any time, thought, or energy into affirming it either. And if the person they choose as a partner in marriage happens to be Jewish, fine, but if not – well, that is all right too. In other words, a large number of third and fourth generation Jews are simply drifting away from Judaism through ignorance, apathy, and intermarriage.

But another increasingly large number of American Jews of the third and fourth generation are drawing the opposite conclusion. They no longer need to prove their Americanism to themselves or anybody else: they take that for granted. But they know little about their Jewish identity, and they long for sources of meaning in their lives, and so they take steps to find out about their Jewish religion and roots. This process is often stimulated by one of the educational efforts mentioned above. It is aided by the emotional attachment that Jews feel toward Israel, especially if that is accompanied by a trip to Israel. It is fostered too by the fact that in America the "melting pot" theory has gone out of style and has been replaced by the mosaic, where America is pictured as a place where a variety of different groups work together in an exciting experiment of inter-ethnic cooperation and learning and where affirming your own ethnicity is therefore "in." In any case, whatever prods the Jews of this group to begin their search, they often become much more committed to Judaism than their parents ever were – or wanted them to be!

These two groups of third and fourth generation American Jews are very dissimilar, but they are alike in one respect: they will not remain Jewish simply because their parents are. Since Judaism was not a major factor in their parents' lives, they have little of the nostalgia that maintained the Jewish identity of the second generation. They will commit their respect, interest, and obedience to Judaism if, and only if, they are convinced that it is a worthwhile pattern of life and thought for *them*. People, of course, differ in the arguments and experiences which they find convincing and in the form of Judaism that they adopt, but since more than 90% of adult American Jews are now college graduates, they increasingly need and want an approach to Judaism which is intellectually stimulating as well as being morally edifying and socially, emotionally, and spiritually satisfying.

This means that major new efforts are now required in Jewish education, and it also means that the Conservative Movement must become much clearer about its ideology and program. Until recently, Jews joined Conservative synagogues because that was the most comfortable way to remain Jewish and still fulfill their social goal of "making it" in the American society. Now that church membership is no longer required to be socially accepted as a full-fledged American, and Jews no longer feel the need to prove their Americanism anyway, they generally will not join synagogues for those reasons any more. They will affiliate with the Conservative Movement only if they are convinced that it is worth their time and effort. That has meant a decline in membership, but it also means that when people do affiliate with a synagogue, they do so for the sake of its program and not simply because it is the socially accepted thing to do. They continue to be interested in all facets of the synagogue program - religious, educational, cultural, social, and even athletic. And while their choice of a synagogue will always depend to some degree on proximity, aesthetic tastes, and family ties, they are increasingly interested in the ideological stance of a synagogue too. That new degree of seriousness challenges the Conservative Movement to spell out the practices and beliefs that define it.

There were several such attempts in the past,[19] but that was never a primary objective of the Movement. On the contrary, Conservative rabbis and lay leaders reveled in the diversity of opinion and practice within the Movement and were concerned not to cut that off. One of the motivations to add lay representatives to the rabbis on the Conservative Movement's Committee on Jewish Law and Standards, in fact, was to broaden the perspectives which enter into the discussion of Jewish law in our movement, and representatives of the lay arms of the movement -- the United Synagogue, Women's League, and the Federation of Jewish Men's Clubs -- were added to the rabbis and Seminary scholars on the Commission on the Philosophy of Conservative Judaism for the same reason. That concern continues: we certainly do not want to squelch the creativity and liveliness that have characterized the Movement by adopting some rigid definition of what one must believe or do to consider oneself a Conservative Jew. *That would be both Jewishly unauthentic and pragmatically deadening.* On the other hand, though, Conservative rabbis and lay leaders have increasingly felt the need for a clearer specification of the points in Jewish belief and practice where there is substantial agreement in the Conservative community, and a description of the various options that at least currently exist within the Movement in the areas where that consensus does not exist.[20]

They feel that need for two reasons. First, it is clear that most Jews affiliated with Conservative congregations have little or no understanding of what Conservative Judaism is all about, including especially its intellectual approach and the demands that it makes in terms of Jewish practice. That is a very frustrating fact for the rabbis and laypeople who are committed Conservative Jews. Second, it is also clear that the Movement will continue to attract members, commitment, and creativity if, and only if, it communicates what it stands for in a clear, exciting, spiritually meaningful, and intellectually cogent way. As we have seen, most Jews of the third and fourth generations are not interested in the sociological gains of affiliation: they are interested in what the synagogue stands for and what it provides for them and their families in the modern world.

Consequently the Conservative Movement has felt the need to clarify its principles, demands, and goals for its leaders, members, and potential members. It can no longer be the case, as it has been, that Conservative Judaism in the minds of its members is simply a pareve (neutral), halfway house between Orthodoxy and Reform. Conservative Jews must be taught what it means to be a Conservative Jew so that they can appreciate its authenticity, maturity, dynamism, and wisdom.

That will mean that the Conservative Movement can no longer be a "catch-all" movement for virtually all Jews, as it was in the middle of the twentieth century. The very process of defining involves setting limits – the meaning of the Latin words from which the English word "define" comes – and that excludes certain practices and beliefs. Thus as the Conservative Movement has defined itself more clearly, it has experienced defections on both the left and the right. The Reconstructionist Movement established its own seminary for training rabbis with its ideology in 1968, and it is no longer the case that all rabbis and synagogues which identify as Reconstructionist also identify as Conservative – although some still do. Some on the far right of the movement left in the mid-1980s, largely over the issue of ordaining women as Rabbis, ultimately establishing their own seminary too. These have not represented major losses in numbers of people, but it has nevertheless been painful to experience these events on both personal and ideological levels.

Personally, many of the people involved were and continue to be friends and colleagues, and they left only with reticence and sadness when they felt the Conservative movement to be too slow, in one case, or too fast, in the other, in accommodating tradition to modernity. Ideologically, the loss of some individuals on the far left and right portions of the Conservative Movement's spectrum make it less rich and less able to accommodate a broad spectrum of beliefs and practices. These developments, however, painful as they have been, have also made the stance of Conservative Judaism much more explicit and distinctive, and so people who participate in Conservative synagogues, schools, youth groups, and camps now understand much more clearly what they are saying about themselves as Jews in becoming part of the Conservative movement.

One important effort to articulate the Conservative understanding of Judaism was the publication in 1988 of *Emet Ve-Emunah: Statement of Principles of Conservative Judaism,* the movement's first official statement of its philosophy. That document, to which we shall refer in later chapters, was the product of the Commission on the Philosophy of Conservative Judaism, which, as we have noted, included representatives of all of the major arms of the movement. This sourcebook, first published in 1977 and now being updated to take account of the many developments in Conservative thought and practice over the last nineteen years, is another effort to explain the ideas, actions, and feelings which define and motivate Conservative Judaism.

We have seen how Conservative Judaism developed. We are now going to look briefly at the institutions which it comprises – the members of the family, as it were – and then, in the next two chapters, we are going to consider the practices and beliefs that define Conservative Judaism so that your affiliation with it may become informed and intelligent.

QUESTIONS

1) Describe the changes that took place in the needs and desires of first, second, and third generation American Jews. Why was Conservative Judaism only minimally successful in affiliating the first generation and immensely successful in the second generation?

2) What forms did Conservative Judaism take on in the second generation which were borrowed from American Protestantism? Why were those forms adopted? Which of them persist? Which have been changed or dropped? Why?

3) What is the reaction of third-generation American Jews to their Judaism as described in this material? Test that description by answering the following questions and sharing your answers with the other members of your discussion group:

a) Think of all your Jewish friends (not only those in USY). Have any left Judaism by actively converting to another religion? How and why do you think that occurred? What are the reactions of their parents to the conversion?

b) Which of your friends would you describe as drifting away from Judaism? Why do you classify them that way? Why are they drifting? What is the reaction of their friends or parents?

c) Which of your friends are more committed to Judaism than their parents? How do you know that? What prompted them to be that way? What is the reaction of their friends and parents to this? Remember that commitment to Judaism is not only a matter of observing rituals, as important as they are; Jewish commitment also involves study, social action, Jewish communal activities, and moral sensitivity.

d) The descriptions in this section are obviously generalizations, and that means that there are undoubtedly exceptions. Can you think of any of your Jewish friends who plan on continuing more or less the same patterns of Jewish identification as their parents now practice? Why is that? Are you interested in having your children identify Jewishly as you do? If so, how do you plan on carrying out that objective?

e) Can you estimate what percentage of your friends fall into each of categories (a), (b), (c), and (d) above? Does that disturb you? If so, what do you plan on doing about it?

f) Where do you fit in the above categories? Are you happy about that? If you had your way, would you have every American Jew act as you do? Why or why not?

4) Answer the following questions yourself first. Then ask some of your Jewish friends. Then ask your parents and some of their friends so that you can determine whether there is any difference in the generations.

a) Would you say that you are an Orthodox, Conservative, Reform, or secular Jew (i.e., a Jew who identifies as a Jew in primarily non-religious ways)?

b) What do you mean by your answer in (a)?

c) How would your parents answer (a)? What would they mean?

5) Which of the following do you think is an important part of what it means to be a Conservative Jew? In each case explain your answer and how Reform or Orthodox Jews might differ:

    I)   Observance of the Jewish dietary laws (kashrut) in your home.
    ii)   Observance of the Jewish dietary laws when eating out.
    iii)   Affiliation with a Conservative synagogue.
    iv)   Speaking Hebrew.
    v)   Reading Hebrew.
    vi)   Contributing to Jewish tzedakot (charities).
    vii)   Spending time in Israel.
    viii)   Making aliyah (settling in Israel).
    ix)   Participating in Sabbath Services.
    x)   Participating in High Holy Day Services.
    xi)   Praying daily (publicly or privately).
    xii)   Having a Passover Seder.
    xiii)   Lighting Sabbath candles and saying the Kiddush on Friday night.
    xiv)   Working in a shelter for the homeless or in a nursing home for the aged.
    xv)   Engaging in interfaith discussions.
    xvi)   Observing Shabbat.
    xvii)   Building a Sukkah at your home for Sukkot.
    xviii) Maintaining regular Jewish study throughout your life.
    xix)   Not cheating on tests.
    xx)   Dating only Jews.
    xxi)   Marrying a Jew.
    xxii)   Once married, having children if one can.
    xxiii) Believing in God.
    xxiv) Believing in life after death.
    xxv) Believing that the Torah is the word of God.
    xxvi) Eating bagels and lox.
    xxvii) Knowing Israeli dances and songs.

(Note: Keep your own answers and those of the people you ask. After you have read Chapters III and IV, answer the questions again. How accurate were you? How accurate were the other people you asked? Does that have any implications for what the Conservative Movement must do?)

6) Have you ever been asked to explain your personal level of religious and ritual observance? How did you feel when answering the question?

ACTIVITY:

There was a tremendous immigration of Jews from the former Soviet Union into North America during the 1980's and 1990's. Since most of these individuals had virtually no Judaic knowledge, great efforts were made to "introduce" them to Judaism and to educate them about their heritage. Many USY chapters also made special efforts to reach out to teenagers in these families. How would you have tried to accomplish these goals? What do you think will happen to the coming generations of these families, in terms of their Jewish identity. Compare these efforts to those of the late 19th century to "Judaize" American Jews.

_____

_____

_____

_____

_____

_____

_____

_____

_____

_____

6. The Builders of the Conservative Movement

It is fitting that we end this historical section with a list of some of the people who have had a major influence on Conservative Judaism together with a brief description of the nature of that influence. The list and the descriptions are, of course, incomplete, but both have deliberately been kept short in the hope that you will remember at least some of the major figures involved. Those interested in more detailed information on this should consult the books listed in the bibliography, especially _Architects of Conservative Judaism_, by Herbert Parzen, _Conservative Judaism in America: A Biographical Dictionary and Sourcebook_ by Pamela S. Nadell, and Appendix A in _The Emergence of Conservative Judaism_, by Moshe Davis. So as not to prejudge history, this list, in the order of date of birth, has been confined to those who had a major impact on Conservative Judaism in the past and who have already passed on, thus transferring the mantle of leadership to those who bear it today.

Sabato Morais (1823-1897), the founding President of the Jewish Theological Seminary Association in 1886. A Sephardic Jew born and raised in Italy, he served as hazzan of the Mikveh Israel congregation in Philadelphia and received the first honorary doctorate ever conferred upon a Jew by the University of Pennsylvania.

Solomon Schechter (1847-1915), the second President of the Seminary (from 1902 to 1915) and founder and first President of the United Synagogue of America. Under his leadership, the Seminary obtained a distinguished faculty and a new, dynamic momentum. He made the Rabbinical School exclusively a graduate school so that rabbis would have a broad education in general culture in addition to their knowledge of Judaica, and he expanded its scope to offer doctoral programs. The Jewish Museum and the monetary foundations for a Seminary library came into being during his administration. Before his association with the Seminary, he was renowned for realizing the importance of the materials that S. A. Wertheimer had discovered in the Cairo Genizah (a burial vault of old Hebrew and rabbinic texts attached to an ancient synagogue there) and for mobilizing the effort to unearth and publish them. He was a staunch proponent of "positive-historical Judaism" and coined the translation "catholic Israel" in speaking about his concern for, and the authority of, Klal Yisrael. In establishing the United Synagogue, he transformed the Conservative scholarly approach into the Conservative Movement. His list of goals, included in his address to the founding meeting of the United Synagogue, says as much about the movement as the man: (a) order and decorum in the synagogue; (b) sermons and teaching in the English language, the language of America, rather than Yiddish; (c) selection of rabbis and teachers who are scientifically trained and educated in institutions wherein scientific techniques and research are fully utilized; (d) use of the newest methods in religious school instruction; (e) religious education for women and their adequate participation in the work of the congregation as well as in the movement; (f) Hebrew in the school and the synagogue; (g) a rounded religious education program including the preparation of books under expert supervision for the various members of the constituent congregations; (h) retention of worship as the primary feature of the synagogue; (i) rejuvenation of the Jewish home through the introduction of observances and ceremonies; (j) conservation of the dietary laws.[21]

Mathilde Schechter (1859-1924), founder of the National Women's League in 1918 to, as she said it, "serve the cause of Judaism by strengthening the bond of unity among Jewish women; and by learning to appreciate everything fine in Jewish life and literature, to instill the beauty of our ancient observances in the hearts of children.... to cherish the various ceremonies of Sabbath and the holidays ... to teach their significance intelligently..."

Cyrus Adler (1863-1940), the third President of the Seminary (1915-1940) under whom the Seminary built the three buildings on 122nd Street and Broadway in New York that house most of its operations to this day. He was influential in putting the Seminary on a solid financial and administrative footing and in bringing Solomon Schechter to head the reorganized Seminary in 1902. At the urgent pleas of all concerned, he served successively as Chairman of the Seminary's Board of Directors, President of the United Synagogue, and President of the Seminary. He also helped to found and direct The Jewish Publication Society, the American Jewish Historical Society, Dropsie College, the *Jewish Quarterly Review*, the Jewish Welfare Board, the American Jewish Committee, and the Joint Distribution Committee. He was truly an institution builder for the American Jewish community in general and for Conservative Judaism in particular.

Mordecai M. Kaplan (1881-1983), creator of the Reconstructionist ideology and member of the faculty of the Seminary for more than 50 years. A clear, powerful speaker, writer, and teacher, he had a direct, major influence on Conservative rabbis for two generations and, through his writings, has continued to influence Jewish life and thought after his death to this day. In his writing and teaching, he relentlessly forced himself and others to be clear about what they mean and say. His central idea of understanding Judaism as an evolving, religious civilization (an idea that we shall examine in detail in Chapter IV) has been almost universally accepted within the Conservative Movement, but his ideas about God and about what should be done in the area of Jewish observance have not been widely adopted. (The one exception is the Bat Mitzvah ceremony; he initiated that institution by creating a Bat Mitzvah ceremony for his own daughter in 1922.) He also accorded equal status to women in the prayer service at his synagogue from the 1930s on. He was among the moving forces that led to the founding of the United Synagogue of America, and it was his idea to establish a University of Judaism in Los Angeles which would foster all of the various elements of the Jewish civilization (including art, dance, music, language, literature, etc.) and not just its religion. In many ways, Dr. Kaplan was a central figure in the ideological development of Conservative Judaism because he forced both his admirers and his detractors to think through their positions thoroughly.

Louis Finkelstein (1895-1991), fourth president and Chancellor of the Jewish Theological Seminary of America from 1940 to 1972, and prolific writer on the talmudic period. During Dr. Finkelstein's administration, the programs of the Seminary were greatly expanded (to include The Cantors Institute and Seminary College of Jewish Studies, the Bernstein Pastoral Psychiatry Center, the Herbert Lehman Institute of Ethics, the Conference on Science, Philosophy, and Religion, the Melton Research Center, and the "Eternal Light" radio and television programs). In addition, the Seminary built its American Student Center in Jerusalem in 1963. Dr. Finkelstein, in conjunction with Dr. Saul Lieberman, the leading talmudic scholar at the Seminary, exerted a strong right-wing influence on the Conservative Movement during his chancellorship.

Simon Greenberg (1901-1993), Rabbi of Har Zion Temple in Philadelphia (1925-1946), Provost of the Seminary (1946-1951), Executive Director of the United Synagogue (1950-1953), one of the founders of USY, President (1955-1963) and moving force behind the founding of the University of Judaism in Los Angeles, Vice-Chancellor of the Seminary, and former President of the Rabbinical Assembly. Dr. Greenberg made his influence felt in virtually every institution and activity of the movement. One of Conservative Judaism's most articulate and persevering spokesmen, he stressed the centrality of the Jewish people, the importance of Zionism, the religious character of American civilization, and the importance of Hebrew in Jewish education. He is the author of a number of books and articles in Jewish thought, Jewish education, and American Jewish history, including a pamphlet on Conservative Judaism.

Abraham Joshua Heschel (1907-1972), Professor of Jewish Ethics and Mysticism at the Seminary from 1946 until his death, and world-renowned as a philosopher of religion, as an activist for civil rights in the United States and for Soviet Jewry, and as a spokesman for Judaism to the non-Jewish world.

Robert Gordis (1908-1992), Rabbi of Temple Beth El of Rockaway Park, New York from 1931 until his retirement in 1968, founder of the first Conservative day school, former President of the Rabbinical Assembly and of the Synagogue Council of America, and Rapaport Professor in the Philosophies of Religion and Professor of Bible at the Seminary from 1940 to his death. Dr. Gordis was a major influence on all three major institutions of the Conservative Movement and was an articulate spokesman for the centrist position in the Movement in both law and ideology. He wrote one of the first pamphlets specifically designed to explain Conservative ideology in 1946 and fittingly was called upon to serve as Chair of the Commission on the Philosophy of Conservative Judaism, the panel which produced the first official statement of Conservative ideology, Emet Ve-Emunah, in 1988.

Moshe Davis (1916-1996) as Dean of the Teachers Institute and Provost of the Seminary, he established Leaders Training Fellowship and was a prime mover in the founding of the Camp Ramah movement. He was also the first program editor of the Seminary's "Eternal Light" radio programs and its first television programs, entitled "Frontiers of Faith." He codirected the Seminary's American Jewish History Center before moving to Israel to head the Institute of Contemporary Jewry of the Hebrew University in Jerusalem.

Gerson D. Cohen (1924-1992), Chancellor of the Seminary from 1972 to 1985, under whom the Mathilde Schechter Residence Hall, a gift to the Seminary by the Women's League for Conservative Judaism, was completed and the new library building was built. Under his chancellorship, women were admitted to the Seminary's rabbinical school for the first time.

B. *The Structure of The Conservative Movement*

The Conservative Movement is composed of academic institutions, professional organizations, and lay groups, each with its own committees and activities. The Movement is one movement by virtue of the fact that the three groups cooperate in a number of different ways, partly through formal "Joint Commissions" and partly in more informal ways. Moreover, the three groups share common goals and a common ideology - although they sometimes interpret and apply them differently.

Since new programs are constantly being created by the constituent arms of the movement, and since new institutions emerge from time to time as well, no list can be complete. Moreover, a long list will probably not be helpful to the readers of this volume. The description which follows of the structure of the Conservative Movement, then, is admittedly partial and current, but it should give readers a good, general sense of the members of the Conservative Movement's institutional family, the organizations which all, in one way or another, help people live as Conservative Jews.

In reading the following list, look for the following things:

(1) Notice the variety of programs which the Conservative Movement includes in an effort to serve the needs of the contemporary Jewish community.

(2) Take note of programs in this list in which you would like to participate, either now or in the future, and write to them for more detailed descriptions of their programs.

1. The Academic Centers of the Conservative Movement

a) The Jewish Theological Seminary of America, 3080 Broadway, New York, NY 10027.

Includes an undergraduate college, professional programs for the training of Conservative rabbis, cantors, and teachers, and Masters and doctoral programs to prepare scholars of Judaica. Auxiliary programs include a supplementary high school program (Prozdor); the Ramah camps; the Jewish Museum (1109 Fifth Avenue in New York); the Institute for Religious and Social Studies; the Melton Research Center; the Bernstein and Brand Foundation counselling centers; and the Eternal Light radio and television programs.

b) The University of Judaism, 15600 Mulholland Drive, Los Angeles, CA 90077.

Offers an undergraduate liberal arts college, professional programs for the education of Conservative rabbis, educators, and managers of synagogues and federation agencies, and a Masters program in Jewish studies. Auxiliary programs include Camp Ramah in California and its year-round conference center; the Whizin Center with training programs for Jewish family educators and a research institute (Synagogue 2000) for planning the shape of synagogue life in the future; the Wagner program to train volunteers to help people cope with a variety of life situations; and a large Department of Continuing Education.

c) The Bet Midrash (The Seminary of Judaic Studies), 4 Avraham Granot Street, P.O. Box 8600, 91083 Neve Granot, Jerusalem, Israel.

A branch of the Seminary, it provides one year of rabbinic studies for those in the rabbinical schools of the Seminary and the University of Judaism in addition to offering programs to prepare Conservative rabbis and educators for Israel. Auxiliary programs include the Tali school system, Ramah camps in Israel, the Schocken Institute for Jewish Research, and outreach efforts to Jews in the former Soviet bloc.

d) The Seminario Rabbinico Latinamericano, Jose Hernandez 1750, 1426 Buenos Aires, Argentina.

Offers programs to prepare Conservative rabbis and educators for Latin America. Auxiliary programs include Ramah camps in Argentina and Chile and a kashrut certification system for Latin America.

44

2. The Professional Organizations of the Conservative Movement

a) **The Rabbinical Assembly, 3080 Broadway, New York, NY 10027.**

The international association of Conservative rabbis, now with over 1400 members, it includes about one hundred women rabbis, with the first admitted to its ranks in 1985. It runs a number of activities for the educational, social, and professional welfare of its members; determines the Conservative interpretation of Jewish law through its Committee on Jewish Law and Standards; coordinates rabbinic efforts on behalf of Israel and social action projects; and publishes books and other materials for use by rabbis and Conservative laypeople, including the journal, *Conservative Judaism*, a journal published in cooperation with the Seminary, and many fine materials for worship.

b) **Cantors Assembly, 3080 Broadway, Suite 613, New York, NY 10027.**
Jewish Educators Assembly, 106-06 Queens Blvd., Forest Hills, NY 11375.
Jewish Youth Directors Association, 155 Fifth Ave., New York, NY 10010.
North American Association of Synagogue Executives, Adath Jeshurun Cong.,
1109 Zane Ave. N., Golden Valley, MN 55422.

These organizations provide programs to augment the skills of their members and to insure the highest standards among the professionals serving congregations. Each of these associations cooperates with the United Synagogue in operating a placement service to aid congregations in obtaining qualified personnel.

3. The Lay Organizations of the Conservative Movement

a) **The United Synagogue of Conservative Judaism, 155 5th Avenue, New York, NY 10010.**

The organization of Conservative synagogues in North America with a membership of about 800 congregations, its influential work extends to the fields of Jewish education, youth activities, congregational programming, leadership development, congregational standards, social action, and Israel affairs. It accomplishes this through the publication of *The United Synagogue Review*; its network of regional branches, each with its own commissions, departments, and committees; its international office in New York; and, of course, through the programs and activities of the individual synagogues

45

themselves. The United Synagogue's Solomon Schechter Day School Association sets standards for Conservative day schools and provides a forum for them to share ideas. The United Synagogue also sponsors a Jerusalem Center for Conservative Judaism, which coordinates and creates new activities throughout Israel, together with Mercaz, the Conservative Zionist organization. United Synagogue Youth, the publisher of this volume, is part of the Department of Youth Activities of the United Synagogue.

b) **Women's League for Conservative Judaism, 48 East 74th Street, New York, NY 10021.**
Women's League for Conservative Judaism serves as the parent body for 700 affiliates in North America and in Israel, reflecting the multi-faceted concerns of modern Jewish women. Each of its branches conducts an annual conference, programs in cooperation with local synagogues, workshops, and study groups. *Outlook*, the Women's League magazine, has appeared quarterly since 1930. Active in world affairs, Women's League is an accredited, non-governmental observer at the United Nations. The Women's League has been directly involved with educational needs of the Seminary and the University of Judaism through the Torah Fund.

c) **Federation of Jewish Men's Clubs, 475 Riverside Drive, Suite 244, New York, NY 10115.**

Unifying close to 400 Men's Clubs affiliated with Conservative synagogues in North America, the Federation promotes appreciation of the Jewish heritage together with involvement in Jewish communal and synagogue life. The Federation, in cooperation with the University of Judaism, has published the Art of Jewish Living Series of books about the Sabbath, Passover, Hanukkah, and mourning rites to teach families of a variety of configurations how to mark those events in their homes. The Federation has also sponsored a program which has enabled over 100,000 people to gain Hebrew literacy so that they can participate in services. The Federation's magazine, *The Torchlight*, and a variety of Federation pamphlets are all part of its program for adult Jewish education. The Federation of Men's Clubs also sponsors the Tikvah program at several Ramah camps for Jewish youth with developmental disabilities.

d) **The World Council of Synagogues, 155 Fifth Avenue, New York, NY 10010.**

As the international arm of the Conservative Movement, the World Council of Synagogues is comprised of member congregations in 22 countries around the world.

4. "Joint Commissions"

These joint commissions generally include representatives from several arms of the movement. They include:

> The Joint Commission on Jewish Education
> The Joint Commission on Social Action
> The Joint Placement Commission
> The Joint Prayer Book Commission.

This last Commission and the Rabbinical Assembly are responsible for publications used in most Conservative synagogues. You are probably familiar with some of them: *Siddur Sim Shalom, The Sabbath and Festival Prayer Book, Weekday Prayer Book, Mahzor for Rosh Hashanah and Yom Kippur, The Feast of Freedom* (a Haggadah for Passover), *The Bond of Life* (for a house of mourning), *Megillat Esther with Introduction, New Translation and Commentary,* and others. These books include major innovations dictated by the philosophy of the Conservative Movement to make the liturgy reflect the language, concerns, and ideas of the Jewish community of the present in the framework of the hallowed traditions of the past. So, for example, modern English is used in translating the prayers, references to sacrifices are primarily historical, and the prayerbooks include liturgical reactions to the Holocaust and Israel's independence.

Finally, nationally there is a **Conservative Movement Leadership Cabinet** and a **Conservative Movement Forum,** consisting of representatives of all the arms of the movement, which meets periodically to coordinate activities and initiate joint efforts. Several regions have similar bodies which meet for the same purposes.

All of these organizations are responses to the needs of our movement to teach and live Judaism in the vibrant way it should be known and lived. The organizations gain their importance from the sacred tasks to which they are devoted.

CHAPTER III
JEWISH LAW WITHIN THE CONSERVATIVE MOVEMENT

The Torah, the foundation of Judaism, contains 613 commandments (commonly called "*Taryag Mitzvot*" since תַּרְיַ״ג "*Taryag*," is the Hebrew numerical equivalent of 613). Almost all of them tell you to *do* something or not to *do* something; none of them says "*believe* something" or "don't *believe* something" with the possible exception of the first of the Ten Commandments. Judaism has certainly always included a number of beliefs which serve as the source and rationale for observing the commandments, and we could probably even describe a mainstream Jewish position on many issues; but it has largely left it to the individual to decide the particular form of belief to adopt, as long as the person continues to observe Jewish law. Consequently, we will first examine the way in which Conservative Judaism treats Jewish law; then, in Chapter IV, we will turn our attention to Jewish beliefs.

A. The General Approach of Conservative Judaism to Jewish Law: Tradition and Change

In 1958 Rabbi Mordecai Waxman edited a book entitled *Tradition and Change*. That title has virtually become the motto of the Conservative Movement. As Rabbi Waxman himself explains it,

> Reform has asserted the right of interpretation but it has rejected the authority of the legal tradition. Orthodoxy has clung fast to the principle of authority, but has in our own and recent generations rejected the right to any but minor interpretations. The Conservative view is that both are necessary for a living Judaism. Accordingly, Conservative Judaism holds itself bound by the Jewish legal tradition, but asserts the right of its rabbinical body, acting as a whole, to interpret and to apply Jewish law.[1]

The first thing that you must understand about the Conservative approach to Jewish law is that *Conservative Judaism requires observance of the laws of classical Judaism*, including the dietary laws (*kashrut*), the Sabbaths and Festivals, daily and Sabbath worship, and the moral norms of the Torah, Prophets, and Sages. It is *not* the case that you are "Orthodox" if you observe the dietary laws or Shabbat, as many American Jews think: Conservative Judaism requires that too! Following the *mitzvot* is the "Tradition" part of the motto "Tradition and Change," and it is the reason why the Movement is called "the *Conservative* Movement"; as we have seen, its founders wanted to *conserve* Jewish law. That *must* be the case because

49

we have seen, its founders wanted to *conserve* Jewish law. That *must* be the case because Conservative Judaism insists upon studying the tradition historically, and through the ages acting in accordance with the *mitzvot* has always been a key factor in what it means to be a Jew. Only observant forms of Judaism are historically authentic.

On the other hand, the *content* of Jewish law – that is, the specific ways in which Jewish law is to be observed – has not been the same in all periods of history. On the contrary, there have been many changes in Jewish law, including additions, deletions, and modifications. For example, Simhat Torah is a major festival in the Jewish year that has no roots in the Bible or Talmud: it developed in the Diaspora and is celebrated even in Israel, where the second day of Yom Tov (on which it occurs in the Diaspora) is not observed. Similarly, the *kippah* has become a universally recognized Jewish symbol only in the last four centuries. On the other hand, some laws have been dropped, sometimes out of necessity (e.g., all of the laws relating to the ancient Temple), sometimes out of choice (e.g., the acceptance of "the law of the land" in place of all Jewish civil and criminal legislation in rabbinic, medieval, and, to an increased extent, in modern times), and sometimes out of disuse (e.g., some of the laws of purity). And finally, Jewish laws have been modified in form. For example, in talmudic times there was a mandatory full year period between engagement *(erusin)* אֵרוּסִין and marriage *(kiddushin)* קדוּשִׁין with separate ceremonies for each; since the Middle Ages, both ceremonies are done together under the wedding canopy, separated only by the reading of the *ketubbah* כְּתֻבָּה (wedding contract).

All three types of changes – additions, deletions, and modifications-- have occurred constantly and pervasively in Jewish law. Some of those changes occurred gradually and unconsciously, but many were consciously designed by rabbis in specific generations to make observance of Jewish law possible, relevant, and uplifting in their time. As we shall see, the Rabbis of the Talmud and Middle Ages saw it as their responsibility to make such changes under the authority entrusted to them in the Torah, specifically, in Devarim 17. Consequently, it not only is a fact that changes *have* occurred; it is also that changes *must* be introduced at times if the requirements of the Torah are to be carried out. In fact, *not* to make the necessary adjustments in Jewish law would be to abandon the tradition!

That poses a major problem, though: how do you balance tradition with change? It is easy to accept all of tradition: you simply follow whatever code you choose (the sixteenth-century Shulhan Arukh is a popular choice) blindly and mechanically. That may require a lot from you in terms of action, but it certainly does not require any judgment on your part or attention to the complications of modern life. You practice Judaism as if nothing had changed in the last

Tradition, for there have been numerous responsa during that period of time that have changed Jewish law substantially. It is, however, an approach adopted by all too many Jews who want to return to the Tradition, largely out of ignorance or misplaced zeal. On the other hand, to change the Tradition at will or to give it little weight in deciding how to practice Judaism is to create your own religion. The whole point of the Conservative Movement is that to practice Judaism authentically you must combine tradition with change. In other words, we need to achieve the *balance* expressed by the "and" in the motto "Tradition and Change."

That is the general approach of the Conservative Movement to Jewish law. Before you can understand that fully, however, you need to know three things:

> (1) You will need to consider the evidence for the assertion that Jewish law has always been a matter of tradition and change. So far you have only been shown a few concrete examples of that process, but you deserve to see much more of the theory and practice of traditional Jewish law if you are to be convinced of that.

> (2) You will also need to understand the various approaches to explain the authority of Jewish law. After all, if human beings can change it, how is it divine in any way? And if it is not divine, why does it have any more authority than any system of law created by human beings -- or, for that matter, any authority at all?

> (3) Even if you accept the notion that Jewish law should involve tradition and change, how do you put that into practice? Which traditions and which changes? And who decides? What procedures has the Conservative Movement developed for such decisions?

In sections (C), (D), and (E) of this chapter, we will try to answer those questions in turn, but first you must learn (or review) a few important facts about the history and literature of Jewish law so that you can be familiar with the terms and concepts.

QUESTIONS:

1)   Why is it that Conservative Judaism insists upon observance of Jewish law?

2)   If both Orthodoxy and Conservatism require observance of *kashrut*, Shabbat, etc. how are they different?

(Hint: Recall the material in Chapter II, and answer the question in terms of how each understands the origins of Jewish law. Also answer this question in terms of how each determines the content of Jewish law and how each views other customs, if you can. You will be able to answer this question more fully once you have completed this chapter.)

3)   "I know a lot of Conservative Jews who do not observe *kashrut* and *Shabbat*." Explain how this can be true even though the Conservative Movement requires observance.

(Hint: distinguish levels of affiliation with the Conservative Movement, from one who simply feels like a Conservative Jew, to those who join a Conservative synagogue, to those who participate actively in the activities and programs of that synagogue, to those who take the ideology seriously and make it part of their daily lives.)

4)   Give some specific examples of how Jewish law has added observances, dropped some, and modified some. Classify each change according to these categories: technology, values (e.g., feminism), new freedoms (e.g., ability to go to college), other.

5)   Which of the examples that you gave in answer to Question (4) were brought about by a conscious decision of some rabbi or group of rabbis and which just developed as customs of a certain segment of the Jewish People? Can you think of comparable examples in the practices of American society – i.e., some that came into being through custom? Why is a greater percentage of Jewish law determined by custom than in American law? (Consider the fact that Jews are scattered, that there is no central legislature for Jewish law, modern communications, etc.)

6)   "*Not* to make the necessary adjustments in Jewish law would be to abandon the tradition!" Why?

7)   In what ways is it harder to be a Conservative Jew than an Orthodox or Reform one? Why bother, then?

ACTIVITY:

Ask your parents and grandparents what they feel have been the greatest changes in the world and in society since their youth. Think about how these changes have impacted upon Judaism. Make a list of what you feel will be the greatest changes in the coming generation and how they will effect Judaism. How do you feel Judaism should respond to these changes, while maintaining the halakhic integrity of the Movement? How might Conservative Judaism's solutions be different from other Movements'?

_____

_____

_____

_____

_____

_____

B. The Historical Development of Jewish Law

In order to aid you in keeping track of what happened when, keep your finger on the following 2 pages with the Time-Line of Jewish Law as you read this section. Don't worry: the terms will be explained in the pages following, and you will not need to know all of the dates and names. All of this information is being included so that the Time-Line can serve as both a guide and a reference for you and so that you can understand the basis for a major claim of this chapter and of Conservative Judaism, namely, that Jewish law has always been characterized by tradition and change. You should also refer to the "flow chart of halakhah" on page 276. This will give you a good picture of how everything fits together.

1. The Formation and Writing of the Oral Law: 444 B.C.E. - 200 C.E.

The biblical Book of Nehemiah, Chapters 8-10, records a very important ceremony. The Jewish People had been exiled from Jerusalem to Babylonia after the destruction of the First Temple in 586 B.C.E. A group of them returned to Israel in 539 B.C.E. with the permission of the Persians (who had conquered the Babylonians) and by 516 they had rebuilt the Temple. In the middle of the next century Ezra and Nehemiah built a wall around Jerusalem, and they got permission from the Persian king to use the Torah as the law of the Jews there. To make that work, they had to inform the people of the contents of the Torah, and so they

TIME-LINE OF JEWISH LAW

c. 1700 B.C.E*   - Abraham
c. 1290 B.C.E.   - Exodus from Egypt; Moses
c. 1000 B.C.E.   - David

c. 950 B.C.E. - 586 B.C.E. - The First Temple Period (Biblical laws and Prophets)
722 B.C.E.   - Fall of Northern Kingdom: 10 tribes become "lost"
586 B.C.E.   - Fall of Southern Kingdom: exile to Babylonia

c. 516 B.C.E. - 70 C.E. - The Second Temple Period
516 B.C.E.   - Some return to Israel under Haggai and Zekhariah
444 B.C.E.   - Ezra: a) Institutes synagogue and prayer service

  b) Canonized the Torah by reading it publicly in Jerusalem on Sukkot

  c) Appoints the Men of the Great Assembly (which is probably an early form of the institution later known by the Greek name "Sanhedrin"); they are scholars, judges, and legislators

444 B.C.E. - 70 C.E. - Development of the Oral Tradition
70 C.E. - 200 C.E.   - Period of the Tanna'im (organized Oral Law)

(A) Their decisions are contained in:
  (1) The Mishnah - R. Judah Ha-Nasi (6 Sedarim, 63 Massekhtot; Hebrew)
  (2) The Tosefta - R. Hiyya and R. Oshaiah
  (3) Baraitot - known only through their appearance in the Gemara

(B) Their legal interpretations of biblical verses appear in *Midr'shai Halakhah*:
  (1) The Mekhilta - on Exodus
  (2) The Sifra - on Leviticus
  (3) The Sifre - on Numbers and Deuteronomy

200 C.E. - 500 C.E - Period of the Amora'im

(A) *The Babylonian Talmud (Gemara)* compiled by Ravina and Rav Ashi c. 500 C.E. (same order as Mishnah; Babylonian Aramaic)

(B) *The Palestinian (Jerusalem) Talmud (Gemara)* compiled c. 400 C.E. (same order as Mishnah; Palestinian Aramaic; much shorter than the Babylonian Talmud)

---

*B.C.E. = Before the Common Era; C.E. = In the Common Era.

B.C.E.=B.C., and C.E.=A.D., but since "B.C." (Before Christ) and "A.D." (anno domini, in the year of our Lord) refer to Jesus as Lord, many Jews use the notations employed here. When it is clear that dates refer to the Common Era, "C.E." (or "A.D.") is often dropped.

500 - 650 *- Period of the Sabora'im*

650 - 1050 *- Period of the Geonim* (in Babylonia). The responsa literature

c. *1000 - 1250* *- Period of the Commentators and Early Posekim.* (in Spain, France, and North Africa)

1013 - 1073	- R. Isaac of Fez ("Alfasi," "Rif")
1040 - 1105	- R. Sh'lomo Yitzhaki ("Rashi")
c. 1100 - 1275	- Tosafot (e.g., Rabbenu Tam, Ri, etc.)
1135 - 1204	- Maimonides ("Rambam") (*The Mishneh Torah; The Guide for the Perplexed*)

1250 - 1550 *- Period of the Rishonim* (in Spain, France and North Africa)

1195 - 1270	- R. Moses b. Nahman (Nahmanides, "Ramban")
1233 - 1320	- R. Solomon b. Abraham ibn Adret ("Rashba")
1250 - 1327	- R. Asher ben Yehiel ("Rosh," "Asheri")
1270 - 1343	- R. Jacob ben Asher (*Arba'ah Turim or "The Tur"* – 4 rows or parts: *Orah Hayyim, Yoreh De'ah, Even-Ha'Ezer, Hoshen Mishpat*)
1550	- R. Joseph Karo (*The Shulhan Arukh* - the order of the Tur)

1550 - present *- Period of the Aharonim* (primarily in Eastern Europe and the Eastern Mediterranean)

c. 1650	- R David ben Samuel Ha-Levy (*Turei Zahav* = "Taz")
c. 1650	- R. Shabb'tai b. Meir Ha-Kohen (*Siftei Kohen* = "Shakh")
1720 - 1797	- R. Elijah, the Gaon of Vilna
1863	- R. Solomon Ganzfried (*The Kitzur Shulhan Arukh*)
1829 - 1908	- R. Yehiel M. Epstein (*Arukh Ha-Shulhan*)
1838 - 1933	- R. Israel Meir Kagan (*Mishnah Berurah*)

read it to all of the people assembled. The princes, Levites, and Kohanim bound themselves to it in writing and the rest of the people swore an oath to abide by it.

Why was that so important? That depends upon your theology. If you accept Orthodox belief, all of the Torah had already been given at Sinai some 800 years earlier, and this was merely a rededication to it. If you study the Bible historically, as the Conservative Movement does, then this is nothing less than the Jewish Philadelphia, the time in which the Torah became the Constitution of the Jewish People. Until that time many of the biblical laws and stories had been known and accepted by the people, but they had not been put together as one document. In fact, the Torah contains many materials from widely different time periods and places, and that is why some of the laws and stories actually contradict each other.[2] It was only in Ezra's time that the Torah became "canonized"' -- that is, that it received its final form and became the authoritative constitution of the Jewish People. In any case, on either interpretation, the Torah had certainly achieved that status by the time of Ezra (if not earlier).

Ezra is credited by the tradition for doing something else that is of major importance for Jewish law. Chapters 4 and 13 of Devarim (the last book of the Torah) forbid adding to the commandments of the Torah or subtracting from them. In other words, the Jewish constitution is different from the American Constitution in one critical point of method: the Jewish constitution lacks an amendment clause. In fact, it forbids the entire legislative procedure. Chapter 17 of Devarim, however, allows and even requires that a judicial system be established for each generation with complete authority over that generation:

> If a case is too baffling for you to decide, be it a controversy over homicide, civil law, or assault -- matters of dispute in your courts -- you shall promptly repair to the place which the Lord your God has chosen, and appear before the levitical priests, or the magistrate in charge at the time, and present your problem. When they have announced to you the verdict in the case, you shall carry out the verdict that is announced to you from that place which the Lord chose, observing scrupulously all their instructions to you. You shall act in accordance with the instructions given you and the ruling handed down to you; you must not deviate from the verdict that they announce to you either to the right or to the left. Should a man act presumptuously and disregard the priest charged with serving there the Lord your God, or the magistrate, that man shall die. Thus you will sweep out evil from Israel: all the people will hear and be afraid and will not act presumptuously again.
>
> (Devarim 17:8-13)

Moses had established a judiciary long before (cf. Shemot 18), but Ezra reinstituted the judiciary in the Second Temple period (Ezra 7:25-26). It was called the כְּנֶסֶת הַגְּדוֹלָה (the

56

Great Assembly). In later periods the central governing body of the Jewish community was called by the Greek equivalent, Sanhedrin. Historians differ as to the exact nature and procedures of these institutions, but as far as we can tell, some such central governing body existed from the time of Ezra (444 B.C.E.) to the demise of the Sanhedrin in 361 C.E. According to tradition, there were 71 judges in the Sanhedrin. When one retired or died, the remaining members would elect a new member from among those who had passed the equivalent of the Bar Examination in those days (called סְמִיכָה), thus demonstrating that they were learned in the law. You could not qualify by being elected by the people, or by having land or money, or through inheritance. You needed to be educated in Jewish law and certified as such. From Ezra's time on, then, Judaism increasingly became an aristocracy of the learned – but an aristocracy which even a humble shepherd like Rabbi Akiba could join if he put his mind to it.

The Sanhedrin passed down its decisions from generation to generation in oral form. That may seem strange to you because the American system of law largely depends upon written materials. If you lived in England, though, that would not seem strange to you at all because among the English there is a long tradition of oral decisions, called "the common law." In fact, after the constitutional revolution in England, the House of Lords, which functions as the Supreme Court, voted in 1698 to ban and punish publication of their decisions altogether. No more written reports of the House of Lords cases appeared until 1784.

Why the oral form? There are several important reasons recorded in rabbinic literature:

1) God specifically gave some laws orally, so how can we dare to change their form? (*B. Temurrah* 14b, *B. Gittin* 60b).

2) God was afraid that if the laws were written, the Gentiles would discover them and either steal them for themselves, thus weakening the uniqueness and identity of the Jewish People, or else misinterpret them and use them to undermine rabbinic authority (*Tanhuma Buber*, Ki Tissa, 58b; *Bamidbar Rabbah* 14:10).

3) It is simply impossible to write down all of the laws that were part of the oral tradition (*Bamidbar Rabbah* 14:4).

4) Many of the laws are demanding and consequently seem strange. There is a much better chance of explaining the laws and encouraging people to observe them if they are taught in the context of an intimate, teacher-student relationship rather than in a cold, difficult scroll (*B. Gittin* 60a - 60b).

5) Only if the Oral Law remained oral could Jewish law retain sufficient flexibility to be able to adapt to new situations (*B. Hullin* 6b-7a). This is especially important in view of the Torah's prohibition against adding to it legislatively (Devarim 4:2 and 13:1), as we discussed earlier.

As a result, the decisions of the Sanhedrin were handed down orally from the time of Ezra onwards. You are probably wondering how they could have survived in that form. After all, human memory is short and inaccurate, and so how was it that the decisions did not just get forgotten or hopelessly confused? The answer is an ingenious system that the Rabbis invented for preserving the decisions. Recognizing that some people are better at memorizing things and some people are better at analyzing them, they chose a group of people skilled at memorization to be members of the guild of memorizers, called "*Tanna'im*," תַּנָּאִים or "repeaters." When the Sanhedrin had reached a decision, the President of the Sanhedrin would teach it to the head of the Tanna'im, who, in turn, would teach it to the second-in-command, and so on, until the entire group knew it. It was their job, then, to repeat it constantly (hence their name) and to supply it when requested by the Sanhedrin in the course of its discussions of other issues. They were, in other words, a sort of human memory bank.

That system worked well until the second century C.E. The Second Temple had been destroyed by the Romans in 70 C.E. After that time, many political and religious restrictions were imposed upon Jews, culminating in the Hadrianic persecutions and the Bar Kokhba Revolt in the 130's C.E. Consequently, despite all of the considerations that led them to hand down the tradition orally and leave it in a loose form, they decided, reluctantly, to organize it in a fixed form so that it would not get lost. Rabbi Akiba, Rabbi Meir, and Rabbi Yose each compiled a collection of those decisions, but the edition that gained almost immediate authority was the "*Mishnah*" מִשְׁנָה by (or in the name of) Rabbi Judah, the President of the Sanhedrin, probably because he held that position.

> **Definition**: The MISHNAH is the collection by Rabbi Judah Ha-Nasi (the President) of the decisions of the Sages from roughly 444 B.C.E. to 200 C.E.

Another collection which gained some popularity and authority was the *Tosefta* תּוֹסֶפְתָּא (literally, "the addition"), which is another edition of the decisions of the Sages in that time period. In addition, some of the decisions which do not appear in either of these two collections are mentioned in the discussions of the Mishnah that took place in the centuries following its compilation. Those decisions are called "*Baraitot*" בָּרַיְתוֹת (literally, "the outside ones," because they are outside of the Mishnah), and they are recorded in the Talmud, which is the record of the later discussions about the Mishnah.

The Mishnah is organized according to subject matter, divided into six *Sedarim* סְדָרִים ("Orders"; singular, "*Seder*"-- just like the name for the ceremony which follows a set order on Passover). The six *Sedarim* are, in turn, divided into *Massekhtot* מַסֶּכְתּוֹת ("tractates" or "books"; singular, "*Massekhet*"). There are 63 *Massekhtot* in the Mishnah, each on a specific subject, although other topics are sometimes included. A list of the *Sedarim* and *Massekhtot*, together with a brief description of the content of each appears in Appendix V; that list will give you an idea of the scope of Jewish law and will enable you to get used to the names of the books in this critically important source of the Jewish tradition.

There is another type of literature that comes from this time period (444 B.C.E. - 200 C.E.). It is *Midrash Halakhah*, מִדְרָשׁ הֲלָכָה which is the interpretation (= "*Midrash*") of the legal sections (= "*Halakhah*") of the Torah. Since there are very few laws in Bereshit, there is only Midrash Halakhah on the last four books of the Torah, collected in the three compilations listed in (B) on the Time-Line. Each book is arranged according to the order of the Bible, so that the comment on Shemot 21:11, for example, is followed immediately by the comment on Shemot 21:12, even though the two verses speak about totally different matters.

The laws of the Bible are not organized by topic; in fact, the laws on any given subject may appear in several places in the Bible. Since the Midrash Halakhah is a line-by-line interpretation of the legal sections of the Bible, it is not arranged by topic either, and that makes it rather cumbersome for a judge to use. Moreover, the Midrash Halakhah often records several different possible interpretations of a verse without coming to a decision as to which one of them is the law. It should not be surprising, then, that the Mishnah, which is arranged by topic and which records decisions, gained almost immediate authority since it was *that* book which judges could most easily use in making their decisions when a case came to court. (Moreover, as we mentioned before, it carried the name and authority of Rabbi Judah, the President of the Sanhedrin.) On the other hand, the Mishnah rarely supplies the reasons for its decisions, and consequently the Midrash Halakhah is often used by later rabbis who need to know the rationale behind a law in order to apply it to a new or difficult case -- just as American judges deciding difficult cases will use the *Congressional Record* in addition to the *United States Code* in order to determine the intent of Congress in passing legislation, and will use the written opinions of previous judges in order to know how to apply their rulings. As a result, both the decisions themselves [(A) on the Time-Line] and the reasoning that led to the decisions [(B) on the Time-Line] were preserved, but the Mishnah and Tosefta have greater authority than the Baraitot or Midreshai Halakhah in the sense that they were more commonly used in court.

2. The Period of the Amora'im and the Talmud: 200 - 500 C.E.

In the next several centuries, leadership of the Jewish community increasingly passed over to the Babylonian Jewish community. A large group of Jews had been living there ever since the destruction of the First Temple (remember that only a small percentage of that group had returned to Israel with Ezra). Between 200 and 500 C.E., that community lived rather securely under Persian rule. Great law schools were developed there in which the Mishnah was discussed and applied to new circumstances. Those discussions were kept in oral form for the same reasons that we considered earlier. Once again, though, political and economic conditions at the end of this period forced the discussions to be organized. This time it was the increasing pressure on the Jews by radical Zoroastrian rulers in Persia that endangered the chain of tradition and convinced the Rabbis that their discussions must be organized and edited if they were not to be lost.

The record of those discussions is called, in Hebrew, the *Talmud*, תַּלְמוּד from the Hebrew word meaning "to learn," since it consists of the discussions which record how the rabbis learned and interpreted the Mishnah. Sometimes the Talmud is called the "*Gemara*," גְמָרָא from the Aramaic word which also means "to learn."

In Israel the Jews that remained lived under Roman rule and were not allowed to teach or practice their religion during some parts of this period. They did succeed, however, in establishing one academy in Tiberias which was far from the centers of Roman power in Palestine. The rabbis there often had to meet in hiding, but they did manage to carry on discussions of the Mishnah in which they too applied the law to new cases. As the Roman Empire was beginning to crumble, the law and order that Rome had guaranteed (however oppressive it may have been at times) disintegrated, and once again the rabbis felt the need to write a record of their discussions in order to preserve them.

> ### Definition:
> The TALMUD (or GEMARA) is the record of the discussions about the Mishnah
> that took place in Babylonia between 200 and 500 C.E. and in Israel between
> 200 and 400 C.E. (There are therefore two Talmuds, a Babylonian Talmud and
> a Palestinian Talmud.)

The Palestinian Talmud is sometimes called "The Western Talmud" ("*Talmud Ha-ma'aravi*") or, more commonly, "The Jerusalem Talmud" (the *Talmud Yerushalmi*) -- even though the discussions it records did not take place in Jerusalem. The Babylonian Talmud is called, in Hebrew, the *Talmud Bavli*. Because the Babylonian community was closer to the center of

Arab power and the trade routes in the next major period of Jewish history, the Babylonian Talmud spread to many more Jewish communities than the Palestinian Talmud did and consequently became more authoritative – that is, became the standard way Jews understood and practiced Judaism in most places of the world. Therefore, whenever people refer simply to "The Talmud," they almost always have the Babylonian Talmud in mind.

Since both Talmuds are discussions of the Mishnah, the order and divisions of the Talmud are the same as the order and divisions of the Mishnah (see list in Appendix V). However, a few *Massekhtot* consist only of Mishnah without the explanatory Talmud.[3]

There is one other type of rabbinic literature that was produced in this time period (although most of it was not compiled until later). It is the *Midrash Aggadah,* מִדְרָשׁ אַגָּדָה the interpretation (= "Midrash") of the non-legal sections of the Bible (= "Aggadah"). Since there is much more Midrash Aggadah than Midrash Halakhah, the Midrash Aggadah is often simply called "The Midrash." The purpose of the rabbinic comments was to stimulate the intellect and enhance commitment, not to decide legal issues. In rabbinic terminology, the Aggadah was intended "to draw the heart of a person."[4]

Because the Midrash Aggadah did not determine matters of community practice, there was no need to establish a uniformity of viewpoint within the Midrash Aggadah; on the contrary, in view of its purpose, that would have been counterproductive since different things stimulate and motivate each one of us. The Midrash Aggadah therefore contains a potpourri of views on a number of subjects. That makes it interesting and fun, but it sometimes also makes it difficult to determine whether there was any consensus on a given issue.[5] Furthermore, since Jews did not have to know the material in the Midrash Aggadah in order to know what was expected of them as Jews, the Midrash Aggadah was not committed to writing until the Middle Ages, although much of the material dates from talmudic times. The Midrash Aggadah is recorded in a number of collections, but perhaps the most famous are the group known as "*Midrash Rabbah*" מִדְרָשׁ רַבָּה (literally, "the large Midrash"), which is a line-by-line commentary on the Five Books of Moses and the Five Scrolls (Shir HaShirim, Ruth, Eicha, Kohelet, and Esther), all of which are read in the synagogue at some point during the year and therefore especially subject to comment. We will use the Midrash Aggadah in this chapter, along with sections of the Mishnah and Talmud, to see the way in which the Rabbis thought about their legal authority and activity and, in the next chapter, to examine their views on God, humanity, and other philosophical issues.

Key to references in the Mishnah, Talmuds, and Midrash: References to biblical books traditionally are cited by book, chapter and verse (e.g., Shemot 12:2 [or, in English, Exodus

12:2 or Ex. 12:2]). References to the major collection of Midrash Aggadah, known as *Midrash Rabbah*, can easily be confused with biblical references because they also refer to book, chapter and verse. The letter *R* is added, however, indicating that it is a reference to the Midrash Rabbah (e.g., Shemot R. 28:6 [or, in English, Exodus R. 28:6]).

References to the Mishnah begin with "M." for Mishnah and then record the tractate, chapter and law (e.g., *M. Bava Kamma* 4:2). References to the Babylonian Talmud, which commonly (but not always) begin with "B" or "B.T." for Babylonian Talmud or "T.B." for Talmud Bavli, follow the same tractate scheme as the Mishnah, but talmudic references can be recognized immediately because page numbers followed by the letter a or b are used instead of chapter and law (e.g., *B. Bava Kamma* 83b or, simply, *Bava Kamma* 83b). While most books in English are numbered consecutively, with one number on the one side of the page and the next number on the opposite side, the Talmud's numbers refer to both sides of the page, and so an "a" following the number refers to the first side of the page as one reads the book, and "b" refers to the second side of the page. Fortunately, the page numbering of the Bomberg edition of the Babylonian Talmud, the first complete printing of the Talmud (1520-23), has been universally accepted, and so sections are always cited according to that numbering; that makes it clear to everyone living any time after that printing at least what page is being discussed.

Sections of the Palestinian Talmud are always preceded by "J" (or J.T. or T.J.) for Jerusalem Talmud or "P" (or P.T.) for Palestinian Talmud. Because the Palestinian Talmud was not as well-known or authoritative, no edition of it ever became widely used. Therefore, citations to it are usually to the chapter and law of the Mishnah on which the comment appears as part of the discussion (e.g., *J. Pe'ah* 4:1) or sometimes to the page number and column in the one-volume edition of the Palestinian Talmud (e.g., *J. Pe'ah* 17d).

3. The Periods of the Sabora'im and Geonim: 500 - 1050 C.E.

The period between 500 and 650, during the waning years of Persian rule, is the period of the Sabora'im, who standardized the text of the Talmud and expanded some sections of it in order to explain them.

Mohammed, who preached in the early 600s, died in 632. He founded a new religion known as "Islam," meaning "submission," because its major teaching is that everyone must submit to *Allah* (God). Since Mohammed did not require that the submission be willing, those who followed him were quick to use military means to gain the submission of the people of the world to the will of God as they saw it. By 711 they had conquered almost all of the known world, from India to Spain. At first they were very zealous in trying to get everyone to convert to Islam, but they soon found that they did not have the manpower to do that. They were simply spread too thin. As a result, they let certain communities rule themselves (specifically, the Jews, Christians, and Zoroastrians) as long as they paid taxes to the caliph, and then the Moslems used their limited manpower to defend their realm and enforce their religious demands on other groups within it.

This policy gave the Jewish community a great deal of internal freedom. They took part in government, commerce, and the professions and practiced Judaism with few restrictions -- at least in most times and places during this period. There was an official liaison of the Jewish community to the government called a "Resh Galuta" רֵישׁ גָּלוּתָא ("Head of the Diaspora"), but the real power in Jewish law rested with the *Geonim* גְּאוֹנִים . The Geonim (singular, "Gaon") were heads of the two major law schools in Babylonia, one in Sura and one in Pumbedita. When Jews had questions of Jewish law, they would ask the most learned Jew in the community. If that person did not know how to answer, he (women were rarely involved in this process, if at all) would write the question to one of the Geonim, who would write a response. In that way the *responsa* literature (singular, "responsum") developed. In Hebrew it is called *she'elot u'teshuvot,* שְׁאֵלוֹת וּתְשׁוּבוֹת " questions and answers."

While determining Jewish law through questions and answers first became popular during the Geonic period, that method has persisted to this day. In fact, most discussions of Jewish law today center around *teshuvot* (responsa) written in response to a specific case or question. That enables Jewish law to be responsive to the specific issues which each Jew or Jewish community faces and thus helps Jewish law to stay current and relevant. During most of the period between 650 and today, however, it was hard to know whether responsa had already been written on a given issue because most often a rabbi would simply answer a question orally, and even if the answer was written down, it often was just a letter to the person who asked the question. The responsa of rabbis who were known for their expertise in Jewish law and who were admired for their personal qualities were sometimes later published in collections of their responsa, but that meant that one could only know whether a responsum relevant to your question had been written if one had access to, and knew, all of the books of responsa literature that had been published. Now, however, some 300,000 responsa have been computerized by Bar Ilan University in Israel, and one can buy a computer disc with all of them on it. That still does not eliminate the need for learning how to reason legally -- any more than a similar computer program for American law (Lexis) eliminates the need to go to law school -- but it sure makes finding material which might possibly be relevant to a given question much easier. This new technological development, plus the ability of responsa to respond to particular circumstances, has made responsa the primary way in which issues in Jewish law are addressed in our day.

4. The Commentators, Posekim, Rishonim, and Synods: 1000 - 1550 C.E.

Due to a drought in the Middle East and a decentralization and shifting of Arab power to the West, Jews moved to the western part of the Muslim empire in North Africa, Egypt, and Spain in the tenth and eleventh centuries. Simultaneously small numbers of Jews were being attracted to Western Europe by favorable commercial and communal policies offered to them by the Christian kings there. The political instability of Spain during the eleventh century and the persecutions which the Jews suffered at the hands of fanatic Muslim rulers of the twelfth century impelled more Jews to live under Christian rule in France and, later, in Germany. The majority still lived under the Muslims during this time period, but a significant number found themselves under Christian domain.

In the first centuries in which Jews lived under the Muslims, Muslim society was culturally pluralistic and open, in which the most wide-ranging philosophic questions were raised. Jews took part in these discussions along with everyone else. The time that they spent in studying secular subjects inevitably lessened the time that they had to learn about Judaism. Moreover, the discussions themselves cast doubt on fundamental Jewish beliefs and practices. This led to the development of Jewish philosophy, where people like Saadia Gaon, Judah Halevi, and Moses Maimonides sought to explain and justify the beliefs and practices of Judaism to Jews themselves and to those of other faiths.

Gradually, though, persecutions against Jews became an increasingly common phenomenon in both the Muslim and Christian countries in which Jews lived. This was especially true during the Crusades (the first one was in 1096) and the expulsions of Jews from the countries of Western Europe from the late twelfth century through the sixteenth century.

Under these circumstances two types of legal literature were necessary. First of all, since Jews were scattered, they could no longer learn the traditional interpretations of the Bible and Talmud orally. Consequently, rabbis like Rashi wrote commentaries on those books so that they could be studied by Jews everywhere.

But most Jews did not have the time or ability to study, and so there was also a need for codes which could tell Jews in a simple, organized way what was expected of them as Jews. The Talmud, after all, is a running discussion, often with no final conclusion, and, moreover, a number of decisions had been made during the Geonic period. Consequently, people began to write codes.

One of the most famous codes is Maimonides' *Mishneh Torah* מִשְׁנֶה תוֹרָה ("second to the Torah" or "the instruction of the Torah"). As Maimonides explains in the Introduction, he wanted to create a code such that Jews could read the Torah and then read his code, and through reading those two books they would know what Jewish law requires. All Jewish learning that Jews could do after that would be "frosting on the cake," as it were.

The Hebrew term for such codifiers is "*Posekim*" פּוֹסְקִים (singular, "*posek*"). Sometimes the commentators and codifiers of this period are also called "*Rishonim*," רִאשׁוֹנִים and sometimes that term is reserved for those who wrote commentaries and codes after 1250 C.E. or so. In any case, the term "*Rishonim*" ("first ones") is used for the commentators and codifiers who wrote *before the Shulhan Arukh* שֻׁלְחָן עָרוּךְ was produced in 1565 (hence the name), while *Aharonim* אַחֲרוֹנִים ("the last ones") is used for those who wrote after the *Shulhan Arukh*.

The *Shulhan Arukh* is a code written by Joseph Karo. Its name means "a set table"; through it Karo wanted essentially to spoonfeed Jewish law to the Jewish masses, making it simple and clear. In point of fact, Maimonides' *Mishneh Torah* is better organized and clearer than the *Shulhan Arukh* is, but the *Shulhan Arukh* enjoys greater authority. The reason is that Karo was a Sephardic Jew (i.e., from the Mediterranean basin). After he wrote his code, a rabbi by the name of Moses Isserles wrote comments to each section where the customs of the Ashkenazic community (i.e., the Jews living in Eastern Europe) differed from those of the Sephardim. His comments he cleverly titled *Mappah*, the tablecloth to Karo's set table. Because of the existence of the *Mappah*, the *Shulhan Arukh* together with the notes by Isserles reflected Jewish law as it was practiced in all of the then-known Jewish world (the communities in China, India, Ethiopia, and Yemen excluded). That was the last code of Jewish law for which that claim can be made. Consequently it is used widely even today.

One other important aspect of this period is the synods or councils that took place and the *takkanot* (revisions; literally, "fixings"of the law) that they produced. To solve the numerous problems that arose due to the persecutions of the Crusades, the ruthless taxation of the feudal lords, and the general anarchy that prevailed, the French and German Jews of the tenth to the fourteenth centuries formed synods where representatives of the various communities gathered, usually at the call of one of the great leaders of the people and often in conjunction with one of the large commercial fairs. (We must remember that the rabbis and laymen who constituted the membership of the synods were usually not salaried officials but rather businessmen and workers of sufficient learning to be the leaders of their respective communities, and hence a trade gathering was the most convenient opportunity for the discussion of intercommunal problems.) These synods often acted as an appellate court for members of a community who were not satisfied with the way their local officials had handled their case. They also functioned in legislative roles, laying down numerous *takkanot* תַּקָּנוּת (singular, "*takkanah*"), or revisions, of the law. They are often ascribed to the most prominent member of the group so that they are identified with his name and thus gain greater respect and authority, but many takkanot specify that a whole group of rabbis, representing a variety of communities, were involved in promulgating the new ordinance.

To give you an idea of exactly how far-reaching these revisions were, here is a list of *Takkanot* of Rabbenu Gershom (c. 963-1028) taken from Louis Finkelstein, *Jewish Self Government in the Middle Ages* (New York: The Jewish Theological Seminary of America, 1924,1964), a book which presents many of the original sources on this topic:

The Takkanot of Rabbenu Gershom

1)   *Ordinances Regarding Marriage Law*

a) Takkanah Against Plural Marriage

Although polygamy had not been common among Jews for centuries, especially after Rabbi Ammi in the third century laid down the rule that no one may marry a second wife against the will of his first wife (*Ketubbot* 65a), nevertheless there must have been some specific instances of polygamy (perhaps among the wealthier classes) that prompted this ordinance. It was officially binding only on the French and German communities represented at the synod, but it achieved such wide respect that Spanish rabbis often felt compelled to enforce it on German Jews who came within their jurisdiction, and the writer of the Book of the Pious, living in Germany in the thirteenth century, demands the same respect for biblical and rabbinic laws as is paid to this ordinance of R. Gershom! (Res. R. Hayyim Or Zarua,182).

b) Takkanah Against Compulsory Divorce

Both biblical and rabbinic law enable a man to divorce his wife virtually at will. The Rabbis instituted monetary obligations that the husband must pay his wife if he decides to divorce her, but that apparently was not enough of a deterrent to divorce. R. Gershom therefore ruled that no man may divorce his wife against her will. For the Rhine communities, he also ordained (or the synodal representatives of those communities accepted his suggestion) that no divorce should be executed without the consent of the community's representatives. Later generations strengthened this *takkanah* by ordaining that any writ of divorce delivered in violation of it was null and void in prohibiting the husband from remarrying, although the fact that such a writ fulfilled talmudic requirements made it valid for all other purposes. The only exceptions to this *takkanah* were if the woman had accepted baptism or had voluntarily abandoned him, in which cases the husband could issue a writ of divorce and remarry without her consent.

66

2) Moral Ordinances

a) Against Insulting Penitent Converts

The number of forced conversions in R. Gershom's day must have been considerable in view of the *takkanah* he made prohibiting anyone to insult converted Jews after their return to Judaism.

b) Protecting the Privacy of Letters

R. Gershom forbade a person to read someone else's letters without permission. This ordinance was of special importance in days when mail delivery by government agencies was practically unknown in Europe and private messengers were often the source of fraud and blackmail.

3) Civil Ordinances

a) The jurisdiction of the local courts of the communities extends not merely to the members of the community, but to any Jew who may happen to come within their city.

b) The right of interrupting the prayers because a defendant refuses to come to court or because the court refuses to summon a defendant is guaranteed, but it is limited to cases where the plaintiff has complained three times in public at the end of the service. If he finds no response from the community, he may prevent them from holding public worship until his wrongs are righted.

c) If the synagogue building is owned by a member of the community, he may not prevent any other member from attending public services except by closing it to everyone.

d) Anyone losing an object may publicly declare a *herem* (ban) in the synagogue, compelling any person having knowledge of the finder to inform against him.

e) No Jew may rent a house of a Gentile who had unjustly evicted a former Jewish tenant. (This *takkanah* suggests the existence of very cramped Jewish quarters even in these early centuries in the Middle Ages since it is designed to present a united front against ruthless landlords.)

f) The minority in any community must accept the ordinances of the majority and abide by them.

These synods probably based their authority on the acceptance of their respective communities. The members of the communities took a vow that they and their descendants would accept the synod's decisions. In that way, Jewish law was changed considerably.

5. The Aharonim: 1550 C.E. - Present

The three types of legal literature that we have seen -- responsa, codes, and revisions -- continued on into the last four centuries, when Jews lived primarily in Eastern Europe, Muslim lands, and, in this century, in North America. In the nineteenth century the Neo-Orthodox and Reform Movements developed, and in the twentieth century Conservative Judaism became a movement (and not just a way of studying classical Jewish texts) with the inauguration of the United Synagogue of America, as we have seen. Rabbis in each of those movements created legal responses to the new realities of the modern world, according to their separate philosophies, and they continue to do so today. We have explained the interpretation of Jewish history that each Movement uses as the basis for its approach to Jewish law. In the next section we shall examine the sources upon which the Conservative Movement bases its interpretation of Jewish history and its claim to authenticity as the proper form of Judaism, both historically and pragmatically.[6]

QUESTIONS:

1) What does "canonize" mean?

   How and when did Ezra canonize the Torah?

   What are the Orthodox and historical understandings of that? Why is what he did important according to either understanding of that event?

2) On what biblical authority did Ezra appoint a group of judges? How were new members appointed to that group when someone died or retired?

3) Why did the Mishnah attain almost immediate authority? Give several reasons.

4) Why were Jews reluctant to write the laws down?

   What forced them to organize the previous legal materials in the time of the Mishnah? the Talmud? the Posekim?

5) Why has the *Shulhan Arukh* gained as much respect and authority as it has?

6) What were the synods? What did they produce and on what did they base their authority? Do we have any gathering similar to the synods today?

7) Compare your knowledge about the origins of Jewish law with the origins of American law. How important is it to understand the origins of law?

C. Tradition and Change in Rabbinic Literature

Where does Jewish law come from? Does it allow any changes?

If you were to answer these questions on the basis of what the Bible says, you would probably say that God gave the law, and no changes are allowed. That certainly is the explicit meaning of the two passages in Devarim (4:2 and 13:1) in which Jews are told "not to add anything to what I command you or take anything away from it, but keep the commandments of the Lord your God which I enjoin upon you." It is also the general impression that the Bible gives in that the laws are given at Mount Sinai in an overpowering event, with thunder, lightening, and other features to make one think, "Hands off! This is God's law, and don't you dare tamper with it!" The understanding of the origins and functioning of Jewish law that most Jews have is usually based on these biblical stories alone.

Judaism, however, is NOT identical with the religion of the Bible. Judaism is based upon the way in which the Rabbis of the Talmud and Midrash interpreted the Bible (in contrast to non-religious, Christian, Muslim, and other Jewish interpretations of it). Consequently, it is crucial to see how *the Rabbis* would have answered the questions with which this section began.

1. The Substitution of Interpretation of the Torah for Prophecy

When we consult the rabbinic sources, we discover some important and surprising things. First of all, the Bible claims that God spoke to Moses and the Prophets directly, and it leaves open the possibility of future prophets (e.g., Devarim 18:15-22). The Rabbis, however, claimed that God ceased to make His will known through prophecy shortly after the destruction of the First Temple:

a) The Primacy of the Revelation to Moses:

#1)   When the latter prophets, Haggai, Zekhariah, and Malakhi died, the Holy Spirit departed from Israel. (*B. Sanhedrin 11a*)

תנו רבנן: משמתו נביאים האחרונים חגי זכריה ומלאכי נסתלקה רוח הקודש מישראל.

#2)   The Holy One, blessed be He, said: "Twenty-four books [the Hebrew Bible] have I written for you; beware and make no addition to them." For what reason? "Of making many books there is no end" (Kohelet

69

12:12). He who reads a single verse which is not from the twenty-four is as though he read in "the outside books." Beware of making many books [to add to the Scriptures], for whoever does so will have no portion in the World to Come. (*Bamidbar Rabbah 14:4*)

אמר הקב"ה כ"ד ספרים כתבתי לך הזהר ואל תוסף עליהם למה עשות ספרים הרבה אין קץ כל מי שקורא פסוק שאינו מכ"ד ספרים כאלו קורא בספרים החיצונים הוי הזהר עשות ספרים הרבה שכל העושה כן אין לו חלק לעולם הבא.

Furthermore, the Rabbis introduced distinctions in the authority of the prophets who had prophesied before the destruction of the First Temple, claiming that Moses' prophesies were most authoritative because his vision was clearest and most inclusive:

#3)   What was the distinction between Moses and the other prophets?...The latter looked through nine lenses...whereas Moses looked only through one...They looked through a cloudy lens...but Moses through one that was clear. (*Vayikra Rabbah 1:14*)

מה בין משה לכל הנביאים. . .מתוך תשע איספקלריות היו הנביאים רואים. . .ומשה ראה מתוך איספקלריא אחת. . .כל הנביאים ראו מתוך איספקלריא מלוכלכת. . .ומשה ראה מתוך איספקלריא מצוחצחת.

#4)   What the prophets were destined to prophesy in subsequent generations they received from Mount Sinai....Moses gave utterance to all the words of the other prophets as well as his own, and whoever prophesied only gave expression to the essence of Moses' prophecy. (*Shemot Rabbah 28:6, 42:8*)

א"ר יצחק מה שהנביאים עתידים להתנבאות בכל דור ודור קבלו מהר סיני. . .משה שאמר כל דברי הנביאים ושלו וכל שהיה מתנבא מעין נבואתו של משה היה.

#5)   Forty-eight prophets and seven prophetesses spoke prophecies for Israel, and they neither deducted from, nor added to, what was written in the Torah, with the exception of the law to read the Book of Esther on the Feast of Purim. (*B. Megillah 14a*)

תנו רבנן: ארבעים ושמונה נביאים ושבע נביאות נתנבאו להם לישראל ולא פחתו ולא הותירו על מה שכתוב בתורה חוץ ממקרא מגילה.

b) New Revelations from God Through Interpretation Exclusively:

In place of prophecy, the Rabbis greatly expanded the judicial powers that the Torah had created in Chapter 17 of Devarim, and they claimed that *their interpretations were the new and only way in which God spoke to humankind:*

#6)   R. Abdimi from Haifa said: Since the day when the Temple was destroyed, the prophetic gift was taken away from the prophets and given to the Sages. – Is then a Sage not also a prophet? – What he meant was this: although it has been taken from the prophets, it has not been taken from the Sages. Amemar said: A Sage is even superior to a prophet, as it says, "And a prophet has a heart of wisdom" (Tehillim 90:12). Who is (usually) compared with whom? Is not the smaller compared with the greater? (B. Bava Batra 12a)

אמר רבי אבדימי דמן חיפה. מיום שחרב בית המקדש ניטלה נבואה מן הנביאים וניתנה לחכמים. אטו חכם לאו נביא הוא? הכי קאמר: אע"פ שניטלה מן הנביאים מן החכמים לא. ניטלה. אמר אמימר: וחכם עדיף מנביא שנאמר: (תהלים צ') ונביא לבב חכמה מי נתלה במי?

They even denied authority to new revelations (that is, ways in which God spoke to us anew) claimed by members of their own sect, as in this remarkable story:

#7)   We learned elsewhere: If he cut it [the material for an oven] into separate tiles, placing sand between each tile, Rabbi Eliezer declared it pure, and the Sages declared it impure....On that day Rabbi Eliezer brought forward every imaginable argument, but they did not accept them.

Said he to them: "If the law agrees with me, let this carob tree prove it!" Thereupon the carob tree was torn a hundred cubits out of its place - others affirm, four hundred cubits. "No proof can be brought from a carob tree," they retorted.

Again he said to them: "If the law agrees with me, let the stream of water prove it." The stream of water then flowed backwards. "No proof can be brought from a stream of water," they rejoined.

Again he urged: "If the law agrees with me, let the walls of the schoolhouse prove it," whereupon the walls began to fall. But Rabbi Joshua scolded them, saying: "When scholars are engaged in a legal dispute, what right have you to interfere?" Therefore they did not fall in honor of Rabbi Joshua, nor did they resume an upright position in honor of Rabbi Eliezer, and they are still standing there inclined.

Again he said to them, "If the law agrees with me, let it be proved in Heaven." Whereupon a Heavenly Voice cried out: "Why do you dispute with Rabbi Eliezer, seeing that in all matters the law agrees with him."

But Rabbi Joshua arose and exclaimed: "It is not in Heaven" (Devarim 30:12). What did he mean by this? Rabbi Yermiah said: "That the

Torah had already been given at Mt. Sinai; therefore we pay no attention to a Heavenly Voice, because You [God] have long since written in the Torah at Mount Sinai, `One must follow the majority'" (Shemot 23:2).

Rabbi Nathan met Elijah (the Prophet) and asked him: "What did the Holy One, Blessed be He, do in that hour?" "He laughed with joy," he replied, "and said, `My children have defeated Me, My children have defeated Me.'" (B. Bava Metzia 59a - 59b).[7]

תנן התם: חתכו חוליות ונתן חול בין חוליא לחוליא. רבי אליעזר מטהר וחכמים מטמאין. . .
תנא: באותו היום השיב רבי אליעזר כל תשובות שבעולם ולא קיבלו הימנו. אמר להם:
אם הלכה כמותי - חרוב זה יוכיח. נעקר חרוב ממקומו מאה אמה ואמרי לה: ארבע
מאות אמה. אמרו לו: אין מביאין ראיה מן החרוב. חזר ואמר להם: אם הלכה כמותי אמת
המים יוכיחו. חזרו אמת המים לאחוריהם. אמרו לו: אין מביאין ראיה מאמת המים. חזר
ואמר להם: אם הלכה כמותי כותלי בית המדרש יוכיחו. הטו כותלי בית המדרש ליפול.
גער בהם רבי יהושע. אמר להם: אם תלמידי חכמים מנצחים זה את זה בהלכה אתם מה
טיבכם? לא נפלו מפני כבודו של רבי יהושע. ולא זקפו מפני כבודו של רבי אליעזר.
ועדין מטין ועומדין. חזר ואמר להם: אם הלכה כמותי מן השמים יוכיחו. יצאתה בת קול
ואמרה: מה לכם אצל רבי אליעזר שהלכה כמותו בכל מקום? עמד רבי יהושע על רגליו
ואמר "לא בשמים היא" (דברים ל'). מאי לא בשמים היא? אמר רבי ירמיה: שכבר נתנה
תורה מהר סיני: אין אנו משגיחין בבת קול. שכבר כתבת בהר סיני (שמות כ"ג) אחרי
רבים להטות. אשכחיה רבי נתן לאליהו. אמר ליה: מאי עביד קודשא בריך הוא בההיא
שעתא? אמר ליה: קא חייך ואמר נצחוני בני. נצחוני בני.

If that does not make it clear that the rabbinic methodology is significantly different from the biblical one, nothing will! The Rabbis clearly and consciously shifted the operation of the law from the Prophets to the judges, from revelation to interpretation. Why did they do that? Undoubtedly part of the reason has to do with problems in using revelation.

c) Distinguishing True Prophecies and Interpretations From False Ones:

The Bible itself struggles to create a way of distinguishing true prophets from false ones (Devarim 13:2-6; 18:9-22), and Jeremiah, especially, complains of the many false prophets in his time (e.g., Jeremiah 14:14; 23:25, 32; 27:10, 14, 16; 29:23, etc.). The problem of identifying and weeding out false prophets was a continuing problem for the Rabbis -- especially in light of the many people in their time roaming the hills of Judea claiming to be prophets (Jesus included). Thus they said:

> #8) To what are a prophet and a Sage to be compared? To a king who sent his two ambassadors to a state. For one of them he wrote, "If he does not show you my seal, do not believe him"; for the other he wrote, "Even if he does not show you my seal, believe him." Similarly, in

regard to a prophet, it is written, "If he gives you a sign or a portent" (Devarim 13:2) [believe him], but here [in Devarim 17:11, concerning judges] it is written, "You shall act in accordance with the instruction which they shall give you" [even without a sign]. (J. Berakhot 1:4)

נביא וזקן למי הן דומין? למלך ששולח ב' פלמטרין שלו למדינה. על אחד מהן כתב: אם אינו מראה לכם חותם שלי וסמנטירין שלי אל תאמינו לו. ועל אחד מהן כתב: אע"פ שאינו מראה לכם חותם שלי האמינוהו בלא חותם ובלא סמנטירין. כך בנביא כתיב ונתן אליך אות או מופת.

This is an especially forceful endorsement of rabbinic authority because Devarim 13, which is quoted here, says that even if the prophet gives you a sign or portent and it comes true, nevertheless you should not believe in the prophet if he tells you to follow another god or disobey God's laws "for the Lord your God is testing you" (Devarim 13:4). Rabbis, though, are to be followed even without a confirming sign or portent. The following source demonstrates exactly how far this rabbinic authority goes:

#9)   "According to the sentence...of the judges shall you act, you shall not deviate...to the right or to the left" (Devarim 17:11). Even if they demonstrate that that which seems to you right is left, and that that which seems to you left is right, listen to [and obey] them.

(Sifre Devarim 154)

ועל המשפט אשר יאמרו לך תעשה. . .לא תסור. . .ימין ושמאל. אפילו מראים בעיניך על ימין שהוא שמאל ועל שמאל שהוא ימין שמע להם.

On the other hand, another strain within the tradition maintains that rabbinic rulings, just like prophetic revelations, are to be judged for the propriety of their content before being obeyed as authoritative law:

#10)   You must not deviate from the verdict that they announce to you either to the right or to the left" (Devarim 17:11). You might think that this means that if they tell you that right is left and left is right, you are to obey them; therefore the Torah tells you, "to the right or to the left," [to indicate that] when they tell you that right is right and left is left [you are to obey them, but not otherwise]. (J. Horayot 1:1)

יכול אם יאמרו לך על ימין שהיא שמאל ועל שמאל שהיא ימין תשמע להם. ת"ל ללכת ימין ושמאל שיאמר לך על ימין שהיא ימין ועל שמאל שהיא שמאל.

73

d) Maintaining Legal Continuity:

Besides the problem of distinguishing between true prophets and false ones, there is yet another problem with prophecy. If you accept it, then the law is always subject to changes or complete cancellation at a moment's notice because God could conceivably announce completely new rules through a prophet - or at least a prophet could claim that God had done so. In other words, accepting prophecy spells legal chaos. Consequently the Rabbis in the above story (Source #7) were well advised to reject divine intrusions into the lawmaking process and to claim that God had had His say once and for all. So part of the reason for substituting interpretation for prophecy is because of the problems inherent in using prophecy -- namely, the difficulty of distinguishing true prophets from false ones and the legal chaos which prophecy can cause.

e) The Need for Interpretation to Know What the Torah Means:

The Rabbis emphasized interpretation of the Torah as the way to know the will of God also because they were convinced that the Torah needs interpretation, that even the accepted revelation in the Torah could not stand alone. There are sects of Christians who are "fundamentalists." They try to make their decisions in life solely on the basis of the Bible. There also have been sects of Jews who have tried to do that, including the Karaites (who were strongest in the ninth and tenth centuries but who still exist today) and, to a lesser degree, the Sadducees. (Even though these sects tried to rely solely on the Bible, they themselves found it necessary to develop their own tradition of interpretation.) The Rabbis, however, claimed that living by the Bible alone was impossible since its verses are open to many different interpretations:

#11) "Is not My word like a hammer that breaks a rock in many pieces?" (Jeremiah 23:29). As the hammer causes numerous sparks to flash forth, so is a Scriptural verse capable of many interpretations. (B. Sanhedrin 34a)

וכפטיש יפצץ סלע (ירמיהו כ"ג). מה פטיש זה מתחלק לכמה ניצוצות - אף מקרא אחד יוצא לכמה טעמים.

#12) It happened that a heathen came before Shammai and asked him, "How many Torahs do you have?" He answered, "Two – the written and the oral." He [the heathen] said, " With respect to the written Torah I will believe you, but not with respect to the Oral Torah. Accept me as a convert on condition that you teach me the former only." Shammai rebuked him and drove him out with contempt. He came before Hillel with the same request, and he accepted him. The first day he taught him the alphabet in the correct order, but the next day he reversed it. The heathen said to him, "Yesterday you taught it to me differently!" Hillel replied, "Do you not have to depend upon me for the letters of the alphabet? So must you likewise depend upon me for the interpretation of the Torah." (*B. Shabbat* 31a)

תנו רבנן: מעשה בנכרי אחד שבא לפני שמאי אמר לו: כמה תורות יש לכם? אמר לו: שתים. תורה שבכתב ותורה שבעל פה. אמר לו: שבכתב - אני מאמינך. ושבעל פה - איני מאמינך. גיירני על מנת שתלמדני תורה שבכתב. גער בו והוציאו בנזיפה. בא לפני הלל. גייריה. יומא קמא אמר ליה: א"ב ג"ד. למחר אפיך ליה. אמר ליה: והא אתמול לא אמרת לי הכי? אמר לו: לאו עלי דידי קא סמכת? דעל פה נמי סמוך עלי.

#13) "The words of the wise are as goads...They are given from one shepherd" (Kohelet 12:11), that is, the words of the Torah and the words of the Sages have been given from the same shepherd [Moses]. "And furthermore, my son, be careful: of making many books there is no end" (Kohelet 12:12) means: More than to the words of the Torah pay attention to the words of the Scribes. In the same strain it says, "For your beloved ones are better than wine" (Shir HaShirim 1:2), which means: The words of the beloved ones [the Sages] are better than the wine of the Torah. Why? Because one cannot give a proper decision from the words of the Torah, since the Torah is shut up [cryptic and therefore ambiguous] and consists entirely of headings...From the words of the Sages, however, one can derive the proper law because they explain the Torah. And the reason why the words of the Sages are compared to goads (*darbanot*) is because they cause understanding to dwell (*medayerin binah*) in people [a play on words].
(*Bamidbar Rabbah* 14:4)

דברי חכמים כדרבונות. . . נתנו מרועה אחד ד"ת ודברי חכמים מרועה אחד נתנו ויותר מהמה בני הזהר עשות ספרים הרבה אין קץ ולהג הרבה יגיעת בשר (קהלת יב) ויותר מהמה בני הזהר יותר מדברי תורה הוי זהיר בדברי סופרים וכן הוא אומר (שיר א) כי טובים דודיך מיין טובים דברי דודים מיינה של תורה למה שאין אדם מורה כראוי מד"ת מפני שהיא סתומה וכולן סימנין. . . אבל מתוך דברי חכמים אדם מורה כראוי מפני שהם פורשים את התורה ולכך נמשלו דברי חכמים כדרבונות מפני שהן מדיירין בינה בבני אדם.

f) The Need for Interpretations to Retain Flexibility and Relevance:

Moreover, interpretation is necessary not only because the Torah on its own is ambiguous; it is also necessary if Jewish law is to retain sufficient flexibility:

#14) If the Torah had been given in a fixed form, the situation would have been intolerable. What is the meaning of the oft-recurring phrase, "The Lord *spoke* to Moses?" Moses said before Him, "Sovereign of the

Universe! Cause me to know what the final decision is on each matter of law." He replied, "The majority [of the judges] must be followed: when the majority declares a thing permitted, it is permissible; when the majority declares it forbidden, it is not allowed; so that the Torah may be capable of interpretation with forty-nine points *for* and forty-nine points *against*." (*J. Sanhedrin* 22a)

א"ר ינאי אילו ניתנה התורה חתוכה לא היתה לרגל עמידה מה טעם וידבר ה אל משה.
אמר לפניו רבונו של עולם הודיעני היאך היא ההלכה. אמר לו אחרי רבים להטות רבו
המזכין זכו. רבו המחייבין חייבו. כדי שתהא התורה נדרשת מ"ט פנים טמא ומ"ט פנים
טהור.

In fact, the Rabbis considered new interpretations and expansions of the law not only necessary, but also desirable. God wants us to make new applications of the Torah, just as the King in the following rabbinic story wants bread and not just wheat:

#15) A king had two slaves whom he loved intensely. He gave each one a measure of wheat and a bundle of flax. The intelligent one wove the flax into a cloth and made flour from the wheat, sifted it, ground it, kneaded it, baked it, and set it [the bread] on the table on the cloth he had made before the king returned. The stupid one did not do a thing [with the gifts the king had given him].

After some time the king returned to his house and said to them: "My sons, bring me what I gave you." One brought out the table set with the bread on the tablecloth; the other brought out the wheat in a basket and the bundle of flax with it. What an embarrassment that was! Which do you think was the more beloved?

[Similarly] when the Holy One, Blessed be He, gave the Torah to Israel, He gave it as wheat from which to make flour and flax from which to make clothing through the rules of interpretation.

(*Seder Eliyahu Zuta*, Chapter 2)

למה הדבר דומה? למלך בשר ודם שהיה לו שני עבדים. והיה אוהבן אהבה גמורה ונתן
לזה קב חיטין ולזה קב חיטין לזה אגודה של פשתן ולזה אגודה של פשתן. הפקח שבהן
מה עשה? נטל את הפשתן וארגו מפה ונטל את החיטין ועשאן סולת בוררה טחנה ולשה
ואפה וסידרה על השלחן ופרס עליה מפה והניחה עד שלא בא המלך. והטפש שבהן לא
עשה ולא כלום. לימים בא המלך בתוך ביתו ואמר להן בניי הביאו לי מה שנתתי לכם.
אחד הוציא את [פת] הסולת על גבי השלחן ומפה פרוסה עליו. ואחד הוציא את החיטין
בקופה ואגודה של פשתן עליהן. אוי לה לאותה בושה אוי לה לאותה כלימה. הוי אומר
איזה מהן חביב? זה שהוציא את השלחן ואת [פת] הסלת עליו. . .אלא כשנתן הקב"ה
תורה לישראל לא ניתנה להם אלא כחיטים להוציא מהן סולת וכפשתן להוציא ממנו
בגד. ניתנה בכלל ופרט. ופרט וכלל.

g) God's Command That We Interpret the Torah:

Finally, human interpretation and application of the law is necessary because God Himself required it in Chapter 17 of Devarim. Thus *not* to interpret the law anew in each generation would be to disobey God's Law!

> #16) No man should say, "I will not observe the precepts of the elders" (i.e., the Oral Law), since they are not of Mosaic authority (literally, contained in the Torah). For God has said, "No, my son, but whatever they decree for you, you must perform," as it says, "According to the Torah which they (i.e., the elders in days to come) *shall* teach you shall you do" (Devarim 17:11): for even for Me do they [the Rabbis] make decrees, as it says, "when you (i.e., the rabbis) decree a command, it shall be fulfilled for you" (i.e., by Me, God) [a playful interpretation of Job 22:28]. (*Pesikta Rabbati*, ed. Friedmann, 7b)

לא יאמר אדם איני מקיים מצות זקינים הואיל ואינם מן התורה אמר לו הקב"ה לאו בני אלא כל מה שהם גוזרים עליך קיים שנאמר על פי התורה אשר יורוך (דברים י"ז: י"א) למה שאף עלי הן גוזרין שנאמר ותגזור אומר ויקם לך (איוב כ"ב: כ"ח).

> #17) It is written, "For this commandment is not in heaven" (Devarim 30:11, 12). Moses said to the Israelites, "Lest you should say, `Another Moses is to arise and to bring us another Law from heaven,' therefore I make it known to you now that it is not in heaven: nothing is left of it in heaven." R. Hanina said: "The Law and all the implements by which it is carried out have been given, namely, modesty, beneficence, uprightness and reward." (*Devarim Rabbah* 8:6)

לא בשמים היא (דברים ל') .אמר להן משה: שלא תאמרו משה אחר עומד ומביא לנו תורה אחרת מן השמים. כבר אני מודיע אתכם "לא בשמים היא" שלא נשתייר הימנה בשמים. ד"א אמר רבי חנינא: היא וכל כלי אומנותה ניתנה: ענותנותה צדקה וישרותה ומתן שכרה.

2. Retaining Coherence in the Law

That is all well and good, but with all of these interpretations, how is there to be any coherence in the law -- any sense that, despite the many different understandings and applications of the law, this is still one, reasonably consistent, system? And how are the various interpretations of the word of God in any sense such that they continue to have divine authority?

a) The Law Will Remain Coherent Because All Decisions are Based on What Comes From God:

Those are hard questions, but the Rabbis faced them squarely. They answered the question of coherence in three ways. First of all, the tradition would remain coherent despite the many variations of opinion because they all derive from God:

> #18) Lest a man should say, "Since some scholars declare a thing impure and others declare it pure, some pronounce a thing to be forbidden and others pronounce it to be permitted, some disqualify an object while others uphold its fitness, how can I study Torah under such circumstances?" Scripture states, "They are given from one shepherd" (Kohelet 12:11): One God has given them, one leader [Moses] has uttered them at the command of the Lord of all creation, blessed be He, as it says, "And God spoke *all* these words" (Shemot 20:1). You, then, should, on your part, make your ear like a grain receiver and acquire a heart that can understand the words of the scholars who declare a thing impure as well as those who declare it pure, the words of those who declare a thing forbidden as well as those who pronounce it permitted, and the words of those who disqualify an object as well as those who uphold its fitness. Although one scholar offers his view and another offers his, the words of both are all derived from what Moses, the shepherd, received from the One Lord of the Universe.
>
> (*Bamidbar Rabbah* 14:4)

שמא יאמר אדם הואיל והללו מטמאין והללו מטהרין הללו אוסרין והללו מתירין הללו פוסלין והללו מכשירין היאך אני לומד תורה מעתה ת"ל נתנו מרועה אחד אל אחד נתנן פרנס אחד אמרן מפי אדון כל המעשים ב"ה שנאמר (שמות יט) וידבר אלהים את כל הדברים האלה אף אתה עשה אזנך כאפרכסת וקנה לך לב שומע את דברי המטמאין ואת דברי המטהרין את דברי האוסרין ואת דברי המתירין את דברי הפוסלין ואת דברי המכשירים...אע"פ שזה אומר טעמו וזה אומר טעמו דבריהם של אלו ושל אלו כולם ניתנו מן משה הרועה מה שקיבל מיחידו של עולם.

b) The Law Will Remain Coherent Because Jews Have a Sense of Its Coherence as the Ongoing Legal Story of the Jewish Community:

In other words, however much the interpretations of various rabbis may vary, they are all interpretations of one document, the Torah, and they will all be cohesive because God, the Author of that document, can be presumed to be consistent. In somewhat the same way, American law is consistent because it all derives from the framework and powers that were established in the Constitution – however much it has changed since then.

Second, the tradition will be cohesive because there is a sense of continuity within the tradition itself. There is a famous story in the Talmud which illustrates that. When Moses visits the academy of Rabbi Akiba, who lived some 1400 years after him, he does not even understand what Rabbi Akiba is saying, let alone agree with it. Nevertheless Moses is comforted when Rabbi Akiba cites one of the new laws in Moses' name because that indicates that Rabbi Akiba and his contemporaries understood themselves to be part of the ongoing tradition which stretches back to Moses and there is thus a sense of continuity in the tradition, however much it has changed in form:

#19)   Rav Judah said in the name of Rav: When Moses ascended on high, he found the Holy One, blessed be He, engaged in affixing crowns to the letters [of the Torah]. Said Moses: "Lord of the Universe, who stays Your hand?" [that is, is there anything lacking in the Torah so that additions are necessary?]

He answered, "There will arise a man at the end of many generations, Akiba ben Joseph by name, who will expand upon each decorative marking heaps and heaps of laws." "Lord of the Universe," said Moses, "permit me to see him." He replied, "Turn around."

Moses went and sat down behind eight rows [of R. Akiba's disciples and listened to the discourses on the law]. Not being able to follow their arguments, he was ill at ease, but when they came to a certain subject and the student said to the teacher, "From where do you know it?" and the latter replied, "It is a law given to Moses at Sinai," he [Moses] was comforted. Thereupon he returned to the Holy One, blessed be He, and said, "Lord of the Universe, You have such a man and You give the Torah by me?!" (*B. Menahot* 29b)

אמר רב יהודה אמר רב: בשעה שעלה משה למרום מצאו להקב"ה שיושב וקושר כתרים
לאותיות. אמר לפניו: רבש"ע מי מעכב על ידך? אמר לו: אדם אחד יש שעתיד להיות
בסוף כמה דורות ועקיבא בן יוסף שמו שעתיד לדרוש על כל קוץ וקוץ תילין תילין
של הלכות. אמר לפניו: רבש"ע הראהו לי. אמר לו: חזור לאחורך. הלך וישב בסוף
שמונה שורות ולא היה יודע מה הן אומרים. תשש כחו. כיון שהגיע לדבר אחד אמרו
לו תלמידיו: רבי מנין לך? אמר להן: הלכה למשה מסיני נתיישבה דעתו. חזר ובא לפני
הקב"ה אמר לפניו: רבונו של עולם יש לך אדם כזה ואתה נותן תורה ע"י?

Incidentally, this story also clearly indicates that the Rabbis realized that there had been changes in the law.

This sense of continuity is dependent, of course, on having people who have studied the Torah sufficiently to carry on its spirit and substance in new settings, and the Rabbis were keenly aware of what happens to the law's coherence when those to whom it is entrusted do not know it thoroughly:

#20) When the disciples of Shammai and Hillel increased who had not served [that is, studied with] their teachers sufficiently, dissensions increased in Israel and the Torah became like two Torahs.

(*B. Sotah* 47b)

משרבו תלמידי שמאי והילל שלא שימשו כל צורכן רבו מחלוקת בישראל ונעשית תורה כשתי תורות.

But they also were convinced that the continuity and consistency that they sensed was real, that the law in its present form, however different from the Torah, is the direct extension of it:

#21) Moses received the Torah from Sinai and handed it down to Joshua, and Joshua to the elders, and the elders to the prophets, and the prophets handed it down to the men of the Great Assembly. (*M. Avot* 1:1)

משה קבל תורה מסיני ומסרה ליהושע ויהושע לזקנים וזקנים לנביאים ונביאים מסרוה לאנשי כנסת הגדולה.

#22) At the same time when the Holy One, blessed be He, revealed Himself on Sinai to give the Torah to Israel, He delivered it to Moses in order — Scripture, Mishnah, Talmud, and Aggadah. (*Shemot Rabbah* 47:1)

בשעה שנגלה הקב"ה בסיני ליתן תורה לישראל אמרה למשה על הסדר מקרא ומשנה תלמוד ואגדה.

Again, the comparison to American law is instructive. Judges can make revolutionary decisions, but in so doing they must tie those decisions to already existing laws and precedents. This process preserves a sense of continuity within the American legal system so that, in philosopher Ronald Dworkin's terms, Americans can have a sense of their law as an ongoing, connected, legal story, however much that story develops in surprising ways.

The Supreme Court's decision in 1954 requiring integration of the public schools is a good example of how law changes and yet retains a sence of coherence. Segregated schools clearly continued to exist in the United States after the First and Fourteenth Amendments to the Constitution became law, and the framers of those Amendments certainly did not intend to outlaw such schools in passing them. Moreover, the Supreme Court itself specifically upheld the constitutionality of segregated facilities in 1896. Nevertheless, in 1954 the Supreme Court declared segregated schools unconstitutional and based their decision on the First and Fourteenth Amendments in order to preserve a sense of continuity and consistency in the law. Shades of Rabbi Akiba!

c) The Law Will Remain Coherent Because Decisions Among Various Options are Made:

Third, Jewish law would retain its coherence because it includes a way of making decisions. All opinions could be aired in discussion, and, in fact, all are to be considered "the words of the living God," but in the end a decision must be made:

#23)   R. Abba stated in the name of Samuel: For three years there was a dispute between the School of Shammai and the School of Hillel, the former asserting, "The law is in agreement with our views, "and the latter contending, "The law is in agreement with our view." Then a Heavenly Voice announced, "The utterances of both are the words of the living God, but the law is in agreement with the rulings of the School of Hillel."

Since, however, "both are the words of the living God," what was it that entitled the School of Hillel to have law fixed in agreement with their rulings? Because they were kindly and modest, they studied their own rulings and those of the School of Shammai, and they were even so humble as to mention the opinions of the School of Shammai before theirs. (B. Eruvin 13b)

אמר רבי אבא אמר שמואל: שלש שנים נחלקו בית שמאי ובית הלל הללו אומרים הלכה כמותנו והללו אומרים הלכה כמותנו. יצאה בת קול ואמרה: אלו ואלו דברי אלהים חיים הן והלכה כבית הלל. וכי מאחר שאלו ואלו דברי אלהים חיים מפני מה זכו בית הלל לקבוע הלכה כמותן? מפני שנוחין ועלובין היו ושונין דבריהן ודברי בית שמאי ולא עוד אלא שמקדימין דברי בית שמאי לדבריהן.

There is a famous instance in the Mishnah in which the authority of the President of the Sanhedrin was asserted forcefully when it was called into question. Until the fourth century C.E., there was no fixed Jewish calendar. Instead witnesses would come to the Sanhedrin during the day and testify that they had seen the first sliver of the new moon on the previous night. The President of the Sanhedrin would then declare that day the first day of the new month. There were some special rules to make sure that the calendar would never be too much out of step with the movements of the sun and the moon, no matter whether there were witnesses to the new moon or not, but the fixing of the dates of the calendar did depend to a large extent on the testimony of witnesses. You can imagine how important this was: after all, if the first day of the Hebrew month Tishre, for example, was declared to be on a Monday, then that day was Rosh Hashanah, no work should be done, special services should be held, and Yom Kippur would be ten days later, on the Tuesday night and Wednesday of the following week. If, on the other hand, the first day of the month were declared to be on Tuesday, then both Rosh Hashanah and Yom Kippur would take place a day later, and all of the special laws of the High Holy Days should be observed then. With this as a background, you can understand the story in the following Mishnah and why it is important:

81

#24)　On one occasion two witnesses came and said: "We saw the new moon at its expected time [the night after the 29th day of the previous month], but on the next night it could not be seen" [when it should have been even larger and clearer]. Yet Rabban Gamliel [who was President of the Sanhedrin] accepted them as true witnesses [assuming that they did not see the moon on the next night simply because clouds covered it.]

Rabbi Dosa ben Harkinas said, "I maintain that they are false witnesses," and Rabbi Joshua ben Hananiah said to him, "I see the strength of your arguments.

[Since Rabbi Joshua was Vice-President of the Sanhedrin, Rabban Gamliel felt that it was necessary to assert the authority of the President and the accepted procedures forcefully.] Rabban Gamliel sent a message to him [Rabbi Joshua], saying, "I order you to come to me with your staff and money on the day on which, according to your calculations, Yom Kippur falls." Rabbi Akiba went and found him [Rabbi Joshua] in distress [since he would have to publicly violate the laws of Yom Kippur on the day which he thought to be Yom Kippur].

He [Rabbi Akiba] said to him [Rabbi Joshua]: I can prove [from the Torah] that everything which Rabban Gamliel has done, he has done [correctly], for the Torah says, "These are the appointed seasons of the Lord, holy convocations, *which you shall proclaim* in their appointed season" (Vayikra 23:4) [which means]: whether they are proclaimed at their proper time or not, I [God] have no other "appointed season" but these [which you – that is, the People Israel through its official decision-making body, the Sanhedrin – declare].

He [Rabbi Joshua] then went to Rabbi Dosa ben Harkinas [who had agreed with Rabbi Joshua that the witnesses were false but who nevertheless] said to him: "If we call into question the decisions of the Court of Rabban Gamliel, we must call into question the decisions of every single court that has existed from the days of Moses to the present day....

So he [Rabbi Joshua] took his staff and his money in his hand and went to Yavneh to Rabban Gamliel on the day on which Yom Kippur fell according to his own calculation. Rabban Gamliel stood up, kissed him on his head, and said to him, "Come in peace, my teacher and my pupil: my teacher in wisdom, and my pupil in that you have accepted my decision." (*M. Rosh Hashanah* 2:8-9)

82

באו שנים ואמרו: ראינוהו בזמנו ובליל עבורו לא נראה וקבלן רבן גמליאל. אמר
רבי דוסא בן הרכינס: עדי שקר הן. אמר לו רבי יהושע: רואה אני את דבריך.
שלח לו רבן גמליאל: גוזרני עליך שתבוא אצלי במקלך ובמעותיך ביום הכפורים שחל
להיות בחשבונך. הלך ומצאו רבי עקיבא מצר אמר לו: יש לי ללמוד שכל מה שעשה
רבן גמליאל עשוי שנאמר (ויקרא כג) "אלה מועדי יי מקראי קדש אשר תקראו אתם" -
בין בזמנן בין שלא בזמנן אין לי מועדות אלא אלו. בא לו אצל רבי דוסא בן הרכינס
אמר לו: אם באין אנו לדון אחר בית דינו של רבן גמליאל צריכין אנו לדון אחר כל
בית דין ובית דין שעמד מימות משה ועד עכשיו. נטל מקלו ומעותיו בידו והלך ליבנה
אצל רבן גמליאל ביום שחל יום הכפורים להיות בחשבונו. עמד רבן גמליאל ונשקו
על ראשו אמר לו: בא בשלום רבי ותלמידי: רבי בחכמה ותלמידי שקבלת את דברי.

The situation became more complicated when the Sanhedrin ceased to exist and there was no longer a central authority in Judaism, but there are still ways in which decisions are made in Jewish law, thus preserving its continuity. In some places and times, Jewish communities have been sufficiently organized to have a centralized court system for a community or a group of communities. We have seen an example of that in the synods of the Middle Ages. When that is not possible, each community follows the decisions of its local rabbi, its *mara d'atra* ("the teacher -- or master -- of the place") and the court that he often chairs, for each community is *commanded* to establish a court:

> #25)   Courts should be established in Israel and outside it, as it says, "Such shall be your law of procedure throughout the generations in *all* your settlements" (Bamidbar 35:29), from which we learn that the courts must be established in Israel and outside it. So why does the Torah say, "in all the settlements which the Lord your God is giving you" (Devarim 16:18)? To teach you that in Israel you establish courts in every district and city, but outside Israel only in every district. (Tosefta *Sanhedrin* 3:5; cf. *B. Makkot* 7a)

סנהדרין נוהגת בארץ ובחו"ל שנא' (במדבר ל"ה. כ"ט) "והיו אלה לכם לחקת משפט
לדורותיכם בכל מושבתים" בארץ ובחו"ל אם כן למה נאמר (דברים ט"ז. י"ח) "שופטים
ושוטרים תתן לך בכל שעריך"? אלא בא"י עושין אותן בכל עיר ועיר ובחו"ל עושין אותן
פלכים פלכים.

That means, of course, that there are many different decisions being made on any given issue in the various places in which Jews live, but even then there is a general rule to coordinate the decisions in order to give Jewish law coherence. Maimonides summarizes it clearly:

> #26)   After the Supreme Court [Sanhedrin] ceased to exist, disputes multiplied in Israel: one declared something "impure," giving a reason for his ruling, [while] another declared it "pure," giving a reason for his ruling; one forbade [something], the other permitted [it].

83

In case there is a difference of opinion between two scholars or two courts, one pronouncing "pure" what the other pronounces "impure," one declaring "forbidden" what the other declared to be permitted," and it is impossible to determine the correct decision, if the controversy is with regard to a scriptural law, the more stringent view is followed; if it is with regard to a rabbinical law, the more lenient view is followed. This principle holds in post-Sanhedrin times, and it determined the law even at the time of the Sanhedrin if the case had not yet reached that tribunal. It governs whether those who hold different views are contemporaries or live at different times. (Maimonides, *Mishneh Torah*, The Book of Judges, "Laws Concerning Rebels," Chapter I, Laws 4 & 5.)

משבטל בית דין הגדול רבתה מחלוקת בישראל: זה מטמא ונותן טעם לדבריו וזה מטהר ונותן טעם לדבריו זה אוסר וזה מתיר. שני חכמים או שני בתי דינין שנחלקו שלא בזמן הסנהדרין או עד שלא היה הדבר ברור להם בין בזמן אחד בין בזה אחר זה אחד מטהר ואחד מטמא אחד אוסר ואחד מתיר אם אינך יודע להיכן הדין נוטה - בשל תורה הלך אחר המחמיר בשל סופרים הלך אחר המקל.

Moreover, since Jews have lived under many different conditions in the scattered places in which they have found themselves, it probably is a good thing that the court in each area makes decisions appropriate to its particular setting. Jewish law thereby gains the necessary flexibility to enable it to work in many different times and places. Nevertheless, there is a clear way of making decisions wherever Jews live and that, together with the sense of continuity and the dependence upon one Torah that we discussed earlier, gives Jewish law coherence and a reasonable degree of consistency.

The second question posed above goes to the very root of the authority of Jewish law: with all of the various interpretations of the law and the new applications of it, how is it in any sense divine? After all, the Rabbis explicitly claimed that it is the *human* judges in each generation that have the authority to make decisions in Jewish law, that God no longer has the right or authority to determine the law even if He wants to (remember Source #7 above), and so how is Jewish law as the rabbis interpret it God's word any more?

That is the crucial question, and it is important to remember why it arises in the first place. On the one hand, the Rabbis clearly wanted to retain divine authority for Jewish law: there may be many reasons to observe it, but the most important one by far is that it is the will of God. On the other hand, the Rabbis had to assert the right of rabbis in each generation to interpret and apply the law for the reasons we discussed above: the difficulties of using prophecy as a legal guide; the ambiguity of the Torah, especially in regard to how it is to be applied to new situations; the need to retain flexibility in the law in order to enable it to function under new circumstances; and the commandment of God Himself that judges in each generation take on the responsibility of interpreting the law.

3. Affirming the Divine Authority of the Law

a) How the Rabbis Justified the Divine Authority of Their Rulings:

There is no simple way of affirming both the divine authority of the law and the right of human beings to interpret it. The Rabbis, in a style typical of them, claimed two opposite things in order to assert the truth of both of them. On the one hand, they claimed that all later developments in the law were already revealed at Sinai:

> #27) What is the meaning of the verse, "And I will give you the tablets of stone, and the law and the commandment, which I have written, so that you may teach them" (Shemot 24:12)? "Tablets of stone," [that refers to] the Decalogue; "law" [refers to] the Pentateuch; "commandment" [refers to] the Mishnah; "which I have written" [refers to] the Prophets and Hagiographa [Writings]; "so that you may teach them" [refers to] the Gemara. The verse [thus] teaches that all of those sources were given to Moses on Sinai. (B. Berakhot 5a)[8]

> ואמר רבי לוי בר חמא אמר רבי שמעון בן לקיש: מאי דכתיב (שמות כ"ד) "ואתנה לך
> את לוחות האבן והתורה והמצוה אשר כתבתי להורתם"? לוחות - אלו עשרת הדברות תורה -
> זה מקרא והמצוה - זו משנה אשר כתבתי - אלו נביאים וכתובים להרתם - זה תלמוד
> מלמד שכולם נתנו למשה מסיני.

> #28) Even that which a distinguished student was destined to teach in the presence of his teacher was already said to Moses on Sinai.
> (J. Pe'ah 17a)

> אפילו מה שתלמיד ותיק עתיד להורות לפני רבו כבר נאמר למשה בסיני.

Consequently, since all of the interpretations, extensions, and revisions of the law by the rabbis of all generations to come were already revealed at Sinai, they carry God's authority. On the other hand, the Rabbis were aware that many of their interpretations and laws were new (see Sources #7 and #19 above), and they even held that it is God's desire that the Rabbis create new laws in each generation (see Sources #14 and #15 above). Moreover they claimed that these new interpretations were the form in which God revealed His will to us in post-biblical times (see Source #6 above). The Rabbis therefore also said this:

> #29) When God revealed His presence to the Israelites, He did not display all His goodness at once, because they could not have borne so much good; for had He revealed His goodness to them at one time they would have died....When Joseph made himself known to his brothers, they were unable to answer him because they were astounded by him

85

(Bereshit 45:3). If *God* were to reveal Himself all at once, how much more powerful would be the effect. So He shows Himself little by little. (*Tanhuma Buber*, Devarim, 1a)

כי בשעה שהקב״ה מגלה שכינתו על ישראל אינו [מגלה] עליהם כל טובתו כאחת מפני שאינן יכולין לעמוד באותה טובה שאם יגלה עליהם טובתו בפעם אחת ימותו כולם. . . צא ולמד מיוסף שבשעה שנתוודע לאחיו לאחר כמה שנים. . .ולא יכלו אחיו לענות אותו כי נבהלו מפניו הקב״ה על אחת כמה וכמה אלא מה הקב״ה עושה להם מגלה להם קימעא קימעא.

#30)   Matters that had not been disclosed to Moses were disclosed to R. Akiba and his colleagues. (*Bamidbar Rabbah* 19:6)

דברים שלא נגלו למשה נגלו לר״ע וחביריו.

How is it possible that everything was revealed at Sinai and yet new things are revealed each day? Actually, it is not as contradictory as it seems. If you have ever read a good story as a child and then again when you were older, you will know how that can be. You understood the story in one way the first time, but the second time you might have seen completely new levels of meaning in it. The text was the same, but it said something new to you because you were different. You were older and could relate the story to more areas of life. You also could appreciate more of the themes of the story. *Alice in Wonderland*, for example, is not just a funny story about a girl who has a crazy dream. It is also a satire on many different types of people and includes even some interesting problems of logic. You certainly did not see it that way when you read it at age seven or eight (or, alas, saw the movie!), but you may be able to understand it that way now.

Similar things could be said about the stories in the Bible. If you have considered them only as stories, you have missed a great deal of their meaning. The Bible is *at least* good literature, and you need to study it again many times as a teenager and as an adult to understand it maturely. The reason why people call it a classic is because it says important things about life, but you need to be trained to recognize the various levels of meaning that it has.

Law operates in a similar way. On the one hand, with the exception of the last sixteen amendments, the Constitution of the United States is the same as it was in 1791, when the Bill of Rights was ratified. Its meaning, however, has extended far beyond the intentions of its framers, for judges, lawyers, and scholars have carefully examined its every phrase in applying it to new problems and circumstances. It has even changed meaning a number of times as the Supreme Court has reversed itself or greatly narrowed or expanded the application of its previous rulings. *Yet, in an important sense, all of the later developments were already inherent in the original Constitution because they all are derived from the governmental bodies that it established and the general principles that it enunciated.* The Constitution is understood and applied in many novel ways each year – or, in more theological terms, many new, previously undiscovered meanings and applications are revealed in it as time goes on. But all of the new meanings are dependent upon the Constitution which established the structure for those interpretations and applications in the first place. That is the sense of continuity in law to which we previously referred.

The exact same thing is true about Jewish law. On the one hand, every interpretation and application of Jewish law that ever has been, is, or will be was already revealed at Sinai because every one of them comes directly or indirectly from the procedures and principles that the Jewish constitution, the Torah, established. Even the *takkanot* (revisions) that rabbis have enacted over the centuries are based upon the Torah's authorization of judges to act on behalf of Jewish law in every generation. The *takkanot* may represent a change in the content of the law, as their name implies, but they nevertheless are part of Jewish law because they were enacted by its duly authorized representatives. Similarly, and more importantly, each time that a Jewish court or judge decided to interpret the Torah or Talmud in one way and not another, the meaning of those texts changed. Sometimes the texts were given meanings that they had never had before through this process of *midrash* (interpretation), and sometimes several possible alternative interpretations were cut off by this process.

In any case, whether a given verse in the Torah was being expanded or contracted in meaning or application, that was possible only because the Torah established the ground rules and procedures of Jewish law. In that sense, *every* later development in Jewish law, no matter how far removed in content from the simple meaning of the Torah, was already revealed to Moses at Sinai. On the other hand, in every generation the Torah is given new meanings and applications, and in that sense "matters that had not been revealed to Moses were revealed to Rabbi Akiba and his colleagues."

b) How the Rabbis Used Their Divine Authority in Far-Reaching Rulings:

The authority of Jewish law does not diminish, then, as it is applied anew in every generation. It *must* be so interpreted and applied if it is to continue to live, and the Rabbis clearly recognized that. So far we have seen that in what the Rabbis *said*, but the evidence is more overwhelming if we consider what the Rabbis *did*. Through using the methods of exegesis (interpretation) that they developed (some of which are contained in "The Baraita of Rabbi Ishmael," found in the early part of the daily Shaharit service in some prayerbooks), they totally annulled some biblical laws and, in other areas, created new laws.

87

For example, the Bible requires capital punishment for a whole variety of offenses, but the Rabbis created court procedures for capital cases which were so demanding that it became virtually impossible to obtain a capital conviction in Jewish law. To give you an idea of what they did, here are some of the requirements that they instituted:

(1) The culprit must be warned by two witnesses immediately before he or she committed the act that it is unlawful and carries the death penalty. (After all, the accused may not have known that the act is illegal or punished so severely, and how can you hold people liable for a penalty as severe as death for transgressing a law that they never knew?)

(2) The accused must have responded, "Even so, I am going to do it," for otherwise one cannot be sure that the culprit heard the warning.

(3) The defendant must have committed the act within three seconds after hearing the warning because people forget things and if the culprit forgot the law we do not hold him or her responsible for a penalty as serious as death.

(4) The witnesses may not be related to each other or to the culprit.

(5) There must be at least one judge on the court who votes to acquit the defendant, for otherwise the court might be prejudiced against him or her -- which, by the way, is the exact opposite of the requirement in American law for a unanimous jury.

Some of these requirements -- and some of the other things that the Rabbis required -- are clearly implausible extensions of principles that are reasonable in a different form, and the Rabbis certainly knew that. They had decided, though, to outlaw the death penalty, despite the numerous times the Bible requires it, and they used court procedures to accomplish that. Put another way, they interpreted the death penalty out of existence, and they realized that result and the issues involved fully:

> #31) A court which has put a man to death once in a seven-year period is called "a hanging court" [literally, a destructive court]. Rabbi Elazar ben Azariah says, "Even once in seventy years." Rabbi Tarfon and Rabbi Akiba say, "Were we members of the court, no person would ever be put to death." Rabban Simeon ben Gamliel retorted, "If so, they would increase shedders of blood [murderers] in Israel." (*M. Makkot* 1:10)

סנהדרין ההורגת אחד בשבוע נקראת חבלנית. רבי אלעזר בן עזריה אומר אחד לשבעים שנה. רבי טרפון ורבי עקיבא אומרים אלו היינו בסנהדרין לא נהרג אדם מעולם. רבן שמעון בן גמליאל אומר אף הן מרבין שופכי דמים בישראל.

On the other hand, while the Rabbis effectually nullified the death penalty, they created a whole structure of Sabbath laws far beyond those in the Bible – to the extent that they themselves said:

> #32) The laws of the Sabbath...are like mountains hanging by a hair, for they consist of little Bible and many laws. (*M. Haggigah* 1:8)
>
> הלכות שבת. . .הרי הם כהררים התלויין בשערה שהן מקרא מועט והלכות מרובות.

Thus the Rabbis of the Talmud and Midrash clearly and consciously changed Jewish law as evidenced both by what they said and by what they did, adding a number of laws, dropping some, and changing the form of some.

Two things must be emphasized about this. First of all, they considered their actions authorized by God because *they* – the Rabbis themselves – were the ones appointed by the Torah to interpret and apply it in every age.

In other words, in the Jewish law, as in American law, the Constitution establishes some laws together with bodies to interpret and apply those laws. In both systems the interpretations in later generations may vary widely from the original intention of the constitutional laws – even to the extent of nullifying them – *but the new interpretations carry constitutional authority because they are made by the bodies which the Constitution establishes.* This is the reason why lawyers cite recent court decisions about the Constitution rather than the Constitution itself, and that is also the reason for the Geonic rule in Jewish law that *hilkhita kebatra'ai,* ("the law is according to the last, [that is, the most recent] authorities"). In both cases, it is the *forms* (institutions) established by the Constitution which determine its meaning, even to the point of effectively canceling sections of its contents, and it is because the new rulings issue from the duly authorized bodies that they carry constitutional authority.

Secondly, and perhaps more importantly, with all of the changes that the Rabbis instituted, they did *not* think that "anything goes," that they could play completely fast and loose with the law. On the contrary, for them it was clearly a matter of *"tradition* and change." In fact, all of the changes that we have mentioned have meaning only if one accepts the authority of the law in the first place. If that is not the case, then the whole legal system is not a matter of practical concern, and changes in it are irrelevant. The Rabbis dared to make the changes that they did because they took the law seriously. They practiced it, honored it, and were deeply concerned with its continuing authority and viability. *It is the law which defines Jews as Jews;* without it there is no point to their separate identity:

#33) ["...they rejected My rules and spurned My laws. Yet even then, when they are in the land of their enemies,] I will not reject them or spurn them [so as to destroy them, annulling my Covenant with them]" (Vayikra 26:43-44). All the good gifts that were given them were taken from them. And if it had not been for the Book of the Torah which was left to them, they would not have differed at all from the nations of the world. (*Sifra* 112c)

לא מאסתים ולא געלתים לכלותם. . והלא כל מתנות טובות שנתנו להם נטלו מהם. ואילולי ספר תורה שנשתייר להם לא היו משנים מאומות העולם כלום.

#34) Our Rabbis have taught: Once the wicked government decreed that Israel should no longer occupy themselves with Torah. Then came Pappos b. Judah and found R. Akiba holding great assemblies and studying Torah. He said to him, "Akiba, are you not afraid of the wicked government?"

He replied, "I will tell you a parable. What is the matter like? It is like a fox who was walking along the bank of the stream and saw some fish gathering together to move from one place to another. He said to them, `From what are you fleeing?' They answered, `From nets which men are bringing against us.' He said to them, `Let it be your pleasure to come up on the dry land, and let us, me and you, dwell together, even as my ancestors lived together with your ancestors.' They replied, `Are you he of whom they tell that you are the shrewdest of animals? You are not clever, but a fool! For if we are afraid in the place which is our life-element, how much more so in a place which is our death-element!' So also is it with us [Jews]: If now, while we sit and study Torah, in which it is written, `For that is your life, and the length of your days' (Devarim 30:20), we are in such a plight, how much more so, if we neglect it." (*B. Berakhot* 61b)

תנו רבנן: פעם אחת גזרה מלכות הרשעה שלא יעסקו ישראל בתורה בא פפוס בן יהודה ומצאו לרבי עקיבא שהיה מקהיל קהלות ברבים ועוסק בתורה. אמר ליה: עקיבא אי אתה מתירא מפני מלכות? אמר לו: אמשול לך משל למה הדבר דומה? לשועל שהיה מהלך על גב הנהר וראה דגים שהיו מתקבצים ממקום למקום אמר להם: מפני מה אתם בורחים? אמרו לו: מפני רשתות שמביאין עלינו בני אדם. אמר להם: רצונכם שתעלו ליבשה ונדור אני ואתם כשם שדרו אבותי עם אבותיכם? אמרו לו: אתה הוא שאומרים עליך פקח שבחיות? לא פקח אתה אלא טפש אתה. ומה במקום חיותנו אנו מתיראין במקום מיתתנו על אחת כמה וכמה אף אנחנו עכשיו שאנו יושבים ועוסקים בתורה שכתוב בה (דברים ל') "כי הוא חייך וארך ימיך" כך אם אנו הולכים ומבטלים ממנה - על אחת כמה וכמה.

4. The Significance of the Law to the Jewish People

Israel's acceptance of the Torah was the reason why it had a special covenant with God:

> #35) If it were not for My Torah which you accepted, I should not recognize you, and I should not regard you more than any of the idolatrous nations of the world. Therefore I entered into a covenant with you [Moses] and with Israel. *(Shemot Rabbah 47:3)*

> שאלולי תורתי שקבלתם לא הייתי מכיר אתכם ולא הייתי מביט בכם משאר עובדי כוכבים. לפיכך כרתי אתך ברית ואת ישראל.

Moreover, the Torah is Israel's gift to God and the world, and through it Israel gains not only worth, but beauty:

> #36) God said, "If you read the Torah, you do a kindness, for you help to preserve My world, since if it were not for the Torah, the world would again become 'without form and void...'"
>
> The matter is like a king who had a precious stone, and he entrusted it to his friend and said to him, "I pray you, pay attention to it and guard it, as is fitting, for if you lose it, you cannot pay me its worth, and I have no other jewel like it, and so you would sin against yourself and against me; therefore, do your duty by both of us, and guard the jewel as is fitting." So Moses said to the Israelites, "If you keep the Law, not only upon yourselves do you confer a benefit, but also upon God," as it is said, "And it shall be a benefit for us" (Devarim 6:25).
>
> [Even though the direct meaning of the verse is that it will be to our merit as a people to obey God's law, the midrash takes "us" to mean God and Israel, not just the people of Israel, and the word *tzedakah* -- "righteousness"-- it takes to mean benefit, which led to its later signification of "alms." Thus while Moses tells the Israelites to obey the Torah for their own merit before God, the midrash reinterprets it to mean that if the Israelites obey the law, it will be a benefit to both the People Israel and to God.] *(Devarim Rabbah 8:5)*

> אם קריתם את התורה מצוה אתם עושים על עולמי שאלמלא התורה כבר היה העולם חוזר לתוהו ובוהו...למה"ד למלך שהיה לו אבן טובה והפקידה אצל אוהבו א"ל בבקשה ממך תן דעתך עליה ושמור אותה כראוי שאם תאבד לא יש לך מהיכן לפרוע לי ואף אני לא יש לי אחרת כיוצא בה ונמצאת חוטא עלי ועליך אלא עשה מצוה על שנינו ושמור אותה כראוי כך אמר משה לישראל אם שמרתם את התורה לא על עצמכם אתם עושין צדקה בלבד אלא עלי ועל עצמכם מנין שנאמר (דברים ו) וצדקה תהיה לנו.

#37) "You are beautiful, my love, you are beautiful" (Shir Hashirim 1:15). "You are beautiful through the commandments, both positive and negative; beautiful through loving deeds; beautiful in your house with the heave offerings and the tithes; beautiful in the field by keeping the commands about gleaning, the forgotten sheaf and the second tithe; beautiful in the laws about mixed seeds, fringes, first fruits, and the fourth year planting; beautiful in the law of circumcision; beautiful in prayer, in the reading of the *Shema*, in the law of the *mezuzzah* and the phylacteries [*tefillin*], in the law of the palm-branch (*lulav)* and the citron (*etrog);* beautiful too, in repentance and in good works; beautiful in this world and beautiful in the world to come.

(Shir Hashirim Rabbah 1:63)

"הנך יפה רעיתי הנך יפה יפה" (שיר א'). הנך יפה במצות הנך יפה בגמילות חסדים הנך יפה
במצות עשה הנך יפה במצות לא תעשה הנך יפה במצות הבית בחלוק תרומה
ומעשרות הנך יפה במצות השדה בלקט שכחה ופאה ומעשר עני וההפקר הנך יפה
בכלאים הנך יפה בסדין בציצית הנך יפה בנטיעה הנך יפה בערלה הנך יפה בנטע
רבעי הנך יפה במילה הנך יפה בפריעה הנך יפה בתפלה הנך יפה בקריאת שמע הנך
יפה במזוזה הנך יפה בתפילין הנך יפה בסוכה הנך יפה בלולב ואתרוג הנך יפה
בתשובה הנך יפה במעשים טובים הנך יפה בעולם הזה הנך יפה בעולם הבא:

#38) R. Jonathan said that this verse [the famous words in Joshua 1:8, "You shall meditate on it (the Torah) day and night"] were neither command nor obligation, but blessing. The Holy One, blessed be He, said: "Joshua, the words of the Torah are so dear to you that the Book of the Torah will never depart from your mouth." In the School of R. Ishmael it was taught: The words of the Torah are not to be to you a burden, but, on the other hand, you are not free to excuse yourself from them."

(B. *Menahot* 99b)

ר' שמואל בר נחמני א"ר יונתן: פסוק זה אינו לא חובה ולא מצוה אלא ברכה. אמר לו
הקדוש ברוך הוא: יהושע כל כך חביבין עליך דברי תורה? לא ימוש ספר התורה הזה
מפיך. תנא דבי ר' ישמעאל: דברי תורה לא יהו עליך חובה ואי אתה רשאי לפטור
עצמך מהן.

Consequently, if you do not observe the Law, say the Rabbis, you might as well not have been created:

#39) Rabbi Yohanan ben Zakkai said: If you have learned much Torah, do not take credit for yourself, for you were created for that purpose.

(M. *Avot* 2:9)

רבן יוחנן בן זכאי...היה אומר: אם למדת תורה הרבה אל תחזיק טובה לעצמך כי לכך
נוצרת.

#40) Rava said: If someone fulfills the Torah not for its sake [that is for an ulterior motive], it were better had he or she never been created.

(B. Berakhot 17a)

וכל העושה שלא לשמה נוח לו שלא נברא.

In sum, then, the Rabbis of the Talmud and Midrash, who were the framers of Judaism and gave it its distinctive cast, held unequivocally that a Jew must observe the Torah's laws. They also held, though, that the Torah was not given once and for all at Sinai but rather must be interpreted and applied anew in each generation. Only if that happens can the Torah continue to be an important concern of Jews, a program for living. The alternative is to let it petrify into a relic of history. Thus it is not so much "tradition and change" as it is *"tradition, which includes change."*

If the Torah is to retain a reasonable degree of consistency, however, it cannot be left to every individual to decide which laws to keep intact, which to change, and how. That must be done together as a community, and in Section (E) of this chapter we will discuss more fully the process by which communal decisions are made in Jewish law.

Changes, though, make sense only if you observe the law in the first place, and that raises the critical question: Why accept the authority of the Torah's laws and teachings at all? Until now we have assumed that Jews accept the Torah's law as binding, and we have discussed how the Jewish tradition defined the content of that law. But why should I observe the law in the first place?

As you might imagine, responses to that important question differ among Jews, and even within the Conservative Movement approaches vary. We will turn to study a number of the responses in the next section.

QUESTIONS:

1) "Judaism is NOT identical with the religion of the Bible but is rather based upon the way in which the Rabbis of the Talmud and Midrash interpreted the Bible."

a. Why is that?

b. How could that fact help you if you were approached by a Christian missionary who supports her claims using (her interpretation of) verses from the Bible?

c. What significance does the sentence in (1) have for Jewish law?

93

2) (a) "You shall not add anything to what I command you or take anything from it...." (Devarim 4:2; Devarim 13:1 is similar).

(b) "You shall act according to the instructions that they [the judges] give you and the ruling that they hand down to you...." (Devarim 17:11).

> How does (a) make Jewish law different from American law?
>
> On what authority, then, have the Rabbis changed Jewish law?
>
> *(Hint: Consider (b) and distinguish between the legislative and judicial functions of government.)*

3) If changes occur in Jewish law through judicial interpretation, what is left of the command in (1a) not to add or subtract anything from the commandments of the Torah? In answering, consider the following sources:

a. How do we know that we may not add [other fruits to the four of] the *lulav* or to the [four biblical selections in the] *tefillin*? The Bible says. "Do not add to them" (Devarim 13:1). How do we know that we may not use less [than what is required]? The Bible says "Do not subtract from them" *(ibid.).* How do we know that if he [the Kohen] began blessing the [three] priestly blessings he should not say [as a fourth blessing], "Since I began to bless, I will say also `May the Lord, God of your fathers, bless you'"? The Bible says, "[Do not add to] the thing [which I have commanded you," where the word for "thing" (davar) is the same word in Hebrew for "word," implying] even a word you should not add to it. *(Sifre* on Devarim 13:1, Re'eh, Section 82; see also *B. Sanhedrin* 88b and *B. Rosh Hashanah* 28b)

b. The Rabbis based [the authority of] all of their ordinances on the prohibition "You shall not turn aside" (Devarim 17:11). *(B. Berakhot* 19b)

c. Comment of Joseph Karo, author of the *Shulhan Arukh,* on Devarim 4:2: "That, however, does not imply that the enactments of the code of Moses could never be added to or modified as new conditions warranted the change, provided all such modifications were not proclaimed as new revelations from on High." (Cf. also Sources #6 and 7 above).

4) List and explain the five reasons given in the text for the Rabbis' transfer of legal authority from the Prophets to the judges. Can you think of any other reasons?

5) How does Jewish law hold together and remain reasonably consistent despite all of the changes that have occurred in it? Give three ways, and compare them to American law.

6)   What two ways have Jews used in order to make legal decisions? When has each been used? What are the advantages and disadvantages of each?

7)   We will examine the basis for the authority of the law in the next section. Assume for now what the Bible says in several places – namely, that Jewish law is binding because God gave it. With all of the changes that human beings have introduced into Jewish law, how can it retain its divine authority?

(Hint: explain how it is possible that every later development in Jewish law was already revealed at Sinai and yet new laws are revealed each day. Compare this to American law.)

8)   a. Give some examples in what the Rabbis *said* to indicate that they knew that they were changing the law.

b. Show how what they *did* also illustrates that.

c. Why is it that changes in the law are significant only if you accept the authority of the law in the first place?

d. What reasons do the Rabbis give for the importance of observing the law?

(Note: Another USY sourcebook, Mitzvah Means Commandment, discusses nine different reasons which the Bible gives for obeying the commandments and five others which the Rabbis provide. According to our classical sources, then, one should live by the commandments not only because one wants to gain God's reward and avoid God's punishment, but also, among other reasons, because one loves God, one promised God in the Covenant, the commandments are internally wise and therefore it makes good sense to live by them, because they mark us off and identify us as Jews, and because we strive to be holy. See that book for more extensive explanations of these and other motives to live one's life in accordance with the commandments.)

e. In what sense, then, do the Rabbis of the Talmud and Midrash believe in tradition and change -- or, better, in tradition, which includes change?

D. The Question of Authority: Orthodox, Reform, and Four Conservative Theories of Revelation

Why should Jews observe the *mitzvot*? The Bible gives many answers to that question (again, see my other USY sourcebook, *Mitzvah Means Commandment*, for a discussion of them), but the most common one is simply that God commanded us at Sinai to do so. There God revealed (showed) His will to us, and so philosophers say that "revelation" occurred there. The Bible is careful to describe that event in impressive terms: there was lightning, thunder, and earthquakes (Shemot 19:16, 18), and the whole group of 600,000 Israelites witnessed what happened there (Shemot 12:37).

More importantly, that event made the law binding on Jews for all generations to come:

> It was not with our fathers that the Lord made this covenant, but with us, the living, every one of us who is here today. Face to face the lord spoke to *you* on the mountain out of the fire. (Devarim 5:3-4; see also Devarim 29:9-14)

> Know, therefore, that only the Lord your God is God, the steadfast God who keeps His gracious covenant to the thousandth generation of those who love Him and keep His commandments, but who instantly requites with destruction those who reject Him — never slow with those who reject Him, punishing them instantly. Therefore observe faithfully the Instruction, the laws, and the norms with which I charge you today. (Devarim 7:9-11)

As the above citations indicate, there are two reasons why the Law that God gave at Sinai is eternally binding. First, our forefathers made a covenant (agreement) with God in which the Israelites were promised the land of Israel and the status of being God's Chosen People in return for observing His commandments, and so we must observe the *mitzvot* because we promised to do so. You might say to yourself that it is not fair that you should be bound by what your ancestors promised, but that would not be right: you should understand the event at Sinai as if you yourself were there and participated in the promise. As the Haggadah of Passover phrases it:

> In every generation a person must look upon him/herself as if he or she personally had come out from Egypt, as the Bible says: "And you shall explain to your child on that day, "It is because of what the Lord did for *me* when *I* went free from Egypt'" (Shemot 13:8). For it was not alone our forefathers whom the Holy One, praised be He, redeemed, but He redeemed us together with them, as it is said: "He freed us from there to bring *us* to, and give *us*, the land that He promised on oath to our forefathers." (Devarim 6:23)

(Incidentally, the same is true for secular law. The constitution of the country in which you live is binding upon you even though you were never asked whether you approve of it. Simply identifying as one of its citizens and reaping the benefits of citizenship obligate you to obey it. You may never have promised obedience to it in words, but your actions indicate "tacit [silent] consent," as the political philosopher Thomas Hobbes said. Similarly, international agreements do not have to be renewed with each new government or generation: they bind both parties forever unless there is a specific time limit in the original agreement or unless both parties agree to renegotiate the agreement.)[9] Secondly, the Law of Sinai is eternal because God, who gave it and enforces it, is eternal.

Why, then, should we go any further? Why should we not simply say that you should observe Jewish law because its root is in the Torah, and that is the will of God?

Many do say that, but some do not, and even those who do hold that position feel compelled to deal with two problems in that assertion. The first concerns the act of revelation, and the second revolves around its product:

(a) In regard to the *act* of revelation, we ask: What happened at Sinai? How do we know that it was God speaking? Perhaps the whole account of the revelation at Sinai is simply a product of someone's imagination. Even if God did speak, how do we know that He was understood correctly?

(b) In regard to the *product* of the act of revelation— that is, the Torah — we ask: Is this the direct transcription of God's words? If so, how do we explain some of the contradictions in its laws (e.g., Passover is to be celebrated for seven days according to Shemot 13:6, Vayikra 23:6, and Devarim 16:3, but for only six days in Devarim 16:8; Shemot 20:21 permits the erection of a sanctuary anywhere, but Devarim 12:4-5 restricts the sanctuary to a single shrine in all of Israel)? And what about the variations in its stories (e.g., the different orders of Creation depicted in Chapters One and Two of Bereshit, and the different paths described for the Israelites in Bamidbar 20:21 and Devarim 2:4)? And how do we explain the similarity of some of its laws (e.g., eye for an eye) and stories (e.g., flood stories) to those of the nations surrounding the Israelites during biblical times? And what about the variant versions of the Bible that we have? Even if God revealed His will at Sinai, human beings have copied it and interpreted it throughout all the generations, and so how can we be assured that what we have in hand is anything like what God gave, and how do we know that our interpretation of it is anything like what God intended then -- or wants us to do now?

	SOME EXPONENTS OF THE APPROACH	1) METHOD OF STUDY
ORTHODOX	Berkovits, Lamm	No distinction between *Peshat* and *Derash*: meaning of text = meaning that traditional commentators assigned to it.
CONSERVATIVE I	Leeser, Kohut, Schechter (?) Roth	HISTORICAL METHOD: Distinguish between *Peshat* and *Derash*: determine *Peshat* through literary and historical analysis.
CONSERVATIVE II	Bokser, Gordis Routtenberg	"
CONSERVATIVE III	Existenialists: Jacobs, Schorsch, Heschel, Gillman Objectivists: Lieber, Dorff	"
CONSERVATIVE IV (= Reconstruction tendency)	Kaplan, Eisenstein, Green, Teutsch, Schulweis	"
REFORM	Petuchowski, Borowitz, 1937 Guiding Principles 1976 Centenary Perspective	"

2) THE NATURE OF REVELATION	3) THE AUTHORITY OF THE BIBLE LAWS AND IDEAS	4) MAN'S ABILITY TO CHANGE THE BIBLE'S LAWS AND IDEAS
Verbal Revelation: The Torah, including both the Written and Oral Traditions, consists of the exact words of God. He gave it all as one piece at Sinai, and we have those words in hand.	God's will	None, since God revealed the answers to all future questions at Sinai and man does not know more than God. *Exceptions:* 1) Applications to new situations (which were also revealed at Sinai). 2) Choice of one position in the codes or responsa over others.
Continuous Revelation: God dictated His will at Sinai and other times. It was written down by human beings, however, and hence the diverse traditions in the Bible.	God's will	Same as Orthodox (but usually choose the lenient position in the codes) *plus* 3) Places where there are clear scribal errors. 4) Clear borrowings from other cultures. That is, distinguish the divine and human elements in our texts.
Continuous Revelation: Human beings wrote the Torah, but they were divinely inspired.	God's will	Human beings *can* change them because rabbis in each generation may be inspired to a new Midrash; they *must* because the rabbis of each generation are charged with the responsibility to keep Jewish Law viable by balancing tradition and change.
Continuous Revelation: The Torah is the human record of the encounter between God and the People Israel at Sinai. Since it was written by human beings, it contains some laws and ideas which we find repugnant today.	1) God's will 2) Covenant with God and the Jewish People of past, present and future.	We continue to have encounters with God, and the law must be changed to reflect the new understanding of God's will that results from these encounters. It is the rabbis, representing the community, and not every individual on his own, who must determine the content of Jewish law in our day.
No Revelation: Human beings wrote the Torah. No claim for divinity of the product.	1) Tradition (custom) 2) Internal Wisdom	Communal authorities in each generation can and must help individuals reconstruct Judaism with current and meaningful customs and ideas, but observance of rituals is *voluntary*; an organized creative community of the future could establish and enforce *moral* laws.
Progressive Revelation: The Torah is God's will written by human beings. As time goes on, we get to understand His will better and better (= "progressive revelation")	1) Moral laws come from God. 2) Ritual laws have no authority because: a) prophets cancelled them. b) Rabbinic laws were intended for specific periods only.	Every *individual* decides both what and how to obey.

These are hard questions, but it is necessary to face them squarely if you are ever going to understand the authority behind Jewish law. This is especially important for the Conservative Movement because from its beginning it has been based on taking an *historical* approach to the texts of our tradition, and that approach makes the problems listed in (b) all the more compelling, as you will see.

To show you the responses to these questions, it will be helpful to distinguish four separate, but related questions:

(1) *Method of Study*: How should we study the Bible? Should we see it as the direct word of God, or is it a book written by human beings and therefore subject to historical, literary, and philosophical analysis like other books? These are questions concerning the product of revelation, the questions listed in (b) above

(2) *The Nature of Revelation*: Where did the Bible come from? Revelation? If so, how should we understand how that occurred? If not, then why did the people who wrote it call it the word of God?

(3) *The Authority of the Bible's Laws and Ideas*: Is the Bible a special book for us because it carries the authority of God or for another reason – or is it a combination of both? The answer to this question will depend very much on how we answer (1) and (2).

(4) *The Warrant for Human Beings to Change the Bible's Laws or Ideas*: Do people, whether individually or collectively in some forum, have the right or obligation to make such changes? If so, how? The answer to those questions obviously depends upon the answers to (1), (2), and (3).

Despite some variations, the Orthodox answer these four questions in one basic way, and the same is true for the Reform Movement.[10] There are at least four distinct responses in the Conservative Movement. We will consider each of those approaches in turn. To help you keep track of the discussion, keep your finger on the pages containing the chart on the preceding pages. Do not expect to understand everything; some things may even seem confusing at first glance. The entire chart will be explained in the following pages.

Let us now take the positions one by one.

1. Orthodox

The Orthodox affirm that God revealed His will at Sinai in both a Written and an Oral form. The Oral tradition was ultimately written down in Rabbinic literature. It consists of the way in which God wanted the Written law (the Torah) to be interpreted and applied. Consequently, the meaning of any given verse of the Bible is what the Talmud, Midrash, and later commentaries say it is. Thus Eliezer Berkovits, an Orthodox rabbi who was formerly a professor at Hebrew Theological College in Chicago and who now teaches at Bar Ilan University in Israel, maintains: "...every word of the Torah, and, of course, every commandment, has its source in God; but the meaning of the revealed word or commandment is given in the oral tradition, the *Torah she-be'al peh* alone."[11] Moreover the texts of the Bible and Talmud that we have in hand must be understood as the exact word of God because if a human being wrote down God's word, the record of it that we have may be in error. As Rabbi Norman Lamm, President of Yeshiva University, says:

> I accept unapologetically the idea of the verbal revelation of the Torah. I do not take seriously the caricature of this idea which reduces Moses to a secretary taking dictation. Any competing notion of revelation, such as the various "inspiration" theories, can similarly be made to sound absurd by anthropomorphic parallels. Exactly how this communication took place no one can say: it is no less mysterious than the nature of the One who spoke....*How* God spoke is a mystery; how *Moses* received this message is an irrelevancy. *That* God spoke is of the utmost significance, and *what* He said must therefore be intelligible to humans in a human context, even if one insists upon an endlessly profound mystical overplus of meaning in the text. To deny that God can make His will clearly known is to impose upon Him a limitation of dumbness that would insult the least of His human creatures.[12]

That, of course, raises all the questions about the biblical and talmudic texts that we mentioned earlier in (b) and that lead other people to analyze the Bible historically. Rabbi Lamm recognizes that as a problem, but he downplays the evidence:

> Literary criticism of the Bible is a problem, but not a crucial one. Judaism has successfully met greater challenges in the past. Higher Criticism [applying literary analysis to the Bible] is far indeed from an exact science. The startling lack of agreement among scholars on any one critical view; the radical changes in general orientation in more recent years; the many revisions that archaeology has forced upon literary critics; and the unfortunate neglect even

by Bible scholars of much first-rate scholarship in modern Hebrew supporting the traditional claim of Mosaic authorship – all these reduce the question of Higher Criticism from the massive proportions it has often assumed to a relatively minor and manageable problem that is chiefly a nuisance but not a threat to the enlightened believer.[13]

What this effectively means is that Orthodox believers must be intellectually schizophrenic, because they approach the Torah in a totally different way than they study any other book. Orthodox Jews may use their minds and scholarly methods of analysis to understand any other text, but the Bible and Talmud are different. They must understand such classical Jewish texts as the tradition has interpreted them, ignoring or somehow circumventing those factual and intellectual problems which arise from archaeological finds, literary or linguistic analysis, cross-cultural studies, scientific discoveries, and the like.

The advantage of that, of course, is that God Himself is speaking in both the legal and non-legal sections of the Bible, and therefore both are true and authoritative. Moreover, the laws are unchangeably binding. Thus Rabbi Eliezer Berkovits says this:

> As to the meaning of the commandments, even those that apparently have neither ethical nor doctrinal content, one must – as always – refer to the oral tradition, as well as to the continually developing philosophy and theology of Judaism. One may explain the ritual commandments according to Saadia's hedonism, or according to Yehuda Halevi's quasi-mysticism; according to Maimonides's rationalism, or Kabbalistic mysticism, or according to some more sophisticated modern religious philosophy or theology. The commandments, however, remain unchangeably binding.[14]

David Singer, an Orthodox Jew who is editor of the *American Jewish Yearbook*, puts it more bluntly than the rabbis do, but his formulation gives one a good insight into the mindset of Orthodox Judaism:

> "...The line of authority is clear: God issues the marching orders and man obeys. About these marching orders there is nothing at all vague -- we are talking about law, law that encompasses the whole of life and is sharply focused in detail. As for obedience, it entails an urgent feeling of obligation, in which the sole criterion of significance is the will of God. Ludicrous though it may seem to others, for the committed Orthodox Jew, not tearing toilet paper on the Sabbath is a serious religious issue.[15]

If asked about the changes that have in fact taken place in Jewish law, most Orthodox Jews[16] would claim that they were not changes but simply extensions of the Law, and moreover those extensions were already revealed at Sinai. In other words, they would interpret Source #28 in Section (C) of this chapter literally (but perhaps incorrectly) and not as it was explained there.

2-5) Conservative I-IV

All of the other positions listed on the chart take an historical approach to the texts of our tradition. That is, the texts are understood in the context of the times and places in which they were written. A distinction is therefore made between the meaning of the text as it stands (the *peshat*) and the meaning(s) that later generations ascribed to the text (the *midrash*, or *derash*).

Historical analysis reveals that the Torah consists of several documents ("the Documentary Hypothesis") coming from different periods and places and edited together by the time of Ezra (444 B.C.E.). The most common version of this theory identifies four documents within the Torah, labeled J, E, P, and D. In broad terms, the J document refers to the sections of the Torah which refer to God by God's proper name (the tetragrammaton of yod-heh-vav-heh, or "Jehovah," often translated as "Lord"); the E document refers to God as "Elohim," usually translated as "God"; the P document is the priestly code, including much of Vayikra and sections of the other books; and D is Devarim, a document separate from those which make up the first four books of the Torah and whose authors were probably also the authors of Melakhim, Jeremiah, and Eikhah. Sometimes the historical approach is called "biblical criticism" or "the critical approach," not because people who want to study the Bible historically disrespect it and want to diminish its stature ("critical" in the sense of criticize), but rather because studying the Bible historically subjects it to historical analysis (or "critique").

The advantage of understanding the text historically is clear: you do not have to be intellectually schizophrenic, applying different methods of analysis to Jewish texts from those which you use in understanding other texts from the past. On the contrary, you not only admit, but expect that the texts will manifest the influences of neighboring cultures and particular periods in history because you assume that the texts were written by people. But the disadvantage is also clear: you must explain why these texts have particular authority for you as a Jew. If human beings wrote them, why should I assume that they are binding, true or good?

There are at least four distinct answers to that in the Conservative Movement which we will now consider and which we will label Conservative I, II, III, and IV. These are *not* separate organizations within the Movement: they are rather composite pictures created for this sourcebook of positions held by a number of Conservative rabbis. Consequently, after the description of each one of the four general positions on the authority of Jewish law, several specific versions of the position are cited as illustrations.

2) Conservative I

Those who hold this view maintain that -

a) God in fact dictated His will at Sinai and at other times in words. Since the revelation to Moses was by far the clearest and most public, it is the most authentic recording of God's will.

b) The revelation at Sinai and those which followed, however, were written down by human beings, and hence there are diverse sources of biblical literature which one discovers when one studies the Bible historically.

c) From Sinai on, Jewish law and theology are to be identified with the ways in which the leaders (later, the rabbis) of each generation interpreted and applied the laws of the Torah. Hence the authority of Jewish law is based upon the fact that it is God's will, as stated first in the Torah and then by rabbis of each generation.

d) Rabbis are authorized to modify the law for their time, but only with extreme caution, for, after all, they are altering the closest thing that we have to a record of what God said. At the same time, God specifically authorized judges in each generation to interpret and apply the law, and God commanded the people to follow the rulings of the judges of their generation, and so contemporary rabbinic rulings are authoritative expressions of God's will for us, even, in the extreme, when they differ from the plain meaning of the biblical text.

This position retains a direct, verbal revelation at Sinai, and, as such, it can and does claim that all of the laws in the Torah have the express authority of God behind them. At the same time, it openly asserts that God's words were recorded by human beings, and hence this theory can account for the variations in law, ideology, and language in the Bible. The latter feature qualifies it as a Conservative position, for it advocates an historical study of the texts of our tradition – or at least most of them.

This is a "right-wing" view,[*] however, because it claims that God communicated His will to Moses in a direct, verbal way, and consequently it is not easy to dismiss any law as a product of human error, however troublesome it may be. That, after all, would undermine this position's claim that the Torah's authority is ultimately based on God's words to us, however much they were filtered through human understanding and recording. Therefore while advocates of this position might choose the liberal position among those available in the tradition, they are generally not willing to modify the law in the absence of a reasonably strong precedent which already appears in the texts of the tradition. They understand other factors which others use to modify the law – as, for example, moral, social, or economic considerations – as "extra-legal" and therefore only to be used when there is an intensely pressing need and no other recourse to justify a change. This view, in other words, tends to be the most conservative (with a small "c") within the Conservative movement in that it is least likely to institute or accept a change in pre-existing law.

The position that I have described as "Conservative I" was held by a number of the people who were involved in the Conservative Movement in its early years. Rabbi Isaac Leeser, for example, was the first exponent of a modern form of traditionalism in America and in many ways the precursor of Conservative Judaism. When asked by those who doubted the literal truth of the Bible whether God spoke with a voice, Leeser answered: "Let it be clearly understood that our religion is true, not because other systems are false, but because it is based on divine revelation, which to a believer is the only source of truth."[17] In the preface to his English version of the Bible, he wrote: "The translator...believes in the Scriptures as they have been handed down to us, as also in the truth and authenticity of prophecies and their literal fulfillment."[18] Similarly, Rabbi Alexander Kohut, whose views on the teaching of Bible and Talmud were ultimately adopted by the Seminary faculty in the late 1800s and early 1900s, approved of a critical study of the Talmud, the Prophets, and the Hagiographa, [the Writings] but not of the Five Books of Moses: "To us the Pentateuch is a *noli me tangere*! Hands off! We disclaim all honor of handling the sharp knife which cuts the Bible into a thousand pieces"[19] – and, in fact, the Torah was not taught with the critical method in the Rabbinical school of the Seminary until much later.[20] Rabbi Solomon Schechter, the first

---

[*] "Right-wing" generally refers to a position which is least willing to change past patterns of thought or practice. As you go left on the spectrum, you encounter positions which are increasingly willing to reinterpret, modify, or substitute. A position may be "right-wing" in thought and "left-wing" in practice, or *vice-versa*; the spectrum of ideology and the spectrum of observance are two *different* spectra which do not necessarily coincide, although there usually is some correlation between the two, as the descriptions of the various positions in this section will indicate.

president of the reorganized Seminary, described the historical approach on which the Seminary's curriculum was based as follows:

> It is not the mere revealed Bible that is of first importance to the Jew, but the Bible as it repeats itself in history, in other words, as it is interpreted by Tradition.[21]

He was not altogether happy with that, however, and apparently sought to regain the certainty and grandeur of direct, verbal revelation if he could only reconcile it with his commitment to the historical approach:

> But when Revelation or the Written Word is reduced to the level of history, there is no difficulty in elevating history in its aspect of Tradition to the rank of Scripture, for both have then the same human or divine origin (according to the student's predilection for the one or the other adjective), and emanate from the same authority. Tradition becomes thus the means whereby the modern divine [that is, the modern student of theology] seeks to compensate himself for the loss of the Bible, and the theological balance is to the satisfaction of all parties happily readjusted....

> How long the position of this school will prove tenable is another question. Being brought up in the old Low Synagogue, where, with all attachment to tradition, the Bible was looked upon as the crown and the climax of Judaism, the old Adam still asserts itself in me, and in unguarded moments makes me rebel against this new rival of revelation in the shape of history. At times the new fashionable exaltation of Tradition at the expense of Scripture even impresses me as a sort of religious bimetallism [a market based on two metals] in which both speculators [traders] in theology try to keep up the market value of an inferior currency [=tradition] by denouncing loudly the bright shining gold [=the Torah] which, they would have us believe, is less fitted to circulate in the vulgar use of daily life than the small cash of historical interpretation.[22]

Early exponents of this view of revelation were wary of applying the techniques of historical scholarship to the Torah in part because they were worried that that would undermine its authority and in part because the first group of scholars to use historical methods in understanding the Pentateuch were German Protestant writers who frankly intended to attack Judaism and the Jewish claim to embody the original and authoritative revelation of God. Solomon Schechter, in fact, called higher biblical criticism "higher anti-Semitism," and Joseph Hertz, in his popular commentary on the Pentateuch, uses every opportunity to rail against the documentary hypothesis.[23]

Modern advocates of the view I have designated as "Conservative I" are much more willing to study not just the Prophets and Writings of the Bible and Rabbinic literature with the historical methods of scholarship, but the Torah itself. For one thing, the anti-Semitism that motivated much of biblical criticism among German Protestant scholars in the late nineteenth and early twentieth centuries (which were also the early years of the Conservative Movement) no longer is a significant factor in it. Jews and Christians have both learned to use that methodology with objectivity. Moreover, the techniques of biblical criticism have proved helpful in clarifying many passages that were either not understood or misunderstood before. Consequently, from the 1950s on, advocates of Conservative I have generally been willing to apply historical and literary techniques to the study of the Bible, including the Torah.

One contemporary exponent of Conservative I is Rabbi Joel Roth, Professor of Talmud at the Jewish Theological Seminary of America and past chair of the Conservative Movement's Committee on Jewish Law and Standards. Rabbi Roth adopts the theory of law of Sir John Salmond and Hans Kelsen (the theory known as "positivism") in distinguishing between legal sources and historical sources. Legal sources are "those sources which are recognized as such by the law itself" because they are in the texts of a legal system's legal literature and have been recognized as authoritative statements of the law by those charged with interpreting and enforcing it. Historical sources, on the other hand, are "those sources lacking formal recognition by the law itself" because they do not appear in such texts and are therefore not recognized by the officers of the legal tradition.

> The myriad tomes [many books] of law, the *corpora* [bodies] of judicial decisions, the various state and local constitutions or charters are all legal sources of the American legal system. As these sources function within the system of American law, the philosophical, political, socio-logical, or economic factors that may have been instrumental in their becoming legal norms are considered to be irrelevant; these factors constitute historical sources, and are not accounted *legally* significant by the system. One reads occasionally of some judge who was forced to render a decision on the basis of a valid statute, the origin of which had been clearly predicated on a reality different from that of the present. However, since the norm had never been amended or abrogated by the system, it remained authoritative and legal, and the judge was compelled to render his decision in accordance with it. His knowledge of the historical antecedents that gave rise to the norm in the first place was irrelevant. He could not decide *legally* in a manner contrary to its dictates.

> The Jewish legal system is no different from any other in this regard. Its recognized legal norms operate independently of the historical sources that may have given rise to them. So long as a norm has not been amended or

abrogated by the halakhic system, its origin as a reaction to Roman practice, as an emulation [copying] of Roman practice, or as a concession to the economic realities of Christian Europe, to suggest only several possibilities, is irrelevant to its validity as a norm of the halakhic system.

For this reason, historical sources are of a unique nature. At the point in time when they influence the introduction of new ideas into the legal system they are extremely important; yet their importance rests solely on the fact that their persuasive powers are sufficient to convince the authoritative *legal* body (or bodies) to incorporate them into the system as *legal* sources. Barring such incorporation, their influence on the legal system is merely potential, not actual, and regardless of their original importance, they fade into *legal* irrelevance once norms based on them are incorporated into the system as legal sources. So singularly unimportant to the functioning of the system are they, then, that inability to reconstruct the historical sources of any legal norm has no bearing whatsoever on the binding and authoritative nature of the norm....

From the fact that historical sources are legally insignificant, it follows that the demonstration by scholars that the true historical sources of a given norm are different from what had generally been assumed is an interesting revelation, but *legally* insignificant....[24]

This distinction between legal and historical sources enables Rabbi Roth to be fully open to studying the historical origins of the law, even during the time of the Torah, because nothing – literally, nothing – in the history of the law is relevant to its authority. That comes from the *grundnorm* (basic ground of authority) of the law, that is, the fundamental concept at the base of a legal system which gives it authority. Those who abide by a legal system must accept that fundamental concept and may do so for any reason which appeals to them. *Why* they accept the legal system's claim to authority is a "metalegal" issue – that is, a matter which stands apart from the legal system itself, usually in the realm of philosophy, theology, or history. The legal system's validity, however, depends only on *the fact that* its adherents accept its fundamental claim to authority, not on *why* they do so.

The concept of the basic norm is complex, yet indispensable. Its complexity derives mainly from the fact that this *grundnorm* is at once "metalegal" and "legal," that is, while its validity is presupposed by the system, it functions *legally* as a norm of the system. Any attempt to prove the validity of the basic norm must belong to a realm other than the legal. To the extent that its validity can be proved at all, the proof must be theological, philosophical, or metaphysical. Yet it is this norm that serves as the ultimate basis of the legal system and has definite legal functions. Put succinctly, the orderly functioning of any legal order requires of its adherents a "leap of faith" concerning the validity of the basic norm of the system. Although leaps of faith do not fall within the realm of law, such a leap of faith is the ultimate validation of the legal system.

Furthermore, it is important to grasp that presupposing the existence of a *grundnorm* is an amoral and nonvaluative act. The fact that a tyrant may have promulgated a constitution, obedience to which is the basic norm of a particular legal system, does not affect its status as a *grundnorm*. A postulated *grundnorm* is a *sine qua non* [indispensable condition] of a legal system, not a statement of the desirability, morality, or positive nature of the system. In many instances, such considerations will vary with the perspective of the viewer. The *grundnorm* of the American legal system was created as the result of an act of rebellion against a legal sovereign. To some, it was a necessary and ethical rebellion; to others, it was an immoral act of rebellion against the British crown. But even to this latter group, the *grundnorm* is the basic norm of the American system. Presupposing the basic norm of the American system is necessary in order to comprehend the functioning of the system, but carries no valuational implications whatsoever concerning the rectitude of the framers of the Constitution in postulating it. Thus, every legal system – democracy, monarchy, dictatorship, benevolent despotism – presupposes a basic norm; that fact, however, is independent of any consideration of the desirability of the system itself.

What, then, is the fundamental concept which underlies Jewish law and gives it its authority? According to Rabbi Roth, it is this: *"The document called the Torah embodies the word and will of God, which it behooves man to obey, and is, therefore, authoritative."*[25]

This immediately establishes the priority and superior authority of any statement of the Torah (*de-oraita*) over later, interpretive statements of the rabbis (*de-rabbanan*), for the Torah is, or is presumed to be, "the word and will of God" while rabbinic statements are those of human beings and, in any case, depend for their authority on the prior authority of the Torah which the rabbis are interpreting and applying. Moreover, in the halakhic system, as in any other legal system, the "truth" of the fundamental concept on which the system bases its authority is irrelevant to that authority, according to Rabbi Roth, once the claim to authority made by that fundamental concept is accepted:

> Whether or not it is "true" that the Torah embodies the word and will of God is of great historical and theological significance, but of no legal significance. Even if one has traced the origins of the Torah to documents called J, E, P, and D, he may have uncovered the historical sources of the legal norms, but he has

in no way abrogated the *grundnorm* of the halakhic system, which is *presupposed* by the system.[26]

In fact, Rabbi Roth is so convinced that historical, biblical scholarship is so irrelevant to the authority of Jewish law – and yet so convinced that it is an important way of studying the text -- that he reformulates the fundamental concept of Jewish law as follows: *"The document called the Torah embodies the word and the will of God, which it behooves man to obey, as mediated through the agency of J, E, P, and D, and is, therefore, authoritative."*[27]

In any case, note that Rabbi Roth ultimately affirms that the Torah is "the *word* and will of God," thus placing him in Conservative I.[28] Note, too, that his particular theory of Jewish law places moral, economic, social, and psychological concerns outside the realm of the law, making them, in his phrase, "extra-legal."

Those who embrace the theories I shall call Conservative II and III do not see the relationship of such concerns to Jewish law in that way. They instead understand moral, economic, social, and psychological issues to be intimately entwined in the law at all its stages, including the reasons why the law was formulated in the first place and the ways it should be interpreted and applied now – even to the extent, if necessary, of changing something in the Torah.

Nobody seriously committed to Jewish law will want to do that very often, but Rabbi Roth's theory diminishes the importance of such factors in interpreting and applying the law to such an extent that they become weak grounds for revision. That, though, is only because he defined the law in the first place as that which appears in the texts of the tradition. Most others within the Conservative movement understand the law much more broadly as the product of the ongoing interactions among the texts of the tradition, individual Jews, the Jewish community, the larger world, and God, and that perspective on the origins and nature of Jewish law often has significant effects for the ways people who hold that view (primarily those in Conservative II and III) interpret and apply Jewish law.[29]

In sum, then, for Conservative I, God spoke a message at Sinai, and belief in the divine authority of that message is the essence of Jewish faith. Such faith does not preclude an objective, historical and literary analysis of the biblical text, however, because it was human beings who wrote down their understanding of God's words in their own language and conceptual framework.

3) Conservative II

This position consists of the following claims:

a) Human beings wrote the Torah at various times and places. That is why the Torah contains diverse documents, laws, and ideas.

b) These people were, however, *divinely inspired*, and therefore their words carry the insight and authority of God.

c) Jewish laws and ideas may be changed for two reasons. First, since the Torah is a combination of divine inspiration and human articulation, we must distinguish the divine and human elements in the tradition and change the latter when circumstances require it. Second, divine inspiration did not happen once and for all at Sinai. The Torah is the document on which Judaism is based, and it therefore has special importance for us; but divine inspiration continues on in the form of new interpretations of the Torah in each generation (*not* through new words or appearances of God — cf. Sources #6 and #7 in Section C of this chapter).

d) When changes are made, they must be made by the *community* in the two ways described in Section (B) — i.e., through rabbinic decisions and communal custom. Only in that way can there be both tradition and change.

This position is widely held in the Conservative Movement, and you can see its advantages almost immediately. On the one hand, the assertion that people wrote the texts of the tradition enables advocates of this approach to accept the results of historical research into those texts fully and openly. Nobody needs to pretend that the Bible consists of one source written at one time and place or that the Jews escaped the influences of outside cultures, and nobody needs to be intellectually schizophrenic in applying totally different *methods* of inquiry to the Jewish tradition from those one uses in understanding any other culture. Moreover, you do not have to blame God for everything in the Bible or claim that every passage there is divine, for the human element in it can be the source of those segments which we now find objectionable and perhaps subject to change. On the other hand, the fact that the Jewish tradition was divinely inspired gives its laws and ideas divine authority. In other words, with this approach you have the best of both worlds, the intellectual and the religious.

That does not come without its own price, however. The first question that one has about this approach is simply this: What does "divine inspiration" mean? How does it operate, and how does it differ from the inspiration of Mozart, the wisdom of Socrates, or the skill of a good baseball player?

There are two distinct answers to those questions within the Conservative Movement, and it is this issue which distinguishes Conservative II from Conservative III below. Advocates of Conservative II claim that God inspired human beings with a specific *message*; those who hold Conservative III maintain that God inspired people with His *presence* by coming into contact with them, but God did not reveal concrete instructions through the inspiration. We will further define and illustrate Conservative III shortly, but now let us examine the ways in which proponents of Conservative II explain their position.

Perhaps the clearest exponent of Conservative II is Rabbi Ben Zion Bokser, z"l, who was rabbi of Forest Hills Jewish Center in New York and served as Chair of the Committee on Jewish Law and Standards. In his book *Judaism: Profile of a Faith* (1963), he warns against "two extremes in the interpretation of revelation or prophecy," in which one understands revelation as either a totally human or a totally divine act. It is both.

> There is no contradiction between the discovery of a historical dimension in the sacred texts of Scripture and the belief that they are disclosures of God's revelation. The human and the divine commingle in all of life. The farmer tills the soil, plants, weeds, harvests, but this does not contradict a dimension of divine providence at work in the same process of bringing food from the earth. For the farmer did not create the earth with its power to fructify the seed placed in its womb, did not create the economy of nature on which his labor depends, he did not stuff the sun with energy, nor fill the clouds with rain, nor did he fashion the seed with its miraculous power to reproduce itself. Throughout nature we witness what is a cardinal belief in Judaism, that man is God's partner in the work of creation.
>
> The partnership between God and man is similarly at work in bringing forth the truth on which our souls are nourished. Man receives a divine communication in the moment when the divine spirit rests on him, but man must give form to that communication; he must express it in words, in images, and in symbols which will make his message intelligible to other men. Out of this need to give form to the truth that is revealed to him the prophet places the stamp of his own individuality upon that truth. He draws upon his own experience, upon the idiom current in his time; he creates images that will be familiar to his people. Thus the truth becomes personalized; it takes upon itself the robes of the world in which it is to enter to perform its work of moral and spiritual transformation. In the process of expression and transmission truth takes on a historical dimension, which the historian can examine by the tools of historical

investigation, but all this in no way invalidates the role of the divine factor, the initial "breathing in" on the prophet of the message which he is called to proclaim to the people of his time.[30]

What is the nature of the divine part of prophecy? It is the push which enables one to be creative, courageous, or insightful beyond his or her normal powers:

> Why doesn't God reveal himself to people nowadays to communicate His will to them? *The answer is that He does.* People who have brought new visions of truth or beauty to the world and who have reflected on the process which underlies their creative acts have often spoken of the sense of receiving their ideas from a Power beyond themselves....

> Maimonides teaches us that every creative act in any field of human endeavor is an instance of the same process which was at work in *prophecy....*

> In its most familiar form prophecy appears in the experience of a "call" which impels certain people to perform heroic deeds in the service of some good cause or to become creative in the fields of theology, politics, science or literature. Maimonides describes this call in words that ring familiar to any one who has probed into any phase of the creative process: "A person feels as if some thing came upon him, and as if he received a new power that encourages him to speak. He treats of science and composes hymns, exhorts his fellowmen, discusses political and theological problems; all of this he does while awake and in the full possession of his senses....

> What normally requires laborious reasoning, and, indeed what laborious reasoning cannot establish, is grasped intuitively and with an overpowering sense of certainty.[31]

Whether you have such an experience or not depends in part upon your own abilities, preparation, and sensitivity. This is no different from creativity in other parts of human life: the unskilled, unlearned, or untalented rarely invents something new. On the other hand, prophecy is not totally within the power of human beings to produce: some Jewish philosophers (Maimonides, for example) say that you have to prepare for it. Others (Heschel, for example) claim that no preparation is possible or necessary.[32] Both groups agree, however, that there can be no prophecy unless God wants to contact you.

In exactly the same way, many people can train themselves assiduously for a given profession, but only some will be ingenious creators of new insights or techniques. Training alone cannot guarantee that. Similarly, in human relationships, you can do all in your power to

113

become friends with someone else, but you cannot create the friendship by yourself: the other person must be willing to respond. When we talk about relationships to God, that has to be the case all the more so.

Still, an ordinary person can have what Rabbi Bokser calls a "secondary revelation" by imagining oneself in the prophet's place while reading the prophet's words:

> The ordinary man may not sense the beauty of a sunset in a direct encounter. But when he reads a poem or looks at a picture glorifying the sunset, his perceptive powers may be ignited, and he too can begin to see and feel the haunting beauty which the sunset discloses. It is similar with the fruits of prophecy. The rest of mankind, not privileged to encounter the divine directly, may be introduced to it through confronting the words of the prophets. The divine haunts every utterance which issues from the prophetic experience. The prophet's words are "magnetized" with the divine power which initially sent them forth into the world. A secondary revelation occurs whenever we study the words of the Torah, and we too come under the spell of the divine.[33]

Moreover, the Jew is *obligated* to try to have such a secondary revelation in that the Jew is required to study the Torah and follow its precepts, thus putting him/herself in the place of the prophet in both thought and act.

Are there any differences between inspiration and revelation? Rabbi Bokser says no:

> We often use the term "inspiration" rather than "revelation." *Inspiration* means literally a *breathing in*. But who is it who breathes in upon the person and directs him to communicate to his fellow man? Every creative act where true inspiration is at work is a continuation of God's disclosure; it is a further unfolding of the light with which God began the order of creation.[34]

Rabbi Max J. Routtenberg, z"l, past president of the Rabbinical Assembly, has identified revelation with even more types of inspiration:

> For those who regard God, as I do, as the sum total of those forces in the universe which make for goodness, for truth, and for beauty, any and every manifestation of these qualities is a revelation of God. When man becomes aware, as he frequently does, sometimes even in a blinding flash, of what "the Lord doth require of him" and it becomes a consuming fire in his bones so that he must do something about it, he has received a communication from God. Man himself may verbalize this intuition and ascribe it to God, but it is a divine inspiration nevertheless. Every impulse to goodness, every quest for truth,

114

every search for beauty is a communication from God; every deed of goodness, every discovery of truth, every expression of beauty is a fulfillment of God's commandments.[35]

On the other hand, Rabbi Robert Gordis, z"l, a congregational rabbi, a professor at the Seminary, and past president of the Rabbinical Assembly, claims that there is a difference in the scope of the message:

> The superlative endowment that causes a Shakespeare to issue from some ordinary English farmers, and a Mozart from some moderately talented musicians, we call "inspiration." In restricting the term "revelation" to the sphere of religious and ethical truth, while using "inspiration" to describe other manifestations of genius, we are not [merely] yielding to convention. There is a qualitative difference between the two phenomena not to be ignored. God's creative power enters man's spirit in countless areas, such as science, art, music, literature, or the social order, each of which is a segment of our existence. All those whom He singles out for greatness in one area or another have been granted His authentic inspiration. But when God reveals a glimpse of His truth, not on one limited aspect of life, but rather on man's total relationship to the universe, when He grants insight into the character of man's nature and duty, the human being that God has chosen as His spokesman has experienced Revelation.[36]

Rabbi Abraham Heschel, z"l, whose approach we shall study in the next section, would add several other ways in which revelation is different from inspiration, with which advocates of Conservative II might agree. Specifically, for Rabbi Heschel a revelation of God differs from any other type of inspiration in that the receiver of a revelation experiences not only a specific message, but that it is God who is giving that message: "Seen from man's aspect, to receive a revelation is to witness how God is turning toward man."[37] Moreover, the prophet feels that he himself is being experienced by God.

> This, it seems, was the mark of authenticity: the fact that prophetic revelation was not merely an act of experience but an act of *being experienced*, of being exposed to, called upon, overwhelmed and taken over by Him who seeks out those whom He sends to mankind. It is not God who is an experience of man; it is man who is an experience of God.[38]

In other words, it is similar to what you experience when you come into contact with another human being; you perceive the other person and his or her message, and you also know that you are being seen and heard by him or her.

The crucial question, though, is the relationship between such acts of divine inspiration and the laws and ideas in the Torah. After all, the whole point of asserting divine inspiration in the first place was to impart God's authority to biblical law and ideology. Therefore, in addition to our questions about the nature of such inspiration, we must ask whether "divine inspiration" is sufficient to invest biblical law with God's authority.

It is that point which is, frankly, somewhat sticky for the advocates of Conservative II. Since the Bible is a combination of the human and divine, how do you distinguish the one from the other? Rabbi Emil Fackenheim, Professor of Philosophy at the Hebrew University, has stated this point well and has proposed an answer:

> The view I have sketched implies that not all 613 commandments are equally binding. Shot through with *human* appropriation and interpretation, both the Torah and the subsequent tradition which is oral Torah inescapably reflect the ages of their composition. But it also follows that it is both naive and un-Jewish to distill, as still binding, "eternal" commandments from a complex composed of both eternal and "time-bound" ones, the latter simply to be discarded. (This is done by old-fashioned liberalism, with its rigid distinction between the "principles" of prophetic ethics and mere external "ceremonial" laws, a distinction which derives its standards from external sources -- Plato, Kant, Jefferson, and the like -- and considers the standards by which it judges to be superior to what is judged by them; this is an inversion of the Jewish view in which God speaking through the Torah does the judging.) A modern Jew can escape his own time-bound appropriating no more than could his fathers; but his interpretation is Jewishly legitimate only if it confronts, and listens to, the revelation reflected in the Torah, which continues to be accessible only through the ancient reflection which is the Torah. Our modern appropriating is both possible and necessary because Sinai is not an ancient event only: the Torah is given whenever Israel receives it. But the act of present appropriation is mediated through the original Sinai. It is this listening appropriation which creates historical continuity.[39]

In other words, there are some parts of Jewish law which uplift people morally, enrich them aesthetically, and give them group identity. Those we would like to call divine and eternal. On the other hand, there are parts of Jewish law which seem to us to be morally degrading, aesthetically offensive, and/or socially useless. (Examples commonly given are the biblical laws sanctioning slavery, requiring the death penalty for violations of the Sabbath, and prohibiting a bastard and his descendants for ten generations from marrying a Jew.) To those, many people would like to deny divine status, claiming that they are the product of the limited vision of human beings at a particular time. A third category consists of those laws in the tradition which are morally, aesthetically, and socially neutral. Those laws most would be willing to continue observing if only to preserve as much of the tradition as possible.

Which laws fall into which category? *That* is the real problem. Rabbi Fackenheim claims that we cannot really tell because our own judgment is limited by the prejudices of the times. The best that we can do is to try to listen to the tradition as well as we can and then apply it to our own times. He claims that each individual Jew should do this. Most of the advocates of Conservative II would agree with Fackenheim that all we can do is to listen to the Tradition and try to apply it appropriately; but they would claim, as the tradition does, that it is the *rabbis* of each generation that should do this because only they have studied the tradition enough to be able to listen to it sensitively. In other words, it should be a decision made on behalf of the community by its religious leaders, as it has been historically, and not a matter for each individual to decide. (It is not an accident that Fackenheim is a Reform rabbi, for, as we shall see below, the Reform movement generally leaves it to individuals to discern God's will.)

Is asking rabbis to distinguish the human from the divine elements of our tradition an effective way to guarantee that the decisions that are made are an accurate expression of God's will? That depends upon your point of view. Advocates of Conservative II would argue that putting the decisions in the hands of the rabbis of each generation does not guarantee wisdom or divinity, but it is the best we can do. Life does not come with guarantees. Besides, the tradition requires that we proceed in this way (cf. Sources #6 and #7 in Section C above).

4) Conservative III

Advocates of this position assert the following:

> a) Revelation is the disclosure of God Himself. It is not the declaration of specific rules or ideas, but rather a meeting between God and human beings in which they get to know each other. This meeting is asserted for different reasons and described in different ways by the existentialist and objectivist thinkers of this group. (These terms will be explained below.) In other words, there are variant understandings of the *act* of revelation.
>
> b) Both schools agree, however, on the nature of the *texts* of revelation: the Torah is the record of how *human beings responded to God* when they came into contact with the Eternal.

c) Jewish law has *authority* for the Jew *both* because it represents the attempt of the Jewish People to spell out *God's will*, as revealed in the ongoing encounter with God, and also because Jews are members of a *covenanted community* and have obligations under that covenant to God and to the Jewish community of the past, present, and future. The divine and communal aspects of Jewish law make it a series of *mitzvot* (commandments), and not just *minhagim* (customs), in contradistinction to the position of Conservative IV below. For Conservative III, both God and the Jewish community command a Jew to act in accordance with Jewish law as it is interpreted in each generation, and the Jew gains a personal contact with both God and the Jewish community every time he or she abides by the *mitzvot*.

d) However, since the Torah was written by human beings, if we want to learn about the origins and meaning of the Bible, we must use the techniques of biblical scholarship as thoroughly and honestly as we can.

e) Moreover, because the Bible is the *human* recording of the encounter between human beings and God during times past, the specific ideas and laws contained therein reflect the practices, values, and attitudes of those times. They may no longer be an adequate expression of our own understanding of what God demands of us now. We in our day have not only the right, but the responsibility, to make appropriate changes in the Tradition that has come down to us so that it will reflect God's will as accurately as possible and accomplish it as effectively as possible in the contemporary world. Since God can be presumed to know and take account of the moral, social, economic, and psychological factors which influence the way in which the law will function in society, we, in interpreting God's will, must take those factors into account as well. In other words, the sanctity and authority of Halakhah attaches to the body of law, not to each law separately; human beings have the right and responsibility to evaluate the laws which have come down to us and change them if pressing moral, social, economic, or psychological factors require that.

f) While every person may have his or her own relationship with God, it is God's encounter *with the Jewish People* as a whole that is of primary importance. The communal character of revelation is, in fact, a distinguishing feature of Judaism. Consequently, changes in the laws of Judaism must be made by the rabbis on behalf of the community, as the tradition requires, and not by individuals on their own. But the entire body of Jewish law, as interpreted by the rabbis of our times, is binding on every Jew as a member of the community covenanted with God and with generations of Jews, past, present, and future.

This view is also widely held in the Conservative Movement. It is popular for the same reasons that Conservative II is – namely, because it combines objective study of the texts of the Tradition with divine authority for its laws and ideas. Advocates of Conservative III often explain that one of their primary motivations in adopting this approach is to preserve a sense of *mitzvah*, of being commanded by God, when observing Jewish law while yet retaining intellectual honesty. Since they do not believe that God gave a specific message for all time, they also tend to be more willing than those who hold Conservative I or II to make changes in Jewish law.

They would, however, encourage caution in making such changes for two reasons. First of all, for the advocates of Conservative III, as for the rest of the Conservative movement, Jewish law embodies what we understand God to want of us, and it is a chief factor in defining us as people. We therefore need to conserve the law more than we need to change it; in fact, the burden of proof rests with the one who wants to alter a law, not with the one who wants to maintain the practices which have come down to us. Second, since we do not know what parts of the system are responsible for its durability, we should not tamper with it too much. In other words, advocates of this position will be more interested in the *results* of the proposed changes than in the strength of the precedents justifying the changes. Therefore, on certain issues, they may be more conservative - that is, less willing to make changes - than those who take a more assured stand on the divinity of the origin of the law.

Advocates of Conservative III agree on all of the points stated above, including the tenet that the authority of Jewish law is in part divine and in part communal. However, Conservative III includes two different ways of describing the divine aspect of Jewish law and a corresponding difference in emphasis on divine and communal factors.

a) The Existentialists:

One group within Conservative III depends heavily on the *existentialist* tradition in philosophy, which emphasizes the *individual 's* experience. Thinkers in this group speak often of the personal encounters which individuals have with God. On the other hand, advocates of this position want to preserve Jewish law, which is communal in nature. Moreover, the most important Jewish contacts with God in revelation and history were interactions between God and the Jewish People as a whole. Therefore existentialist exponents of Conservative III often cite the work of Franz Rosenzweig, who emphasized the importance of having a relationship with God and also considered law to be an aid, rather than an obstacle, to that relationship.[40] Their traditional leanings, however, make them more communally oriented than Rosenzweig's thought is – although they often do not recognize that they differ from Rosenzweig in this way.

Let us consider a few examples of this position. Rabbi Louis Jacobs, rabbi of the New London Synagogue in London, England, has explained it well:

> Both doctrines – that of tradition and that of "progressive revelation" – see revelation in propositional terms. According to the traditional view, God revealed certain propositions all at once, whereas according to "progressive revelation" theory He revealed them gradually. In more recent times a very different (and to many minds far more satisfactory) view of revelation has gained ground. On this view, revelation does not mean that God conveys to man detailed propositions at all, but rather that He enables men to have an encounter with Him of a specially intense form. It is God Himself who is disclosed in revelation. Revelation is an event, not a series of propositions about God and His demands.
>
> The Bible is the record of how men were confronted with God....For all the human colouring of the story, for all that Genesis is a book like other books and so amenable to literary and historical analysis, it is in this book that God is revealed. If God is, then He is to be found in the Biblical record; nowhere else in human literature is He told of so clearly. What applies to the Genesis narrative applies to the rest of the Bible. It is all the record of a people's tremendous attempt – the believer declares a successful attempt – to meet God. The various propositions are, then, not themselves revelation but are the by-product of revelation....
>
> Revelation can thus be seen as the disclosure of God Himself. The rules and regulations, the Torah and precepts, provide the vocabulary by which the God who is disclosed is to be worshipped, in the broad sense of the term. They are a repertoire which has evolved in response to the impact of the original disclosure....
>
> The precepts of the Torah are binding because they provide the vocabulary of worship – always understanding worship in its widest sense. God did "command" them, but not by direct communication – as in the traditional view – but through the historical experiences of the people of Israel. The Rabbis had what we would today call the "fundamentalist" view. They believed in the doctrine of "verbal inspiration"....[But] the idea of a "command" through man – of God, as it were, giving the Torah not so much *to* Israel as *through* Israel – is not entirely foreign to Rabbinic Judaism so that a creative Jewish theology can build on it....
>
> The great difficulty, as we have noted, for upholders of the binding character of Jewish laws is the leap from the intensely personal meeting with God, of which the Bible is the record, to the full acceptance of the detailed laws. These

120

belong not to the actual revelation but to its fallible human recording. Why, then, should they be held to be binding?...

The final work, with its contradictions and errors, is the result of a teaching process, frequently unconscious, in which the record was drawn up of Israel's quest for God and of God allowing Himself to be found. Such an understanding preserves the dynamic quality of the process. Revelation is still to be seen as God's self-disclosure, but what we have called the "vocabulary of worship" is as much a significant factor in the process as the original disclosure.

It need hardly be said that the view we have adopted is certainly not the traditional one. But it does preserve the idea – of the utmost significance for the Jewish religion – that to lead the good life is to obey God's will. The idea of the *mitzvah*, the divine command, can and should be maintained even though intellectual honesty compels us to interpret revelation in non-propositional terms.[41]

Another important proponent of this view is Rabbi Ismar Schorsch, Chancellor of the Jewish Theological Seminary of America. For him, too, the authority of the commandments derives from two sources, the ongoing relationship – or "dialogue" – between God and the Jewish People and the continuing decisions of the Jews of every age to express their response to that dialogue in specific forms of action, the *mitzvot*:

For me, God is both transcendent and immanent, incomprehensible and knowable. Ignorance does not deprive me of a sense of relationship. God is a verb, not a noun, an ineffable presence that graces my life with a daily touch of eternity. I have no doubt that the Sabbath is a foretaste of the world-to-come. The holy is found through the medium of community and commandments.

I deem Torah to be the grand record of the initial and formative dialogue between God and Israel, a book that sparkles with the intensity of ongoing religious experience. Its legal core, set in an exquisite narrative framework, repudiated the values and beliefs of the ancient world even as it borrowed heavily from them. What ultimately made it sacred and binding was its public acceptance at the time of Ezra (and often thereafter). Not for nothing did the rabbis regard him as the equal of Moses.

As a Conservative Jew, I live the Judaism fashioned out of the Bible by the rabbis in Palestine and Babylonia from the 1st to the 6th centuries. While they turned the Torah into the foundation text of Judaism, as symbolized by its central role in the synagogue, they did not hesitate to modify, expand, and even abrogate it through interpretation. In the process, they achieved the paradox of a canon [that is, a set, authoritative body of writings] without closure, a dynamic exegetical [interpretive] culture marked by equal amounts of reverence and responsiveness. The dialogue between God and Israel animates the ferment of rabbinic literature....Theologically, I believe that Conservative Judaism is heir to the mantle of rabbinic Judaism....[42]

Probably the most famous modern proponent of this view is Rabbi Abraham Joshua Heschel, Professor of Jewish Ethics and Mysticism at the Jewish Theological Seminary of America from 1945 to his death in 1972.[43] On the one hand, Rabbi Heschel makes statements like this, in which he seems to hold that God uttered words during acts of revelation, which would place his thought in the rubric I have called Conservative I:

..."God spoke" is not a symbol. A symbol does not raise a world out of nothing. Nor does a symbol call a Bible into being. The speech of God is not less but more than literally real....

The extraordinary qualities of the divine word is in its mystery of omnipotence. Out of God went the mystery of His utterance, and a word, a sound, reached the ear of man. The spirit of His creative power brought a material world into being; the spirit of His revealing power brought the Bible into being....

The Bible is *holiness in words*....Some people may wonder: why was the light of God given in the form of language? How is it conceivable that the divine should be contained in such brittle vessels as consonants and vowels?....And yet, it is as if God took these Hebrew words and breathed into them of His power, and the words became a live wire charged with His spirit. To this very day they are hyphens between heaven and earth.

What other medium could have been employed to convey the divine? Pictures enameled on the moon? Statues hewn out of the Rockies? What is wrong with the human ancestry of scriptural vocabulary?...

If God is alive, then the Bible is His voice. No other work is as worthy of being considered a manifestation of His will. There is no other mirror in the world where His will and spiritual guidance is as unmistakably reflected. If the belief in the immanence of God in nature is plausible, then the belief in the immanence of God in the Bible is compelling.[44]

For him revelation did *not*, in contrast to Conservative II, consist in an inspiration like that which creative people often feel, for several reasons. First, inspirations are usually impersonal: people who have them describe them by saying, "It came over me." Biblical prophets, on the other hand, are keenly aware that they are being addressed by a divine Person, by God Himself. Consequently the prophets themselves describe their experiences of God with the words, "So said God!" Second, inspirations often do not involve a message: inspired people experience a force that carries them beyond their normal powers, but inspirations do not generally consist of words. They are more often inchoate feelings or energy, like being carried along by a wave. Prophecy, however, consists of words that are spoken and heard and a burning desire to transmit them to others. And finally, inspirations are often "one-time things"; even when people experience several inspirations, they do not usually think of them as being related, and the content of the several inspirations is generally dissimilar. By contrast, prophets often connect any given revelation with all previous ones that they have had – that is, they themselves see their various visions as being related experiences – and the content of several revelations is consistent. Consequently, revelation is *not* the same as inspiration:

> In contrast to the inspiration of the poet, which each time breaks forth suddenly, unexpectedly, from an unknown source, the inspiration of the prophet is distinguished, not only by an awareness of its source and of a will to impart the content of inspiration, but also by the coherence of the inspired messages as a whole (with their constant implication of earlier communications), by the awareness of being a link in the chain of the prophets who preceded him, and by the continuity which links the revelations he receives to one another. The words that come to him form a coherence of closely related revelations, all reflecting the illumination and the sense of mission shed by the call. There is both a thematic and a personal unity of experience....What is important in prophetic acts is that *something is said*....Prophecy is an experience of a relationship, the receipt of a message.[45]

All these passages make Rabbi Heschel sound as if he is taking the position I have called Conservative I, and that is indeed where I placed him in the first edition of this book.

Throughout his life, however, Rabbi Heschel always described himself as a phenomenologist, that is, of the school of philosophy which asserts that we human beings experience phenomena and can only respond to them inadequately through our concepts and words. Moreover, in other passages, Rabbi Heschel indicates that the Bible's citations of God's words should not be understood literally as God speaking physical, audible words, but rather such language in the Bible is only a human retelling of the experience of God in human terms, thus placing him sqarely in Conservative III:

As a report about revelation the Bible itself is a *midrash*. To convey what the prophets experienced, the Bible could use either terms of description or terms of indication. Any description of the act of revelation in empirical categories would have produced a caricature. That is why all the Bible does is to state *that* revelation happened; *how* it happened is something they could only convey in words that are evocative and suggestive.

The same word may be used in either way. The sound is the same, but the spirit is different. "And God said: Let there be light" is different in spirit from a statement such as "And Smith said: Let us turn on the light." The second statement conveys a definite meaning; the first statement evokes an inner response to an ineffable meaning. The statement "Man speaks" describes a physiological and psychological act; the statement "God speaks" conveys a mystery. It calls upon our sense of wonder and amazement to respond to a mystery that surpasses our power and comprehension.

There are spiritual facts which are wholly irreducible to verbal expression and completely beyond the range of either imagination or definition.

It was not essential that His will be transmitted as sound; it was essential that it be made known to us. The sound or sight is to the transcendent event what a metaphor is to an abstract principle....

[The prophet's words] are not portraits, but *clues*, serving us as guides, suggesting a line of thinking. This indeed is our situation in regard to a statement such as "God spoke." It refers to an idea that is not at home in the mind, and the only way to understand its meaning is by *responding* to it. We must adapt our minds to a meaning unheard of before. The word is but a clue; the real burden of understanding is upon the mind and soul of the reader.[46]

Thus Rabbi Heschel approvingly cites Rabbi Solomon ibn Adret (c. 1235 - c. 1310) of Barcelona, Spain and Rabbi Judah Loew of Prague (c. 1525-1609) to indicate that "The leading exponents of Jewish thought exhort us *not* to imagine that God speaks, or that a sound is produced by Him through organs of speech,"[47] for, says Rabbi Heschel,

...this is the axiom of Biblical thinking: God who created the world is unlike the world. To form an image of Him or His acts is to deny His existence. Not all reality is material; not all real acts are perceptible to our bodily senses. It is not only by his ear that man can hear. It is not only the physical sound that can reach the spirit of man.[48]

Thus he says that the human beings who were prophets (including Moses) recorded what *they* understood, and thus Rabbi Heschel makes his belief in the human authorship of the Torah very explicit:

> The prophets bear witness to an event. The event is divine, but the formulation is done by the individual prophet. According to this conception, the idea is revealed; the expression is coined by the prophet. The expression "the word of God" would not refer to the word as a sound or a combination of sounds. Indeed, it has often been maintained that what reached the ear of man was not identical with what has come out of the spirit of the eternal God. For Israel could not possibly have received the Torah as it came forth from the mouth of the Lord, for...the word of God in itself is like a burning flame, and the Torah that we received is merely a part of the coal to which the flame is attached....
>
> Out of the experience of the prophets came the words, words that try to interpret what they perceived....
>
> The Bible reflects its divine as well as its human authorship. Expressed in the language of a particular age, it addresses itself to all ages; disclosed in particular acts, its spirit is everlasting. The will of God is in time and in eternity. God borrowed the language of man and created a work such as no men had ever made.[49]

In line with his belief in the human authorship of the Bible, Rabbi Heschel is emphatic in stating that the Bible must be understood as a *literary* work, with many levels of meaning, and using literary analysis and interpretation:

> The surest way of misunderstanding revelation is to take it literally, to imagine that God spoke to the prophet on a long-distance telephone. Yet most of us succumb to such fancy, forgetting that the cardinal sin in thinking about ultimate issues is *literal-mindedness.*
>
> The error of literal-mindedness is in assuming that things and words have only one meaning. The truth is that things and words stand for different meanings in different situations....
>
> The meaning of words in scientific language must be clear, distinct, unambiguous, conveying the same concept to all people. In poetry, however, words that have only one meaning are considered flat. The right word is often one that evokes a plurality of meanings and one that must be understood on more than one level. What is a virtue in scientific language is a failure in poetic expression.

Is it correct to insist that Biblical words must be understood exclusively according to one literal meaning? It often seems as if the intention of the prophets was to be understood not in one way, on one level, but in many ways, on many levels, according to the situation in which we find ourselves. And if such was their intention, we must not restrict our understanding to one meaning.[50]

But even he is not completely convinced of the fruitfulness of modern biblical scholarship — especially in comparison to traditional Jewish interpretations of Scripture:

Israel's understanding of the word was not cheaply or idyllically won. It was acquired at the price of a millennia of wrestling, of endurance and bitter ordeals of a stubborn people, of unparalleled martyrdom and self-sacrifice of men, women and children, of loyalty, love and constant study. What modern scholar could vie with the intuition of such a people? The Torah is not only our mother, it is "our life and the length of our days; we will meditate (on her words) day and night" (Evening liturgy).

Without our continuous striving for understanding, the Bible is like paper money without security. Yet such understanding requires austere discipline and can only be achieved in attachment and dedication, in retaining and reliving the original understanding as expressed by the prophets and the ancient sages.[51]

Thus although Rabbi Heschel says some things which would put him squarely in Conservative I, on balance it appears that he belongs instead to Conservative III, where it is not God, but human beings, who provide the words to describe and respond to their mutual encounter.

Rabbi Neil Gillman, professor of Jewish philosophy at the Jewish Theological Seminary of America, takes a similar view but with a decidedly different twist. Instead of using the language of relationship common to existentialists like Martin Buber and Franz Rosenzweig, as Rabbis Jacobs and Schorsch do, or the language of mystery as Rabbi Heschel does, Rabbi Gillman employs ideas and language from anthropology, the academic study of human physical and cultural development. In that he resembles the objectivists who will be described below, for they too try to base their claims for belief in God and for the authority of Jewish law in phenomena that can be studied and evaluated by anyone, just as anthropologists do. Rabbi Gillman's view of truth, though, is decidedly an existentialist one in that truth claims about God cannot be verified or falsified by a group of people; they can only be true or false for the individual. His approach, then, is a good bridge between the existentialists and the objectivists of Conservative III.

When we say that something is a myth, we usually mean that it is a falsehood, as, for example, in the sentence, "The economic recovery much touted by the current administration is in reality a myth." Rabbi Gillman, though, uses the term as anthropologists do to mean a story which bespeaks our perceptions of the world and the values we find in it. In a myth, many of the characters are metaphors for all of us, so that, for example, the story of Adam and Eve is intended to be, at least in some ways, the story of all men and women, describing aspects of who we are and the world in which we find ourselves.

Such stories are not just entertainment; they are the ways in which a culture conveys its deepest beliefs and values to all of its members -- a much more effective mode of communication, in fact, than any philosophical argument would be. They "reveal" -- that is, they display -- aspects of the world which we encounter, tying them together in the specific way in which a particular culture sees them. The Torah is "revelation" in that sense, for Rabbi Gillman: it is the way in which our ancestors expressed the truths which they discovered about the world and their responses to those truths in feeling and action.

Note that such myths are not just the figments of our ancestors' imaginations; they are instead ways in which our ancestors communicated what is true and important about life. Jewish law, then, gets its authority from the fact that it articulates the values we discover in our encounter with reality and also from its roots in the Jewish community's particular way of responding to those values. In other words, for Rabbi Gillman, as for the other thinkers in Conservative III, the authority of the law comes from two related sources, namely, first that it contains the rules *of our Jewish community*, and second, those rules are based on *our perception of reality (the truth as we know it)*. It is, in other words, how we, as a Jewish community, have perceived and responded to the facts and values which we find in our experience. Note, though, that Rabbi Gillman thinks that we each individually perceive truth and join that community which best expresses our own individual vision, and so even though we must express our Jewish commitments in a community, they are rooted in our own, individual experiences of God -- so much so that for Rabbi Gillman there is no way to verify or falsify such claims about God objectively, but only existentially and individually:

> Whenever I am asked if I believe in God, I respond, "Tell me what you mean by God and I'll tell you if I believe in that God." On this issue, I insist that God transcends human understanding and language. That is what makes God God. To believe that human beings can comprehend God is idolatry, the cardinal Jewish sin.
>
> The alternative to idolatry or worshipful silence is the claim that all characterizations of God are metaphors crafted by human beings. Metaphors

combine to form myths. To the invariable question, "Do we then invent God?" I respond, "No, we discover God and create the metaphors/myths which reflect our varied human experiences of God." My faith is that these experiences are true, not in any objective sense of that term but subjectively, existentially. Our human experiences of God are objectively neither verifiable nor falsifiable. Finally, by myth, I mean not a fiction but rather a structure of meaning whereby human beings make sense of their life-experience. However "broken," that myth remains very much alive for me.

Much of the complex metaphorical system through which Jews have portrayed God remains vital for me. I affirm that God is unique, personal, transcendent; that God cares deeply about human life and history; that God has entered into a special relationship with the Jewish people; and that God creates, reveals, and will ultimately redeem. These metaphors flow from our ancestors' varied experiences of God in nature, history, and in their individual lives, and they have in turn continued to inform the experience of generations of Jews to this day.

Metaphors can reveal, but they can also blind. Therefore I also affirm our own right and responsibility to discard those metaphors which contradict our own experiences of God and replace them with others. Every myth enjoys a certain plasticity; the process whereby Jews reformulate the contents of their myth is what we call midrash.

The claim that Torah is "revealed" by God reflects our ancestors' understanding of how and why their distinctive way of viewing themselves and their world was accepted as authoritative. The biblical account of revelation is classic myth – historiography, not history – or, as Abraham Joshua Heschel put it, itself a midrash. Torah then represents the canonical statement of our myth and our guide for conducting our individual and collective lives in the light of that vision....

The ultimate authority for what entered into Torah *ab initio* [from the beginning], and therefore the ultimate authority for what in Torah remains binding for any future generation, is a Jewish community – not all Jews at one time, but those Jews in any generation for whom the myth remains alive. Inevitably, there will be many different, equally valid Jewish readings of that myth, and hence many different equally authentic Jewish communities. The decision as to what readings are authentically Jewish is arrived at consensually within a committed community of Jews who have a stake in the process and in its outcome.[52]

Several theologians in the Reform Movement have also developed theologies based upon existentialism, especially in the mode of Rosenzweig, and it is instructive to note how their understanding and use of existentialism and Rosenzweig differ from those of the advocates of Conservative III. The Reformers who use this approach speak about the individual's identification with the covenant between God and Israel, but they assert and stress that in the end it is the *individual* who decides how the covenant is to be interpreted and applied, not the community. So for example, Rabbi Jakob Petuchowski, z"l, who was Professor of Rabbinics and Jewish Theology at Hebrew Union College in Cincinnati, says

> "Legislation" is something that is "on the books." A "commandment," on the other hand, is addressed to me personally. Now, it may well be that much of the legislation found in the Torah originated as "commandments" experienced by ancient Israel. But it is also true that, in the course of time, it did become "legislation," and, as such, applicable only to the everyday life of a community governed by this legislation.
>
> The modern Jew, as we have defined him, lacks the awareness of living in such a community, and, therefore, also the prerequisite for re-translating the cold letters of legislation into the personally meaningful and significant sounds of commandments. This is not to say that the modern Jew rejects the idea of "community" as such. Even the non-religious Jew in America is often very community minded. But it just is no longer the kind of community which would accept a 16th-century, or even a 3rd-century, formulation of Jewish Law as its constitutional basis....
>
> By thus stating the diagnosis we have already hinted at the cure. In the first place, the modern Jew must regain the frame of mind in which he is able to experience the "commandment" addressed to him. It is a frame of mind which the Rabbis of old attempted to create, when they insisted that the Revelation at Sinai must be as topical to the Jew as if it had happened to him "*today.*" It is also a frame of mind to which the modern Jew *can* attain, as has been demonstrated by Franz Rosenzweig, both in his thoughts and in his way of life....
>
> Of course, all of this will be marked by a high degree of subjectivity. There is in it none of the certainty which Orthodoxy promises its adherents, none of the matter-of-factness of complying with the established legislation of a body politic. One individual's observance of the Sabbath, for example, is unlikely to be identical with that of another individual. The former might consider that to be forbidden "work" which for the latter is an indispensable ingredient of his Sabbath "delight." But this is the price which will have to be paid. For the majority of modern Jews, it will either be this or nothing at all.

It is a state of affairs well described by Franz Rosenzweig, when he said that what we have in common nowadays is the landscape, and no longer the common road on which Jews walked in unity from the close of the Talmud to the dawn of Emancipation. The best we can do today is to work at our individual roads in the common landscape. Perhaps the future will again know of a common road, or, more likely, of a common *system of roads*.

There is, however, a limit to too much subjectivity, just as there is the need to preserve the "common landscape." In the first place, it must not be forgotten that the modern Jewish individuals, with all their diversities, will, if they are interested in Torah at all, share a common ground and a common aspiration. What does it matter if there are variations in the minutiae of observance, as long as there is a willingness to "observe" at all?! It should be borne in mind that we are speaking of the modern Jew who is anxious to find his way back to the Torah, and not of him who is trying to run away from it.

The second consideration is that the very nature of Torah makes it impossible for the modern Jew to remain an isolated individual. Jewish living, in one form or another, is community living. The Jewish hermit is inconceivable. (The nearest approach we ever had to "hermits," the sectarians who shunned Jerusalem and went to live near the Dead Sea, lived there in highly organized *communities*. The now famous Dead Sea Scrolls arose within a *community* framework.) And, if the old form of the community has broken down at the beginning of the modern era, if its surviving remnants appear to be too artificial to command the modern Jew's devotion, a new form of the "holy community" is already in the making.

The Torah was given to the *People* of Israel. God's covenant is, as we have seen, with the "chosen *people*." Israel's task is to be "a kingdom of priests and a holy *people*." But if the historical identity of Israel, in space and in time, is to remain intact, because without the people there would be no covenant, it follows that, over and above the "commandments" which the modern Jewish individual accepts as his *personal* obligation, there will be others to which he submits as a member of the People of Israel.[53]

Rabbi Eugene Borowitz, Professor of Education and Jewish Religious Thought at Hebrew Union College in New York and Chair of the committee that drafted the latest (1976) statement on Reform ideology for the Reform Movement, is another Reform theologian who uses the notion of covenant extensively. However, like Petuchowski, he also emphasizes the ultimate authority of the individual in determining the content of the covenant in modern times:

The traditional Jew, looking at my observance, will find many of its features strange. He will be particularly perplexed that I interpret *brit* [covenant] in personal rather than in legal terms. But he should be able to recognize (and that is increasingly my experience) that what unites him and me is greater than what separates us. We stand as part of the same Jewish people united in the same basic relationship with the same God....We both believe that this Covenant relationship authorizes and requires communal and individual action. We differ only – though it is a great Jewish "only" – on what constitutes that required action, its substance, hierarchy, and religious weight.[54]

Jewish faith increasingly cannot be the passive continuation of a social heritage which is what it essentially was in previous Jewish generations. The more modern one is, the more one insists that it is a matter of responsible willing. One should choose to be Jewish and resist as non-determinative the claims of family, history, or personal sentiment. That choice, particularly since it is a fundamental commitment of one's life, must be made autonomously to be authentic.[55]

In his latest and most developed statement of his own theology, Rabbi Borowitz distinguishes between Jews and others in the type of relationship the individual has with God: "Like all humankind (the *benei noah*), Jewish selves (the *benei yisrael*) have a grounding personal relationship with God; but where the *benei noah* relate to God as part of a universal covenant, the *benei yisrael* have a particular, ethnic Covenant with God," and thus

In contrast to contemporary privatistic notions of selfhood, the Jewish self, responding to God in Covenant, acknowledges its essential historicity and sociality....With heritage and folk essential to Jewishness, with the Jewish service of God directed to historic continuity lasting until messianic days, the Covenanted self knows that Jewish existence must be structured. Yet as long as we honor each Jew's selfhood with a contextually delimited measure of autonomy, this need for communal forms cannot lead us back to law as a required, corporately determined regimen. Instead, we must think in terms of a *self-discipline* that, because of the sociality of the Jewish self, becomes communally focused and shaped. The result is a dialectical autonomy, a life of freedom-exercised-in-Covenant.[56]

That is, Jews are individuals and make their decisions on their own (they exercise "autonomy"); they do not defer to rabbis engaging in a halakhic process of interpretation, even if those rabbis happen to be liberal-minded.[57] Jews, though, are not just human beings like all others; Jews are born (or converted) into a special Jewish Covenant with God. In response to that Covenant, Jews shape their individual choices in Jewish ways. (Should this

131

last sentence read that in response to the Jewish Covenant individual Jews *should* or *must* shape their individual choices in Jewish ways? Rabbi Borowitz is not clear on this – or on why the imperatives involved in words like "should" or "must" would apply to the Jewish Covenant as he conceives it.) In any case, in the end it is the individual who decides how and when – let alone, if – she or he is going to respond to God in traditional Jewish ways.

One can see in this restatement of Rabbi Borowitz's understanding of Jewish individualism a reflection of recent developments in Reform Judaism, where increasing numbers of Reform Jews are taking on traditional practices because they recognize that "the sociality of the Jewish self" requires communal focus and shaping. At the same time, though, Rabbi Borowitz and those Reform Jews who are now more traditional in their life patterns reaffirm what has always been the chief characteristic of Reform Judaism, namely, the belief that ultimate authority for Jewish choices rests in the individual.

Contrast these statements by Rabbis Petuchowski and Borowitz with Rabbi Schorsch's insistence that what makes the Torah and its subsequent interpretations "sacred and binding was ...[their] public acceptance at the time of Ezra (and often thereafter)," and consider too the following two citations, the first by Rabbi Jacobs and the second by Rabbi Gillman:

> We believe in the God who speaks to us out of Israel's experience; Israel, the covenant people, dedicated to God's service and the fulfillment of His purpose. We believe in the God who, as Frankel said, reveals Himself not alone to the prophets but through Kelal Yisrael, the Community of Israel, as it works out and applies the teachings of the prophets.[58]

> The notion that to be a Jew is to be bound to a covenant that entails specific obligations is the cornerstone of the classic Jewish myth. In our day, the individual Jew is free to choose his or her community, and one of the criteria for so doing is a determination of which commandments are binding for that individual. The Jew makes that decision out of the personal experience of being commanded, but also within the context of Jewish communities of the past and a Jewish community today. Ultimately, though I believe in self-obligation, I cannot function as a religious Jew without a *minyan*, i.e., without a community.[59]

Rabbi Gillman here comes close to Rabbi Borowitz in asserting that a modern Jew's commitment to Jewish law is ultimately a "self-obligation," because in modern democracies everyone is free to choose whether, and how, to be religious. Nevertheless, for Rabbi Gillman, in contrast to Rabbi Borowitz, that individualism is very much restricted by the fact that "I cannot function as a religious Jew without a *minyan*, i.e., without a community," and

132

so the individual Jew's expression of his or her Judaism is shaped much more significantly by the tradition and the community for Rabbi Gillman than it is for Rabbis Borowitz or Petuchowski. That communal role in determining the content of Jewish law in our day is even more obvious in the formulations of Rabbis Jacobs and Schorsch. Thus the traditional Conservative emphasis on the community and the characteristic Reform concentration on the individual are clearly in evidence in the different ways in which Conservative and Reform thinkers interpret and apply an existential approach to Judaism.[60]

b) The Objectivists:

The other group of thinkers of Conservative III are more in the objectivist tradition of philosophy – that tradition which tries to analyze experience in a detached, objective way, appealing to reason ("rationalists") and the experiences ("empiricists") that we all share as much as possible. That is not to say that objectivist thinkers deny personal, emotional experiences or that existentialists neglect reason and shared experiences entirely: both schools must account for both our detached, objective experiences and our involved, personal ones if they are to reflect human experience adequately. But each emphasizes and uses one type of experience more than the other in creating its interpretation of experience ($=$its philosophy).

Applying this now to Jewish law, we find that while the objectivist thinkers of Conservative III may well have personal experiences with God, perhaps even intense ones, they hesitate to base the authority of the tradition on them because such encounters differ substantially in nature and import from person to person. Moreover, we really do not know what happened at Sinai, and it does not help to call it a mystery: we want firmer grounds than that if we are going to base our lives on the Jewish tradition. Consequently, advocates of this position base more of the authority of the tradition on its acceptance by the community of Israel than on the event at Sinai. On the other hand, they recognize the fact that only a religious stance adequately accounts for many aspects of our experience, and they also attribute a special character to Jewish law. In other words, their experience makes them want to assert both communal and divine authority for Jewish law without basing it on a revelatory event. Instead, they point to other features of our experience which indicate God's presence in, and the special nature of, Jewish law.

Some examples will make this clear. Rabbi David Lieber, President Emeritus of the University of Judaism in Los Angeles and current President of the Rabbinical Assembly, clearly employs an objectivist methodology in his understanding of God, and he emphasizes the cohesiveness and shared experiences of the community, another characteristic of an objectivist position. For Rabbi Lieber religion is necessary to have an adequate understanding of humanity, to

133

"provide a way out of the egocentric predicament" – that is, to give human beings an external view of themselves and of humanity as a whole and thereby to demonstrate why people cannot rely on themselves alone or have concern for themselves alone. As he says, "Without a transcendent point of reference, it is difficult for me to see how human beings can be persuaded to make the personal sacrifices required to keep the race from ecological disaster or avoid a struggle for decreasing resources."[61] Religion is also necessary to provide an object of aspiration, a set of worthy goals for which to strive. The law, then, is special because it attempts to express the transcendent in life (that is, that which goes beyond our human understanding or abilities) and because it is necessary if we are going to be able to continue as a covenanted community:

> I consider myself to be a "modernist" for whom reason and experience are the touchstones of knowledge, and not the authority of a text or tradition, hallowed though it may be by centuries of saints and scholars. At the same time, I cannot accept the methods either of the behavioral scientists or of the philosophical analysts as adequate to an understanding of the condition of man. Nor do I believe that they can provide a way out of the egocentric predicament in which man presently finds himself. Moreover, I am impressed by the moral and spiritual insights which have resulted from authentic religious experiences, as well as by their power to move men and mountains and reshape entire civilizations.

> Fundamentally, then, God, the source of all existence, is unknown and forever unknowable. At the same time, He does seem to reveal Himself in human experience in unexpected moments and in a variety of circumstances. In any case, He functions as the symbol of all human aspirations for self-transcendence as the ideal limit of man's notion of supreme value. He is "the `beyond' in our midst," and faith in Him is an awareness of the ideal possibilities of human life, and of man's ability to fashion his life in the light of them....

> For myself, I accept the notion of a religious law as being a corollary of, and flowing from, the notion of the covenant. A community must have rules and regulations to function; its individual members must be guided by norms, standards, and laws. Furthermore, since I do recognize the desirability of maintaining continuity with the past, as well as a measure of unity with Jews the world over, I am prepared to guide myself by those rules and regulations which have been accepted through the ages, provided they do not conflict with my ethical or aesthetic sensibilities. Beyond that, I am anxious to reexamine the whole corpus of Jewish law to point up, wherever possible, its relevance to contemporary social and personal issues – such as war and peace, the rights of minorities and of majorities – and to expand it so that it may speak to those questions for which the tradition offers no guidance to date.

I do this in full consciousness of the fact that I do not believe the law and its details to be of divine origin, but rather Israel's response to what it considered to be the divine call. On the whole, I think that this response was unexceptionable and that it has elevated and ennobled Jewish life throughout the ages. To the extent, however, that the development of the law became an end in itself, and the fundamental principles upon which it was based were forgotten, it did become necessary from time to time for courageous religious leaders and teachers to set themselves against the trend. They had to blaze new paths so that the fundamental respect of the people for the law would not be destroyed, and Judaism might remain relevant to the Jews' highest aspirations and meet the needs generated by new ages and new surroundings.

Ours, it seems to me, is just such an age.[62]

Rabbi Elliot Dorff, the author of your sourcebook and Rector and Professor of Philosophy at the University of Judaism in Los Angeles, subscribes to this position in a somewhat different way. For him, revelation can occur in any event from the most common to the most unusual: what marks an event as a revelation of God is not that the event itself is of a special character, but that it is interpreted as such by a human community. So, for example, the Holocaust may be just another ugly war for most of the world, but it may be a revelation by God of a 614th Commandment for the Jewish People as Emil Fackenheim would claim – a Commandment not to give Hitler a posthumous victory.[63] Whether it is a revelation of God or not depends upon whether the Jewish community accepts it as such. Similarly, the decision of a particular rabbi about a matter of Jewish law may be just his or her opinion (and perhaps one which should be quickly forgotten!), or it may be a revelation from God Himself: which it is depends upon how the Jewish community treats it. Moreover, the Jewish community determines not only what events shall count as revelations; it also decides how those revelations are to be interpreted and applied.

Jewish law, then, is of human authorship, a human, communal response to events which the Jewish community accepts as revelatory. The law is divine because of its internal wisdom (its soundness as a way of living, as demonstrated by experience), its moral goodness, and its durability (strength). Here, as usual, wisdom, power, and goodness are characteristics which we call divine.[64] The authority of Jewish law for the Jew is then a function of both its communal acceptance and its divinity.

Note that while Rabbi Gillman maintains that "My faith is that these experiences are true, not in any objective sense of that term but subjectively, existentially," for Rabbi Dorff religious claims are indeed objectively true – at least as objectively as any human claims to truth can be.

In practical science we can use "the scientific method" to prove or disprove something, but as soon as we go beyond the particular to the level of theory (including scientific theory), that method will not work. Instead, we judge between competing theories in terms of their *clarity*, their *adequacy* to the facts of the case, their *consistency*, their *coherence*, and their *moral import*. That method for determining which theory is "true" – or at least as true as we can tell – is used in virtually every area of inquiry. So, for example, we would use those criteria to decide the historical question of whether the American revolution was caused primarily by economic factors or by ideological ones, or the economic question of whether a nation's economy is best evaluated and stimulated through concern with the amount of money in circulation or the amount of goods, or the literary question of whether Shakespeare's *The Merchant of Venice* is an anti-Jewish polemic or a satire of the Anglican Church in disguised form, or the legal question of whether a given person is innocent or guilty, or the scientific question of whether light is best conceived as a series of waves or packets.

For Rabbi Dorff, we can and should evaluate religious claims in the same way we assess other theories about our experience. When one does that, one can and should maintain that varying religious descriptions of reality are *not* equally true, or true for varying people existentially in differing, individual ways. We can and should have respect for other religions, for people can be intelligent and moral and yet evaluate the evidence differently from the way in which Jews do. Indeed, we can often learn from the strengths and weaknesses of the approaches of other religions. Ultimately, though, being a Jew means that we believe that the Jewish description of reality and the Jewish response to our perceptions in thought, feeling, and action are true and morally appropriate, at least as much as we, the Jewish community, can discern:

> 1) Human moral, intellectual and aesthetic *faculties* distinguish human beings from the animals, in degree if not in kind. As such, these capabilities are a touch of the divine within humanity in the root sense of "divine" as power, for they enable human beings to know, feel, and do things that other animals cannot.

> 2) The structure of the world is an objective base which serves as a criterion for the evaluation of any philosophic theory or moral code; and since I hold that the world was divinely created at least in the sense that its creation involves powers beyond our control, I would be willing to say that God informed us about divinity and the world and gave us Jewish law in an *indirect* way, specifically, by creating the world in such a way that certain formulations of thought and practice fit the pattern of creation better than others. They are, in that sense, wiser than any alternative ways of thinking and acting.

3) I maintain, however, that the specific *content* of human theological ideas and codes of practice is created by human beings and hence is subject to error and change. I agree with William Temple's analysis that revelation occurs *in events which human beings interpret to be revelatory* of truths or norms of conduct, and therefore any event could be a source of revelation, although some may be more impressively so than others. I would also want to stress that, within Judaism, it is the Jewish community of the past and present which decides which events are revelatory and what the content of that revelation is, and that this communal check prevents revelation from being simply the figment of someone's imagination....

4) I would then observe Jewish law (that is, Jewish law would attain its authority for me) both because it is the way *my people* have understood *the demands of God* in the past and do so now and because of its own intrinsic wisdom as a program for satisfying human needs and maximizing human potential in the world as we know it. Similarly, Jewish philosophic views from the Bible to modern times have special relevance to me because they represent the way my people have understood God, human beings, and the world. Both Jewish law and Jewish thought thus require attention to God, the Jewish people, and the interaction between them....

Since I identify conscientiously as a Conservative Jew, the "community" whose ideas and practices define God's word for me in our time is the body of Conservative rabbis and lay people who actively live Conservative Judaism in what they think, say, and do. On legal issues this is defined by the decisions of the Conservative Movement's Committee on Jewish Law and Standards, and on philosophical issues the parameters were defined by the Commission on the Philosophy of the Conservative Movement in its document, *Emet Ve-Emunah: Statement of Principles of Conservative Judaism.* Deciding matters of Jewish law and thought within the context of a Jewish community narrower than all Jews may not be ideal, but it is the way Jewish law has been applied and practiced for most of its history, albeit with greater coherence, and it is inevitable in the pluralistic societies in which we live today.

5) When a particular law is not moral or wise, I must be prepared to change it in consort with the rest of the Conservative community, taking due regard of the weight of tradition in the process. The same is true for specific Jewish beliefs....Evaluating traditional laws and concepts must be done deliberately, and commitment to the tradition requires that the burden of proof rests with the one who wants to change it. Moreover, the need for communal concurrence should help to guard against precipitous changes. No mechanism can guarantee wisdom in such evaluations, however, and no simple rules can be applied to determine when to change an element in the tradition and when not

to....That is why we must entrust such decisions to a committee which is called upon to use their collective *judgment*. We clearly use our own individual experience and reason when responding to the tradition, but for Judaism to retain continuity and coherence, we must discuss our evaluations with the other members of our community and make decisions as a group. That does not guarantee wisdom, but since human beings are not omniscient, that method is the one which holds the most promise for us in knowing the true, the good, and the holy.

6) Even though for lack of knowledge I must suspend judgment as to what actually happened at Sinai, there are elements of the texts attributed to that event which induce me to attach a divine quality to them. These include their scope, their inherent wisdom, and especially the demonstrated viability of the tradition which they fostered over the centuries and throughout many regions of the world.

This clearly does not mean that Judaism's understanding of life is the only possible one. There are obviously other traditions which claim similar authority for their philosophies of life and which have undergone a long period of intersubjective testing, too. Judaism itself recognizes the existence of prophets and saints among non-Jews and does not require Jewish belief or practice of non-Jews, even in judging who has the merit of attaining a place in the world to come. In the end, all descriptions of the world and how we should live in it must be subjected to the same criteria of truth we use to test theories in history, economics, science, literature, and any other academic discipline – namely, their clarity, their adequacy to the facts, their consistency, their coherence, and their moral import. To assert the truth of Judaism, in other words, we must be prepared to subject it to the same standards of truth and goodness which we would use in evaluating any other civilization's view of the world and its pattern of action.

When I do that, the amazing adaptability and endurance of Jewish law and ideology over the ages and in many places indicate to me that Jews have apparently hit upon a pattern of life and thought that fits the structure of human beings and nature well, and so I ascribe truth to Judaism's claims. In fact, it appears to me that Judaism fits the structure of reality so well that I doubt that it could simply be the product of human minds. Consequently, although I cannot unequivocally affirm or deny belief in a verbal communication at Sinai, I do want to claim that the Jewish tradition embodies a degree of foresight, insight and sheer wisdom which is abnormal for human beings, even especially sensitive ones, and that in this sense at least it is a revelation of divine (super-human) truth and will.[65]

Note that these more objective, detached arguments on behalf of Jewish belief and Jewish law do not mean that the thinkers who propose them are blind to the personal aspects of religious commitment. On the contrary, Rabbi Dorff and other exponents of an objectivist approach have, in their writings, described how the personal and objective factors of their religious faith intertwine.[66] It is just that these "objectivist" exponents of Conservative III choose to emphasize publicly observable facts rather than private, personal experiences in arguing for Jewish belief and observance.

5. Conservative IV (=Reconstructionist tendency)[67]

The fourth position on the source and authority of Jewish law within the Conservative Movement is this:

a) Human beings wrote the texts of the Tradition. The authors were, in many cases, trying to capture the experience of the sacred in writing what they did, but God is not the author.

b) All talk of a Chosen People is both in error and dangerous: other peoples have their own special vocation to develop and express their own traditions, which are not necessarily worse than ours, and so to call ours "chosen by God" is erroneous; moreover, doing so risks that Jews will think of themselves as morally superior and that others will hate us for that attitude.

c) Nevertheless, Jewish law has authority for us, depending upon the specific law, either as a moral norm or as one of the "folkways" (*minhagim*, customs) of our People. In general, Jewish law should be observed in order to give our People continuity and coherence. If particular laws become offensive or fall into disuse, however, they should be changed or dropped.

d) If the Jewish community succeeds in organizing itself into a cohesive, active group as the Kehillah was in medieval Europe, then communal methods for deciding issues in Jewish law and communal sanctions for it would make sense. Until such time, the individual Jew will make these decisions. That is as it should be in the area of ritual practices, for in a democratic society with freedom of religion any attempt to coerce Jews to obey Jewish law would not work and would in fact be counterproductive. In the realm of moral norms, however, that inability to enforce the law is not desirable, and we must strive to create a Jewish community with real initiative and authority in such matters.

Rabbi Mordecai Kaplan, z"l, was the creator and clearly the major spokesman for this view, which he named "Reconstructionism." A few paragraphs from two of his writings will articulate this approach nicely:

> Instead of assuming the Torah "to be divine revelation," I assume it to be the expression of ancient Israel's attempt to base its life on a declaration of dependence upon God, and on a constitution which embodies the laws according to which God expected ancient Israel to live. The declaration is spelled out in the narrative part of the Torah, and the constitution is spelled out in the law code of the Torah.[68]

> Our position is that those *mitzvot* which, in tradition are described as applying "between man and God" should be observed, insofar as they help to maintain the historic continuity of the Jewish People and to express or symbolize spiritual values or ideals which can enhance the inner life of Jews. *Their observance, however, should be reckoned with, not in the spirit of juridical law, which is coercive, but in the spirit of a voluntary consensus based on a general recognition of their value.* We shall, therefore, refer to our approach to Jewish ritual observance as *the voluntarist approach.*

> In advocating that approach to Jewish ritual, we are not taking an antinomian attitude [that is, one which argues for having no laws at all], as Dr. [Robert] Gordis contends that we do. We insist that the concept of Jewish peoplehood which is basic to the whole Reconstructionist position involves the translation of ethical principles into concrete laws and institutions. We deplore and are endeavoring to correct the communal disorganization which has made the Jewish People impotent to enforce standards of ethical behavior in the relations of man to man....

> *To achieve the purposes of ritual, even from the voluntarist viewpoint, calls for a formulation of norms or standards.* These norms must be determined by the two-fold purpose of contributing simultaneously to Jewish survival and the enrichment of the Jewish spiritual life....These considerations, rather than *halakhic* precedent and legalistic interpretation, should, in our opinion determine the development of Jewish ritual for the Jew of today.[69]

Rabbi Ira Eisenstein, z"l, the first president of the Reconstructionist Rabbinical College after its founding in 1968, voiced a similar view:

> Despite what the Torah claims for itself — and what some people still claim for it — I believe that it is a human document, reflecting the attempt of its authors to account for the history of the Jewish people, and for the moral and ethical

insights which its geniuses acquired during the course of that history. It is "sacred literature" in the sense that Jews have always seen in it the source and the authority for that way of life and that view of history which gave meaning and direction to their lives.

I can understand why our ancestors believed the Torah (and its authoritative interpretations) to have been "divine revelation." For me, however, those concepts and values explicitly conveyed or implied in it which I can accept as valid represent *discovery*, partial and tentative glimpses into the true nature of human life. I find in the Torah adumbrations [outlines] of ideas which I believe to be of enduring worth, and true insights into the unique laws which govern the relations of people and peoples.

Some of these ideas and values – that man is created in the image of the divine, that life is sacred, that man is his brother's keeper, that society must be ruled by law, that justice and compassion are the highest virtues, that moral responsibility is the most authentic form of ethics, that man must serve as a "partner to God" in perfecting this world, etc. – have exerted a tremendous influence upon Western civilization. I do not, however, infer from this fact that the Jews are the chosen people. I see no justification for ascribing metaphysical status to what is merely historical fact. Nor do I believe that the Jews are entrusted with any kind of mission in the sense of a preordained function in this world. I do, however, believe that Jews, as a people, have an opportunity to make a contribution to society which is uniquely their own.[70]

Rabbi Arthur Green, who served as president of the Reconstructionist Rabbinical College after Rabbi Eisenstein, moved Reconstructionism to welcome more mysticism into its theology, contrary to the identification of God with nature (naturalism) in the thought of Kaplan and Eisenstein, but his view of the authority of the commandments remains similar to theirs:

In ways I do not claim to understand, Universal Mind is also Universal Heart; we reach inward toward it by emotional openness as well as by contemplative detachment. Awareness of this underlying and all-pervasive oneness of being leads me to feelings of awe and wonder, to a desire to be present to it always....It thus causes the impulse within us to need religious expression and to create forms through which we all attain deeper knowledge and awareness of the One. In that sense you may say that the essential forms of our religion are "revealed": they are our human creative response to the divine presence that makes itself known within us....

I believe that the most essential message of Judaism is that each of us is created in the image of God. We exist for the purpose of teaching that message...In their imperative form, these self-expressions of the One reveal themselves as ten commandments, the binding power of which I fully affirm.

As a tradition-embracing Jew, I hear the voice of my Beloved [God]... calling to me from within many of the commandments, customs, and teachings of the Jewish people. That same Beloved, of course, also calls to me from treetops, from within great music, and from "behind the lattice-work" of the Song of Songs...[71]

Note that in Rabbi Green's formulation of the Reconstructionist ideology, more than in either Rabbi Kaplan's or Rabbi Eisenstein's, the *mitzvot* are much more clearly responses to experiences of God (in that way he is close to the theologies of Conservative III thinkers), but also note that he never talks about those responses being mediated, much less regulated, by the Jewish community; they are instead personal responses of individual Jews (and in that way he is closer to Reform thinkers).

Rabbi David A. Teutsch, current president of the Reconstructionist Rabbinical College, stresses, in contrast to Rabbi Green, that God is to be found in nature and that halakhic decisions are to be made in community, and in these ways he returns to the ideology of Mordecai Kaplan, whom he mentions by name:

I very much feel the presence of the divine in nature, in community, and in the workings of my own heart. It is up to us to seek God, however, because God is not a divine person Who intrudes in our life or makes individual decisions, but rather the unifying dimension of our reality that is the ground of meaning and morality....

The Torah represents the record of the earliest efforts of the Jewish people to discover the divine in human history and shape our shared life in light of the divine. Thus the Torah reflects both its historical context and profound insights into moral and spiritual truth. The shared communal life that has developed out of Jewish interpretations of Torah embodies the moral and spiritual tasks that have long been central to the Jewish people's commitments.

I believe that Mordecai M. Kaplan, the founder of Reconstructionism, was right when he said that one of the unique characteristics of the Jewish people is our concern with what has ultimate importance in human life. The *mitzvah* system leads to an awareness of the transcendent value in human life and guides us to living in a moral and spiritual fashion that has redemptive power not only for us as individuals, but for us as a collective. Those actions recommended by Jewish tradition – both old and new – which achieve that end are truly *mitzvot*. Those parts which are only historically bound or out of keeping with the best values and practices of our time are no longer *mitzvot*.

Central to our struggle as Jews is the obligation to distinguish those parts of our inherited tradition that continue to have meaning from those that do not. This struggle can only take place authentically in the context of Jewish community, which provides the essential experiences that shape our inheritance of Judaism, our consciousness, and our intuition. It is the community that provides a sense of continuity and the fundamental context for the development of Jewish identity. It is also the community that as a collective can point toward the divine and make moral and spiritual demands upon its members.[72]

Finally, Rabbi Harold Schulweis, Rabbi of Congregation Valley Beth Shalom in Los Angeles, shares this view. In the following he attacks some of the weaknesses of the other positions that we have considered:

...The Torah is the selective record of Israel's extraordinary religious interpretation of its collective experience during the formative period of its career. The origin of Torah lies not in an extramundane source which has cast down absolute truths upon a receiving people, nor is it the arbitrary projection of human inventiveness flung upward. Torah is rooted in the matrix of a living organism, in a people which discovers out of its experience with failure and fortune the powers of godliness residing within it and its total environment. Torah as revelation is the product of Israel's creative transaction with history....

The sanctity of Torah-revelation lies not in the perfection of its authorship nor in its absolute finality. The Torah is holy not because it is the last word, but because it is the first self-conscious word of Judaism which reveals the direction of its moral thrust. The holiness of Torah does not require that its contents be held as infallible or immutable....

To argue, as is fashionable among so many contemporary theological statesmen, that Torah admits of some human elements and then to offer no way of determining where divine initiative ends and where human interpretation enters, is to avoid the heart of the question. To claim *that* revelation occurs without commitment to follow *what* revelation demands, or to proclaim the will of God without offering grounds for distinguishing true from false revelation, is to offer a vacuous form-revelation without content or criteria. In my interpretation, the divine element of Torah-revelation comes not vertically from a superperson whose will descends upon us, but horizontally from a people engaged in the process of complex interaction within history. Real events and ideal visions acting upon each other yield the *sancta* of Judaism, and these values named sacred are ever being validated in the experience of this people....

While one can understand the psychological value of such belief [in Israel as the chosen people] during years of isolation and humiliation, one cannot on such pragmatic grounds justify its morality or truth. Modern attempts to hold on to the concept of "chosen people," but to redefine its contents remain unconvincing. There are those who explain that God-chosenness does not establish political superiority but only results in a *noblesse oblige* directive to lead a life of holiness; but this fails to recognize that such a claim to higher spiritual obligation remains an aristocratic conceit which demeans all other peoples by lowering our moral expectation of their behavior.

The effort at compensatory parceling-out of divinely designated racial or national gifts – e.g., philosophy to the Greeks, administration to the Romans, religious genius to the Jews – both caricatures nations and peoples and presumptuously offers the greatest prize to Israel as God's witness on earth.

The modern suggestion that God's choosing of Israel really means Israel's choosing of God is as valid a translation as turning X's owing Y money into Y's owing X money. The propositions are clearly not symmetrical. Moreover, if to be chosen means to choose, then which group holding a concept of God is not equally chosen by God?...

Rejection of the doctrine of chosenness in no way denies the uniqueness or value of a people, its style of life in theory and practice. Uniqueness must not be confounded with the theological claim that one people is distinguished by God from all others as He distinguishes light from darkness, the sacred from the profane, the Sabbath from the weekday.[73]

6. Reform

In Chapter II we discussed the way in which the early (or "classical") Reform Movement interpreted Jewish history. You will remember that for the Reform thinkers of the nineteenth century and the first four or five decades of the twentieth, the essence of Judaism was construed as morality and belief in God, a combination demonstrated most clearly in the literature of the Prophets. The legal developments during the talmudic period and the Middle Ages were temporary measures designed for those periods only; they have no authority today, when Jews no longer need laws to enable them to survive under governments hostile to Jews. On the contrary, the governments of Western Europe and America are fair to all because of the Enlightenment ideas on which they are based. We should respond in kind, taking an active role in modern society and embracing the Enlightenment emphases on the individual and on reason. Many of the rituals of Judaism should be disbanded because they hinder the integration of Jews into modern society.

The theory of revelation which accompanied that interpretation of history is called "progressive revelation." According to that doctrine, God reveals His will to human beings through the use of human reason and moral striving. Each individual can be the recipient of revelation (in that sense) if he or she will only pay attention to the evidences of God in the natural and moral orders of the universe and deduce from that what God requires of him or her. (You can see strong Enlightenment influences here in the emphasis on the individual and on morality.) Moreover, as humanity has more and more experience on this earth, human knowledge of what is and ought to be grows, and so the scope and accuracy of revelation progresses as time goes on (hence the name "progressive revelation"). This, then, explains why Jewish law of previous eras is not binding, and why it is the individual who decides what to observe in Reform Judaism. Several planks of the Columbus Guiding Principles of 1937, which was the second official ideological statement of the Reform Movement (after the Pittsburgh Platform of 1885), will illustrate this theory and its implications:

1937 Columbus Guiding Principles:

Nature of Judaism. Judaism is the historical religious experience of the Jewish people. Though growing out of Jewish life, its message is universal, aiming at the union and perfection of mankind under the sovereignty of God. Reform Judaism recognizes the principle of progressive development in religion and consciously applies this principle to spiritual as well as to cultural and social life.

Judaism welcomes all truth, whether written in the pages of scripture or deciphered from the records of nature. The new discoveries of science, while replacing the older scientific views underlying our sacred literature, do not conflict with the essential spirit of religion as manifested in the consecration of man's will, heart and mind to the service of God and of humanity....

Torah. God reveals Himself not only in the majesty, beauty and orderliness of nature, but also in the vision and moral striving of the human spirit. Revelation is a continuous process, confined to no one group and to no one age. Yet the people of Israel, through its prophets and sages, achieved unique insight in the realm of religious truth. The Torah, both written and oral, enshrines Israel's ever-growing consciousness of God and of the moral law. It preserves the historical precedents, sanctions and norms of Jewish life, and seeks to mold it in the patterns of goodness and of holiness. Being products of historical processes, certain of its laws have lost their binding force with the passing of the conditions that called them forth. But as a depository of permanent spiritual ideals, the Torah remains the dynamic source of the life of Israel. Each age has the obligation to adapt the teachings of the Torah to its basic needs in consonance with the genius of Judaism....

145

The Religious Life. Jewish life is marked by consecration to these ideals of Judaism. It calls for faithful participation in the life of the Jewish community as it finds expression in home, synagogue and school and in all other agencies that enrich Jewish life and promote its welfare....

Judaism as a way of life requires, in addition to its moral and spiritual demands, the preservation of the Sabbath, festivals and Holy Days, the retention and development of such customs, symbols and ceremonies as possess inspirational value, the cultivation of distinctive forms of religious art and music and the use of Hebrew, together with the vernacular, in our worship and instruction.

These timeless aims and ideals of our faith we present anew to a confused and troubled world. We call upon our fellow Jews to rededicate themselves to them, and, in harmony with all men, hopefully and courageously to continue Israel's eternal quest for God and His kingdom.[74]

At the conference of Reform rabbis at which the Columbus Guiding Principles were adopted, Rabbi Samuel Schulman, one of the most respected and scholarly liberals of his time, proposed a substitute version because he recognized and objected to the great stress on individualism and reason:

> ...we must courageously confront the issue of absolute and unlimited individualism in our own body; but if there are such absolute individualists, then let us continue without a platform because platforms, while they seemingly unite, also divide if they are written with strength. Therefore, I wrote the paragraph on authority. Individualism had to be met; therefore I said that science is not self-sufficient, that it does not cover the whole of life, it is not the whole of truth.[75]

The Guiding Principles were adopted without his amendment, however, by a vote of 110 to 5.

Two things should be noted about this. First of all, the theory of progressive revelation should not be confused with the doctrine of "continuous revelation" which characterizes positions II and III in the Conservative Movement. "Continuous Revelation" means that God continues to manifest His will through the rabbinic interpretations of the Torah in each generation. That may involve changes in the law, but the new law is not necessarily better or worse than the previous law. Moreover, it is the rabbis acting on behalf of the community that define the content of God's revelation in our day.

In contrast, "Progressive Revelation" assumes continual progress in that we will get to know more and more of God's will for humanity as time goes on. Moreover, in this theory it is the individual who determines the content of revelation as it has progressed to our day by applying her or his reason to nature as well as to the texts of the Jewish and other traditions.

Thus the two theories differ in (a) the people who are considered the modern recipients of revelation and who are entrusted with deciding its content (the rabbis or individuals of each generation); (b) the methods those people are supposed to use in making their decision (reason, attempting to apply past Jewish law to modern circumstances, or reason applied to everything in human experience); and (c) the degree of desirability of maintaining practices and ideas in past records of revelation. In each of these ways, the theory of continuous revelation has greater respect for the past than the theory of progressive revelation has, and those who believe in continuous revelation will, as a result, exert a stronger effort to incorporate the wisdom and practices of the Jewish past into our thought and action in the present.

The second point that should be noted is that Reform Judaism has changed in the last forty years or so, with a decided shift to more traditional patterns of observance. A number of Reform Jews (male and female) now wear skullcaps (*kippot*) during services, much more Hebrew is used in Reform liturgy now than was previously the case, and some Reform Jews observe the dietary laws (*kashrut*). In general, the hostility to many rituals has dissolved, and in its place there is an openness and a willingness to experiment with various elements of traditional practice. Along with this has come a new respect for the classical Jewish sources: other sources of knowledge and morality are still to be used, of course, but the Torah, Talmud, Midrash, and Codes are taken more seriously now.

This development is still largely confined to the rabbis, however, and even they are by no means unanimous in this shift. Moreover, the classical Reform insistence that it is the individual who must decide what to observe is as strong as ever. This was clearly in evidence in 1985, when the Central Conference of American [Reform] Rabbis passed by a large majority a resolution disparaging intermarriage; in view of the Reform emphasis on autonomy, though, it was left to individual rabbis to decide whether to officiate at them or not. In contrast, Conservative rabbis may not even be present at an intermarriage, let alone officiate at one. In other areas as well there remains a significant difference between the Reform and Conservative Movements in the degree to which classical Jewish law is observed by both rabbis and laypeople.

Both the changes and the elements which have remained constant in the Reform approach are manifest in the theories of revelation and Jewish law of Rabbis Petuchowski and Borowitz, discussed in contrast to the existentialist version of Conservative III above. The constancies and changes within Reform Judaism over the last four or five decades are also apparent in the latest, official ideological document of the Reform Movement, "Reform Judaism: A Centenary Perspective," adopted in June, 1976. As you read a brief excerpt from it below, notice the extent to which the statement specifies the Jewish observances it encourages. Take particular note of the last sentence in this excerpt, which carefully balances, on the one hand, a duty of all Reform Jews to "confront the claims of the Jewish tradition" while at the same time upholding a parallel duty to exercise one's own autonomy intelligently, with commitment and knowledge. The document thus embodies a stronger appreciation of the tradition than appeared in the Pittsburgh (1885) or even in the Columbus (1937) platforms, even to the point of stating that it makes claims on us, but it explicitly preserves the autonomy which is at the heart of the Reform approach to Judaism:

Reform Judaism: A Centenary Perspective (1976):

Torah.   Torah results from the relationship between God and the Jewish people. The records of our earliest confrontations are uniquely important to us. Lawgivers and prophets, historians and poets gave us a heritage whose study is a religious imperative and whose practice is our chief means to holiness. Rabbis and teachers, philosophers and mystics, gifted Jews in every age amplified the Torah tradition. For millennia, the creation of Torah has not ceased and Jewish creativity in our time is adding to the chain of tradition.

Our Obligations: religious practice. Judaism emphasizes action rather than creed as the primary expression of a religious life, the means by which we strive to achieve universal justice and peace. Reform Judaism shares this emphasis on duty and obligation. Our founders stressed that the Jew's ethical responsibilities, personal and social, are enjoined by God. The past century has taught us that the claims made upon us may begin with our ethical obligations, but they extend to many other aspects of Jewish living, including: creating a Jewish home centered on family devotion; life-long study; private prayer and public worship; daily religious observance; keeping the Sabbath and the holy days; celebrating the major events of life; involvement with the synagogue and community; and other activities which promote the survival of the Jewish people and enhance its existence. Within each area of Jewish observance Reform Jews are called upon to confront the claims of Jewish tradition, however differently perceived, and to exercise their individual autonomy, choosing and creating on the basis of commitment and knowledge.[76]

QUESTIONS:

1) Which of the positions do you find most satisfying? least satisfying? In each case, why?

2) As far as you can tell, does any of the positions require specific beliefs about the nature of God? the People Israel? Zionism? Jewish art?

3) What unites the four Conservative positions? That is, what do they share? What distinguishes them as a group from the Orthodox and Reform positions?

4) In each of the following issues, try to determine whether the four Conservative positions would be able to come to a common decision or would have difficulty doing that. In each case, explain your answer.

   a) Using English in services.
   b) Allowing women to read the Torah during services.
   c) Prohibiting cremation.
   d) Having a Bat Mitzvah ceremony for girls.
   e) Permitting travel to the synagogue on Shabbat for those who cannot walk there.

ACTIVITY:

Working in groups of two or three, fill out the following worksheet summarizing the six views of revelation and law which we have studied in this chapter.

According to this view...	THE NATURE OF REVELATION	AUTHORITY OF THE BIBLE'S LAWS AND IDEAS	MANS ABILITY TO CHANGE THE BIBLE'S LAWS
ORTHODOX			
CONSERVATIVE I			
CONSERVATIVE II			
CONSERVATIVE III			
CONSERVATIVE IV			
REFORM			

E. Living Jewish Law as a Conservative Jew

In the previous sections of this chapter, we have discussed the historical development of Jewish law and the ways it changed throughout history (Sections B and C). We have also discussed the basis of authority for Jewish law and the ability to change it as seen by four different positions within Conservative Judaism (Section D). Those discussions were crucial for understanding how the Conservative Movement makes decisions in Jewish law, which we will describe in this section.

Because the Conservative Movement has tried from its beginning to preserve Judaism *as it has developed historically*, you need to know the history of how Jewish law has developed. As you will see, the method which the Conservative Movement uses to make its decisions combines the major methods used in the past, and its entire approach of "tradition and change" (or "tradition, including change") continues the view and methods of the rabbis of the last two thousand years. You also need to know the varying positions within the Conservative Movement regarding revelation, the authority of the law, and the ability to change law in order to be able to understand why Conservative rabbis and synagogues vary in their practices in specific areas of Jewish law.

How, then, are decisions in Jewish law made within the Conservative Movement? The first important thing to realize about this topic – and perhaps the most important – is this: since acting in accordance with the *mitzvot* has always been a key factor in what it means to be a Jew, *Conservative Judaism requires observance of the laws of classical Judaism*, including the dietary laws (*kashrut*), the Sabbaths and Festivals, daily worship, and the moral norms of the Torah, Prophets, and Sages. That is why we are called the "Conservative" Movement, or, in Hebrew, "Masorti" (traditional): we intend to conserve the tradition by studying it and practicing it.[76] Only through such observance can one identify authentically with what Judaism has stood for over the centuries. Consequently, the Movement invests as much talent and energy as possible into Jewish education of all sorts and on all levels, including schools, youth groups, camps, conventions, educational trips to Israel and other Jewish communities, adult education programs, and publications such as this. *The emphasis and major efforts of Conservative Judaism, then, is NOT how we can or should change Jewish law; it is rather on motivating and helping Jews to observe it.*

1. The Communal Nature of Jewish Law Within the Conservative Movement

The Conservative Movement realizes, however, that sometimes the law must change -- just as it has historically -- so it can effectively tie people to the Jewish tradition and influence their lives. Deciding when such additions or modifications are necessary, and how they should be made, requires considerable judgment and risk, and consequently the Conservative Movement has made the decision a *communal* matter for both rabbis and laymen. That happens within the Conservative Movement through the same three historical mechanisms by which Jewish law has traditionally developed -- namely, by decisions of the local rabbi, by decisions of a communal body, and by custom.

a) *The Local Rabbi:*

In the vast majority of cases, when a question is raised in Jewish law, it is answered by the local rabbi, the *mara d'atra*, the "teacher of the place." That person gains the right to make such decisions by virtue of his or her education as a rabbi and by his or her election as the rabbi of the congregation, marking the respect which the community has for this person interpreting Jewish law for them.[77] Historically, most such questions and answers were communicated orally, and that remains true to this day. Sometimes a rabbi may have to check some sources and think about an issue for a few days before answering, but usually the answer, like the question, remains in oral form.

In some cases, though, communities without a rabbi have historically written to one and have received a written answer. Sometimes rabbis faced with a question which they did not know how to answer consulted with other rabbis with known expertise in that area of Jewish law, and the second rabbi would then write back his answer (until very recently, it was invariably "his" answer since women rabbis are a very new phenomenon). That literature is the responsa literature about which we spoke in Section B, called in Hebrew "*she'elot u'teshuvot,*" questions and answers. That kind of consultation among rabbis goes on to this very day, but now it often happens over the telephone and even by FAX or e-mail. In the end, though, it is the local rabbi who still makes the decision in this process.

b) A Central, Communal Institution: The Committee on Jewish Law and Standards:

In Jewish history, though, there were some places and times when there was a central agency to make decisions of Jewish law for an entire region or community. That was true in one form or another during all of the following times and places:

1) During the time of the Sanhedrin, which lasted possibly from as early as the time of Ezra (450 B.C.E., although probably under a different name and with a different structure) or at least from the first century C.E until 361 C.E.;

2) During the time of the Geonim in Babylonia (650-1050 C.E.), for they functioned both as the court of first inquiry for some Jewish communities and the court of last review for others worldwide;

3) From the eleventh to the early seventeenth centuries, when rabbis in western and central Europe met at commercial fairs for business reasons and used the opportunity to meet in "synods" to make decisions in Jewish law for the Jewish communities of the Rhineland and France;[78]

4) Between approximately 1550 and 1764, when the Council of Four Lands determined Jewish law and other matters of public policy for much of Eastern European (especially, Polish) Jewry; and

5) Today in the Jewish communities of England, France, and Israel, there is an institution called the [Orthodox] Chief Rabbinate, and that officially determines Jewish law for those communities. Because all of those nations guarantee religious freedom, however, the Chief Rabbinate in each of those countries cannot function as the sole religious authority for the Jews there. Indeed, in all three cases, the Conservative and Reform movements are attempting to provide non-Orthodox options for the Jews there.

In line with these precedents, the Conservative Movement has a Committee on Jewish Law and Standards (sometimes called "the Law Committee") to determine Jewish law for the Conservative Movement. When a rabbi thinks that a given question should be addressed on a movement-wide basis, or when an arm of the Movement must make a decision of halakhic policy for its functions, the rabbi or an authorized representative of the branch of the Movement may send the question to the Chair of the committee. The Chair then assigns the question to one of the members of the committee, and he or she writes a formal rabbinic ruling on the question. In addition, any Conservative rabbi may write a *teshuvah* (an answer to an halakhic question)* for consideration by the committee.

.

The word "*teshuvah*" may be familiar to you from the High Holy Days, where it means "return" [to God, or to the right path], sometimes translated "repentance," from the Hebrew *lashuv*. Here it means "answer," from the Hebrew word *lehashiv*, meaning both "to return" an object to its owner and "to answer." The fact that the word "*teshuvah*" has all these meanings, however, should not be confusing because the contexts in which they are used in these varying ways are quite different, and so the context will alert you to the intended meaning.

The Committee on Jewish Law and Standards consists of twenty-five rabbis, fifteen of whom are chosen by the President of the Rabbinical Assembly directly, five of whom are recommended to the Rabbinical Assembly President by the Chancellor of the Jewish Theological Seminary of America, and five of whom are recommended to the President of the Rabbinical Assembly by the President of the United Synagogue of Conservative Judaism (but all rabbis on the committee must be members of the Rabbinical Assembly). In addition, there are five lay members (that is, non-rabbis) appointed by the President of the United Synagogue of Conservative Judaism who participate actively in the discussion and may even write a *teshuvah* for consideration by the Committee, but who do not vote. The members are each chosen for five-year terms (which are sometimes renewed), and an effort is made to insure that the Committee represents a variety of different ages, geographical locations, ideological positions within the movement, and areas of expertise in Jewish law so that it can represent the movement fairly. In recent years, as women have been ordained as rabbis, several women rabbis and laypeople have been appointed to the committee.

Each *teshuvah* is subjected to considerable discussion, usually first by a subcommittee charged with the general area of Jewish law in which a particular question falls and then by the full committee. *Teshuvot* (the plural of *teshuvah*) are often revised as a result of those discussions before a vote is taken.

If a given *teshuvah* gets six votes or more, it becomes a *valid option* within the Conservative Movement. That means, of course, that there may be more than one validated option within the movement on a given issue, and there are indeed some matters for which two or more options have been approved. The structure of the Committee on Jewish Law and Standards deliberately allows for that pluralism so that the spectrum of religious practice within the Conservative community can be expressed together with the legal reasoning which justifies the various validated positions. When two or more *teshuvot* are approved on any given issue, then the decision returns to the local rabbi, who chooses the one which best fits his or her own understanding of Jewish law and the needs of his or her community. In most cases, though, there is only one validated option, and that reflects the other side of the coin – namely, that there is much in common in the practice of Conservative Jews.

In a few cases, a matter is considered so important that a *teshuvah* is introduced as a possible standard of the movement. Until now these have been situations in which Reform practice has varied from the tradition and the Conservative movement has wanted to reaffirm our commitment to the traditional practice in a very definitive and public way. If a *teshuvah*, then, is introduced as a possible standard of the movement and is approved by four-fifths of the Committee on Jewish Law and Standards present at a regular meeting, four-fifths of the entire committee polled by mail (since a quorum for a meeting is one more than half), and by a majority of those voting on the matter at the next Rabbinical Assembly convention, then it becomes a standard of the movement. A rabbi or a synagogue which violates a standard is subject to dismissal from the movement.

So far there are three such standards:

OFFICIAL STANDARDS OF THE CONSERVATIVE MOVEMENT

1. A Conservative rabbi or cantor may not attend, let alone officiate at, the marriage of a Jew to a non-Jew, even if the ceremony is a purely civil ceremony, and Conservative synagogues may not be used for such weddings. (Responsum of Rabbi Aaron Blumenthal, adopted as a Standard in 1972).

2. Jews who have been divorced in state law must give (in the case of a man) or receive (in the case of a woman) a Jewish writ of divorce (a *get*) before being allowed to remarry (unless the original marriage is annulled by a rabbinic court). (Resolution, Rabbinical Assembly Convention, 1975)

3. Jewish identity is defined by being born to a Jewish woman or being halakhically converted to Judaism. (Responsum of Rabbis Joel Roth and Akiba Lubow, adopted as a Standard by the Committee on Jewish Law and Standards, May, 1985; Resolution, Rabbinical Assembly Convention, 1986).[79]

There are obviously many, many Jewish laws which the Conservative movement assumes and shares but which have not been made standards. No Conservative synagogue, for example, will intentionally have a non-kosher kitchen, and no Conservative synagogue will sponsor activities which involve writing or the exchange of money on Shabbat. Conversely, Conservative prayer services will be primarily in Hebrew no matter where you go. Every Conservative synagogue will make provision for the ongoing Jewish education of Jews of all ages, and every Conservative institution will see the moral imperatives of our tradition as binding in its own activities and will strive in some way to improve the world (*tikkun olam*). This broad group of shared commitments of Conservative Jews — and there are many more than the ones just listed — need not be put into standards because they have not been seriously challenged as standards by which we should live as a movement. Individual Jews, of course, may live up to these standards in their lives to a greater or lesser degree, but they join the Conservative movement knowing that the movement stands for this broadly shared set of practices, and, in many cases, they join, in part, because they want to be affiliated with institutions who understand and practice Judaism as the Conservative movement does.

c) *Following a Sample Teshuvah Through the Law Committee:*

To enable you better to understand the process by which questions are considered by the Committee on Jewish Law and Standards, it will be helpful to trace a sample *teshuvah* through the processes of the Committee. I will use as our example an actual question which the Committee is, as of this writing, still in the process of considering.

Jews suffer from problems of infertility far more than the general population does. That is, in large measure, because Jews postpone thinking seriously about marriage until after college and graduate school, and so they only begin to try to have children in their thirties. With all of our advancements in medicine, though, the ideal age for both men and women to procreate is still 22. People can clearly have children before and after then, but as one gets older, and especially after age thirty-five, the chances grow significantly slimmer with each passing year. Because of these Jewish educational patterns and the enduring medical facts about human physiology, many Jewish couples find that they cannot have children when they are ready to try, and that, in turn, has led to many questions about whether Jewish couples may use some modern medical advances to help them. The Committee on Jewish Law and Standards has therefore, in recent years, dealt with a series of questions revolving around infertility, including the permissibility of using in vitro fertilization, artificial insemination using the husband's sperm, artificial insemination using a donor's sperm, egg donation, and adoption as ways of having children.[81]

One other form of assisting couples is surrogate motherhood. When the wife can produce an egg and the husband can produce viable sperm, but the wife cannot, for some reason, carry the fetus to term, the couple may engage the services of another woman to carry their baby through pregnancy. The couple's own genetic materials are then inserted into the woman's uterus through in vitro fertilization. This is "gestational surrogacy," in that the surrogate mother is used solely for gestation (that is, carrying the fetus during the months of its development in the womb, the period of "gestation"); the baby's genes come completely from the couple. When the wife cannot produce an egg, then the husband's sperm is artificially inserted into the surrogate mother's womb, hopefully to unite with one of the surrogate mother's own eggs. This is called "ovum surrogacy" since the surrogate mother provides not only a womb for gestation but also an egg, or "ovum." May Jews use either or both of these techniques to overcome infertility?

The question was sent to the Committee on Jewish Law and Standards by a rabbi who had been asked by a couple about this. The Chair, currently Rabbi Kassel Abelson, added the question to the list of questions circulated to all members of the Committee before each meeting, asking members to sign up to write a *teshuvah* on those issues on the list in which they have some special expertise or which especially interest them for some other reason. Rabbi Elie Spitz volunteered to write on this topic, in part because he had had experience with a number of couples who had used surrogacy and he had therefore already done some thinking and research on it.

If nobody volunteers to write on a given topic, Rabbi Abelson will directly ask a member to take on the assignment or choose to write on the topic himself. Sometimes, if it is clear that the Committee needs to respond to a given issue because it occurs frequently in contemporary Jewish life or has arisen quite publicly on society's agenda, Rabbi Abelson will ask a member to write about it even though it has not officially been posed as a question to the Law Committed by a rabbi or an arm of the Movement. During the summer of 1996, for example, Rabbi Abelson asked Rabbi Elliot Dorff to write about assisted suicide after the United States Supreme Court agreed to take two cases from the Ninth and Second Circuit Courts, both of which had ruled that the right to ask for assistance in suicide and the right to provide it were both guaranteed by the Constitution. Rabbi Dorff had already written about that topic in another context, and so he had already done most of the research needed and was therefore willing and able to write a *teshuvah* on the subject expeditiously.

When Rabbi Spitz completed the first draft of his responsum on using surrogate mothers to overcome infertility, he sent that draft to the Chair of the Law Committee's Subcommittee on Bioethics, the subcommittee appropriate for a question such as this. The Chair distributed it by mail to the members of the subcommittee, who discussed it at their next meeting. The points made during that discussion caused Rabbi Spitz to rethink some aspects of his responsum, and so he made several changes in it. That is the purpose of bringing a *teshuvah* to the appropriate subcommittee first: it enables an author to hear reactions to a first draft so that the *teshuvah* can be refined before it is presented to the entire Committee on Jewish Law and Standards. Unlike the Senate and House of Representatives of the United States Congress, where a subcommittee must approve bills by majority vote for them to be brought to the entire Senate or House for a vote, the procedures of the Law Committee do not require subcommittee approval; the subcommittee's review of a draft of a responsum is only to provide advice to author.

Rabbi Spitz's revised responsum was then thoroughly discussed by the Law Committee. After that discussion, it was clear that there were two distinct issues: one was the legitimacy of using a surrogate mother to overcome infertility, and the other was the Jewish identity of the child if the bearing mother was not Jewish. There was some opposition to surrogacy itself,

157

but there was even more to considering the child to be Jewish if the surrogate mother was not Jewish, even in gestational surrogacy, where the egg comes from the Jewish wife in the couple. Rabbi Spitz therefore decided to divide his *teshuvah* into two separate questions, one on the permissibility of surrogacy itself and the other on the Jewish identity question. He also saw that he needed to address the additional points raised against surrogacy itself. No vote was taken on his *teshuvah* after that first discussion (which, in this case, lasted for more than two hours!) so that Rabbi Spitz could make these revisions. As of this writing, Rabbi Spitz has submitted his third draft for the Committee's consideration, and, in the meantime, Rabbi Mackler has submitted a paper articulating objections to Rabbi Spitz's reasoning and conclusions. Both of these papers will be discussed at an upcoming meeting.

If Rabbi Spitz's responsum permitting surrogacy gains six or more votes, then rabbis may use its reasoning, cautions, and conclusions in advising couples about using this technique to overcome infertility. If the second part of Rabbi Spitz's paper — which makes the child Jewish if the genetic materials are from Jews, even if the bearing mother is not Jewish — fails to get six votes, then those who use a non-Jewish surrogate mother will need to have their child go through the rites of conversion to make the child Jewish. If Rabbi Mackler's paper objecting to surrogacy also gets six votes or more, then the issue will revert to each rabbi as *mara d'atra* (teacher of the community) to decide which of the two positions better matches his or her own understanding of Jewish law and the sensitivities of the community he or she serves.

If either or both of the *teshuvot* on this issue are validated, those decisions will be reported to rabbis in the monthly newsletter sent to all Conservative rabbis. In addition, in 1994 all Conservative rabbis were sent a comprehensive listing and summary of all responsa validated by the Law Committee, and each year the Secretary of the Committee sends additional pages with the responsa approved during the past year so that rabbis can add them to each section of the looseleaf notebook which contains these summaries. If some specific issue is of special interest, rabbis may ask the office of the Rabbinical Assembly to send them the full text of any responsum on that issue approved by the Committee. All validated responsa are also reported to the laypeople of the movement in the summary of Law Committee decisions which the Chair writes for *The United Synagogue Review*, the quarterly magazine which goes to every home affiliated with a Conservative synagogue. A few *teshuvot* — generally those on especially significant topics — are sent in their entirety by mail to the entire membership of the Rabbinical Assembly or are published in the journal, *Conservative Judaism*. Ultimately, all approved *teshuvot* are published in volumes of the responsa of the Committee on Jewish Law and Standards over a period of years. As of this writing, the volume that includes the responsa validated in the years between 1980-1985 is available, and the one for the years 1985-1990 is soon to be published. Now that authors of *teshuvot* are being asked to write their responsa using a specific format and to submit them on computer diskette, publication of these volumes will hopefully become more timely.

Although this example has been used to illustrate the procedures of the Committee on Jewish Law and Standards, it is important to remind Jews that infertility, the problem which led to writing this responsum in the first place, is a major problem for Jews. The best way to increase your chances of avoiding that problem is to marry and to begin to have children earlier than Jews commonly do in our day. Jewish teenagers need to think seriously of choosing a college attended by a substantial number of Jews so that they can have a community not only for Jewish educational, cultural, and religious activities, but, frankly, for social and romantic reasons as well. Jews also need to think about looking for mates in their college years. Finding a husband or wife is, of course, not a matter of your choice alone, and you should definitely not think less of yourself or of your college or graduate career if you have not found a spouse during those years. At the same time, you should put yourself in a community for college and graduate school where the chances of meeting someone you will wish to marry are high, and you should not think of your graduate school years as too soon to marry and to begin to have children. The pressures of graduate school are no more than those of the first years in your chosen profession, when you are trying hard to make a good impression on your superiors. In the end, with all of our new technology, only 50% of infertile couples can be helped to have children, and then only with considerable financial and psychological costs, and so here, as elsewhere, an ounce of prevention is definitely worth a pound of cure. In light of the demographic problems of the Jewish community, these considerations are critical for the welfare of both the couple themselves and the Jewish people.

d) Central, Communal Institutions: Other Sources of Standards Within the Movement:

In addition to the Committee on Jewish Law and Standards, there are other bodies within the Conservative Movement which have created standards for various aspects of the movement. The deliberations of these bodies do not have the force of Jewish law; that is restricted to the decisions of the Law Committee and of each communal rabbi acting as *mara d'atra*. The standards which come out of these other bodies within the movement are therefore not "standards" in the technical sense described above with regard to standards approved by four-fifths of the Law Committee and a majority of those voting at the Rabbinical Assembly convention. Violation of these standards therefore does not lead to expulsion from the movement.

They are serious standards for behavior nevertheless. The standards by which any given community lives often appear in forms other than law, and they are often not enforced by courts of law and police agencies, if at all. So, for example, subgroups within a society, like a football team, may have special rules which govern the members of the team and which they must obey or face discipline by, or expulsion from, the subgroup. Another form of standards consists of the mores by which people in a given community are expected to live. These are enforced more by social pressure than by formal, established disciplinary measures.

Standards of both types within the Conservative Movement include, but are not limited to, the following:

I. The Solomon Schechter Day School Association has established religious and academic standards for schools which want to affiliate with the Association. Similarly, each of the schools of higher learning within the Movement has established religious and academic standards for students and faculty in their programs.

ii. The United Synagogue of Conservative Judaism has established a minimum of six hours of instruction per week for supplementary schools within the movement. That kind of standard is, by its nature, different from the curricula which the same body has developed for supplementary schools, where each school is encouraged to choose its area of emphasis (e.g., Bible, prayer, Jewish holidays and life cycle rituals, Jewish ethics) and to follow a model curriculum for schools choosing a given emphasis.

iii. The Federation of Jewish Men's Clubs and the Women's League for Conservative Judaism have criteria for membership which must be satisfied for individuals or groups to become part of those organizations.

iv. A very different kind of standard was established by the new *Rabbinic Letter on Intimate Relations*, written by Rabbi Elliot N. Dorff for and with the Rabbinical Assembly's Commission on Human Sexuality. The purpose of that educational document was to inform Conservative Jews of the moral, as well as the *halakhic*, standards by which they should conduct their relationships, including their most intimate ones. The Letter does not speak of enforcing those standards through some sort of formal mechanism; rather, the standards described there stand as a statement of expectations for members of our movement and goals for which they should strive. Even though such standards cannot be enforced -- and maybe especially because they are not to be enforced -- they appeal to the best in Conservative Jews, describing *not* what they *must* do to remain members of the movement or of a group within it, but what they *should* do to achieve the moral standard that we expect of ourselves as a community, a community with a God-given mission to be not only morally decent, but holy.

e) The Power of Custom in Jewish Law:

The decision of the shape of Jewish law, including when change of traditional law is necessary and when, conversely, traditional law needs to be reenforced, is a communal matter at the congregational level as well. Jewish law has always been the product of an interaction between the rabbis and the general Jewish community. That is the reason for the power of *minhag* (custom) in Jewish law. In the Conservative Movement, congregations are increasingly getting involved in the discussion of important issues in Jewish law, and that is precisely as it should be, for no law has authority unless it becomes part of the concern and practice of the community.

Jewish law often motivates Jews to create new customs in order to embellish Jewish life, as, for example, the practice of singing and swaying together before and after reciting the blessings of Havdalah, or the practice of saying a group of psalms before the Friday evening service as a way of welcoming the Sabbath (*Kabbalat Shabbat*), a custom initiated by the Jewish community in Safed in the sixteenth century.

Sometimes, though, the interaction goes in the opposite direction, where custom is the primary root of our practice and even of later rabbinic rulings based upon that custom. So, for example, a practice which Conservative Jews take for granted is that men and women sit together for services, but that originated simply as the custom of North American synagogues, without an official ruling confirming and justifying it. It was only decades after Conservative congregations sat that way for services that the Committee on Jewish Law and Standards confirmed that "there is no specific prohibition in Jewish law of mixed seating (rather it is a custom), and therefore this question is to be decided by each congregation as guided by its rabbi."[82] Many of the new ways in which women now participate in services began as the practices of some Conservative congregations and only after some time were analyzed and justified legally by the Committee on Jewish Law and Standards. So, for example, the Bat Mitzvah ceremony (and what is done at such a ceremony), calling women to the Torah, and having women serve as leaders of services have all begun as the practices of some Conservative congregations and then, when the practices spread, they were examined legally by the Committee on Jewish Law and Standards.[83] Custom, then, is an important way in which decisions in Jewish law are made communally within the Conservative movement.

This structure is a combination of the two traditional ways in which Jewish legal decisions were made – namely, by majority vote of a central body, when a given Jewish community was sufficiently organized to have a body, and/or by the decision of the local rabbi (the "*mara d'atra*," or "teacher of the community"). This structure also explains why you probably have observed considerable differences in the practices of Conservative synagogues and rabbis. It is important to realize that these differences do *not* represent a lack of decisiveness or commitment on the part of the Movement; they rather reflect the fact that the Conservative Movement wants to deal with life as it actually is, and that requires that it be open to differences among people and communities. This plurality may make some of us uncomfortable at times, but life does not lend itself to a neat, unchanging structure, and so people must learn to accept changes in law without at the same time discarding it completely. This is the approach of Jewish law historically, and it is the approach of the Conservative Movement.[84]

2. The Grounds Which the Conservative Movement Recognizes for Changes in Jewish Law

Whether a given issue arose from increasingly widespread customary practice within Conservative congregations or from rabbinic initiatives, sometimes the Conservative Movement has instituted changes in Jewish law. Such changes can be additions to the received law, deletions from it, or modifications in its form. The reasons for those changes have varied from case to case, as you would expect.

Sometimes changes in technology created new living conditions to which the law had to be applied. For example, the widespread availability of the car has meant that Jews do not necessarily live within walking distance of the synagogue any longer, and that raises questions about how to foster Shabbat observance among Conservative Jews. The majority opinion on that issue, as decided by the Committee on Jewish Law and Standards in 1950, is reproduced at the end of this chapter together with a dissent so that you can see the varying ways in which Conservative rabbis have wrestled with making Shabbat a real experience for Jews when they do not live in densely populated areas, making travel to the synagogue necessary if the community is going to get together for Shabbat activities at all. This *teshuvah* has been the subject of ongoing debate within the Conservative movement, and your study of it will hopefully engage you in a discussion not only of the specific legal issues involved, but also of the broader educational and policy concerns which it raises.

Sometimes new historical realities have been the grounds for changes, as, for example, in the decisions of the Conservative Movement to add special prayers for the State of Israel in Sabbath and Festival services and in Grace after Meals throughout the year and to treat Israeli Independence Day as a formal, religious holiday, both liturgically and programmatically.

Sometimes new social or educational realities have been the motivation for changes. The most wide-ranging example of that is the multitude of issues that have been, and are being, discussed and acted upon within the Conservative Movement in redefining the rights and responsibilities of women in Jewish law in light of their new educational and social status. Summarizing these factors and more which motivate changes in Jewish law – whether they be additions to it, deletions from it, or changes in form – *Emet Ve-Emunah: Statement of Principles of Conservative Judaism*, the first movement-wide statement of Conservative philosophy (1988), says this:

> Following the example of our rabbinic predecessors over the ages, however, we consider instituting changes for a variety of reasons. Occasionally the integrity of the law must be maintained by adjusting it to conform to contemporary practice among observant Jews. Every legal system from time to time must adjust what is on the books to be in line with actual practice if the law is to be taken seriously as a guide to conduct. New technological, social, economic, or political realities sometimes require legal action. Some changes in law are designed to improve the material conditions of the Jewish people or society at large. The goal of others is to foster better relations among Jews or between Jews and the larger community. In some cases changes are necessary to prevent or remove injustice, while in others they constitute a positive program to enhance the quality of Jewish life by elevating its moral standards or deepening its piety.[85]

As the last sentence of that paragraph indicates, one factor that has consistently played a major role in Conservative thinking and action is the area of ethics. In many Conservative decisions moral injustice, or the opportunity to encourage greater moral sensitivity, has been the primary motivation for revising the law.

In this last respect, the Conservative Movement has acted quite differently from both the Orthodox and Reform. The Orthodox would not consider modern ethical sensitivities as sufficient grounds to change the law: for them, the law as it has been formulated over the centuries must be binding. Put another way, for them the *halakhah* (the specific form which the law has taken) controls the *aggadah* (the ethical and theological values of Judaism). In contrast, the Conservative Movement maintains that one major purpose of the law in the first place is to concretize moral values, and so the specific form of the law can and should be changed if it is not effectively doing that. In other words, the *aggadah* should control the *halakhah*. Moreover, the Rabbis of the Talmud and Middle Ages themselves changed Jewish law for moral reasons, and consequently *not* to do so would be to violate the tradition!

On the other hand, the Reform Movement does not connect its concern with morals to a corresponding concern for Jewish law. For them the law may suggest some approaches to solving moral problems, but it is to be seen as purely advisory. No specifics of the law are binding – either moral or ritual. In response, the Conservative Movement claims that Jewish law must be considered authoritative if we are to retain our identity and heritage. Moreover, Jewish law contributes in crucial ways to moral practice, theory, and sensitivity, and therefore to abandon it is to sacrifice a major reservoir of moral encouragement, education, and insight. We therefore must pursue our moral goals through Jewish law, but the form of Jewish law must change from time to time if it is to aid us effectively in fashioning ourselves after God's image.

Emet Ve-Emunah affirms the stance described above in very strong terms: halakhah as we interpret and live it must "embody the highest moral principles." While the document indicates that some within the movement are willing to amend Jewish law through formal legislation (*takkanah*), if need be, in order to accomplish this, and while others are not willing to go that far, in practice the Conservative Movement has never issued a *takkanah*, and so that debate, at least as of the date of this writing, remains on the level of theory. The critical point, then, is that the Conservative movement is fully committed to ensure, through its interpretations of Jewish law and through its practice of it, that Jewish law articulates "the highest moral principles" and stimulates us to strive to achieve them:

> We affirm that the halakhic process has striven to embody the highest moral principles. Where changing conditions produce what seem to be immoral consequences and human anguish, varying approaches exist within our community to rectify the situation. Where it is deemed possible and desirable to solve the problem through the existing halakhic norms, we prefer to use them. If not, some within the Conservative community are prepared to amend the existing law by means of a formal procedure of legislation (*takkanah*). Some are willing to make a change only when they find it justified by sources in the halakhic literature. All of us, however, are committed to the indispensability of Halakhah for authentic Jewish living.[86]

Three points ought to be emphasized about the Conservative approach to interpreting Jewish law for our day: (1) The Conservative Movement does not introduce changes in Jewish law just to make life easy; it does so to make Judaism live in the modern world. Sometimes that requires adding new laws, and sometimes that requires dropping or modifying traditional ones, and the Conservative Movement has acted in each of these ways, always with the goal in mind of enabling Judaism to be effective in our lives. (2) Introducing such changes is not a departure from the tradition. On the contrary, not to do so is to abandon the tradition! (3)

In the present day, the overwhelming need is to teach Jewish practices and ideas together with an appreciation for the differences of opinion and practice that have always characterized Judaism. It is to that task that most of the efforts of the Conservative Movement are directed and to which we shall now turn.

3. Educating and Guiding Conservative Jews in Fulfilling the Mitzvot

Until now we have spoken about how Jewish law is defined in its developing context. Most of Jewish law, however, does not change very much from generation to generation. The task of the Conservative Movement with regard to such laws – and, for that matter, with regard to those laws which are in the process of changing – is to teach Jews why and how to observe the law as it currently stands. In many ways, this is the most important charge which we have as a movement, for Jewish law can be real for people and a significant part of their lives only if they know how and why to observe it in the first place.

Toward that end, the Conservative movement has sponsored countless numbers of educational programs, including, but not limited to, all of the following:

* formal classes for Jews of all ages on living Jewishly

* family services, youth services, and learners' minyanim to teach people how to pray in a Jewish way

* weekend retreats and summer encampments for children, for adults, and for families to demonstrate Jewish living concretely as well as teach about it

* informal educational activities, such as discussion groups on specific mitzvot, whether ritual or moral, or social action projects designed to teach the various mitzvot associated with tikkun olam while living themout

* pilgrimages around North America and to Eastern Europe and to Israel to learn about our roots and hopes for those communities while living Jewishly on a day to-day basis

* study groups to fulfill the mitzvah of *Talmud Torah*, and so on

In addition, the various arms of the Conservative Movement publish magazines not only to inform members of the organization's activities but also to teach them about important aspects of what it means to be a Jew. The Rabbinical Assembly and the Jewish Theological Seminary of America publish *Conservative Judaism*, a journal of scholarly articles designed not only for rabbis, but for any Conservative Jew who wants to study Jewish issues in a more in depth manner. Arms of the movement have also published many books to help Conservative Jews learn about their faith, including some specifically designed to teach them how to live a Jewish life. Many of the books in the USY series of sourcebooks are designed for that purpose, and United Synagogue has also published a number of other books in this vein, including, for example, the popular guide to the Jewish dietary laws by Rabbis Samuel Dresner and Seymour Siegel entitled *The Jewish Dietary Laws*. The University of Judaism and the Federation of Jewish Men's Clubs have jointly published the *Art of Jewish Living Series*, with books by Dr. Ronald Wolfson of the University of Judaism faculty on how to celebrate Shabbat, Passover, and Hanukkah and how to participate in Jewish mourning rites, all with attention to how families of various ages, sizes, and forms can successfully incorporate traditional Jewish practices into their lives in a meaningful way. The Rabbinical Assembly has just published *It's a Mitzvah! Step-by-Step to Jewish Living*, by Rabbi Bradley Shavit Artson, to help Conservative Jews make *mitzvot* part of their lives in a gradual, "step-by-step" approach. These are just some of the publications produced by the arms of the movement in order to teach Conservative Jews how to make the mitzvot of Judaism an integral part of their lives.

One should note that these activities and publications do not deal with the ritual aspects of Judaism alone, as important as they are. Conservative publications include such USY sourcebooks as *We are Family, Community and Responsibility in the Jewish Tradition, ...Who Makes People Different: Jewish Perspectives on the Disabled*, and *When Life is in the Balance: Life and Death Decisions in Light of the Jewish Tradition*. In addition, the Rabbinical Assembly has just published "`This Is My Beloved, This Is My Friend': A Rabbinic Letter on Intimate Relations*" to help teenagers and adults learn Jewish laws and morals regarding sexual and family matters so that they might conduct their sexual activity with those norms in mind.

The Conservative Movement engages in many educational efforts in order to make the mitzvot an integral part of the lives of Conservative Jews. These include the ongoing *teshuvot* of individual rabbis and of the Committee on Jewish Law and Standards in dealing with current issues in Jewish law. In light of all these activities and publications, one can say, without exaggeration, that we are truly an educational movement.

4. Making Conservative Judaism Significant in Your Life

We have seen how Conservative Judaism emerges from classical Judaism, interpreting and applying Jewish law anew in each age, and we have seen how that requires that we develop a tolerance for pluralism, for understanding that other serious Jews may respond to our heritage in ways different from yours personally or even from the entire spectrum within Conservative Judaism. We have also analyzed the various theories which explain why we should live our lives within the framework of the *mitzvot*, which describe, in other words, the grounds for the authority of the *mitzvot* in revelation and in the Jewish People.

Judaism, though, is not a religion which allows theory to suffice. In response to their religious commitments, Jews have produced deep and often ground-breaking thinking on a whole host of important issues, but in the end Judaism requires practice. It demands that we live by our faith commitments in our daily lives, that we translate our words to our deeds.

This means that in our own day Conservative Jewish leaders, rabbinic and lay, are increasingly straightforward about the need for Conservative Jews to abide by God's commandments as understood and applied within our movement. The very purpose of Conservative Judaism in the first place, after all, is to conserve authentic, traditional Judaism in the modern intellectual, spiritual, and social setting. To do that, one must infuse one's life not only with the concepts and values and feelings of Judaism, but also with the actions it commands. If your Jewish commitment is going to be serious, it must be manifest not only in the way you think and feel, but also in the way you act.

In the modern world, this is easier said than done. When Jews lived in ghettos, they often had little choice but to follow Jewish law as everyone else in the town or village did. If one failed to do that, one would be socially ostracized. Conversely, since everyone else in town abided by Jewish law, it was easy to fall in line and follow suit.

We now live, however, under conditions of political and religious freedom. No government is going to insist that you remain in the ghetto and abide by its rules. That freedom, of course, is, in many ways, a blessing, for it enables you and all other Jews to choose their careers, their place of residence, and their form of religious expression.

On the other hand, though, that same freedom is also a challenge, for one can easily fall into ignoring religious and moral issues altogether, leading one to a rather empty life. One can also lose touch with community: America's individualism and materialism all too easily entice us to concern ourselves only with our own needs, wants, and material comforts. That kind of individualism and materialism, as comfortable and even exciting as they may be for a time, ultimately lead to a meaningless life, one devoid of community, of family and communal rituals to mark the passages of life and of the seasons, of moral purpose, and of sacred mission.

Judaism provides all of those things, but at a price. Its price is that one makes a serious effort to incorporate Jewish practice into one's life. Nobody is saying that Judaism should be the whole of your life; school, work, sports, entertainment, art, music, dance, spending time with friends, and, of course, love are all part of what makes life worthwhile. Judaism, though, puts all of those activities and associations into a larger context, giving them structure, perspective, community, roots, hope, and a proper place in a life filled with meaning.

How, then, does one begin? With Judaism, as with everything else in life, it is not smart to jump in, as it were, going from abiding by none of the commandments to trying to abide by them all. Those who do that generally leave the world of Jewish practice just as quickly as they entered it, sometimes even resenting it in the bargain. It is much better to add one thing at a time, taking some time for the new *mitzvah* that you have assumed to become part of your life. Once that is comfortably part of your everyday thinking and acting, you can begin the process of incorporating yet another *mitzvah* into your life.

Two important cautions before you begin. First, it is absolutely critical that you do *not* look down on others who practice Judaism in ways different from the way you adopt. The temptation for some who are beginning to live according to Jewish law is to make some aspect of Judaism part of their lives and then to disdain all Jews who fail to abide by that law -- or even those who observe it differently. *Observing Jewish law does not give you warrant to think more of yourself at the expense of others; quite the contrary, observing Jewish law should motivate you to value others more and treat them better than you have in the past.*

Second, remember that your new patterns of living will almost inevitably have an effect on the others in your life, especially those in your home. If you are living with your parents, remember that the Torah commands honor (Shemot 20:12) and respect (Vayikra 19:3) of parents just as much as it commands the dietary laws and Shabbat. If you are living with college roommates or apartment mates, remember that your decision to abide by some aspects of Jewish law is yours, not theirs, and you do not have a right to impose your decision on them. In both living situations, and frankly in any other, the key to this whole process is mutual respect and calm communication. Parents and Jewish friends may feel threatened in their own sense of Jewish identity by your sudden desire to become more seriously Jewish, and they therefore may react with defensiveness or even anger. If you present this, though, as your acquisition of more of your heritage without intending anything negative about them, then parents and friends may well react with questions but also with a willingness to work this out to everyone's satisfaction. It is all in the way you handle this with those who are near and dear to you.

These cautions are important, of course, on a pragmatic level – that is, so that you succeed in finding a way to adopt new Jewish practices. Doing this with love, respect, and understanding is even more important, though, from the standpoint of Jewish law. You do not want those around you to hate you for this and therefore also the new practices you adopt; that would be a *hillul ha-Shem*, a desecration of God's Name. You want them rather to appreciate and honor you for this, even if they themselves do not follow your lead, so that they value what you are doing; that would make this effort a *kiddush ha-Shem*, a sanctification of God's Name.[87] One should always, of course, treat others with respect and decency, but in the process of deepening one's Jewish identification decency is required not only for moral and practical reasons, but for religious ones as well.

The Torah, according to the Rabbinic numbering, includes 613 commandments. Even though a large number of them are no longer applicable because they depended on the existence of the Temple in Jerusalem with its sacrifices, and even though others apply only to agriculture in the land of Israel, that still leaves quite a sizable number of commandments to fulfill. The problem may seem even more overwhelming once one recognizes that the Rabbis added quite a few to the Torah's list. As a result, in the history of Jewish law, there have been many attempts to articulate the essence of Jewish observance in much shorter lists. The Talmud itself says that David summarized all of the Torah's commandments in eleven, [First] Isaiah in six, Micah in three, [Second] Isaiah in two, and Amos or Habakkuk ultimately in one, namely, "Seek me and live" (Amos 5:4) or "The righteous person shall live by his faith" (Habakkuk 2:4)".[88] Another, famous rabbinic story recounts Hillel's response to the heathen, who asked to learn the entire Torah while standing on one foot. Hillel said, "Do not do to others what is hateful to you" contains the whole of the Torah but that then one must go and study the rest of it to see how everything flows from that principle and to learn how to live one's life in accordance with it.[89] In addition, we have seen that Maimonides and Joseph Karo, among others, wrote codes of Jewish law in order to try to summarize its requirements in a shorter, clearer, and more organized form than they appear in the Talmud so that Jews of all levels of education could easily know what was expected of them as Jews.

Writing in the same vein as these earlier formulations, Rabbi Jerome M. Epstein, Executive Vice-President of the United Synagogue of Conservative Judaism, presented a Dvar Torah at the 1995 United Synagogue biennial convention in which he outlined a list of eight behavioral expectations of the ideal Conservative Jew, and those have been reprinted in a brochure entitled "The Ideal Conservative Jew: Eight Behavioral Expectations." While even Rabbi Epstein would maintain that this list is not exhaustive, it does provide a nice measure by which Conservative Jews can evaluate their Jewish commitment. It also can help those Jews intending to become more serious about their Jewish devotion to identify where they want to start and where they have yet to go. With these purposes in mind, we shall reprint Rabbi Epstein's list here.

The Ideal Conservative Jew...

1) ...supports a Conservative synagogue by participating in its activities.

Judaism is a communal religion and our Jewish lives are infinitely enriched when we play an active part in a synagogue community.

*Attend services on *Shabbat* and Festivals.
*Participate regularly in a daily *minyan*.
*Support synagogue social justice programs.
*Attend synagogue social events.

2) ...studies as a Conservative Jew a minimum of one hour per week – or, in the case of full-time students, six hours per week.

Our approach to study is distinct. We study texts critically and we bring knowledge from other disciplines to help us better understand our own heritage. At the same time, we approach the text with a commitment to preserve our sacred traditions.

Jewish study is essential because it allows us to appreciate our past, understand our present, and chart where we wish to go in the future.

*Attend synagogue adult [or youth] education classes.
*Spend time reading Jewish books.
*Discuss Jewish issues with your family/friends.
*Study the Torah portion each week.
*Take advantage of the Internet and other modern resources for Jewish study.

3) ...employs learned Jewish values to guide behavior even when it conflicts with personal feelings or inclinations.

Judaism is meaningful only if it affects the way we live our lives. Our tradition teaches that study is meaningful only if it leads to action. Judaism must have a strong voice when we make daily decisions in our lives.

*Learn what Judaism teaches about the critical issues of our times.
*Act on the teachings of Judaism.
*Don't follow the crowd: follow what our tradition teaches to be right.

4) ...increases personal Jewish living out of commitment as a result of thought, by adding a minimum of three new *mitzvot* a year.

Conservative Judaism is unique in its approach to *halakhah* and *mitzvot*. For us, *halakhah* is both evolving and binding. Each of us must continue to grow in our commitment and observance.

*Add new *mitzvot* to your *Shabbat* observance.
*Climb the ladder in your observance of *kashrut*.
*Become more aware (and observant of the *mitzvot* of *gemilut hasadim* (acts of loving-kindness).
*Add to your observance of *mitzvot* connected with the family.
*Look for opportunities to recite *berakhot*.

5) ...employs the values of *tikkun olam* to help in the world's continual repair.

We are God's partners in safeguarding His creation. A Conservative Jew does not just believe in repairing the world, but works towards that goal. The Conservative Jew is not only pained by human suffering, but does something to relieve it.

*Participate in synagogue social justice programs.
*Give *tzedakah* regularly.
*Volunteer to work for a local homeless shelter.
*Make *bikkur holim* (visiting the sick) a regular activity.

6) ...makes decisions about Jewish behavior only after considering the effect these decisions will have on *Klal Yisrael* [the entire Jewish people].

Klal Yisrael, the unity of the Jewish people, is a central value of the Conservative Movement. In making decisions about our lives or our religious practices, we must think about their impact on the entire Jewish community. We must avoid taking actions that will divide us from other Jews.

*Make an effort to be involved in synagogue programs to ensure their success.
*Make personal decisions only after considering how they will affect the greater community.
*Consider the impact your choices will have on the health of your community.

7) ...increases ties and connections to Israel.

Since its inception, the Conservative Movement has believed in, and helped to further, the cause of Zionism. As Conservative Jews, we must find ways to increase our ties to Israel in concrete ways.

*Join MERCAZ (the Conservative Zionist Organization).
*Travel frequently to Israel.
*Send your children on Israel programs.
*Support Israel financially.
*Consider making *aliyah* (immigrating to Israel).

8) ...studies to increase his or her knowledge of Hebrew.

Hebrew, as a language, unites us with Jews across time and space. It is the eternal language of our people and connects us with Jews in Israel and throughout the world. It is also the Jewish language of prayer and study. Yet for many of us, it is not a language but a series of letters we can read but not understand.

It is imperative that we not only maintain Hebrew in our services but increase our personal knowledge of Hebrew as a language.

*Take classes in Hebrew as a living language.
*Study the prayers and their meanings.
*Plan to study at an *ulpan* in Israel.

In each of the eight categories, Rabbi Epstein describes some reasons why the goal is important, and he provides some examples (marked with an asterisk) to indicate how one might begin to accomplish that goal. Since Rabbi Epstein's presentation and the brochure based on it were addressed to adults, some of his specific suggestions must be adjusted for use by high school and college students, but the necessary revisions will be quite obvious and will, in any case, apply to young adults in the not-too-distant future.

Rabbi Epstein's list may surprise you in its breadth. You may have thought of Jewish obligations strictly in ritual terms. Jewish ritual life is indeed extremely important. As Rabbi Epstein captures in this presentation, however, the *mitzvot* also entail other sorts of imperatives: to study our tradition and its language; to build connections with a synagogue and with the rest of the People Israel in your local community, in Israel, and worldwide; to support synagogues and other Jewish institutions both financially and by participating in their activities; to make moral decisions in one's life in consonance with the Jewish tradition; and to work for the improvement of the world.

Many Jews express the seriousness of their Jewish commitments in some of these ways and not in others. It is important to recognize the contributions to Jewish life which they are making in what they do; one certainly should not denigrate anyone who is positively affecting the life and future of Judaism and the Jewish People. At the same time, one should strive in one's own life to incorporate more and more of these ways of being a serious Jew so that one's Jewishness is not one-sided. Judaism is too rich a tradition for that, and God's demands are to great. As Rabbi Tarfon said, "The day [that is, life] is short, and the work [of accomplishing God's ends] is great; the workers [that is, we human beings] are lazy, but the reward is great, and the Owner of the house [that is, of the world, namely, God] pushes us on." (*Avot* 2:20).

In the end, it is the old story: you can get out of it only what you put into it. No human being will coerce you into doing any of the things on Rabbi Epstein's list or any of the other aspects of what it means to be a Jew. To be a serious Conservative Jew, though, is to be humane and human in the fullest and finest senses of those words, and we do that by living out in our actions the values and concepts which Judaism teaches us. To be a serious Conservative Jew is, in other words, to carry our enormously wise and noble heritage from our ancestors through our own lives to our descendants.

QUESTIONS:

1) What is "the first – and perhaps the most important" thing that one should realize about Jewish law within the Conservative Movement?

   What ritual practices are involved in being a committed Conservative Jew? List some moral norms that you think would be included.

2) How would the style of life that you described in Question #1 differ from that of a committed Reform Jew? a committed Orthodox Jew?

3) Compare the style of life of a committed Conservative Jew, as you described it in Question #1, with your understanding of what a Conservative Jew is in answer to the questions at the end of Chapter One.

   Are there differences between the picture of a committed Conservative Jew described above and the idea that most Jews have of what identifies a Conservative Jew? If so, what are those differences? How do you explain this lack of understanding? What is the Conservative Movement doing in an attempt to correct it?

4) Describe the mechanisms by which the Conservative Movement makes decisions in Jewish law. How does that mechanism combine the three ways in which decisions in Jewish practice have been made historically – i.e., majority rule of the rabbis, the *mara d'atra* ("teacher of the place"), and *minhag* (custom)?

5) Explain how it is that the practices among Conservative rabbis and synagogues may vary on specific issues. Give some examples.

6) To give you an idea of the scope of issues which have been treated in Conservative discussions of Jewish law, here is a list of some of the questions which have been treated by the Conservative Movement's Committee on Jewish Law and Standards:

   I) Is abortion of a defective fetus permitted in Jewish law?
   ii) May infertile couples use donor insemination, egg donation, or surrogate mothers to have children?
   iii) May machines and medications be withdrawn from a dying patient? May artificial nutrition and hydration be withdrawn?
   iv) May a Jew have his or her skin tattooed or body pierced?
   v) May a minor read from the Torah?

vi)   May Jews on campus use a room in a building with a cross on the roof?

iii)   Are all cheeses kosher?

iv)   Are all gelatins kosher?

v)   May Shabbat services be videotaped?

vi)   What is Jewish law regarding current advertising practices?

vii)   What is Jewish law regarding the sport of hunting?

viii)   May a physician perform a circumcision?

ix)   Does one follow Jewish mourning practices for a non-Jewish parent?

x)   Is it permissible to distribute condoms to Jewish adolescents because of fear of AIDS?

xi)   Privacy in cyberspace: To what extent must people protect themselves and others from intrusion in cyberspace, and under what circumstances may information communicated in cyberspace be disclosed to other people?

In addition, as indicated above, the movement has published a number of educational materials designed to inform Jews of the laws and moral norms of Judaism, for unless Jews know them they cannot possibly incorporate them into their lives. This includes matters as important and as personal as the new Rabbinical Assembly *Rabbinic Letter on Intimate Relations.*

a) What is the authority of an individual rabbi's responsa (*teshuvot*)? How would the authority of responsa by individual rabbis differ from the authority of a responsum (*teshuvah*) validated by the Committee on Law and Standards? How would each of those differ from the authority of a standard approved by the necessary majorities of the Committee and the Rabbinical Assembly?

b) What is the authority of the educational publications of the movement, that is, those which intend not to make any new decisions in Jewish law, but simply to inform people what Jewish law is on a given issue and to teach them why and how to abide by it?

c) Would you ever ask your rabbi some of the questions listed above? Are there any subjects which you think would not or should not be treated in rabbinic responsa? in Jewish educational materials? If so, why? If not, why not?

7)   One matter that has been treated in various ways by Conservative rabbis is the issue of riding on the Sabbath. To give you an idea of the variety of opinions, the process of making decisions, and the issues which are of concern in making decisions in

Conservative law, we have included two opposing responsa on the subject. After you have read them consider the following questions:

a) What reasons are advanced by those in favor of permitting riding? Are they happy about the prospect of people riding on Shabbat? Why not? Why do they permit it then? What restrictions do they place on this permission?

b) What arguments does Rabbi Novak advance in opposition to the decision? Is he using a different methodology in reaching his decision, or is he simply weighing factors differently?

c) Is there a connection between these varying positions to the four positions on Jewish law described in Section D of this chapter? If so, what is it? If not, why not?

d) What authority does the first responsum have in light of its acceptance by the Committee on Jewish Law and Standards? How does that differ from the authority of Rabbi Novak's responsum, which is the responsum of an individual rabbi?

e) Arrange a debate on this issue in your group. Each side should read the entire set of materials and be prepared to advance its own position and attack its opposite as strongly as possible. Other materials may also be used in preparation for the debate.

f) In view of the difference of opinion on this issue within the Conservative Movement, what do you think should be the policy in activities sponsored by the Movement as a whole – e.g., U.S.Y. conventions, Camp Ramah, etc.?

ACTIVITY:

As illustrated by Rabbi Jerome M. Epstein's "Eight Behavioral Expectations," it is incumbent upon each Conservative Jew to make a Commitment to ensure the strengthening and survival of Judaism. Using your knowledge of Judaism, your beliefs and your values, make a Commitment now which you will try to keep. Don't make a promise that is unrealistic. On the other hand, choose something that will require effort and Commitment.

SELF- CONTRACT

I, _____ , because I want to _____

promise myself that I will_____

_____

_____   _____
Signature of contract maker   Signature of witness

Date:_____

The first responsum is taken from Mordecai Waxman, ed., *Tradition and Change* (New York: The Rabbinical Assembly, 1958), pp. 351 ff. The second selection is from David Novak, *Law and Theology in Judaism* (New York: Ktav Publishing House, Inc., 1974) Series I, Ch. 3.

A RESPONSUM ON THE SABBATH

(Rabbis Morris Adler, Jacob Agus and Theodore Friedman)

This is the first of two sets of responsa on the questions of riding...on the Sabbath. The responsum printed below is the collective effort of three men who prepared it for the approval of the Law Committee of the Rabbinical Assembly. It secured the support of a majority of the Law Committee and it was subsequently presented at a convention of the Rabbinical Assembly (1950).

Sheelah:

As a rabbi in Israel, I turn to you my Colleagues, for assistance in a question both theoretic and practical which has caused me concern and anxiety. One cannot serve a congregation for any time without being depressed and disheartened by the widespread disintegration of Sabbath observance among our people. This breakdown of one of the major institutions in Jewish life is too deep and too prevalent to be countered by preachment and exhortations. Sermons declaring the pre-eminence of the Sabbath in Jewish life or extolling its spiritual beauty and social significance are politely received by our congregants but exert no influence on their practices or habits.

Yet the American Jew is not innately resistant to religious forms and values. I find among many in my congregation a fine receptivity to Jewish teaching and a marked interest in Jewish affairs. Some recognize the lack of spiritual satisfactions in their present mode of living and evince eagerness not alone for instruction in Jewish ideas but likewise for guidance in their practical conduct as Jews.

They are Jews who not only have been born into the modern, industrial world, but have also been educated in its institutions and have been mentally and psychologically shaped and moulded by its approaches, attitudes and activities. To ignore this fact and to speak to them as if they were the identical counterparts of their East European forbears is to engage in futile rhetoric. On the other hand, to overlook the spiritual alertness and interest as well as the healthy Jewish pride and desire for Jewish identification which motivate them is to doom to atrophy those characteristics which hold forth greatest promise for the future of American Jewish life. To do nothing, or to mouth easy formulas that have a respectable past behind them, is to abandon to the haphazard forces of the pervasive secular environment much of the richest potential for Jewish living in this land.

I know, dear Colleagues, that the question of the Sabbath, as indeed of Jewish religious life, has agitated you as it has disturbed every earnest and thinking Jew. It cannot be met on a level of individual action since the problem is far too aggravated for such a necessarily fragmentary approach to it. In addition, were every rabbi to work in terms of his individual judgment, the confusion and disharmony in our midst would be greatly intensified.

Our Conservative movement must marshall its forces to meet the problem I have described. I therefore turn to you to ask for guidance in instructing my people as to our view as a movement on the Sabbath disciplines, our best thought as to its proper observance and a practical program by which its meaning may be better understood, its spirit more widely shared, its sanctities more greatly respected by the congregations that look to us, as Conservative rabbis, for guidance and instruction.

PLACE OF SABBATH -- PAST AND PRESENT

Teshubah:

The question raised by our colleague penetrates to the basic core of Judaism and touches likewise the most difficult and aggravating problem in contemporary Jewish life. A question of such scope cannot be simply or readily answered. We have deliberated through many months and have focused upon this problem our most earnest thought. We seek a solution, humbly and prayerfully aware of the fact that we are dealing with one of the central sanctities of our tradition. The feeling that a Sabbath-less Judaism is no Judaism governs our consideration and motivates our reverent approach to the complex issues which are associated with so fundamental a problem. The colleague who has directed his quest to us has rightly suggested that as spiritual leaders in Jewry we would be remiss in our calling were we content to leave the Sabbath to its fate, to be further buffeted about by the compelling pressures of the changed outer world in which we live and by the dictates generated by a greatly altered inner world of ideas and attitudes which we have come, as modern men, to inhabit.

To overlook the former is to sacrifice relevance; to ignore the second is to violate integrity. Our duty as rabbis is not exhausted when we cite the law as it has been understood and practiced, and ignore the conditions of life in the midst of which, or the thoughts of men by whom that law is to be followed. One of the great responsibilities of this age in our history is to release the life-giving and life-enriching powers that inhere in our tradition, by relating that tradition to modern life. Changing conditions threaten an inert system of law. The Halachah lived and functioned in our history because it has traditionally been characterized by resiliency and responsiveness to life. The very designation of Jewish law as Halachah suggests its capacity for movement, and reveals the intent of its architects and builders to charge it with a genius for vital adaptability to the moving and changing scene.

It is out of a faith in the significant meaning which our historic tradition can and should have for us today and out of our conviction that modern Jews have a capacity for spiritual living and Jewish loyalty that we seek an answer to the question addressed to us by our colleague.

The preservation of the Sabbath spirit and of Sabbath practices is an indispensable element in any

178

program for the Jewish future. The Sabbath has always served Israel as a "sanctuary in time," when, released from the deadening drudgery of daily duty, the Jew could soar to the highest realm of his human possibilities. The Sabbath was the most eloquent manifestation of the covenant with God into which Israel had entered and to the fulfillment of which its history is dedicated. The Sabbath helped to naturalize the Jew in a world of spiritual values and sensitivities, and made the Shekinah, the presence of God in human life, felt and experienced by even the humblest. It is impossible to overstate the role the Sabbath played in the spiritual and social economy of Judaism, or to exaggerate the widening circles of influence which it sent forth to the farthermost bounds of Jewish life.

We feel convinced, however, that never before was the Sabbath called upon as urgently to play its creative part in Jewish living as in our time. We could understand most vividly the full meaning of the saying of our sages (ירושלמי ברכות פ"א) שקולה שבת כנגד כל מצותיה של תורה "The Sabbath is equal in value to all the precepts of the Torah." Into a world whose landscape is dominated by visible and massive monuments to human ingenuity and power, the Sabbath quietly but firmly brings the humbling and saving message of man's dependence upon God. Our modern environment, built as it has been by the drives for possession and dominion which it stimulated, needs the spiritual overtones of a day overflowing with moral and religious content. The competitive character of the society we live in not only fosters man's acquisitive appetites, but also encourages the view that man stands in the relationship of competitor and antagonist to his fellow-men in the incessant struggle for worldly reward and gain. Sabbath peace and holiness represent not simply a temporary interruption of the daily struggle, but renew with men the deeper and greater truth that men are brothers under the Common Fatherhood of a Universal God....

The Sabbath forges vital and enriching linkages which the modern Jew needs as a man and as a member of an historic group. The Sabbath unites the Jew with his people not on the level of a joint philanthropic enterprise organized to meet an emergency, nor again on the level of a defense against the defamation of the Jewish name or the denial of Jewish rights -- but rather in terms of deeply-felt and experienced identification with the life and history of a people dedicated to a purposeful and benign destiny. Through the opportunities for study and prayer which in the pressure of life, the Sabbath alone offers, the Jew enters the rich world of Jewish ideas and feelings and becomes kin to those eternal contemporaries in Jewish life -- prophet, sage and poet. The Sabbath quickens the spirit and fortifies the meaningful cohesiveness of the Jewish family by rededicating the family altar and by providing a fund of shared spiritual experiences and delights, this in an age in which the family is being subjected to centripetal forces and multiple corrosions. Thus from the Sabbath there can flow into the life of modern Jews numerous streams of spiritual balm and enrichment...

PROGRAM FOR THE REVITALIZATION OF THE SABBATH

We call upon you and upon all our colleagues of the Rabbinical Assembly of America, in concert with the United Synagogue of America, to launch a campaign for Sabbath observance among our people. The campaign should have as its immediate goal the acceptance on the part of the people of the following basic indispensable elements of Sabbath observance. Emphasis on this immediate program should in no wise militate against the ultimate objective -- the cessation of all gainful employment on the Sabbath. It is in the conviction that only the immediate can lead to the ultimate that the following program is proposed.

(A)   The ushering in of the Sabbath at home through the kindling of the Sabbath candles, the recitation of the Kiddush, the blessing of the children, the singing of Sholom Aleichem and other zemiroth.

(B)   All preparations for the Sabbath, such as the Sabbath meals, the tidying of the home, as well as personal preparation, should be completed before the onset of the Sabbath. It is also suggested that there be introduced the custom now prevailing in Israel of adorning the house with flowers for the Sabbath.

(C)   Attendance at public worship at least once on the Sabbath.

(D)   A portion of one's leisure time on the Sabbath should be devoted to the reading of Jewish sacred literature, particulary the weekly Torah portion.

(E)   One should refrain from all such activities that are not made absolutely necessary by the unavoidable pressures of life and that are not in keeping with the Sabbath spirit, such as shopping, household work, sewing, strenuous physical exercise, etc.

(F)   The type of recreation engaged in on the Sabbath should be such as is calculated to enhance one's spiritual personality in its intellectual, social and esthetic aspect.

(G)   Refraining from the use of a motor vehicle is an important aid in the maintenance of the Sabbath spirit of respose. Such restraint aids, moreover, in keeping the members of the family together on the Sabbath. However, where a family resides beyond reasonable walking distance from the synagogue, the use of a motor vehicle for the purpose of synagogue attendance shall in no wise be construed as a violation of the Sabbath, but, on the contrary, such attendance shall be deemed an expression of loyalty to our faith.

We are well aware, in the above connection, that in accordance with Jewish law one may worship at home as well as in the synagogue. We are equally aware, however, that the practice of private prayer has unfortunately fallen into such disuse that only a very minimal number of people engage in prayer unless it be at a synagogue service. Indeed, it is a well-grounded supposition that were it not for synagogue attendance on the Sabbath, there would be no prayer for most of our people from the end of one week to the other. Moreover, when almost every Jew had some measure of competence in understanding the Torah and our sacred literature, many Jews could and did spend time in studying Torah. Today, however, this condition no longer obtains. The average Jew's knowledge of Torah and his Jewish information are gained through the synagogue and in great measure through the sermon which both instructs and inspires our people to live in accordance with our faith. Hence, in our time regular attendance at the synagogue has become a *sine qua non* for the maintenance of Judaism. We are, we sincerely believe, acting in accordance with the spirit of our rabbis when they declare

אין שבות במקדש - "The Sabbath prohibition of *shebuth*[3]" does not apply to the carrying out of the temple ritual. We similarly state in our program for the revitalization of the Sabbath that the traditional interdiction of riding on the Sabbath for the purpose of attending the synagogue service may, in the discretion of the local rabbi, be modified under the conditions we have described above.

PRINCIPLES IMPLIED IN THIS PROGRAM

(1)

Every effort to restore standards of observance among our people is likely to be met with cynical skepticism, as if the process of continuous deterioration were a foregone conclusion. Actually, there were many occasions in Jewish history when the seemingly hopeless process of decay was arrested and even reversed by a determined and courageous act of reconsecration. The Jewish religion does not favor the emotional excesses of the Christian "revivalist" movements, but it fosters the principle of voluntary acceptance of a pattern of life...It is to a nation-wide effort, conceived in the spirit of the love of God and reverence for our tradition, that we must now dedicate ourselves.

At the same time, we must learn to adjust our strategy to the realities of our time and place, in keeping with the realistic genius of the great builders of our faith. Thus, our Sages cautioned us, *tafasta m'rubah lo tafasta* -- "to overreach is to court failure," when you attempt to grasp a great deal, you will grasp nothing. They also advised all builders of fences in Judaism, "it is better to build a fence of ten handbreadths that is likely to stand than one of a hundred handbreadths that is liable to fall," *tov assarah t'fahim v'omed mimeah t'fahim v'nofel* (Aboth D'Rabbi Nathan). It is also well to remember the sage advice, *mutav shelo lomar davar sheaino nishma* -- "it is better not to say a thing which will not be heeded."

(2)

In this spirit it is our consensus that riding to the synagogue on the Sabbath and the use of electric lights in the course of this journey or for other purposes are comprised in the general category of oneg shabbath, the delight of the Sabbath. Before discussing in detail the precepts and laws relating to these two specific enactments, we wish to point first to the general principle of community enactments.

The power of a community to enact ordinances in the field of religious life is virtually unlimited, provided its ordinances are made with the consent of the resident scholars and provided further that they be inspired by the purpose of "strengthening the faith," and intended only for their own time and place. The general impression that Jewish Law is rigidly inflexible and incapable of adjustment or adaptation is completely erroneous....In crucial periods, our Sages did not hesitate to make special enactments for their own time or for a limited period of time, in order to meet the challenge of new circumstances.

---

3   A quasi-labor activity prohibited by the Rabbis in connection with the Sabbath. The purpose of the prohibition was to erect "a fence about the law."

This power of the communities to make special enactments on behalf of the faith, through their spiritual leaders and lay representatives, is in turn a corollary of the principle of development in Jewish Law....

The share of the people in the creation and repudiation of laws is taken for granted in Jewish tradition. The Torah became binding upon Israel only when the twelve tribes accepted it voluntarily at the foot of Mt. Sinai. The power of the minhag to make laws and break them is well-known. It was the duty of the highest rabbinic court to declare an ordinance invalid if the majority of the people did not accept it in their daily practice. When otherwise observant people were living in habitual violation of a Torahitic ordinance and it was considered likely that they would not obey the law if told about it, the rabbis advised that the people be not told that they transgressed the law so as not to induce either feelings of guilt or a mood of rebellion. *Mutav she yihu shoggim v'al yihyu mezidin....*

To sum up, the human share in the making of Jewish Law is both undeniable and inevitable. The greatest authorities of the Medieval and early modern period were cognizant of this need. Thus, Maimonides who formulated the principle of the irreplaceability of the Torah, *(zoth hatorah lo t'hai muhalefeth)* stressed the duty of rabbis to formulate and enact special regulations for their time and place. The court may revoke these ordinances, for a time, even if it be smaller than the first courts, for the rabbinic ordinances are surely not greater than the words of the Torah itself, which the courts are entitled to revoke on a temporary basis...Even as the physician cuts off a hand or a foot in order that the patient might survive, a rabbinic court may teach the violation of some mitzvoth for a time, in order that the totality of Judaism might be preserved. Thus, our ancient Sages declared, "Desecrate for him one Sabbath in order that he might keep many Sabbaths."

The great scholar of the eighteenth century, Rabbi Jacob Emden, declared "that many mitzvoth come into being at different periods in Jewish history, both in respect of permitting the prohibited and in prohibiting the permitted...Thus, it is clear as the sun that the commandments are dependent upon the time, the circumstances and the people of every age. They were not at one time set up in a pattern that is complete and final, but they are subject to additions and modifications, as changing times require."

In the same spirit, the famed glossator of the Shulchan Aruch, Rabbi Moses Isserless, declared in a responsum, "that when new circumstances develop, which were unknown to the ancient authorities, it is permitted to institute new enactments."

THE PROBLEM OF RIDING

The use of an automobile involves the following activities: the kindling of lights, the indirect combustion of gasoline to produce power, and locomotion from one domain to another....The combustion of gasoline to produce power is a type of work that obviously could not have been prohibited before its invention. All acts of burning are prohibited only when performed for specifically described purposes, such as: cooking, heating, lighting or the need of its ashes. Burning for the sake of power was not included in this list. Of course, some heat is produced in the act of combustion, but this result is neither intended nor desired by the motorist. Hence, it falls in the category of פסיק רישא דלא ניחא ליה which is permitted by the latest authorities. The combustion of gas in the carburetor is therefore the type of work, classed as *m'lachah sheainah z'richah l'gufah*, according to the definition contained in Tosafot, Shabbat 94a -- [12]

נראה לר"י. דמלאכה שאינה צריכה לגופה קרי כשעושים מלאכה ואין צריך לאותו צורך כעין שהיו צריכין לה במשכן. אלא לענין אחר. כי הצורך שהיתה מלאכה נעשית בשבילו במשכן הוא גוף איסור המלאכה ושורשו.

While Rashi defined *m'lachah sheainah z'richah l'gufah* differently, we favor the definition of the Tosafists in this matter. Finally, locomotion from one domain to another (e.g. מרשות היחיד לכרמלית) is a rabbinic prohibition; since today there is no רשות הרבים, there can be no Torahitic interdiction involved. As a matter of fact, on the basis of the strictest interpretation of the law, riding would not be prohibited on Sabbath in a public vehicle driven by a non-Jew. Hence we deal here with a prohibition instituted by the rabbis. Their main reason for the prohibition of riding a horse or in a wagon was the fear that it may lead indirectly to the violation of the Sabbath. Thus they said that one may not ride on an animal because the rider may be tempted to break off a branch to use as a whip (ביצה ל"ו) זמורה גזירה שמא יחתוך. The additional reason was given that riding causes a Jewishly-owned animal to labor on the Sabbath -- (ירושלמי ביצה פ"ה) שאתה מצווה על שביתת בהמתך

Obviously, neither reason applies to the automobile. The apprehension that the driver might be moved to fix the car in the event of a breakdown is remote, since its complicated mechanism generally requires the services of an expert.[13]

פירש רש"י שמא יתקן כלי שיר. ומיהו לדידן שרי. דדוקא בימיהן שהיו בקיאים לעשות כלי שירים שייך למיגזר. אבל לדידן אין אנו בקיאים לעשות כלי שירים ולא שייך למיגזר.

The above analysis leads us to the conclusion that riding in an automobile on the Sabbath is at most a rabbinically interdicted activity. When this act prevents the fulfillment of the mitzvah of attending public worship it shall not be considered a prohibited act. We base this conclusion upon the numerous precedents in the Halachah for the setting aside of a rabbinic prohibition when a great mitzvah is

---

12

A labor which, while it necessarily results in a transgression, is neither intended nor desired. Thus *m'lachah sheainah z'richah l'gufa* is a labor which is not performed for its own sake. The Tossafot' definition is that it is a labor which is performed, but not for the need for which it was performed in the tabernacle (which is the basis of the rabbinic description of types of work) but rather as the means of achieving another type of benefit -- e.g., combustion not for the purpose of burning but of achieving movement.

13

Tosafot, Betzah, 30a. -- The Talmud enjoins that one should neither clap his hands on the Sabbath while singing nor dance, lest he injure, and thus be led to repair a musical instrument. Rashi remarks that we may "in our time" both clap hands and dance for "in our time" people are not versed in repairing musical instruments. It has become the work of professionals, so there need be no fear that the ordinary person will undertake it and thus violate the Sabbath.

involved, such as the mitzvah of Yishuv Eretz-Yisrael (Baba Kama 80b, Maimonides Hilchoth Shabbat 6:11, 6:9) and in the case of witnesses who came to testify on the appearance of the new moon, the law of *tehumin*[14] was relaxed by a *takanah* (ordinance) of R. Gamaliel the elder (Mishnah Rosh Hashanah 4:5). We may also cite the frequently quoted general principle regarding the easing of *shebuth* prohibitions when a great mitzvah or public welfare is involved.

חפצך אסור. חפצי שמים מותר (Shabbat 150a)[15]. As we have already indicated, participation in public service on the Sabbath is in the light of modern conditions to be regarded as a great mitzvah, since it is indispensable to the preservation of the religious life of American Jewry. Therefore it is our considered opinion that the positive values involved in the participation in public worship on the Sabbath outweigh the negative values of refraining from riding in an automobile. When attendance at services is made unreasonably difficult, without the use of automobile, such use shall not be regarded as being a violation of the Sabbath.

We cannot too strongly emphasize that our views in regard to the use of electric lights and the automobile on the Sabbath are not separable from the total program for the revitalization of the Sabbath as herein suggested. To take these elements out of the context of the entire national and local effort required for the strengthening of the basic institution of the Sabbath would be to subvert the spirit and the purpose which animate our decision. On the other hand, it shall be understood that in their wisdom and in the light of the conditions prevailing in their respective communities, individual rabbis may find the easements here proposed unnecessary for the achievement of the larger goal herein envisaged. We take into consideration the fact that different situations in particular communities may dictate the application of varying methods.

The crucial question in the issue before us is whether we of the Conservative movement are well advised to labor on behalf of the Sabbath in our own way. Rooted in the consciousness of our people is the conviction that Judaism is the business of the entire Jewish people and that Jewish Law should be changed, if at all, only by the duly constituted authorities of a reunited Israel. Indeed, in ancient times, the present divisions in Jewish life could scarcely have been envisaged. However, we are neither able nor willing to turn back the clock of history. Diversity of opinion is a direct function of democratic freedom, so that whenever outside pressure was relaxed, the variety of thought and feeling which always existed within the Jewish community came to the surface.

Today, the choice before us is not unity or diversity; the first quality is illusory in any positive program of religious dedication. The second quality is inescapable. The only alternatives we face are a policy of continued inaction by all groups, permitting Sabbath observance to sink out of Jewish life, or a resolute attempt, on as broad a front as possible, to set a floor below which respect for the Sabbath-institution shall not fall among our congregants. In setting forth this program of

---

14   The limitation on the distance one is allowed to walk on the Sabbath.

15   Work which you desire to perform for your own benefit is prohibited, but if it is designed to achieve some religious objective, it may be permitted.

Sabbath-observance for our congregations we hope to contribute toward a reversal of the trend of deterioration in all three groups. We earnestly trust that both the Orthodox and Reform movements will be moved to set up and implement similar programs of reconsecration for their respective memberships, with a consequent gain for American Judaism as a whole. Far from widening the present cleavage in American Jewry, such efforts are bound to make allegiance to Judaism more meaningful and to lead to the emergence of a common core of reference for Judaism and respect for its institutions.

The division of Jewry into communities, maintaining their own forms of ritual observance, is not an unprecedented development. Even before the rise of the Reform movement, there were Ashkenazic and Sephardic communities living side by side and employing a parallel set of rabbis, shochtim and cantors. Similarly, the rift between *Mithnagdim* and *Hassidim* demonstrated the capacity of Judaism to make room for a variety of emphases in religious expression, within the general pattern of loyalty to the tradition.

We call upon our colleagues in the Conservative movement to give to the program of Sabbath revitalization pre-eminence in the many duties they are called upon to discharge. אחינו וחברינו, as rabbis in one of the most difficult and confusing ages for Judaism, we must consecrate our greatest efforts to the preservation of the most sacred institution in Jewish life. In our congregations and in the life of our communities we must, by every means at our disposal and through all the influence and energy we command, bring a heightening consciousness of the sanctity of the Sabbath. We must rally about us the most loyal and understanding members of our congregations and prepare a concerted attack upon Jewish indifference, neglect and ignorance. Our movement nationally must mobilize its best talents and its most dedicated spirits and make of the renewal of Sabbath observance the main object of our efforts. This breach in our wall must be repaired and none among us must rest or divert his energies to other work until American Jewish life is made safe for the Sabbath. We regard this responsum as but the humblest of beginnings in that direction.

By tireless activity, by earnest planning and unwearying persistence it may yet be given to us to bring back the Sabbath to its former glory as a reservoir of Jewish spiritual strength, renewal and inspiration. We earnestly pray

ויהי נועם ה אלוהינו עלינו ומעשה ידינו כוננה עלינו ומעשה ידינו כוננהו.

And Let the pleasantness of the Lord God be upon us
And establish Thou the work of our hands upon us
Yea, the work of our hands establish Thou it.

185

RIDING ON THE SABBATH

Rabbi David Novak
[Footnote references have been omitted.]

There was a time in Jewish history when it was assumed that the vast majority of Jews kept the Sabbath. The effects of this collective Sabbath not only extended to human lives but even to the natural world. There are stories about rivers that would not flow on the Sabbath and oxen who behaved towards the human beings around them differently on the Sabbath than on any other day.

Today the Sabbath-observer is in a minority. Although it is true that many contemporary Jews have partial Sabbath experiences, whether synagogue attendance, lighting candles, or eating special foods, fewer have experienced what the prophet described:

> If because of the Sabbath you turn away your foot from pursuing your business on My holy day, and you call the Sabbath a delight and make it honored...then shall you find delight in the Lord... (Isa. 58:13-14)

The reasons for the weakening of Sabbath-observance, especially among modern American Jews, are seemingly economic and demographic.

Earlier in this century, when large masses of Jews were immigrating to this country from Eastern Europe, economic conditions made Sabbath observance an extreme hardship for many of these people. With the breakup of the semiautonomous communities in which these Jews had lived for centuries, the centrifugal forces of emancipation had economic as well as religious and cultural consequences. In Europe Jewish artisans and petty traders to a large extent controlled the market in which they operated. The non-Jewish peasants came to them. Thus the economic patterns of life were a function of the community as a whole, a community regulated by Jewish religious norms. In America these Jews were thrown into an open-market situation controlled by economic and cultural forces outside their community. As such they now had to go to the non-Jewish world to sell their goods and services.

However, the phenomenon of the American five-day week, although not affecting such occupations as retailing, has indeed affected many other Jews, especially with the gradual broadening of the occupational involvement of American Jews. Most people are no longer required to work on Saturday.

Nevertheless, as regards Sabbath-observance, the lessening of the economic problem has almost simultaneously coincided with the development of a demographic problem. With the availability of the automobile to virtually every American family, housing patterns have arisen that have all but eliminated walking as a practical means of locomotion in a community. Religious considerations aside, how many suburban housing-developments have sidewalks? Therefore, the notion of "neighborhood" as previously understood has been radically altered. Most modern synagogues serving suburban areas are beyond reasonable walking distance for a large number of their members. This is why the question about riding on the Sabbath is probably asked more often than any other question of

Sabbath-observance. Indeed, the popular definition of a "Sabbath-keeper" (*shomer shabbat*) is usually expressed in terms of "Does he or she ride on the Sabbath or not?"

Question: What is the source of the prohibition of riding on the Sabbath?

Answer: In Jewish law there are two irreducible sources of perennial authority: (1) the Written Torah, the Pentateuch; (2) the Oral Torah, the traditions ascribed to Moses (*halakhot*), which were kept as if written in the Torah, even though their specific prescription could not be found in the text of the Pentateuch. These two sources were always regarded by normative Judaism as revelations of God's will.

All other legislation is secondary. It has had to justify itself as either: (I) direct interpretation of Scripture (*derash*); (2) indirect interpretation of Scripture (*asmakhta*); (3) protection of scriptural laws by "fencing" them with additional laws (*gezerot*); or (4) adjustment of specific laws in the interest of greater priorities (*takkanot*).

In the area of Sabbath-observance, the Mishnah classifies thirty-nine specific acts (*abot melekhah*) as subsets of the general prohibition: "On the seventh day, a Sabbath unto the Lord your God, you shall do no work..." (Exod. 20:10). These thirty-nine acts were determined by carefully analyzing the different kinds of labor involved in the building of the Sanctuary (*mishkan*) in the wilderness under the direction of Moses. Since the penalty for working on the Sabbath is directly juxtaposed (*semukhim*) in the Torah to the detailed description of the building of the Sanctuary, the rabbis concluded that this was meant to specify just what the Torah meant by "work" in relation to the Sabbath.

Furthermore, the juxtaposition accomplished two things: (1) It demonstrated that the Sabbath as a "Sanctuary in time" had priority over the building of the physical Sanctuary in space. As important as the building of the Sanctuary was, it did not surpass the observance of the Sabbath. This idea was profoundly developed by my late revered teacher, Professor A. J. Heschel, in his book, *The Sabbath*. (2) It established an objective historical criterion for work, which applied to all Jews since the entire people of Israel, men and women, participated in the building of the Sanctuary (Exod. 35:25-26). The only other criterion would be the highly subjective category, "exertion," which would obviously vary from individual to individual. The Sabbath was meant to be a social institution.

Nevertheless, our sages, although using a historical criterion, were interpreting a law whose source is transhistorical. Despite the fact that the labors involved in the building of the wilderness Sanctuary are the paradigm for the labors prohibited on the Sabbath, there was certainly a recognition that the situation in the wilderness was not in every respect identical with subsequent Jewish history.

The revelation of the law in a particular time and place might very well influence its initial meaning, but it certainly did not confine its ultimate meaning. As the Torah states, "...from the day the Lord commanded and henceforth for your generations" (Num. 15:23). To limit the prohibition of work only to labors performed in the Sanctuary would have the effect of relativizing the concept of work on the Sabbath. Such limitation would shrink the hegemony of the law with each new technological innovation or change. Therefore, derivative acts (*toldot*), which are clearly related to the primary acts (*abot*), although not in themselves identifiable with the construction of the Sanctuary in the wilderness, were also prohibited. Since the number of such derivative acts is potentially infinite, their affirmation saves the hegemony of the law from becoming contingent on historical circumstance. Thus the principles of the law, in our case the Sabbath law, are seen as transcending *any* finite period *within* Jewish history, and, therefore, are applicable to *all* Jewish history.

Now there is no specific prohibition of riding on the Sabbath in either of the primary sources of Jewish law. In other words, there is no explicit "You shall not ride on the Sabbath" in either Torah or tradition. Therefore, the prohibition of riding is either a derived prohibition (*toldah*), or a rabbinic "fence" built to protect the Sabbath (*gezerah*).

1. Automobile Driving

The first case of riding to be considered is that of driving an automobile, since this is the most common way most of us ride today. Driving an automobile, although obviously not directly prohibited in sources first published centuries ago, involves three main areas with which the sources most definitely did deal: (1) combustion of fuel; (2) locomotion over distances not normally covered by walking; (3) various preparations required for travel.

Concerning combustion of fuel the Written Torah states, "You shall not kindle fire in any of your dwelling places on the Sabbath day" (Exod. 35:3). "Dwelling places" refers to anywhere one happens to be. Every time one starts his automobile he is igniting the gasoline in the motor.

In 1950 three members of the Rabbinical Assembly presented a responsum that attempted to legally justify riding on the Sabbath, if one's destination were the synagogue. The responsum created a sensation within the Conservative rabbinate and far beyond. What is much less known, however, is that dissenting papers were prepared by Dr. Robert Gordis and Dr. Ben Zion Bokser. These papers, learned and well written though they were, did not really show the halakhic fallacy upon which this whole dispensation (*heter*) was based. They were, rather, elaborations of the dissenters' theological objections.

Since I was only eight years old in June of 1950, I was not personally involved in the heated discussions that accompanied this responsum or the *ad hominem* attacks that were inevitable in such a charged atmosphere. Therefore, I believe that I can be more objective than my predecessors of twenty-three years ago in showing the fallacy of permitting riding on the Sabbath, especially driving an automobile.

The three rabbis (Dr. Jacob B. Agus, Dr. Theodore Friedman, and the late R. Morris Adler) argued that kindling is only prohibited when there is a need for it *as there was a need for it in the construction of the Sanctuary*. Since combustion for energy was not needed in the building of the Sanctuary, this analogy would rule that combustion for energy is not a prohibited form of kindling on the Sabbath. This is presented as the view of the Tanna, R. Simon, as interpreted by R. Isaac the Elder (Ri).

> The combustion of gasoline to produce power is a type of work that obviously could not have been prohibited before its invention. All acts of burning are prohibited only when performed for specially described purposes such as: cooking, heating, lighting or the need of its ashes.

188

> Burning for the sake of power was not included in this list....The combustion of gas in the carburator is therefore the type of work classed as *m'lachah shaina tzrichah l'gufa* [work not needed for itself]...

This reasoning is halakhically inadmissible for the following reasons:

1. Even if this is a correct interpretation of the position of R. Simon, the law is not according to him.

2. Even according to R. Simon the act is certainly rabbinically prohibited (*assur*) even if not actually liable according to scriptural law (*patur*).

3. R. Simon's view concerns removing something on the Sabbath for a negative rather than a positive purpose. Rashi states:

   > It is an act not performed for its own sake, but only to remove something from the actor...for it did not come to him out of choice and he had no need of it, therefore it is not a premediated act [*melekhet mahshabat*] according to R. Simon.

   Thus, according to Rashi, even R. Simon would hold that any act performed for a positive purpose is scripturally prohibited (*hayyab*).

4. The Tosafists point out that an act was prohibited when it was done to accomplish something that would not have existed before (*l'taken yoter mimah shehayah batehilah*). Unless one accepts the position of the ancient Greek physicist Zeno that locomotion does not exist, a position successfully refuted by Aristotle, igniting an engine to drive an automobile certainly accomplishes something.

5. Moreover, it should be noted that even though the Mishnah holds that only constructive acts violate the Sabbath in the scriptural sense (*d'oraita*), the Talmud includes one who injures a fellow man where injury, a negative act, is the motive. Maimonides holds that the reason for this is that the person did something positive; namely, he appeased anger. Therefore, a seemingly negative act had a positive end (*veharay hu k'metaken*). If a purely subjective state of mind is considered a positive end, how much more is combustion for the sake of locomotion, which is an objective fact?

6. It is surprising that these rabbis, who so emphasized that the Halakhah was never "a frigid and frozen mold" should base their reasoning on a view that, if accepted at face value, would rule out any expansion, which is a positive aspect of the development of the Halakhah. As often happens, extremes look alike. What looks like progress is at times regression.

In short, this whole line of reasoning is unacceptable because it violates the two cardinal principles of all reasoning: the principle of contradiction and the principle of sufficient reason. The position of the three rabbis contradicts itself on the one hand by calling for the development of Jewish law, and on the other hand by presenting a standard that would make the definition of work dependent on conditions in the time of Moses. And their position is based on an insufficient use of the sources, in that they present a minority interpretation of a minority opinion.

As regards combustion for the sake of locomotion, if it is not "kindling" (*habarah*) in the original sense (*ab*), then it is certainly "kindling" in the derived sense (*toladah*). Practically, there is no difference between the two. The only difference between the two categories concerns the sacrifices brought for their unwitting (*shegagah*) transgression. The sacrificial system has been inoperative for almost two thousand years.

2. *Riding in a Vehicle Driven by Someone Else*

The next question involved in riding on the Sabbath is the matter of traveling distances not normally covered by walking. The Torah states, "Let everyone remain in his place; let no one go out from his place on the seventh day" (Exod. 16:29). Now what is considered a person's place (*mekomo*)?

The Karaites, a group of Jewish biblical literalists, over a thousand years ago interpreted this verse to mean that on the Sabbath one's place is restricted to home and synagogue. However, in the rabbinic tradition, of which we are the heirs, one's place is interpreted as the normal space of one's community and its outlying areas. These were determined to be the limits of one's city plus two thousand cubits (three thousand feet, or approximately a half-mile). This area is known as the *tehum*. If one wanted to walk beyond this distance he had to make special provision (*erub*) for the extension of this limit another two thousand cubits in any given direction. Because of the great areas of space covered by our metropolitan communities, this is rarely a problem today. Nevertheless, I remember the son of Grand Rabbin Fuchs of Lorraine telling me that his father has to make this special provision regularly in order to travel on foot from his seat in Colmar to visit outlying towns on the Sabbath.

We can thus see that the intention of the law is to keep one in the vicinity of his or her own neighborhood -- "neighborhood" being the area of normal walking distance.

However, a question does arise as to the use of public transportation on the Sabbath under the following conditions: (1) the vehicle is driven by a non-Jew; (2) the vehicle makes regular stops irrespective of the presence of Jewish passengers; (3) its route is confined to the municipal limits; (4) one is not required to pay his fare on the Sabbath (or Festival).

Practically this would be a possibility if one had a pass attached to his or her clothing, enabling the person to ride on a bus, streetcar, or similar public conveyance. The late Sephardic Chief Rabbi of Israel R. Ben Zion Uziel (d. 1954), addressed himself to this question in a responsum written over thirty-five years ago. He admitted that such travel was legally permissible, especially to attend synagogue services. He pointed out that earlier prohibitions of riding were based on the fact that animals were being used to work on the Sabbath, something the Torah explicitly forbade. Nevertheless, more general theological concerns influenced him to refuse to allow this halakhic leniency in actual practice.

His main point was that the Sabbath must be kept in the spirit of the law as well as in its letter. This desire to extend the physical and spiritual rest of the Sabbath was behind the rabbinic institution of *shebut* -- the prohibition of acts resembling work, even though not work in the technical legal sense. R. Uziel quotes both Maimonides and Nahmanides on this general point. More specifically, he quotes the leading nineteenth-century authority. R. Moses Schreiber of Pressburg (Hatam Sofer, d. 1839), who prohibited such travel because it creates both physical and mental tension inconsistent with the spirit of Sabbath rest. Nevertheless, R. Uziel points out that the anxiety meant is that of a business trip, and this would not be the same as a trip to the synagogue for Sabbath worship. On the basis of this distinction he dismisses R. Schreiber's prohibition and permits such riding, provided the other preconditions are present. R. Uziel claims that if tension is the key factor (*gufo na ve'nad*), then travel on foot ought to be prohibited too. However I would say that in our day the mere experience of being in traffic creates far more tension for the rider than for the pedestrian, irrespective of what his purpose in riding is.

In a subsequent edition of his responsa published twelve years later R. Uziel emphasized to a rabbi in Bombay that anyone who "fears and trembles for the word of the Lord" ought not ride in *any* vehicle on the Sabbath and Festivals, irrespective of the conditions. Why R. Uziel so abruptly changed his view is unknown to me. I can only suspect that his dispensation met with strong rabbinical opposition and that he yielded, "inclining after the majority."

The problem with this kind of travel is that public transportation in our day inevitably involves direct payment and other preparations not in keeping with the Sabbath. The Talmud states, "One is not to ride on an animal on the Sabbath lest he go beyond the limits of travel [*tehum*] and even more so lest he cut a twig to prod the animal." The limits of travel were marked for pedestrians, but, as Rashi pointed out, one riding may overlook them. Furthermore, various auxiliary acts, such as carrying money, identification, and automobile-repair tools, are the modern equivalents of "cutting a twig to prod the animal." This point was brought out in the bitter criticism of several members of the Rabbinical Assembly following the presentation of the responsum of the three rabbis in 1950.

Moreover, there is the problem of the Jew who drives his or her car to the synagogue on the Sabbath to attend services. Should this person be told to stay home? Here one must know who is asking the question about riding to the synagogue on the Sabbath.

If the person is already a Sabbath-observer, I do not hesitate to inform him or her not to ride to the synagogue. In one particular case, an observant man in my congregation fractured his leg before Rosh Hashanah. The only way he could attend the synagogue services to hear the blowing of the shofar was to ride. I told him that he should not ride even if this meant he would not hear the blowing of the shofar. After all. our sages prohibited the blowing of the shofar on Rosh Hashanah coinciding with the Sabbath lest people carry the shofar. In other words, the restraining sanctity of the Sabbath or Festival takes precedence even over a positive, Torah-ordained institution. As it happens, God helps those who desire to do His will, and the injured man heard the shofar blown in his home by a teenage member of the congregation. One can always have the full Sabbath at home even without the synagogue but one cannot have the full Sabbath at the synagogue without the home.

On the other hand, there are many people who if told not to ride to the synagogue on the Sabbath would continue riding everywhere *but* to the synagogue. For them the synagogue's influence would be lost altogether. Therefore, it is wiser not to condemn people who are unprepared as yet to become full Sabbath-observers. As the Talmud puts it.

R. Iylaa said in the name of R. Eleazar ben R. Simon that just as one is commanded to say something which will be heard, so one is commanded not to say something which will not be heard.

However, once such people begin to seriously ask about the Halakhah of riding on the Sabbath they are usually at a level where they are ready to translate the synagogue Sabbath experience into their own personal action. I know several people who came by automobile when they began attending Sabbath services. Later, as they came closer to God and the Torah, they stopped riding to services. In some cases this involved purchasing or renting a house or apartment closer to the synagogue. One chooses where to live on the basis of his or her life-priorities. If Sabbath-observance is high on the list of those priorities, one will make it his business to live in the neighborhood of the synagogue. If Sabbath-observance is not high on one's list of priorities, choice of a home will be determined by other considerations. The late Professor Louis Ginzberg (d. 1953) was entirely correct, it seems to me, in refusing to endorse innovations in Jewish Law designed to exonerate Jews "most of whom had long ago denied its authority."

Finally, a fundamental spiritual problem was overlooked by those who felt that they were saving the Sabbath by permitting people to ride to the synagogue. The assumption underlying this dispensation ignores the possibility of repentance (*teshubah*). To tell people who are not living according to the law of the Torah that what they are doing is correct is to close the door of return in their faces. It places a "stumbling block before the blind." The same is true, on the other hand, if we fail to see that riding to the synagogue, although not permissible, is spiritually on a higher level than driving to business or to a place of amusement. In other words, driving to the synagogue may be the beginning of a true return for persons who have never known any other kind of Sabbath.

In practice I have come to the following conclusions:

1. Driving an automobile is prohibited according to scriptural law in a derived sense (*toladah*), if not in an original sense.

2. Riding on a public conveyance where no other preparations are necessary and in a non-Jewish area is almost too remote a possibility to rule on. Moreover, because of the tension and anxiety involved in any vehicular travel today, such travel is inconsistent with the spirit of the law. The whole institution of *shebut* (rabbinically prohibited activities on the Sabbath) is the practical outcome of speculating on the deeper meaning of the Sabbath.

3. Observant Jews should be warned of the prohibition of travel on the Sabbath, even in order to attend synagogue services. Non-observant Jews should be dealt with more cautiously lest their contact with the synagogue be severed and they be further alienated from the Torah.

CHAPTER IV
THE BELIEFS OF THE CONSERVATIVE MOVEMENT

A. *The Interaction of Action and Belief*

You probably have noticed that we began with Conservative Judaism's approach to Jewish law rather than its understanding of Jewish beliefs. That was not by accident. We began that way for two reasons. First, Judaism itself begins that way, as in this famous statement of the Rabbis:

> "They have deserted Me and have not kept My Law" (Jeremiah 16:11). God says, "Would that they had deserted Me and kept My Law, for if they had occupied themselves with the Law, the leaven which is in it would have brought them back to me."[1] (*Pesikta d'Rav Kahana*, XV)

> ‮אתי עזבו ואת תורתי לא שמרו. הלווי אתי עזבו ותורתי שמרו שאילו אתי עזבו ותורתי‬
> ‮שמרו מתוך שהיו מתעסקין בה השאור שבת היה מחזירן אצלי.‬

In other words, Judaism historically has centered on action rather than on faith, and Conservative Judaism does so likewise.

Secondly, while matters of belief are discussed thoroughly within classical Jewish sources, and while we could probably even describe a mainstream Jewish position on many issues, Judaism has largely left it to individuals to decide the particular form of Jewish belief they will adopt, as long as they continue to observe Jewish law. Under pressure from Christians and Muslims, there were some attempts to define a set of Jewish dogmas during the Middle Ages, but no such formulation ever became authoritative such that Jews had to subscribe to that formulation of Jewish belief or else consider themselves no longer to be Jews. This failure of any list of Jewish beliefs to have the power to define people as falling within or outside the Jewish community is a clear indication of how deeply freedom of thought is ingrained in Judaism.

Since many Jews simply assume that freedom of thought is inherent in Judaism, it may be helpful to contrast Judaism with Christianity on this issue. Both Judaism and Christianity assert a set of beliefs and expect that adherents will live out those beliefs in forms of action, but the emphasis in the two religions is different: in Judaism it is on action, with wide-ranging freedom of thought as a result, while in Christianity the stress is on belief, with comparatively little specificity as to the actions which Christians must perform to demonstrate their faith.

Christianity has had a long history of setting its beliefs in official formulations (called "creeds") which Christians are called upon to affirm. This does not mean that intellectual discussion among Christians ceased with the adoption of a creed; quite the contrary, over the course of time, differences in doctrine led to much splintering within Christianity into denominations (in the United States there are more than 150), in some cases over matters of background and style but in others over serious doctrinal issues. This focus on belief within Christianity means that even if you were born into a Christian family, you would not consider yourself to be Christian unless you affirmed a belief in Jesus as Christ, and you would not see yourself as Catholic, Presbyterian, Baptist, etc. unless you believed that particular denomination's formulation of Christian belief.

In Judaism, in contrast, rabbis and philosophers over the centuries have articulated many different understandings of Jewish belief, and laypeople have had yet other understandings. One could not affirm Jesus as the Messiah and still be Jewish, and one could not avow the idolatry inherent in a religion like Hinduism and still be Jewish; that is, there were and are *some* limits on how far one can go in one's beliefs if one still wants to be called Jewish. Thus if one was born Jewish or converted halakhically to Judaism and then later professed belief in some other religion, one became an apostate (a *meshumad*), losing all the privileges of being Jewish (being married or buried as a Jew, counting as part of a minyan, having honors within the Jewish community, etc.), but one continued to be subject to its obligations! (That is the status of "Jews for Jesus," sometimes called "Messianic Jews": they are apostates and therefore are not granted any of the privileges of being Jews.)

The limits of acceptable Jewish belief among those who abide by Jewish law, though, have historically been interpreted very broadly, leading some rabbis in the early modern period to allow even a variety of superstitions and superstitious practices, such as amulets and red ribbons to ward off evil spirits.[2] Thus while Christianity's emphasis on belief has led it to be both precise and demanding in what Christians must affirm but relatively unspecific as to what Christians must do to demonstrate their faith, Judaism's way is exactly the opposite: through Jewish law and ethics, Judaism makes clear demands on what one must do, but because Jewish faith is defined primarily in terms of action, Judaism leaves plenty of room for Jews to articulate the thought behind their faith as they desire. This liberality in thought is one of the main reasons why Judaism is as vital, stimulating, and realistic as it is.

Moreover, it must always be remembered that thought and action are not two separate realms functioning independently of each other. What we think and feel inevitably has an effect on what we do, and, conversely, what we do significantly influences how we think and feel. We are not, after all, separately body and soul, or body and mind; we are whole human beings, created such that every aspect of our being interacts with every other aspect. Forgetting that leads some mistakenly to think that good intentions or feeling Jewish in one's heart is enough, and it leads others to the opposite error of ignoring Jewish beliefs and values in mechanically acting according to Jewish law (what Rabbi Heschel poignantly called "religious behaviorism"[3]). Judaism speaks to our minds and hearts just as much as it speaks to what we do with our bodies, and authentic Jewish faith involves and integrates all of the aspects of our being.

Conservative Judaism embodies that kind of authentic Jewish faith. It seeks to weave our Jewish moral and intellectual commitments into our Jewish practice and into our lives generally, just as it seeks to infuse our actions with the thoughtfulness and moral sensitivity which Judaism demands. Moreover, in the intellectual realm, it affirms basic Jewish beliefs and denies the legitimacy of believing in other religions or in idolatry of any form while still claiming to be fully Jewish; at the same time, Conservative Jews engage in vibrant and free-wheeling discussion and argument as to how Jewish beliefs should be understood and put into practice.

Thus while Conservative Jews as a group believe in God, Torah, and Israel, the interpretations vary widely. In fact, people affiliated with the Conservative Movement have been among the most creative Jewish thinkers during the twentieth century. Thus in thought as in law, Conservative Judaism is true to the classical Jewish tradition as it has developed over the centuries: it has a mainstream position, but it also has many variations on that theme, and the diversity in issues of thought is more extensive than the differences in practice.

Rabbi Solomon Schechter enunciated that position long ago. He speaks of the "theology" of the new approach to Judaism he and other founders of Conservative Judaism were espousing. "Theology," in the narrow sense of the word, is, literally, talk about God. In the broader sense of the word, theologies present views not only of God, but of other religious topics, such as creation, revelation, redemption, prayer, rituals, and morality. While pointing out that "the historical school has never, to my knowledge, offered to the world a theological programme of its own,"[4] he nevertheless wrote an essay entitled "The Dogmas of Judaism" specifically in an attempt to

> ...contribute something towards destroying the illusion, in which so many
> theologians indulge, that Judaism is a religion without dogmas. To declare that
> a religion has no dogmas is tantamount to saying that it was wise enough not
> to commit itself to any vital principles. But prudence, useful as it may be in
> worldly affairs, is quite unworthy of a great spiritual power.[5]

195

There are many versions of Jewish belief, but Judaism does stand for a particular orientation to life.

QUESTIONS:

1) What is a "theology"? Why is it important to have one?

   (Consider the remark of the late Prof. Louis Ginzberg: "Theology is not religion, and yet whoever has any religious experience must have some form of theology. Theology is the articulation of religion."[6])

2) True or false: "You can believe anything you want and still be Jewish." Explain your answer.

3) True or false: "Judaism tolerates more forms of belief than Christianity does." Explain your answer, indicating the features of Judaism and Christianity which lead to their differing relationships to their own beliefs.

4) What is the status of those Jews who fall outside the acceptable limits of Jewish belief? State both the Hebrew word for such people and their legal status in Jewish law -- that is, the parts of the Jewish tradition which still apply to them and the parts which do not. Give some examples of such groups.

5) Are our beliefs and actions totally independent of each other? If so, what do you think leads us to think as we do and to act as we do? If not, give some specific examples of how beliefs affect our actions and how our actions affect our beliefs.

6) For authentic Jewish faith, is it sufficient to act in accordance with the commandments? Is it sufficient to believe the tenets of Judaism? Is it sufficient to join Jewish organizations? Is it sufficient to feel Jewish? If Judaism demands all of these things -- actions, beliefs, associations, and feelings -- and more, what does that say about the nature of Judaism?

7) Describe the stance of Conservative Judaism on Jewish beliefs. What does it demand in the way of beliefs, what does it deny, and what does it allow? How does it understand the relationship between our beliefs, our moral standards, and our actions?

ACTIVITY:

Jewish tradition teaches that a person's beliefs are best evidenced in the way that a person lives his/her life.

Fill in the chart below and see what your beliefs imply about the way in which you act in the world:

IF I BELIEVE THAT...	THEN I SHOULD...
God is just.	Work to ensure that people are treated justly.
God doesn't care about the world.	Not worry about anyone but myself (or I have no choice but to care!).
(Now you continue.)	

B. *The Core of Conservative Beliefs*

What affirmations constitute the mainstream position within Conservative Judaism? From the very beginning of the movement, Conservative Jews had a reasonably clear idea of why they were establishing this new movement. They listed their convictions and their intentions in the Charter of the Jewish Theological Seminary of America (1902) and in the Preamble to the Constitution of the United Synagogue (1913). (A copy of relevant sections of those documents appears as Appendix III and Appendix IV at the end of this book.) As stated there, the purpose of the organizations they were founding was to further traditional Jewish knowledge and practice in a modern setting. That would, in the founders' view, entail observance of the Sabbath and dietary laws, prayer using essentially Hebrew liturgy, Jewish home life, study of our tradition using all the intellectual tools available to scholarship, a strong tie to Israel and Zionism, and fostering good relations with the non-Jewish community, including, presumably, cooperative efforts to improve the world.

These broad outlines of what Conservative Judaism stands for, then, were evident even at the inception. Over the decades of the twentieth century, individual Conservative rabbis and laypeople wrote articles and books about Conservative Judaism, all of which added to the developing consciousness of the nature of Conservative beliefs.[7] It was not until 1988, however, that an official statement of Conservative beliefs was published -- another indication of the ideological vitality and freedom within the Movement. The delay in publishing such a document until then was motivated in large measure by the fact that Conservative Jewish leaders gloried in the pluralism within the movement and did not want to restrict its popularity and vitality by defining too clearly the limits of what was a legitimate form of Conservative beliefs and what was not. Whether intended or not, delaying the publication of such a document until after the movement was a century old had another good result: it provided a reasonable period of time for those within the movement to articulate the beliefs which had emerged out of the experience of living as Conservative Jews.

In the 1970s, though, there was increasing uneasiness with the lack of definition within Conservative Judaism. The last chapter of the first edition of this book (1977) included some comments by movement leaders reflecting that uneasiness. They worried that if the boundaries were completely undefined or defined too broadly, the Movement would lack coherence, and without focus it would not be able to generate passion and commitment. After all, if you stand for everything, you stand for nothing -- or so it seems. Moreover, if you want to attract new numbers of Jews to our fold, then you have to explain why they should become Conservative Jews, and that is virtually impossible to do without a reasonably clear platform. Nobody wanted to ruin the pluralism within the movement, for, as Conservative leaders for decades have rightly perceived, that pluralism is one of Conservative Judaism's real strengths; but some effort at increased clarity and definition was definitely needed. The first edition of this book was written, in part, in response to that need, and hopefully it helped Conservative Jews understand their faith better (as, I trust, this edition will do as well!). This book, though, is the product of one Conservative rabbi who can only claim to describe the movement to the best of his ability.

That limitation was especially important with regard to this chapter of the first edition of this book, for nowhere had the Conservative movement officially described its views on its beliefs, including such central topics as God, prayer, halakhah, the State of Israel, and eschatology (that is, concepts of the end time, including some which describe a world radically transformed from our own and others which speak of a life after death). Individual Conservative thinkers had written books on their own theologies by 1977, the date of the first edition of this book,[8] and the number of such books since then has increased significantly.[9] (You will find a list of many of those books in these last two notes for this chapter in the section of endnotes at the end of this book. The lists in those notes will give you a sense of the great theological productivity in the Conservative movement and can serve as a resource for your own further reading.) The movement as a whole, though, has not officially adopted any of the theologies of its individual members. That is exactly what one would hope, for if the movement endorsed one particular theology over others, it would stifle theological creativity and diversity.

At the same time, even though there was no official formulation of Conservative Jewish beliefs, the movement was not without theological convictions. From the liturgical publications of the movement, the decisions of the Committee on Jewish Law and Standards, the resolutions passed by various arms of the movement, and, most importantly, from the ongoing practices of Conservative Jews personally and institutionally it was clear that Conservative Judaism embraced a belief in God, in the binding character of Jewish law, in the need for regular prayer in the traditional Hebrew liturgy (with a few changes), in the importance of *kelal yisrael* (the Jewish community as a whole) in both the Diaspora and Israel, and in the mission of *tikkun olam* תִּקוּן עוֹלָם (fixing the world) as part of our covenantal charge from God. Even that list, though, was never officially described and endorsed by the movement.

In response to the increasingly felt need to articulate our beliefs as a movement, the arms of the movement, at the initiative of Rabbi Alexander Shapiro, z"l, President of the Rabbinical Assembly at the time, and Rabbi Gerson Cohen, z"l, Chancellor of the Seminary, convened a Commission on the Philosophy of Conservative Judaism. Meeting five or six times per year from 1985 to 1988, the Commission, which included representatives from the major arms of the Movement, ultimately published *Emet Ve-Emunah: Statement of Principles of Conservative Judaism* and two educational guides for teaching it, one for adults (by Rabbis Elliot Dorff and Sheldon Dorph) and one for teenagers (by Dr. Steven Brown).

Emet Ve-Emunah (which means, literally, "truth and faith," the first words after the Shema in the evening service) states the beliefs and commitments of Conservative Judaism in approximately 40 pages. At times it acknowledges that some within the Conservative community believe *x* and some believe *y* about a given subject, a reflection of the pluralism within the movement. For the most part, though, the booklet states the beliefs of Conservative Judaism unequivocally and thoughtfully, describing not only the beliefs themselves but also some of the reasons why Conservative Jews hold them.

Now that *Emet Ve-Emunah* exists, it is important for Conservative Jews to study it, preferably with the aid of one of the two study guides designed to enrich discussion of it. So that readers of this book will have a sense of the core of Conservative beliefs, though, I will list the titles of the sections of that document on the following pages and summarize the points that it makes, sometimes using phrases or sentences from the document itself.

Following the medieval structuring of Jewish belief around God, Torah, and Israel, *Emet Ve-Emunah* is divided into sections on those three topics:

SUMMARY OF EMET VE-EMUNAH

GOD IN THE WORLD

1) God

a. We believe in God, but we understand God in different ways.

b. It is normal and acceptable to have moments of doubt in one's faith and to ask searching questions about Judaism generally and about God in particular. One is not supposed to accept beliefs passively on faith -- or ignore the subject altogether.

c. Some within the Conservative movement picture God as a supreme, supernatural being; others understand God to be a presence and power that transcends us but not the universe.

d. For both views, God is evident whenever we look for meaning in the world and when we work for morality and future redemption.

2) Revelation

a. We believe in God's revelation to us at Mount Sinai and in God's continuing revelation to us through study of Jewish texts and through our lives as Jews.

b. Some believe that God's revelation at Sinai and subsequently consists of God's own words (Conservative I); others believe that God inspired Moses to write what he did and has continued to inspire others (Conservative II); and still others believe that revelation consists of a human encounter with God to which the people involved respond, in part, by trying to articulate the nature and meaning of that encounter (Conservative III).

c. Revelation can take place through our continuing interaction with nature and history and through our Jewish study and action.

3) Halakhah (Jewish Law)

a. Jewish law is indispensable to what it means to be a Jew for theological, communal, and moral reasons.

b. The sanctity and authority of Halakhah attaches to the body of the law, not to each law separately, for throughout Jewish history Halakhah has been subject to change.

c. Change in Halakhah is not done for its own sake or out of disregard for the law; on the contrary, when rabbis change Jewish law, they do so to enable it to respond to the needs and circumstances of the times and to embody new ethical insights and goals.

d. Authority for religious practices in each congregation rests with the rabbi of that congregation (its *mara d'atra*); rabbis may consult the Committee on Jewish Law and Standards, which issues rulings shaping the practice of the Conservative community.

4) The Problem of Evil.

a. No theology can justify the mass slaughter of the blameless, as in the Holocaust, or the seeming randomness with which natural disaster strikes. We deny as false and blasphemous the assertion of some that the Holocaust was the result of its victims' transgressions or of the sins of Jewry as a whole.

b. We must recognize that much of the world's suffering, though, results from the misuses of human free will.

c. When words fail us, when we cannot understand why someone suffers, we can and should nevertheless respond with acts of compassion and healing as well as with the ritual acts of our tradition like *shivah* which help people cope with their suffering or loss.

d. Despite the existence of unjustified suffering, we affirm that all is not chance, that, in general, right-doing does lead to well-being while wrong-doing results in disaster, and that there is a divine plan even when we cannot clearly discern its contours.

5. Eschatology: Our Vision of the Future.

a. We share classical Judaism's hopes for the future, specifically:

    i. on the individual level, that death does not mark the absolute end of a person's identity;

    ii. on the national level, that the Jewish people may be master of its own identity and successful in finding fulfillment as a people; and

    iii. on the universal level, that warfare, disease, and every social evil cease forever and that, conversely, all human beings enjoy a social order based on justice, compassion, and peace.

b. Some Conservative Jews believe classical statements on these matters literally and others understand them metaphorically. Since no one knows what will happen "in the days to come," dogmatism in these matters is philosophically unjustified and potentially hazardous.

c. We affirm a gradualist or evolutionary approach toward achieving Judaism's messianic goals, not one which employs revolutionary and often murderous methods.

THE JEWISH PEOPLE

1. God's Covenant: The Election of Israel

a. "The election of Israel" and "the covenant of Israel" are two sides of the same coin. That is, the Chosen People idea expresses our self-understanding of having a special mission which we promised to fulfill in our mutual promises (our "covenant") with God to transform this world into a Kingdom of the Almighty (*malkhut shaddai*).

b. The idea of Jews being God's Chosen People has been distorted into an expression of moral arrogance, that we Jews claim to be better than other nations. Because of that distortion, and because of the anti-Semitism caused by it, some within our movement would like to replace the Chosen People concept with the idea that each nation has its particular vocation.

c. Whether God has a unique relationship with the People Israel, unparalleled by specific covenants with other people, or whether God has a particular covenant with us and other covenants with other nations, the covenant idea states that we Jews have the mission to be a people dedicated to the service of God and to God's world. This concept thus offers a purpose for Jewish existence beyond our own narrow self-interest.

2. The State of Israel and the Role of Religion.

a. *Religious Freedom*: The State of Israel must preserve religious freedom for Jews as well as for all others. It should permit all rabbis, regardless of affiliation, to perform religious functions such as marriages, divorces, and conversions; failure to do that is to grant religious freedom to people of all religions except Jews!

b. *The Religious Factor*: Israel must balance religious freedom with its identity as a Jewish state, a balance which is often hard to strike. In general, though, without being a theocracy, Israel should reflect the highest religious and moral values of Judaism and be saturated with Jewish living to the fullest extent possible in a free society.

c. *Religious understanding*: We call for maximum dialogue and cooperation between religious and non-religious elements of Israeli society.

d. *The Role of Religion in a Free Society*: religion should act as a moral voice in Israeli society, not as a political power base for religious coercion.

e. *The Uniqueness of Israel*: Israel should be a morally exemplary state. While understanding the bounds of necessary security measures, we affirm that the litmus test of Israel's success in this mission will be its fair treatment of minorities.

3. Israel and the Diaspora.

a. *The Central Role of Israel*: We rejoice in the reborn national homeland in Israel. We understand the State of Israel not only in political and military terms, but in religious terms as well, a product of God's promise to our ancestors and their descendants. Judaism, though, has been land-centered but never land-bound, and through the centuries we have been able to survive creatively and spiritually in the Diaspora (*tefutzot*) as well.

b. *Conservative Judaism and Israel*: The well-being of the State of Israel is a major concern of the Conservative Movement, expressed by our affiliation through *Mercaz* with the World Zionist Organization, our political and economic activities in the Diaspora on behalf of Israel, our pilgrimages there, our members who make *aliyah*, and the many projects we have established there through our *Masorti* synagogues, our rabbinical school, and our educational projects for children and teenagers (the *Tali*

program, Ramah camps, Noam youth groups) and adults.

c. *Various Centers of Jewish life*: We view it as both a misinterpretation of Jewish history and a threat to Jewish survival to negate the complementary roles of *Eretz Yisrael* and the Diaspora. Currently there are various important centers of Jewish life in the Diaspora. Israeli and Diaspora Jews must aid and enrich the other in every possible way.

4. Between Jew and Fellow Jew.

a. We believe firmly in the principle of *K'lal Yisrael*, by which we mean that Jews, irrespective of philosophical or religious persuasion, are part of one people, *Am Yisrael*. All Jews are responsible for all others.

b. We also believe in pluralism among Jews. As the Rabbis said, every Jew at Sinai understood God's message in his or her own way, and while the community must have some coherence, we prize that pluralism just as much as our ancestors did.

c. We call on our fellow Jews in strengthening the local and national umbrella groups which unite us as a Jewish community. We deplore the refusal of some elements of the community to join the rest in common efforts of importance to the Jewish community as a whole.

5. Relations with Other Faiths.

a. As Conservative Jews, we acknowledge without apology the many debts which Jewish religion and civilization owe to the nations of the world.

b. While we are strongly committed to our own faith and pattern of life, we reject triumphalism with respect to other ways of serving God, and we consequently do not missionize among the adherents of other religions in an effort to convert them to Judaism.

c. We similarly insist that other faiths shun triumphalism with regard to Jews and Judaism and that, in particular, they not missionize among our people to convert them to their faith.

d. Theological humility requires us to recognize that although we have but one God, God has more than one nation. It is part of our mission to understand, respect, and live with the other nations of the world, to discern truths in their cultures from which we can learn, and to share with them the truths that we have come to know.

6. Social Justice: Building a Better World.

a. Our tradition calls us to insure justice within society, that we feed the hungry, clothe the naked, and shelter the homeless. Since there are Jews who are downtrodden and oppressed, we have primary duties to take care of them as members of our extended family, but our tradition also demands that we care for the needy of other peoples as well.

b. Halakhah insists that no human being has the right to ignore the spectacle of injustice in order to engage exclusively in a search for God. Piety, ritual, and study are important, but they do not justify or excuse dishonesty or failure to engage in compassionate acts of social action.

c. In our own day, our tradition's demand for *tikkun olam* (repair of the world) requires not only attention to the poor, but also efforts to bring about social policies which will, among other things, eliminate nuclear arms, provide health care for everyone, and assure the integrity of our environment.

LIVING A LIFE OF TORAH

1. On Women.

a. Conservative Judaism affirms the equality of men and women. It therefore initiated the Bat Mitzvah ceremony, changed some language in the traditional liturgy which can be understood to downgrade or ignore women, took steps to remove injustices to women in traditional Jewish law regarding marriage and divorce, and opened all of its educational programs to females as well as males so that they would study the same curriculum together. It also has encouraged women to assume roles of communal service and leadership in both lay and professional capacities.

b. There is a wide spectrum of practice within our Movement with regard to the role of women in Jewish ritual. We include totally egalitarian synagogues and those with only limited roles for women in communal ritual life, and some women in our movement wear *tallit* and *tefillin* while many do not. We all accept Halakhah as the governing framework for Jewish life and therefore seek to root our various practices within it.

2. The Jewish Home.

a. The home is the principal center for Jewish religious life. A Jewish home should be marked by Jewish ritual objects, art, and publications. A Jewish home should be kosher.

b. Jewish activity should abound in a Jewish home. This includes appropriate rituals, conversation about Jewish affairs and moral issues, and Jewish study.

c. The practice of Judaism in the home is the duty and privilege of all Jews, whether single or married, with or without children.

3. Tefillah (prayer).

a. *The Many Forms of Prayer.* We see the world as pervaded by God, and one of our responses is prayer. Jewish prayer includes petition, but it is not restricted to that. Most of the liturgy, in fact, concentrates on other modes of prayer -- on acknowledgement of God's role in our lives, praise of God, confession, return to God (תְּשׁוּבָה teshuvah), thanksgiving, the enunciation of our ideals, and study of our sacred literature. Conservative liturgy includes all of these, usually in their traditional expression.

b. *Keva and Kavvanah:* in accordance with the Jewish tradition, the Conservative Movement affirms the importance of *both* a fixed structure of the times, content, and order of prayer (קֶבַע *keva,* the established parts of Jewish prayer) *and also* feeling, intentionality, meaning, and spontaneity (כַּוָּנָה *kavvanah,* literally, directionality). We cannot always achieve both, but we need to try.

c. *The Spiritual Meanings of Prayer:* Conservative Judaism seeks to make it possible for Jews to gain spiritual meaning in prayer by affecting us in any or all of the following ways:

    I. Enhancing our sense of perspective, appreciation, and meaning.

    ii. Deepening our communal and historical rootedness.

    iii. Increasing our knowledge of the tradition.

    iv. Enriching our sense of beauty and feeling.

    v. Sharpening our moral awareness and improving the moral quality of our lives.

    vi. Affording us a sense of fulfilling those of God's commandments associated with prayer (prayer as a discipline).

    vii. Creating a living link with God.

d. *The Language and Music of Prayer.* One may, according to Jewish law, pray in any language and with any melody, but prayer gains considerably in meaning if it is in Hebrew and uses the proper melodies for the various seasons of the year. Conservative liturgy is therefore primarily in Hebrew with traditional musical modes, and every effort is made to teach Jews how to pray traditionally in that way. At the same time, in accordance with Jewish historical experience, Conservative Judaism is open to liturgical creativity in both words and music, seeking to fit the new into traditional modes so as to be able to take advantage of both the old and the new in singing a new song to God.

e. *A Life Imbued and Inspired by Prayer.* The Conservative movement also teaches that there are prayers and special blessings (*berakhot*) which are to be said in a variety of circumstances, within the synagogue and without, so that we are aware of our relationship with God and our people throughout the day. This brings a sacred dimension into our lives as a whole.

3. Talmud Torah (Jewish Study).

a. *Life-Long Study.* Virtually alone among all religious traditions, Judaism regards study as a cardinal commandment, indeed, a form of worship of God. In Conservative Judaism, *Talmud Torah* is understood to be the obligation and privilege of every Jew, male and female, young and old, no matter how much or how little one knows at present. Moreover, Jewish study should take place in informal as well as formal settings, and in the home as well as in educational institutions. One should truly be a *ben Torah* or *bat Torah,* a learned and learning Jew, throughout one's life.

b. *Methods of Scholarship.* Since its very inception, Conservative Judaism has been committed to studying Jewish texts with both the traditional modes of exegesis and also with the modern, historical methods used to analyze and understand texts from all other civilizations. We study Jewish texts objectively and dispassionately to understand their meaning and place in their time, and also subjectively and passionately to apply them to our own lives, understanding that the two stances vis-a-vis the texts of our tradition are both different and complementary.

c. *Creative Jewish Scholarship*. Jewish study is not confined to materials from our past; it also consists of the creative contribution to the heritage which we will pass on to the next generation. The Conservative Movement fosters such creative Jewish scholarship through its institutions for higher Jewish learning, its publications, its conferences, its museums, its artistic and theatrical productions, and its institutes for the study of specific subjects.

5. The Ideal Conservative Jew

Rather than assimilating or retreating to a ghetto, the ideal Conservative Jew *integrates tradition and modernity* in his or her own life and in the institutions to which he or she belongs. In doing so, the ideal Conservative Jew is:

a. A *willing* Jew, whose life echoes the dictum, "Nothing human or Jewish is alien to me." That is expressed in the person's ritual acts, study, social action, communal responsibilities, and moral efforts in addition to his or her commitment to *K'lal Yisrael*.

b. A *learning* Jew, devoted to continual, life-long learning and to integrating one's Jewish knowledge with one's general knowledge and with one's efforts to transform the world in light of that learning.

c. A *striving* Jew, working to increase the ways in which Judaism and Jewish identity affect the person's thinking, feeling, associations, and action.

A sourcebook of this type cannot possibly summarize all of the various positions that writers affiliated with the Conservative Movement have taken on matters like God, the problem of evil, redemption, prayer, the People Israel and the land of Israel. The scope of the issues discussed and the variety of positions espoused are simply too great.

Instead, we will do two things. We will first note the types of theologies advanced by thinkers associated with the Conservative Movement. These theologies are characterized primarily by their concept of God, but that affects their understanding of other topics like evil, redemption, and prayer, which most of them also discuss. Those interested in one or more of those positions may then consult the books indicated in the endnotes at the back of the book.

Second, we will turn our attention to three issues which we have not yet discussed where the Conservative Movement has placed great emphasis over the years – namely, the People Israel, often sung as well as said, states that "Israel, Torah, and the Holy One, blessed be He, are one" (*yisrael ve'oraita ve'kudsha b'rikh hu had hu.*[10] Since we at least will name the various views of God taken by Conservative authors in the next section of this chapter, and since we discussed Torah at some length in Chapter Three when we analyzed the various views of revelation within the Conservative Movement, the last three sections of this chapter will complete the trilogy with a discussion of the Conservative Movement's understanding of Israel – the people, the land, and the culture.

QUESTIONS:

1) Rabbi Moshe Davis points out two factors which led to theological diversity in even the early Conservative Movement:

> Characteristic of the Historical School in the past century, as of the Conservative Movement in the twentieth, was its comprehension of several theological approaches within itself, instead of one binding system. A variety of theologies characterizes American religion generally, to the extent that European scholars of religion consider the very term "American theology" self-contradictory....

> [In addition] the Jews, (with notable exceptions) did not historically concentrate on systematic theological thought in their literature. Traditionally, Jewish ideas had been derived from the study of the classic texts and were expressed through commentaries and super-commentaries on these texts.... [Thus] systematic theological writing...was not demanded by the American religious tradition, nor did it spring naturally out of the Jewish intellectual past.[11]

Explain the two factors that he mentions.

Can you think of several examples in the Jewish tradition and in the American tradition of varying theologies?

2) Despite the theological diversity in the Conservative Movement, the beliefs listed in this section are shared in some form by most Conservative Jews. Some of these beliefs may seem obvious to you, and some may seem doubtful.

For those that seem obvious, try to describe an *alternative* belief. That way you will understand what is being affirmed by the belief and what is being denied.

For those beliefs that seem doubtful, try to imagine why anyone would affirm them.

3)   Which of the beliefs listed is specific to Conservative Judaism? Explain the belief. What parts of it would an Orthodox Jew deny? a Reform Jew? a secularist (one who denies either the truth of, or need for, religion)? How would an informed Conservative Jew answer each of them in defense of this belief?

ACTIVITY:

Write a short advertisement about yourself - "selling" yourself to a potential employer or college admissions officer. Afterwards, discuss with a partner the difficulty of reducing your whole being to a short advertisement. What things are included and what others are left out? Do you feel this advertisement adequately represents how you would want others to think of you? How is this exercise similar to the development of Emet Ve-Emunah?

_____

_____

_____

_____

_____

_____

C. The Types of Theology Within the Conservative Movement

In the last chapter we discussed four different positions on revelation within the Conservative Movement. Part of the reason why people take different stands on revelation is because of the different conceptions that they have of God in the first place. For example, according to Rabbi Mordecai Kaplan, God is not personal and does not have a will. As a result, God clearly cannot reveal commandments that would express the divine will since God does not have one! Similar remarks would apply to many of the others who hold the view of revelation which we dubbed "Conservative IV." On the other hand, most of those who affirm the other three views of revelation described above, in which God does reveal His will in some way, do so both because they want to ascribe divine authority to Jewish law and also because of their conceptions of God. Specifically, if you believe that God takes an active role in nature and history, then you probably also want to claim that His activity includes an ongoing relationship with humanity in which there is communication between God and human beings in some way. That is not a necessary corollary of belief in a personal God, but it is a common one. So your conception of God influences your view of revelation, which, in turn. influences your view of the authority and flexibility of Jewish law.

There are many more conceptions of God than there are ideas about revelation, however. That is because thinkers who hold several different views of God may nevertheless have similar ideas about the way in which God communicates to us. Consequently, although we could classify the various Conservative views of revelation in four general categories, there are many more variations in ideas about God.

What are some of the views of God that have been proposed by those associated with the Conservative Movement? The following list will give you an idea of the wide variety of theologies that Conservative thinkers have created, including the general schools of thought to which their theologies belong together with some specific examples of the various approaches (in the endnotes) for those interested in following up on any of these. You may well not understand the philosophic terms used in this list, but it is important that you see that the rich abundance of views of which we have spoken does in fact exist in the Conservative Movement.

What, then, are some of the theological approaches that Conservative thinkers have developed? Some have been rather eclectic in their thought, combining elements from a variety of different schools of thought.[12] Others have concentrated on one specific approach. These have included:

- various forms of naturalism and humanism[13]
- panentheism[14]
- rationalism[15]
- Hegelianism[16]
- organic thinking in the style of Alfred North Whitehead[17]
- atheistic existentialism[18]
- several types of theistic existentialism[19]
- phenomenology[20]
- mysticism[21]
- narrative theology[22]
- spiritualism[23]

What do these views have in common such that they are all views of God? The conceptions listed above are very different, but, generally speaking, when thinkers speak about God, they are referring to the fact that there are many parts of our experience which are beyond our understanding or control. The Hebrew word "el" (translated "god") connotes "power," and

209

the divine aspects of our experience are the overpowering ones. In addition, most Jewish theologies identify God with the manifestations of goodness and justice in our experience. In saying that these elements of power and goodness are divine, a religious person is saying that they are superhuman, beyond human comprehension and control.

That is a very general description of the meaning of the term "God" so that you understand what parts of human experience motivate people to talk about God in the first place. Defining each of the approaches listed above and the specific version of them which each of the above philosophers has taken would turn this sourcebook into a book on Jewish theology rather than a description of the Conservative Movement. Consequently, we will not be able to do that here. The reader is urged, however, to choose at least one or two of the above thinkers and read the books listed in the endnotes. That is important not only to understand some of the views within the Conservative Movement, but also, and more importantly, to help you develop your own ideas in this area.

A mature Jew cannot reasonably rely on the picture of God gained during childhood and then accept Judaism or reject it on that basis. Your childhood understanding of mathematics was not sufficient for your adult years, and your childhood understanding of God – or of Judaism in general – is no better. A mature, intelligent Jew would have to take the time to read at least two or three of these books so that he or she can make decisions about God and Judaism out of knowledge and not out of ignorance. If one or two of the above list do not immediately strike your fancy, additional suggestions can be found at the end of this book in the section entitled "For Further Reading."

QUESTIONS:

1) Why are understandings of revelation related to conceptions of God?

2) What do most of the conceptions of God have in common? Give some examples in your own daily experience of elements that might be called divine (super-human).

   (Hint: consider the attributes and activities which the Bible and prayerbook ascribe to God.)

3) Have half of the members of your group read one of the books listed in the footnotes to this section, and half read a book by a different thinker. Ask two or three of each group to present the views of the thinker they read, either as a panel discussion or as a debate. Invite questions and challenges from the audience.

D. The People Israel

As we mentioned above, there is a popular medieval Jewish maxim that "God, Torah, and Israel are one." The Reform, Orthodox, and Conservative Movements would all agree with that aphorism in that each would affirm the importance of all three elements of Judaism, but each of the movements emphasizes one of the three factors over the other two -- at least in practice. The Reform began by denying interest in the peoplehood of Israel and the authority of many Jewish laws; for them God is the center of Judaism. The Orthodox might agree that God is the center, but even more important for them is what we are supposed to do in obedience to God; consequently for the Orthodox the Torah (and especially its formulation in the *Shulhan Arukh*) is the most important element of the three. (They therefore like to call their version of Judaism "Torah-true Judaism.") For the Conservative Movement there is no question that God and Torah are crucial parts of Judaism, but both of those can become realities in life only if the People Israel make them so. The Rabbis of the Talmud and Midrash said something similar:

> "You are My witnesses," declares the Lord, "and I am God" (Isaiah 43:12). That is, *when* you are My witnesses, I am God, and when you are not My witnesses, I am, as it were, not God.
>
> (*Midrash Psalms* on Psalm 123:1; cp. *Pesikta d'Rav Kahana*, ed. Mandelbaum, p. 208, and *Mekhilta, Shirata*, Beshallah, ed. Lauterbach, Vol. II, p. 28).

ואתם עדי נאם-ה ואני-אל (ישעיה מ"ג. י"ב) אם אתם עדי נאם ה אני אל ואם אין אתם עדי
כביכול אין אני ה.

This concern with the People Israel has been part of Conservative ideology from the very beginning. You will recall Solomon Schechter's concept of catholic Israel from Chapter Two. Schechter's idea of catholic Israel was in part a rejection of the Reform position that Jews are only devotees of a religion and not members of a people as well. Schechter claimed that Jews must regard themselves as members of a people which includes not only the Jews of the present, but those of the past and future as well. This should give a Jew pride and a sense of rootedness, and it also has implications for the way in which a Jew identifies as a Jew. To do that authentically, Jews must see themselves as part of the ongoing Jewish people and must express that in action by observing the laws and customs of the Jewish People. Otherwise Jewish identity is only a matter of the mind and emotions and not a way of life, as it always has been.

Similarly, the Jewish community of the present must see itself in the line of Jewish communities of the past and future and must make its decisions with those communities in mind. This idea is often called "vertical democracy." To understand that term, imagine a vertical time-line, extending from the beginnings of the Jewish People at the bottom and extending upward to the future. The concept of "vertical democracy," then, means that Jews are members of a people consisting not only of the Jews living in many places at this time (that is looking at Jewish peoplehood "horizontally" on the time-line), but also of Jews living at many points in the past and future, up and down the time-line. Consequently in making their decisions, Jewish communities must take account of the concerns and attitudes of the present, but they must also consider the standards of the past and the expectations of the future, giving them a vote as well. Thus Schechter's concept of catholic Israel emphasizes the People Israel as a crucial factor in both the identity of the individual Jew and the character of the Jewish community.

The emphasis on Jewish peoplehood has also had other implications for the activity of the Conservative Movement. One has been an abiding concern for Jews of all persuasions and places. The founders of the Conservative Movement did not want to establish a new movement. On the contrary, they wanted to create a seminary and an organization of synagogues which could include Jews of all persuasions. Thus the early leaders of Conservative Judaism participated in the founding of the Union of American Hebrew Congregations and Hebrew Union College in 1873 and 1875. They broke away from the Reform group and founded the Jewish Theological Seminary only after "the trefah banquet" and the Pittsburgh Platform made it clear that the differences between the two groups were too great to remain as one. Even afterward there was an attempt at union. When Isaac Mayer Wise died in 1900, it was proposed to unite the Historical School and the Reform group on the theory that the radical turn that the Reform group had taken had been solely due to his leadership.[24] The objections to Jewish practice among the Reformers turned out to be more widespread and more deeply rooted than anticipated, however, and so the effort failed.

On the other side of the spectrum, Henry Pereira Mendes, who served as Acting President of the Seminary from the death of Sabato Morais in 1897 until the appointment of Solomon Schechter in 1902, was the founder of the Union of Orthodox Jewish Congregations in 1898 and continued as its president for several terms of office. The Union gradually shifted away from the synagogues tied to the Historical School, however. Schechter again tried to avoid splintering by involving the Orthodox in the Seminary, and for most of his life he saw Conservative Judaism as simply a "tendency" within Judaism and not as a separate movement. He failed, though, to convince the Orthodox to be part of a wider, traditional community.

Because those on the right and the left could not be brought into a wide coalition of all elements of the Jewish community, it was only the synagogues which adopted the approach of the Historical School which became part of the United Synagogue of America which Rabbi Schechter established in 1913. Even the name he gave this new organization, though -- the United Synagogue of America -- betokened the fact that he still hoped that ultimately the other elements of the Jewish community would join forces with the centrists and form a truly *united* group of synagogues in America. (It was only on November 18, 1991 that the organization's name changed to the United Synagogue of Conservative Judaism. Since it had long been apparent that the other groups would not join us in this effort at unity, and the drive for increasing clarity in what we stand for as Conservative Jews and our pride in taking that stance dictated that the very name of the organization specify that the United Synagogue consists of synagogues committed to Conservative Judaism.)

Despite the inability of Rabbi Schechter and his successors to create a broad, American version of Judaism to which all American Jews would subscribe in some form, the Conservative Movement has consistently sought to enlist the participation of other groups of Jews wherever possible, sometimes to the detriment of its own economic interests. Conservative Jews have thus been disproportionately involved in communal organizations like the United Jewish Appeal and local federations, and Conservative leaders have often been the ones initiating joint efforts for the entire Jewish community. These are all concrete expressions of Conservative Judaism's strong commitment to *k'lal yisrael.*

There is another interesting way in which the Conservative emphasis on the entire People Israel has manifested itself. Ashkenazic Jews (i.e., Jews whose ancestors lived in Eastern Europe) form the bulk of American Jewry and hence of Conservative Jewry, but from its very beginnings the Conservative Movement has enjoyed the active involvement of many Sephardic Jews (i.e., those descended from residents of the Mediterranean basin, Syria, Iraq, Iran, and Yemen). Sabato Morais, the first President of the Seminary, and Henry Pereira Mendes, who served as Acting President of the Seminary from 1897 to 1902, were both of Sephardic origin. In our own day the founder and first secretary of the Sephardic World Union were Professor Jose Faur, and Rabbi David Algaze, a former Seminary faculty member and a rabbi trained at the Seminary, respectively. The tradition of Western scholarship from which the Seminary sprang has created ties of spirit and substance between the Conservative Movement and the Sephardic community.

Yet another manifestation of the Conservative Movement's emphasis on the entire People Israel has been the efforts of the Movement to promote the welfare of Jews who are suffering economically and politically in places around the world. So for example, although the Jewish community at large did not take an interest in the plight of Soviet Jewry until the late 1960s, individuals who identified with the Seminary and with Conservative Judaism expressed a deep concern in the plight of Russian Jews as far back as the 1880s. These included:

Louis Marshall - a prominent attorney and patron of the early Seminary, whose legal, political and personal efforts led to the termination of American plans for a foreign trade agreement and a treaty with Russia in response to the Russian refusal to allow Jews to visit Russia and continual pogroms there.

Jacob Schiff - the strongest financial supporter of the Seminary and Conservative Judaism during Schechter's years in America and a powerful financier, prevented Russia from entering many European and American money markets, thus damaging the Russian economy. He also arranged for a $200 million loan to Japan which financed Japan's successful war against Russia. In gratitude for his help, Schiff became the first private citizen to dine with the Emperor and to be made an honorary Japanese nobleman, receiving from the Mikado the Second Order of the Sacred Treasure of Japan.

Israel Friedlaender - a professor at the Seminary, popular educator, Jewish youth worker, and ardent cultural Zionist, traveled to Russia in 1920 to bring encouragement and goods to Russian Jewry. During his exhausting travels in the Ukraine, he and his companion were attacked and murdered, apparently by bandits, but possibly by government agents who were unsympathetic to his mission. Thus a Seminary professor became the first American martyr in the struggle for the rights of Soviet Jewry.

Some forty years later, when Soviet Jewry had been forgotten by American Jewry, another Seminary professor, Abraham Joshua Heschel, awakened the American community to their plight. He continued to speak up for Soviet Jewry when no one else would, and supported the Student Struggle for Soviet Jewry and other organizations and programs aimed at helping Russian Jewry. He encouraged Elie Wiesel to visit Russia and write about his experiences. Wiesel did so in *The Jews of Silence*. The issue of Soviet Jewry rose to the top of the agenda of American Jewry's concerns in the 1960s, 1970s, and 1980s in no small measure because of Rabbi Heschel's long and hard efforts and because of powerful words like these:

> We plead, we implore the leaders of Russia: Let our people live in dignity or let our people go: *Let them live or let them leave!*

> The Jews of Russia are deprived of the right to express themselves, so we American Jews must utter their cry, must serve as their voice. We shall not be quiet. We shall not keep our peace until we pierce the crust of the world's conscience and the Russian Jews are granted their rights.

The time to act is now. A few years hence and there may be no Jews left in Russia to be saved. We must be prepared for a long and bitter battle that will require all our heart and all our strength. Our spiritual integrity is at stake. To fight for human rights is to save our own souls.

I do not want future generations to spit on our graves, saying: "Here lies a community which living in comfort and prosperity, kept silent while millions of their brothers were exposed to spiritual extermination."[25]

And since the fall of the Soviet Union, the Conservative Movement has initiated programs in Russia, Georgia, the Ukraine, and in other parts of the former Soviet bloc to help to revive Jewish life there. These include Ramah camps, teachers training institutes, and the like. The Conservative Movement is also involved in helping new *olim* (immigrants to Israel, literally, "those who go up" to the Holy Land) from Russia, Ethiopia, and elsewhere learn how to live as Jews in the Jewish homeland.

In all these ways, then, the Conservative Movement's commitment to the People Israel has taken concrete form.

E. *Zionism and Israel*

To us it seems obvious that a Jew must be a Zionist. Jews may disagree about how to express their support for Israel, and they may disagree with some of the policies of the State of Israel; but in our day only a small minority of Jews would claim that Judaism can be separated from Zionism.

That was not always the case. Until the establishment of the State of Israel in 1948 and even for a number of years thereafter, there were significant groups of Jews who actively opposed the founding of a Jewish state in Palestine. One plank of the Reform Movement's Pittsburgh Platform (1885) specifically stated that "We consider ourselves no longer a nation, but a religious community, and therefore expect (no)...return to Palestine...nor the restoration of any of the laws concerning the Jewish state." While there were some strong Zionists in the Reform camp like Stephen S. Wise, there were major elements of the Reform Movement opposed to Jewish nationhood in Palestine or anywhere else. They saw Zionism as a nationalist movement which would impede the progress of universalism. They also thought that it would prevent Jews from being "a light unto the nations" because Jews could not act as a model for others if they were concentrated in only one corner of the world. They must be "in the midst of many peoples as dew from the Lord, as showers upon the grass" (Micah

5:6) to do that. Thus it was mostly people affiliated with the Reform Movement who belonged to the American Council for Judaism, an organization of rich and powerful Jews who actively worked against Zionism.

Similarly, while there were Orthodox supporters of a Jewish state in Palestine, many Orthodox leaders opposed it on the grounds that only the Messiah could legitimately lead the Jews back to Zion. If Jews created the state on their own, they would be forcing God's hand and thus committing a sacrilege. To this day there are elements of the Orthodox community, including the Agudat Yisrael party in Israel's government and other Orthodox Jews who refuse to take part in the national life of Israel in any way, who still see the State of Israel as a secular state like any other, with no particularly Jewish character and certainly no legitimate claim to be the hoped-for, third Jewish commonwealth.

It is only the Conservative Movement that has never had a strong anti-Zionist wing. On the contrary, Sabato Morais, the first President of the Seminary, was a member of the *Hovevei Zion* ("Lovers of Zion") organization in Philadelphia, and Solomon Schechter, the second President of the Seminary, wrote a pamphlet in 1906 entitled "Zionism: A Statement," in which he publicly and powerfully explained the reasons for his allegiance to Zionism.[26] Later he was to call Zionism "the most cherished dream I was worthy of having."[27] There were some, like Cyrus Adler and Jacob Schiff, who were not Zionists as early as that, but they later became supporters of the Zionist Movement. The vast majority of those associated with Conservative Judaism from its very beginnings were active Zionists throughout their lives.[28]

Remember that Conservative Judaism emphasizes the People Israel, so this early and constant concern for founding a state for the Jewish People in the Jewish homeland is easy to understand. Also, since Conservative Judaism considers religion to be the core of the Jewish civilization, you can easily understand how the Zionism of Conservative leaders from Schechter onward differed from the secular Zionism of people like Herzl and Ben Gurion. For the latter, Zionism was a means of solving the problem of anti-Semitism in Europe. They thought that if Jews formed a state like any other state and left the countries of Europe, they thought, anti-Semitism would cease. Consequently their interest in Zion was a political interest, and their hopes for the new state were purely political hopes.

For Schechter and later Conservative leaders, on the other hand, both the motivation and hopes for Zionism were different. The motivation stemmed from the longings and literature of Jews throughout the ages to return to Israel. The hopes were for a state which would foster the moral, cultural, and religious growth of the Jews living there and, through them, of Jews throughout the world. If it did not become that, Schechter warned, Zionism could become

216

a danger for Jews and Judaism because it would give Jews the false impression that Judaism amounted to nothing more than living in a secular Jewish state. Schechter was convinced that such a Judaism could not long endure. (Incidentally, he was right. The secular leaders of present-day Israel are increasingly interested in teaching Judaism to the younger generation. This is because many young Jewish Israelis see themselves simply as citizens of Israel and not as Jews, contributing, among other things, to larger numbers of Israelis leaving Israel to live elsewhere and to increasing problems of crime and drugs within Israeli society. The leaders now realize that *they* could create a secular, idealistic society only because they grew up in homes which were deeply Jewish. In so doing they were living off the benefits of their parents' convictions and practices. They themselves did not provide that background for their own children, however, and hence Israel is suffering from the problems of other secular societies.) As Rabbi Robert Gordis put it, "Zionism without Judaism has no roots; Judaism without Zionism will have no fruit."[29]

The distinction between secular Zionism and the religious-cultural type of Zionism of the Conservative Movement also has important implications in another area, the relationship of Jews to Israel and the Diaspora. If your motivation and hopes for Israel are solely political, then the only way to be a true Zionist is to live in Israel, as Ben Gurion publicly declared. On the other hand, if you see Israel as the religious and cultural center of world Jewry, then you are not denying the legitimacy of the Jewish communities of the Diaspora. On the contrary, you might even say that the existence of Jewish communities outside of Israel is necessary for the cultural, political, and economic well-being of Israel. That has been the attitude of Conservative Judaism all along, and it is articulated, as we have seen, in *Emet Ve-Emunah*: "the Jewish communities of both Israel and the Diaspora are legitimate and important for the future of Jews and Judaism. "

The Zionism of the Conservative Movement has taken concrete form in a number of ways. As you may know, Conservative rabbis and laypeople have been among the chief fund-raisers for Israel throughout the years. As early as 1927, Rabbi Israel Goldstein reported that the Zionist Organization of America looked upon the Conservative rabbinate "as the rabbinical bulwark of American Zionism."[30] But Conservative support for Israel does not stop there. The Conservative Movement has made a real effort to expose Jews of the Diaspora to the people, culture, and land of Israel through educational trips there and through publication of study materials for the use of teachers and students in the Diaspora. Since the 1960s, Camp Ramah and USY have included a select group of Israelis on their educational staff so that North American Jewish teenagers can come into direct contact with living representatives of Israel. Conversely, the Conservative Movement (called the Masorti, or "traditional," movement in Israel) has also created synagogues, schools, materials, and youth groups in Israel in order to expose Israeli youngsters and adults to Conservative Judaism.

217

The Conservative Movement has had some problems in Israel, however, and you should be aware of them. When the State of Israel was founded, a compromise was made between the secular and religious populations there in order to gain the support of as many inhabitants as possible and in order to give Israel a distinctly Jewish character. According to the terms of the compromise, matters of personal status are handled by the religious authorities of the various religions, and all other matters come under the jurisdiction of the government and the secular courts. "Matters of personal status" include especially marriages, divorces, and conversions, and the rabbinate designated in the compromise is the Israeli Orthodox rabbinate. This means that Israeli Jews have no choice in these matters: since there is no civil marriage or divorce in Israel, and since the only religious authorities empowered to perform marriages, divorces, and conversions for Jews are the Orthodox rabbis, Israeli Jews must use their services and submit to their interpretation of Jewish practice. This is the case despite the fact that 85% of the Israeli populace do not identify themselves as Orthodox. The compromise also has meant that Conservative rabbis have not been able to perform recognized marriages, divorces, and conversions in Israel and that Jews who have been divorced or converted by Conservative rabbis in the Diaspora often have difficulties if they become citizens of Israel. Since non-Jews may choose to be married or divorced by whichever religious authorities they choose, or by state authorities, Israel effectively has freedom of religion in these matters for everyone but Jews.

Moreover, Israeli rabbis, synagogues and religious education are not financed by local communities, as they are in the United States: they are funded by the government. Since the Orthodox rabbinate is the only one officially recognized in Israel, Conservative rabbis, synagogues, and educational programs have been deprived of virtually all government funding - despite the fact that much of the money which the government raises comes from taxes on the entire Israeli population (not just the Orthodox element) and from donations of Conservative and Reform Jews living in the Diaspora. This problem is exacerbated by the parliamentary structure of Israeli government, for each of the two major parties over the years has had to include the small, Orthodox parties in a ruling coalition in order to have more than a majority of votes in the Knesset. In return for agreeing to be part of such a coalition, the Orthodox parties have been able to insist on being appointed as heads of the ministries of education and religion, among other government posts, and they have exerted an influence on government policies completely disproportional to their numbers in Israeli society. They have then used their political power to deprive Conservative and Reform institutions of any of the money allocated by the government to religious and educational institutions.

This is clearly an intolerable situation, and Conservative leaders in Israel and North America may have to take strong steps to rectify it, both in the Diaspora and in Israel. That may mean, among other things, that Conservative Jews in the Diaspora will be asked to have their local federations apportion a healthy percentage of the money going to Israel directly to Conservative (and Reform) institutions in Israel so that the Orthodox stranglehold on the government cannot siphon it off to Orthodox institutions. If that fails, Conservative Jews may have to investigate other means to ensure that our institutions are adequately funded. In Israel, the Conservative movement has already pursued remedies in the courts, but the Israeli Supreme Court, which has been quite supportive of Conservative Movement law suits for privileges and funds, does not, by Israeli law, have the authority to overrule an act of the Knesset, and so the Orthodox have been able to force the ruling coalition to override Supreme Court decisions in these matters – in fact, even if not in theory. Clearly yet stronger measures must be taken. Such measures will be important not only for the future of the Conservative Movement in Israel, but also for the future of Judaism among the 85% who are not Orthodox and for the future of freedom of religion in Israel.

In the meantime, the Conservative Movement has made major strides in meeting the religious needs of Israel. There are more and more Conservative synagogues, youth groups, and day schools there in addition to institutions like the Center for Conservative Judaism and the Seminary for Jewish Studies (Bet Midrash), which, among other activities in Israel and in Eastern Europe, ordains Israelis as Conservative rabbis and trains teachers for Israeli schools. Moreover, many Conservative rabbis fill important positions in the universities and teacher-training institutes of the country. The Tali system of education, organized and largely staffed by teachers educated by our Israeli Seminary, now enriches the Jewish curriculum of more and more of Israel's "secular" schools. Hopes are high for the success of these projects as well as many others that the Conservative Movement is undertaking in Israel.

QUESTIONS:

1) How does the Conservative emphasis on the People Israel explain the early and continual support of Zionism by the Movement?

2) Why were many of the Orthodox Movement anti-Zionist until the founding of the State? Why were many of the Reform Movement anti-Zionist until then? How do you think Conservative leaders would have answered those reasons to be anti-Zionist?

3) How does the Zionism of the Conservative Movement differ from the secular Zionism of people like Herzl and Ben Gurion? Why does the Conservative Movement differ in that way? Do you agree? Why, or why not?

4)	What is the Conservative attitude toward living in the Diaspora? in Israel? (Consider the statements of *Emet Ve-Emunah* on this, summarized in Section B of this chapter above.) How and why is that different from the secular Zionist position on this issue? What is your opinion on this difficult question? Can you see why others might have a different view?

5)	In answer to Question #4 you described the Conservative position on Zionism. Given that position, how should Zionism be taught in Conservative schools, camps, and USY? How was it taught in the Conservative schools, camps, or youth groups you have attended? How would this differ from the way Zionism is taught in Orthodox schools? in secular Zionist groups like Habonim and Young Judaea?

6)	Describe some of the activities of the Conservative Movement in the Diaspora which express its commitment to Israel. What are some of the programs that it has established in Israel because of this commitment?

	(You might want to turn back to the list of Conservative organizations and programs at the end of Chapter Two of this sourcebook.)

7)	What are we learning from Israel about our Jewish identity? What are the Israelis learning from us? (Notice that it is a "two-way street"!)

8)	What problems is the Conservative Movement having in Israel? How would you go about seeking a solution to those problems?

ACTIVITY:

Kol Yisrael arevim zeh la-zeh - "All Jews are responsible for each other"

Make a list of all the examples within the Jewish community which you think applies to this statement.

_____

_____

_____

_____

F. Judaism as a Religious Civilization

Schechter's concept of catholic Israel put emphasis on the People Israel and its role in determining Jewish law and ideology. This paved the way for an insight by Rabbi Mordecai Kaplan which has shaped the character of Conservative Judaism in many ways. In his book, *Judaism as a Civilization*, Kaplan declared that Judaism must not be viewed exclusively as a religion. It certainly is a religion with beliefs and ritual practices like other religions, but there also are distinctly Jewish forms or subjects for art, music, dance, literature, and diet, and there is a Jewish homeland and a Jewish language (Hebrew). These elements go well beyond what we normally include within the concept of a "religion"; they are part of what we call a civilization. Consequently, Judaism must be seen as a *civilization* if it is to be understood adequately.

One practical upshot of this conception of Judaism is that Jews must learn and develop their non-religious ties to the Jewish civilization as well as their religious ones. That means that synagogues should become Jewish centers with Jewish cultural and social activities, as well as religious ones. Institutions of higher Jewish learning should include courses and performances in Jewish arts, music, drama, and dance as well as work in the texts, practices, and ideas of the Jewish tradition. Thus when Kaplan's idea of founding a University of Judaism was realized in Los Angeles, it included among its first schools a School of Fine Arts.[31] Similar considerations led the Seminary to establish the Jewish Museum in New York. *All* of the civilizational aspects of Judaism are important parts of what it means to be a Jew, and hence all must be taught, developed and practiced.

One example of this has been the devotion of the Conservative Movement to Hebrew, both as the language of tradition and also as the mode of expression for modern literature and conversation. The Orthodox Movement in the Diaspora has largely neglected the study of Hebrew language and literature. Part of the reason for that is the belief that Hebrew is a holy tongue and should not be used for communication that is not religious in nature. Even classes in Judaica are sometimes taught in Yiddish or English. The Reform Movement long ago dispensed with Hebrew even in worship in favor of the vernacular, although the New Union Prayerbook, *Gates of Prayer* (1975), uses much more Hebrew than the former Union Prayerbook, which was in use for eighty years before that. Both movements have changed in recent years under the impact of the State of Israel, but Hebrew is still not high on the agenda of Orthodox or Reform schools. In contrast, Conservative Judaism, with its emphasis on both preserving continuity with the Jewish historical past and creating a vibrant Jewish present, has concerned itself intensely with both classical and contemporary Hebrew language and literature. This has been true ever since the Second Rabbinical Conference of those who desired change in Judaism took place in Frankfurt in 1845. At that time Zecharias Frankel, one of the ideological fathers of the Conservative Movement, left the Conference when it adopted the proposals of Abraham Geiger, the Reform leader, to drop Hebrew from the services and curriculum. Frankel then said,

It was in vain to point out that the Hebrew language must be safeguarded like a precious gem, for the sacred documents are written in it, and the understanding of these documents must not be lost as once it was amongst the Hellenistic Jews. In vain it was stressed [by me to the participants in the conference] that, once Hebrew disappears from prayer, it will be lost altogether, for it will then be banished from the schools and thus another religious element will have disappeared from their already sparse curriculum. In vain was religious sentiment appealed to, for this should be significant in prayer, which is heightened by the sacred sound of Hebrew. In vain it was emphasized that Hebrew prayer especially is a characteristic mark of the religious community of the Jew, for through it the Jew, wherever he meets another Jew, would recognize him as his co-religionist would recognize his temple as his own house of worship, and find his prayer to be his own.[32]

Later on Solomon Schechter was to express a similar view:

...It is not necessary to dwell here at length on the vital importance of Hebrew, the Sacred tongue. It is the great depository of all that is best in the soul-life of the Congregation of Israel. Without it we will become a mere sect, without a past, and without a literature, and without a proper Liturgy, and severed from the great Tree which is life unto those that cling to it. Hellenistic Judaism is the only one known to history which dared to make this experiment of dispensing with the Sacred Language. The result was death. It withered away and terminated in total and wholesale apostasy from Judaism. Let us not deceive ourselves. There is no future in this country for a Judaism that resists either the English or the Hebrew language.[33]

Mordecai Kaplan, Simon Greenberg, and others also stressed the need for learning Hebrew in order to have a viable Jewish present. As Joseph Hertz said, "A Hebrew-less Judaism has no future because it cannot be justly said to have a present."[34]

All of the non-religious aspects of the Jewish civilization are important and have been fostered and practiced within the Conservative Movement. But, as Dr. Kaplan himself stressed, Judaism is a *religious* civilization in that all of the other elements in the Jewish civilization receive their distinctly Jewish character from the Jewish religion. The definition of what constitutes specifically Jewish art, music, or literature is a matter of dispute. Some claim that anything by a Jew or about a Jew is Jewish art. Others maintain that only art by a Jew on a recognized Jewish theme is Jewish art. But all would agree that artistic, musical, or literary creations by Jews on themes from the Bible, Talmud, or Midrash or other parts of the Jewish religion are unquestionably Jewish. That is the case because the Jewish religion is recognized as the core of Jewish identity. Similarly, foods that are popular among Jews and are associated with us vary from community to community, but in all cases the laws of *kashrut* play a major role in determining what can and cannot be classified as Jewish food. So, for example, a cheeseburger would never be thought of as a Jewish food. Even those foods which are popular among Jews are called "Jewish-*style*" if they are not prepared and served in a kosher way: their identity as Jewish foods has been diminished by virtue of the fact that they are not kosher. Hebrew is the Jewish language *not* because Jews spoke it throughout their history: in most periods Jews spoke the language of the country in which they lived. Hebrew is the Jewish language because it is the language of the Bible, Mishnah and Siddur (prayerbook). That is why the founders of the State of Israel spent as much time and effort as they did in learning, teaching, and developing Hebrew as a modern conversational and literary language: it was not the native language of any one of them. And the Jewish attachment to the land of Israel is also a product of the Jewish religion because it is that land which God promised to our ancestors. It is, of course, also the land in which Jews lived for many years, but the historical connection to the land of Israel began and continued largely because of Jewish religious roots there. The Temple could only be in Jerusalem, and only there could the calendar be set. These are the factors that kept Jews longing for a return to Zion and which prevented the large and advanced Jewish communities of Babylonia and Europe from supplanting the importance of Israel, despite attempts to do so at various times in Jewish history. In sum, then, all of the non-religious aspects of the Jewish civilization are important, but they derive their distinctively Jewish identity from the Jewish religion.

As a result, Jewish individuals, communities, and institutions must integrate Judaism into their activities in order to be distinctly and actively Jewish. Any Jewish person or organization which neglects the Jewish religion becomes significantly less Jewish.[35] That, of course, puts a burden upon us to learn and practice the Jewish religion, but nobody ever said that Judaism is easy. If we are honest with ourselves, however, we must recognize that Judaism is the core of Jewish identity, whether we like it or not. Consequently, Conservative Judaism, which tries to be historically authentic, is a *religious* movement, demanding knowledge and practice of the Jewish religion as well as concern for the other civilizational aspects of being Jewish.

QUESTIONS:

1) What is a "civilization"? What is a "religion"? Why does Mordecai Kaplan maintain that Judaism must be viewed as a civilization and not just a religion?

2) In what ways have Conservative synagogues, schools, and youth groups reflected the concepts of Judaism as a civilization?

3) Why is the Conservative emphasis on Hebrew an expression of seeing Judaism as a religious civilization? Give at least two reasons, and show how each of the reasons you give has affected the way in which Hebrew is taught in Conservative schools.

4) Why must Judaism be understood as a *religious* civilization — that is, as a civilization with religion at its core?

5) Can a Jew identify as a Jew without being religious? If so, in what sense is religion the core of Jewish identity?

6) What obligations derive from the fact that authentic Jewish identity is religious identity?

224

CHAPTER V
CONSERVATIVE JUDAISM: LOOKING AHEAD

We have reviewed the history, practices, and ideologies of the Conservative Movement. That constitutes its past and present. What about its future?

That is obviously an impossible question to answer authoritatively, but it is hard to refrain from speculating about it. Moreover, some thought about the future is important for the planning and building that must take place now.

As was noted earlier in this text, there are various committees and councils on the regional and national level in which representatives of all the arms of the movement meeet to discuss issues of communal concern and in order to do some joint planning. It is important that the members of each arm of the movement, and, indeed, of each synagogue, school, group, or chapter do whatever they can to make their own lives as Conservative Jews more vibrant, Jewishly committed, and meaningful, using the full extent of the creativity that they can muster. It is also important that we work together as a movement to plan for our future, for that will avoid the wasting of resources in time, energy, and money which comes out of various groups doing the same thing, and such joint planning will enable each of us to benefit from the ideas and strengths of all the others in the movement.

The readers of this book are most likely the leaders of our movement today or its potential leaders for tomorrow. Leadership demands that you think seriously about the problems and opportunities which present themselves to us, envisioning how we can best overcome our problems and maximize our opportunities. After all, in the end the movement's future depends upon the good sense, the Jewish commitment, and the creativity of each of its members; there is nobody else who will look out for our welfare or insure that we achieve our goals. That burden and that challenge are even more of a responsibility of our leaders of the present and future. It is therefore absolutely critical that you personally get involved in this process of planning for the future.

You undoubtedly have already pondered at least some of the issues which confront us as Conservative Jews. Those issues will clearly change as the years go by, and so one needs to learn how to evaluate situations as they arise, identifying solutions to the problems they present and ways to take advantage of the promise they embody. The Points to Ponder listed below in Section A of this chapter, then, are brought here for two purposes: to alert you to some of the issues and opportunities which we face today as a movement and will most probably face in the near future; and to help you to learn the skills of evaluating circumstances and of identifying ways to overcome their difficulties and to capitalize on their potential for future growth.

Section B then asks you to go beyond dealing with specific points to create an integrated vision of the future of the Jewish community in general and of Conservative Judaism in particular. This level of thinking is, of course, must less rooted in current realities and therefore much more difficult to think of in realistic terms, but when done seriously, it can motivate us to new levels of creativity. As the future participants and leaders of the Conservative Jewish community, it is therefore important that you try your hand at this level of planning for the future as well.

A. *Facing the Future: Particular Points to Ponder*

These Points to Ponder are listed in no specific order, and so in your own thinking and in your discussion with others you should *scan the list quickly first and then focus on the issues which most engage you.* For that matter, if you think of other problems or opportunities, add them to the list and talk about those as well. After all, while I, as the author of this book, am doing the initial work for you in listing many of the most important issues facing the movement today, the first task in any planning for the future is to describe the lay of the land, as it were, identifying problems, resources, and opportunities.

In real leadership roles you will probably find it most productive to concentrate on a relatively small number of issues so that your limited time and energy can be fruitfully devoted to dealing with those, just as I have asked you to do in the last paragraph with the list below. At the same time, though, you must be aware of the wide range of problems and opportunities that exist so that you can make an intelligent choice of which are most pressing.

You must also at least cope with problems, even if you cannot now resolve them, and you will not want to lose important opportunities through your focus on other matters. Moreover, since life does not come in neat packages, you will find that many issues are intertwined with others. For all these reasons, then, dealing effectively with the issues that you choose will demand that you pay at least some attention to the others as well.

Here, then, is a partial list of the issues which confront us as a Conservative Movement. Once you have scanned the list and decided which you think are most pressing (or which are most amenable to solutions), discuss the one or two that you choose within your group. I would

226

then encourage you to forward your conclusions to the people or groups within the movement who are currently working on that matter. After all, that is how we all learn and improve our chances to achieve good things, and that is the first step in taking an active role in the future of the Conservative movement and in your future as a Conservative Jew.

1. Assimilation

According to the 1990 Jewish Population Study sponsored by the Council of Jewish Federations, 59% of North American Jews are not affiliated with any synagogue whatsoever.[1] Of the 5,515,000 "core" Jews, approximately one-fifth of them (1,120,000) classify themselves as Jewish with no religion (they are, in other words, secular Jews). In addition, 210,000 Jews reported being born Jewish but they have converted to another religion; 415,000 had a parent or grandparents who were Jewish but were raised in another faith and practice it (even though they may still consider themselves ethnically Jewish); and 700,000 children under 18 are being raised with another religion even though one of their parents (or, in a few cases, step-parents) is Jewish.[2] Moreover, the study reports, as one would expect, that the chances of someone growing up with a strong Jewish identity increase dramatically if one is raised with synagogue affiliation and participation and, conversely, diminish radically without such affiliation and participation.

All of this means that our major problem as the Conservative Movement is not competition with the other religious movements within Judaism; frankly, we should applaud their successes as we rejoice in our own. The real problem that we all face is assimilation: approximately a third of Jews are not identifying in any meaningful way with their Jewish heritage.[3]

This, of course, has a major effect on their own lives, for they thereby lose the depth, the spirituality, and the moral value which Judaism conveys. It also saps our strength as a Jewish community, for we lose the ideas, the creativity, and the camaraderie which they would bring if they were more actively involved. This is particularly problematic for a religion like Judaism, which is so heavily based in the experience of the community and which, after all is said and done, includes only 14 million adherents in the entire world (0.2% of the world's population, while Christians make up 33% and Muslims 17%). For theological as well as practical reasons, then, every Jew is precious, and we cannot afford to lose any, let alone a third of our numbers, to assimilation.

Questions:

1) How can we stem the tide of assimilation? This itself divides into several different questions, namely, how can we get more secular Jews to affirm the religious part of Jewish identity, how can we bring back into the Jewish fold those who have converted out or are being raised in another religion despite their Jewish parentage, and how can we attract higher percentages of Jews to affiliate with, and participate in, synagogues?

2) How much time, effort, and money should be devoted to trying to win back assimilated Jews as against deepening the knowledge and commitment of those who have already chosen to affiliate? (This is the issue of "outreach vs. in-reach.")

ACTIVITY:

Develop a marketing campaign to try to attract people to affiliate with your synagogue. Choose a specific target population (e.g. singles, young marrieds, etc.) What will you emphasize? How will you reach this population with your message? Be specific.

---

2. Intermarriage

In our free society, Jews meet non-Jews in all sorts of settings on an equal footing. Moreover, while anti-Semitism certainly exists within our society, it has diminished considerably in the last half of the twentieth century, and so many Christians do not find it objectionable to marry a Jew on religious or social grounds. (Some even think that Judaism is just another branch of Christianity!) Under these circumstances, it is not surprising that the rate of marriage of Jews to non-Jews has skyrocketed, such that approximately 25% of Jews getting married between 1985 and 1990 were marrying non-Jews.[4]

This is a problem for both the family and the Jewish community. For the couple, intermarriage poses greater risk of divorce. In fact, marriages between Jews and non-Jews are twice as likely to end in divorce as are marriages of two Jews.[5] Marriage always requires two people of differing temperaments and customs to adjust to each other, and when they come from different religious backgrounds as well, the adjustment is all the harder. Problems of which holidays to observe, of determining the religious education of the children, of balancing the Jewish connections of one of the couple with the (usually) Christian associations of the other, and, in the heat of argument, even some latent anti-Semitism all contribute to making intermarriages a rocky prospect for any couple.

The children of an intermarriage have related problems. Children, no less than adults, want a sense of identity. If the parents decide that the children will be raised in one religion or the other, the children at least have a sense of what their parents want for them, but in such circumstances children often continue to harbor doubts about the depth of their own religious identity. After all, if my Mom or Dad is not what I am, and if she or he even feels uncomfortable in the religious setting in which I am being raised, how much of a Jew or Christian am I? (The child may be fully Jewish or Christian from the point of view of those religions and still feel this way because of the disunity of the parents on this issue.) Often parents reassure themselves by saying that they are going to teach the child both religions and then let the child choose upon reaching the teenage years, but that only makes matters worse because then children inevitably feel that they are choosing Mom over Dad, or the reverse, a choice they do not want to make since they love them both. In such cases, children often embrace no religion at all rather than identify with the religion of either one of their parents.

For the Jewish community, the problems are many. First and foremost, are the children going to be raised as Jews? As much as we might hope that they would be, only 10% of intermarried couples raise their children as Jews. (In contrast, 99% of couples involving a convert to Judaism raise their children as Jews.) The failure of the vast majority of intermarried couples to raise their children as Jews cuts off a significant part of our future as a community.

As a result, the Conservative Jewish community has engaged in a variety of efforts of *keruv* (bringing close) in the hope that the non-Jew will ultimately convert to Judaism and that at least the children will be raised as Jews (and formally converted to Judaism if the mother is not Jewish). In the meantime, the non-Jewish member of the couple may not be a member of the synagogue or participate in any religious role in, for example, the Bar or Bat Mitzvah ceremony of his or her child. All of this makes for a lot of uncomfortable situations among all concerned.[6]

Questions:

1)   Do you feel it is important that Jewish teenagers not date non-Jews? Give reasons for your answer.

2)   How much of the resources of the community – including the time of its rabbis and educators, the money for classes and publicity, etc. – should be invested in efforts of *keruv* (reaching out to intermarried couples)? (Remember that the resources of the Jewish community are limited, and so whatever we invest in this will inevitably mean that we will do less on other important projects.)

ACTIVITY:

Role play the following scenario with one person taking the role of the parent and one as the USY'er. Another option is to write a script and creating the dialogue between the individuals.

> *"Mom/Dad, why are Jews so upset about interdating? Perhaps intermarriage is not acceptable, but dating simply means having a good time, without making a lifelong commitment. Why shouldn't I interdate until the right Jewish person comes along?"*

---

3. Synagogue 2000 and Beyond

Synagogues, for most of Jewish history, were simply places to worship and perhaps hold classes. Rabbi Mordecai Kaplan proposed instead that we create synagogue-centers, where the synagogue would continue to be the place for worship and Jewish study, but would also have facilities for social events, for social action efforts, for meetings of all sorts, for arts and crafts, for theater presentations, and even for athletics. His point was that if we really believe that Judaism is a civilization, the very architecture and organization of our institutions should reflect that perception. Moreover, if people find themselves in the synagogue for some things, they are more likely to learn about other synagogue activities, increasing the likelihood that people would broaden and deepen their Jewish identity. As a result of Kaplan's vision, Conservative synagogues often have facilities for Jewish activities in addition to worship and study.

The synagogue of the twentieth century, though, was largely based in its worship on Protestant models, with people facing front led by rabbis and cantors, who were often clothed in robes. This "cathedral model" of worship stressed decorum and professional leadership. At the same time, though, Conservative youth have been educated at Camp Ramah, USY, and some of their synagogues' own youth services to lead the services themselves. Jews definitely should learn these skills, but once they do, they often want to use them, at least from time to time. As a result, many of the larger Conservative synagogues now offer multiple services on any given Shabbat or Festival morning, some with a formal structure led by professionals and some with an informal structure led by laypeople. Some of the older leaders have seen this development as destructive of the synagogue; after all, should we not all pray together, young and old, parents and children, singles and married, etc.? Such complaints are especially common when those in the alternative service(s) are largely not members of the synagogue and just use it for their purposes. Moreover, quality control becomes hard, if not impossible, when there is nobody specific in charge who can say "No" to something or to someone who is unprepared. Now that many such alternative services consist of synagogue members and have developed their own methods of assuring reasonable quality, however, complaints have diminished, and we are getting used to the new "synaplex" structure.[7]

Questions:

1)   List some reasons for and against switching from a single service for everyone to two or more forms of worship each Shabbat. If a congregation decides to make the switch, what architectural and organizational changes must a synagogue make? How are guidelines to be set to insure that all of the services are within the spectrum of the Conservative movement? What is the role of rabbis and cantors in the new synaplex structure? Do you think that this development is healthy for the synagogue and for Conservative Jews? Why or why not?

2)   The Jewish population has shifted dramatically from two-parent homes with children to a variety of new family configurations -- single-parent families, couples without children, "empty-nesters," widows and widowers, gays and lesbians, and divorced people. Many of these groups have been alienated by the synagogue's orientation toward people who fit into the "traditional" family structure. How can the synagogue be a welcoming and Jewishly growing place for all of these new types of families?

ACTIVITY:

Create your own vision for synagogue 2000 and beyond. What does the building look like? What activities go on there? Who is involved? In what ways? What should Conservative education for children look like in the future? What about Jewish education for teenagers and adults? Think also about the synagogue's youth programs, sisterhood and brotherhood, social action activities, etc. How is it a distinctively Conservative synagogue? How is it different from existing synagogues?

4. Jewish Education

Jewish education has changed considerably in form over the last four or five decades. Many Conservative youngsters are now learning in day schools, and the same phenomenon is now developing in the Reform movement as well. Some of these day schools are independent institutions and some are affiliated with synagogues. Synagogues see the availability of a day school as an important way to convince young parents to affiliate with the synagogue and participate in its activities. Sometimes, though, synagogues do not have the room, the funds, or a sufficient number of students for a day school, and sometimes community leaders think that even if individual synagogues could establish a school, a community school would be better. That avoids the duplication of effort and resources which would occur if each synagogue had its own school, and, in any case, it is good for students from several synagogues to meet each other in one school setting.

Conservative leaders in the first half of the twentieth century were adamantly opposed to day schools because if Jews did not go to public schools, they would be isolated in a Jewish environment and thus not learn to be citizens of their country – and, conversely, non-Jews would not get to know Jews and would therefore see us as alien. By the 1960s, though, increasing numbers of Jews felt perfectly well at home in North America but were worried that their children would not learn enough about their Jewish heritage from afternoon schools alone.

That feeling has increased in recent years, as absenteeism has increased as children of divorced parents are living with the other parent on weekends and can no longer attend a Saturday or Sunday class as part of the curriculum. Moreover, it has become clear that, despite the name "Hebrew schools," few of the afternoon schools have time to teach their students enough Hebrew to function intelligently in Conservative worship, let alone carrying on a conversation in Hebrew or even studying Jewish texts in their original Hebrew. In addition, studies indicate that the depth of the child's future Jewish identity is directly dependent upon the number of hours the child studied Jewish subjects, and there are simply more hours available to day schools than to afternoon schools and they come at times in the day in which children are more likely to be able to concentrate.

On the other hand, though, day school education is expensive, especially if a family has three or four children. If you are a young Jewish parent, you also want to be able to afford to join the synagogue, to participate in non-Jewish activities, to have vacations, and to put away money for your children's college education – in addition to paying for Camp Ramah, USY, etc. The sheer cost of Jewish involvement is thus a major issue for individual Jews and for the

Jewish community as a whole. How are we going to make both formal and informal Jewish education affordable for our children and teenagers?

On the other side of these money questions, how shall we make Jewish education a financially attractive field for our own sons and daughters to consider? As it is, there is a major shortage of qualified, let alone dynamic, teachers and youth leaders, and that will only change when those positions provide enough of a salary to raise a family in reasonable comfort. People going into these fields are almost always idealistic, but they cannot live on their idealism alone.

Curriculum issues also abound. Should there be a common curriculum shared by all day schools and afternoon schools affiliated with the Conservative movement -- or at least a common core? What should the goals of a Conservative education be? What should the goals of USY and Camp Ramah be? How should teenage youth programs like USY and Ramah be tied into formal Jewish education for teenagers?

Adult Jewish education poses its own dilemmas. Judaism teaches that Jewish education is a life-long activity. Do we spend too much time and effort on introductory level classes and not enough on deepening the Jewish education of those who participate actively in our programs? How should these needs be balanced? Many rabbis teach groups of lawyers, doctors, and business people in their downtown offices or in the synagogue during weekday luncheons. Are there other formats which should be tried? How can the new technological advances help us in this? How about a lesson on the Torah portion of the week sent out to the entire congregation on e-mail, for example? In short, what should an effective adult Jewish education program for the 21st century look like?

Finally, higher Jewish education has also changed radically over the last fifty years. Now over 200 universities across North America list at least some courses in Jewish studies (although only twenty or so offer more than a few courses in Jewish areas of study). Undergraduate, graduate, and professional programs at the Jewish Theological Seminary of America in New York and at the University of Judaism in Los Angeles are now educating the Jewish lay and professional leaders of tomorrow. What should the shape of those programs be? We now have, for example, two Conservative rabbinical schools in North America in addition to the ones in Israel and Argentina, and all four schools also educate future teachers and educational administrators for our movement. What should characterize the curriculum of the training programs for our rabbis, cantors, and educators of the future? That, in turn, depends, at least in part, on what rabbis, cantors, and educators in the future are going to be called upon to know and to do. What do you imagine that will be?

Questions:

1) If you were the Education Vice-President of your synagogue, would you want to offer both a day school and an afternoon school? Why or why not? How would you balance the resources being allotted to each of them? Explain.

2) What should be the goals of Jewish day schools and afternoon schools? How much instructional time do you think you need to accomplish those goals?

3) What would characterize a Conservative school? What would differentiate it from a Reform or Orthodox school?

4) What should the Jewish community do to make Jewish involvement – and especially Jewish formal and informal education – affordable?

5) Camp Ramah began as a summer camp for children, and now many Ramah camps offer family camps and adult weekends. USY began as a high-school-age youth group for Conservative congregations, but it now includes programs for middle-school children and for college students. Both began as American programs, and they both now have programs for Americans to learn in Israel in summer and during the year and for Israelis to participate in Ramah day camps in Israel. In what ways, if any, should the roles and structures of Camp Ramah and USY change in the years to come?

6) What should be the goals of adult Jewish education? If you were in charge, what kind of program would you create for your synagogue? Why is adult Jewish education important in the first place?

7) What new uses of modern technology would you employ to further the aims of Jewish education for children? for teenagers? for adults?

8) What should be available in the way of Jewish studies in the college that you choose, even if you do not plan to major in that? Why? Should the college be one which grants credit for a junior year at a university in Israel?

5. Men and Women

Many changes have occurred in the roles of men and women in society generally over the last fifty years and in Conservative Jewish life in particular. The Conservative practice of having men and women sit together in worship was in place by the early years of the twentieth century; the first Bat Mitzvah was celebrated by and for Mordecai Kaplan's daughter in 1922; in the 1950s the Committee on Jewish Law and Standards introduced a clause into the *ketubbah* (Jewish wedding contract) to insure that women who have been divorced in state law but whose husbands refuse to give them a Jewish writ of divorce (a *get*) are nevertheless able to remarry in Jewish law as well;[8] in 1954 the Committee approved women having *aliyot* to the Torah; in 1973 and 1974 the Committee permitted women to count as part of a *minyan* and to act as leaders of prayer; in 1983 the Jewish Theological Seminary of America voted to admit women to its rabbinical school; and in synagogues across the country women have taken on leadership roles, including many who have served as president of their synagogue.

These changes, however, have not come with ease. After all, on the emotional level alone, they have required people accustomed to sharp role differentiations between males and females in Jewish ritual life to adjust to women doing a number of things previously reserved for men. That, of course, parallels the emotional adjustments that we have all made in regard to women serving in traditionally male roles in society generally – and men serving in some roles previously restricted in fact, if not in law, to women. In the case of Jewish ritual life, however, there is the important complicating factor of Jewish law, especially for the Conservative movement, which sees itself bound by Jewish law even if it also understands that Jewish law changes over time. These emotional and legal issues have meant that Conservative institutions have adopted a range of policies on these issues, with the resulting conflicts over what should be the policy for regional or national events. Moreover, some people on the right have left the movement as a result of their opposition to these changes, while some on the left have left the movement because the changes were not occurring fast enough.

Questions:

1) Have you experienced a shift in policy on the role of women in your synagogue or in some other group affiliated with the Conservative movement? How was the change introduced? What, if any, were the reasons given? How did you feel about it? Do you think such changes in the movement have been made too rapidly? too slowly? Explain.

2)   When Conservative Jews meet together in regional or national events, or in nationally sponsored institutions like USY or Camp Ramah, how should the variations in practice within the Conservative movement with regard to the role of women be accommodated? Does the majority practice always win? Is the language of "win" and "lose" appropriate here at all, or are we better off with ideas of pluralism?

3)   Some have pointed out that women serving in roles traditionally held by men alone not only puts new people in those roles but changes the nature of the roles themselves -- or, at least, may do so. Do you think that women serving as rabbis, for example, will, as a group, approach that role differently than men do as a group? Or are the individual differences among the various people who are rabbis more important in the way they function than the difference in gender? What about women as presidents of synagogues? as students in courses in Jewish studies? in rabbinical school?

4)   Some have maintained that the impetus for the changes in the roles of women within the Conservative Movement has been feminism and the changes it has engendered in society in general rather than the values of traditional Judaism itself. Even those who argue, on the other side, that the Jewish tradition itself has over time increasingly strengthened the status of women vis-a-vis men and that recent changes are in line with that trajectory inherent in the tradition must, in fairness, acknowledge that recent social changes have had a significant impact on the discussion within the Jewish tradition. Does it affect the authority of Jewish law if contemporary social and moral perspectives are significant factors in deciding how to interpret and apply Jewish law now?

In answering, review the section from Emet Ve-Emunah on Jewish law, discussed in Chapter Three, Section E, above, and think about (i) the authority which rabbinic Judaism ascribes to the rabbis of each generation to apply the law to the circumstances of their own generation; and (ii) the role of custom in determining Jewish law, with Schechter's related insistence on acknowledging the role of catholic Israel in determining Jewish law. On the other hand, should Jewish law just mirror current values and practices in general society? How do you think that the Conservative Jewish community, which is committed to traditional Jewish law with its inherent openness to change, should balance these competing concerns?

5)   For the first hundred years of the Conservative movement, the daily minyan in most Conservative synagogues consisted almost exclusively of men, and usually of those old enough to retire. What do you think that the daily minyan will look like in the years to come?

6)	Even those who support egalitarianism might agree that equal does not mean same, that men and women, as groups, may be equal in their rights and maybe even in their abilities, but that does not mean that they are the same. Indeed, some recent studies by scholars like Deborah Tannen indicate that men and women even express themselves differently in speech patterns and therefore often do not understand each other. Should gender differences be reflected in Jewish rituals in any way, even in an egalitarian setting? For example, should some parts of the service be led only by men and others only by women? Should women be required to wear *tefillin* to be counted as part of a minyan, or are the black leather straps an inherently male form of dress? Should women's *tallitot* or headdress in worship be different in style than men's? Should women being honored with an *aliyah* be required to wear these garments altogether?

6. Pluralism Within Our Movement

The issues surrounding the roles of men and women are just one of the arenas where there are differences in the ideas and/or practices of members of the Conservative movement. In 1968, some liberal members of the movement (the "left") created the Reconstructionist Rabbinical College, thus ending the time when all Reconstructionists were also Conservative Jews. After the decision of the Jewish Theological Seminary of American to ordain women, the most traditional members of the movement (the "right") created its own rabbinical school and disaffiliated from the Conservative Movement. While this splintering in each case involved small numbers of people and a small percentage of the members of the Conservative movement, each of these splits was emotionally wrenching. Moreover, these events made it clear that the Conservative Movement could no longer be, as it was in the middle of the twentieth century, all things to all people. These losses on the right and on the left have therefore raised some hard theological and legal questions about how the large numbers of Conservative Jews (still the largest movement in North America) should handle the variations in thought and practice among its members.

Questions:

1)	Name some areas other than those involving the relative roles of men and women where institutions within the Conservative movement have different practices. Think, for example, of the nature of services, the educational curriculum and ambience of schools, the degree of commitment to social action activities vs. prayer vs. study, etc. What makes all these institutions Conservative?

237

2) The differences from one synagogue, or school, or camp, or youth group to the next are, in some ways, a healthy variety which the movement offers its members. Why is that healthy? Why is it traditionally Jewish for there to be such variations?

    (*Consider source #23 in Chapter Three, Section C, and consider the variety of forms of Judaism which have existed historically.*)[9]

3) Review the way in which Jewish legal decisions are made in the Conservative Movement (Chapter Three, Section E). How is that designed to preserve the ability of individual congregations to shape their own form of Jewish practice and yet retain coherence within the movement? Do you think that that structure for making halakhic decisions within the movement can successfully sustain this balance? If so, explain why, and if not, explain what changes should be made to achieve both pluralism and coherence of practice in the decades to come.

4) Review the way in which the Conservative movement has approached matters of Jewish belief (Chapter Four). Has the publication of *Emet Ve-Emunah* effectively defined who is a Conservative Jew in belief and who is not? Explain your answer.

5) In the end, do you think that there are more things that unite Conservative Jews than divide them, or the reverse? Explain.

6) What would you suggest we should do to increase our sense of being one movement while yet preserving a healthy pluralism?

7. Relations With the Other Movements in Judaism and With Non-Jews

Recent Efforts by the Conservative Movement to work together with the other movements in Judaism have largely failed. The Synagogue Council of America, which had served as an umbrella organization for synagogue leaders from all movements, dissolved, and its replacement, the National Council of Synagogues, includes only the non-Orthodox branches of Judaism. Fewer and fewer rabbis participate in local Boards of Rabbis, which are supposed to bring together rabbis of all the movements for joint meetings and activities. Many Orthodox groups, in fact, refuse even to attend a community event held in a Conservative or Reform synagogue, even if no food is being served and so conflicting standards of *kashrut* are not an issue. Moreover, some Orthodox groups have taken money from the community as a whole for their schools, synagogues, and *mikva'ot* and then have refused to participate with the rest of the community on joint projects and have denied access to Conservative and Reform rabbis to *mikva'ot* for purposes of carrying out the rite of immersion for converts whose education has been supervised by those rabbis.

The Reform movement, on the other hand, in 1985 officially accepted patrilineal descent as conveying Jewish identity. That is, instead of adhering to the traditional definition in Jewish law of a Jew being a person who is born to a Jewish woman or converted to Judaism according to the requirements and procedures of Jewish law, the Reform movement will now recognize as Jewish a person whose father is Jewish but whose mother is not, provided that some measures be taken to raise the child as a Jew. While this approach might recommend itself to us now because of its egalitarianism and its recognition of the importance of the father's role as well as the mother's in raising a child, historically one could be a Jew by birth only if one's mother was Jewish. One might imagine that a *takkanah* (amendment to the law) might be passed to change this traditional definition of a Jew by birth, but the Jewish community as a whole does not have a mechanism to change its criteria of membership, even if it wanted to do so, and it seems divisive and dangerous for one group of Jews to make that change without agreement from the others. The Conservative and Orthodox movements, on the contrary, have reasserted their commitment to the traditional definition of who is a Jew. The Reform move, then, has created a whole group of people who are Jewish according to some and not according to others, and that, among other things, threatens the ability of Jews from the various movements to marry each other.

Relations with other religions, especially Christianity, have improved considerably since the publication of the Vatican II document, *Nostra Aetatae*, subsequent Vatican documents on the Jews,[10] and parallel documents among many Protestant groups. Some on the Christian right, however, still missionize heavily among Jews, and anti-Semitism still exists. Moreover, conversion by Jews to Christianity and to various Oriental religions has increased markedly in recent decades, and the rate of intermarriage between Jews and people of other religions is strikingly higher than it was, both the result, in part, of Jews being so thoroughly accepted within the non-Jewish world. At the same time, productive dialogue between Jews and Christians, in particular, has taken place regionally, nationally, and internationally in recent decades, resulting in new levels of understanding, cooperation, and friendship. There have even been a number of theological writings on how one can be thoroughly committed to one's own religion and yet appreciate and learn from the religions of others.[11]

Questions:

1) How shall the Conservative Movement seek to repair the damage that has been done in relationships with the other movements over the past several decades? What new initiatives in cross-denominational cooperation should it try? How?

2) Why is it important for Jews of all ideologies to work together on a number of projects in the first place? Conversely, on what issues is it right and proper that there be separate movements with different ideologies, practices, and programs?

3) Why is it important to create good relations of mutual understanding and cooperation with the non-Jewish community? That is, why is it not a good idea to ghettoize ourselves? Give both theological and practical answers to these questions.

4) What are the limits of the relations we should forge with non-Jews?

ACTIVITY:

Write a personal (imaginary) letter to the Pope. The letter should describe your Jewish commitment and what you feel should be the relationship between Christians and Jews. Include any questions, suggestions, or criticisms of the church's actions towards Jews and of Jewish actions towards Christians.

8. Israel

The issues involved in our relationships with other Jews and with non-Jews have direct implications not only for Conservative Jews living in the Diaspora, but also for the Jews and non-Jews of Israel. With regard to the non-Jews of Israel, we clearly want to support freedom of religion in Israel, in accordance with its Declaration of Independence, but does that extend to missionary efforts on the part of any non-Jewish religion there? The State of Israel allowed the Mormons to construct a center in Jerusalem on condition that they not missionize among Jews. Is that a reasonable restriction on their freedom of religion? More pervasively, the State of Israel is self-consciously a Jewish state, as manifested in its calendar, its language, its laws (e.g., El Al, the national airline owned by the State of Israel, is prohibited from flying into and out of Israel on Shabbat), and even the Star of David on the Israeli flag. What does that say to the non-Jews living in Israel?

With regard to the Israeli Jewish community, we noted in Chapter Four the problems that the Conservative movement is having there in procuring government money for its synagogues and schools on a fair basis with the monies the government allots to Orthodox institutions. Israel does not have a separation of church and state, as the United States does, and so religious institutions, including non-Jewish ones, are funded by the Israeli government; to date, however, the monies apportioned to Jewish institutions have been given almost exclusively to Orthodox ones. In addition, while people of other faiths may choose any clergyperson they want to perform their marriages and divorces, Jews must use the Orthodox rabbinate. Both of these factors make the freedom of religion guaranteed by the Israeli Declaration of Independence a freedom for people of all religions except Jews.

And then there is the stance of the Conservative Movement toward *aliyah*, that is, moving to Israel to live there (literally, "going up" to Israel). A number of texts within our tradition, from the Torah on, either assume that most Jews are going to live in Israel or see it as a *mitzvah* to live there. On the other hand, some texts in our tradition, from the Talmud on, do not see it as a *mitzvah* to move there, and, after all is said and done, the vast majority of Jews (including rabbis) over the centuries have not lived in Israel.[12] Moreover, some maintain that if everyone made *aliyah,* that would not be good for Israel (since it does not have the room) and historical experience indicates that it would not be good for the Jewish People either: we should not "put all our eggs in one basket," as it were, even if that basket is Israel. These conflicting factors and perspectives have led to sharply conflicting feelings and practices within the Conservative Movement vis-a-vis *aliyah.*

Questions:

1) How, in your view, should Israel balance its Jewish character with its democratic character? In particular, how can it be a distinctly Jewish state and yet grant meaningful freedom of religion to people of other faiths?

   (You might think of other democracies with established, government-sponsored churches, such as England, where Anglican Protestantism is the official church, or Italy, where Catholicism is the official church. What has that official status granted to one religion meant for those of its citizens who do not affirm that faith? for those who do? Are these good models for Israel? If so, why, and if not, why not?)

2) How does your view on the integration of Israel's Jewish and democratic elements translate into how you would have the Israelis treat the Palestinians, who are generally either Muslim or Christian? (You may want to distinguish political from religious matters here, but maybe not.)

3) How would you have the Conservative Movement both in the Diaspora and in Israel respond to the Orthodox stranglehold on Israeli government funds for synagogues and schools? on the authority to perform marriages, divorces, and conversions?

4) How, in your view, should Conservative schools, youth groups, and synagogues present the prospect of *aliyah*? Explain your thinking on this issue.

9. Conservative Jewish Ritual Practice

In the middle of the twentieth century, most Conservative homes were kosher, but many families would eat anything outside their homes. A fairly large percentage of Conservative Jews would attend services on Shabbat, but mostly on Friday nights and not on Saturday morning or afternoon. Few refrained from those activities prohibited by Jewish law on Shabbat. Very high percentages of Jews joined a synagogue, if only because to be accepted in American society one had to be "churched." Services, especially in large synagogues, were led almost entirely by the rabbi and cantor, and they were usually dressed in robes. Most Conservative Jews did not pray daily, either in the synagogue or at home, but virtually everyone came to at least some part of the services on the High Holy Days and on those days when the *Yizkor* memorial prayers are recited. Most attended synagogue on Purim evening, but few did the next morning.

Home rituals, like lighting candles on Friday night and on Hanukkah and arranging for a Passover *seder* were common, but few built a *sukkah* or bought a *lulav* and *etrog* for Sukkot. *Havdallah* was largely unknown.

As for life cycle rituals, during the middle of the twentieth century Jewish boys were almost invariably circumcised on the eighth day after their birth with the proper prayers, as according to Jewish law; this usually took place in the hospital since women who gave birth without complications commonly stayed in the hospital for a period of two weeks, and so holding the *brit milah* in the hospital enabled the mother to attend. Girls were named in the synagogue in conjunction with their father's *aliyah*, usually the Shabbat after the baby was born and therefore with the mother and daughter not present. Bar Mitzvah ceremonies took place on Saturday mornings, when the boy would chant the Haftarah and possibly other parts of the service; Bat Mitzvah ceremonies, though, were most often held as part of Friday night services, and exactly what the girl would do to mark the occasion varied widely from synagogue to synagogue. Couples about to be married assumed that the rabbi would determine all aspects of the wedding ceremony, and the *ketubbot* generally included the text alone without any artwork. Funerals were almost all done according to Jewish tradition, but few Conservative congregants participated in a *Hevrah Kaddisha* to prepare the body.

Much of this has changed since then. Large numbers of Jews fail to join synagogues, for it no longer is socially necessary to be churched to be accepted socially within American society (even though the vast majority of Christians do, in fact, belong to churches and some forty or fifty percent attend services weekly). This means synagogue members in our day have consciously chosen to join for one or more reasons, and so a greater proportion of synagogue members now are serious about their Judaism than was the case in mid-century. Moreover, American society generally has shown a renewed interest in ritual and in not leaving it to the professionals alone. Ramah and USY experiences have added to that trend, for those who learn to lead services in their youth often want to continue to participate in a leadership role, at least from time to time, in adulthood. The informality of those settings has also had its effect on how the adults of today want to pray.

In the synagogue, this has meant that increasing numbers of synagogues offer multiple services on Shabbat mornings, varying in the nature of who leads the service, its degree of formality or informality, and perhaps the roles open to women. Some also have learners' minyanim, family minyanim (which usually means services which are geared to parents with their young children), and/or services for children or teens. Whatever the specific offerings, synagogues are now more cognizant of the differing styles of worship needed by the various constituencies within the congregation.

Increased seriousness has also meant that the most well-attended service on Shabbat in many synagogues is now the one on Saturday mornings rather than the late service on Friday nights. A number of synagogues, in fact, have abandoned late Friday night services altogether, or have restricted them to once a month, offering only a traditional service at sunset. Rabbis in diminishing numbers wear robes, and, in general, the service feels less like a Protestant service now than it did in mid-century. Bat Mitzvah ceremonies are now generally on Saturday mornings, and in those synagogues which allow women to participate in the Torah service Bat Mitzvah girls typically do exactly what boys do for their Bar Mitzvah -- that is, read the Haftarah and perhaps all or part of the Torah reading as well. Egalitarian synagogues allow Bat Mitzvah girls (and other female family members or friends) to lead the services as well.

The mid-century patterns of attendance on the High Holy Days and on Purim remain the same. While the new generation seems less committed to Yizkor services *per se*, much larger numbers of members are committed to Festival services for their own sake, and so the number of families that purchase a *lulav* and an *etrog* for Sukkot has increased dramatically in many synagogues. The daily *minyan* remains the province of older men in most Conservative synagogues, but that may soon be changing as those born in Europe pass on and the responsibility to maintain a *minyan* now falls on Jews with more egalitarian convictions. Moreover, those who have grown up through Ramah or USY know that they should pray daily, and so while some do so at home, the need of the congregation to support a daily *minyan* may soon bring many such people to the synagogue for daily services, at least on a rotational basis.

Even the architecture of some new synagogues, especially small-to-medium-sized ones, has changed from everyone facing front toward a raised *bimah* (platform or stage) to the "Sephardic style," where the *bimah* is situated in the middle of the room, with seats surrounding it in the shape of a U and the ark in the front of the room (the opening of the U). Because that arrangement puts the congregation in close proximity to what is going on on the *bimah*, it communicates the expectation that everyone will participate actively rather than passively watch what is happening in front of them, probably at some distance. Even large synagogues, for whom such architectural changes are difficult if not impossible, have sometimes created a thrust platform in front of the *bimah* which is deliberately just a few inches above the level on which everyone is seated so as to convey a warmer, closer feel between those leading the service and the congregation.

As Jewish family education programs have blossomed, and as graduates of Ramah and USY form homes of their own, more and more Conservative families are incorporating a series of home rituals into their lives. In addition to lighting candles for Shabbat and Hanukkah, many families engage in the full range of traditional practices around the Friday evening and Saturday noon table, with the singing of "*Shalom Aleikhem*," the reading of "*Eishet Hayyil*" (Proverbs 31) in honor of the woman of the household, the blessing of children, and *kiddush* before the meal and *zemirot* (Sabbaths songs) and *Birkat Ha-Mazon* (Grace after Meals) thereafter. Many also have a *Havdallah* ceremony in their homes. The Passover Seder is, in increasing numbers of families, not simply a perfunctory reading of the Haggadah, but a major participatory experience, in which people are assigned parts ahead of time and told to plan new interpretations or games to tell the Passover story in ever more innovative ways. Much larger numbers of families build their own *sukkah*, with synagogues offering easy-to-put-up "*sukkah* kits" for those of us who are mechanically challenged (!) and sometimes making it a USY project for teenagers to help families erect their *sukkah*. Families then invite friends (perhaps members of their *havurah*) for meals or for "progressive meals," with people walking from *sukkah* to *sukkah* for different courses.

Since the 1970s, many Conservative synagogues have formed *havurot* (friendship groups), consisting of twenty people or so, usually of roughly the same age, who not only engage in ritual ceremonies together but also study and often socialize together as well. This idea of Rabbi Harold Schulweis[13] helps to make the synagogue less big and unfriendly by breaking it down into smaller groups who interact more personally with each other while also benefitting from the larger numbers of people, the facilities, and the expanded services of the synagogue. It also adds to the participatory nature of Jewish life.

Life cycle events have become ever more participatory and innovative. While the traditional text is usually preserved in the circumcision ceremony for boys, families often hand out sheets of additional readings to all those in attendance, and the parents often explain why they chose the name they did, offer a short *d'var Torah* (or ask someone else to do so), or talk a bit about their feelings of joy over their newborn and what he represents in the line of their family tree. It is no longer the *mohel* and rabbi alone who do the ceremony; it is also grandparents, friends, and the parents themselves. While an *aliyah* for naming a girl is still popular, it is now generally postponed until the mother and daughter can be present. A number of families have, in addition or in place of that, created a *brit banot* or *simchat bat* ceremony to welcome their newborn daughters into the Covenant, sometimes more or less parallel to the readings used for boys and sometimes radically different from those. The same participatory nature of modern circumcision ceremonies for boys characterizes *brit banot* ceremonies for girls as well. Joyous singing, of course, accompanies all of these ceremonies.

Bar and Bat Mitzvah ceremonies follow this line of increasing participation. Parents and other family members may take part in the service, with parents each speaking to their child for a few moments during services or at the *kiddush* following. The Bar or Bat Mitzvah generally writes his or her own interpretation of the Torah or Haftarah reading; even though that is often with some help from the rabbi or parents, the point is for the boy or girl to say something that he or she really means. A number of synagogues have boys (and girls) come to services on the Monday or Thursday before the Bar (or Bat) Mitzvah service to put on *tallit* and *tefillin* for the first time as part of a *minyan*. Some families travel to Israel for this event or after it for an educational trip and possibly another service in Israel to mark the occasion.

Couples about to be married now take a much more active role in understanding and shaping the ceremony itself and in choosing the text and form of the *ketubbah* (wedding document) than they did in times past. In many cases, couples choose to have their *ketubbah* calligraphed with artwork meaningful to them surrounding the text. Increasing numbers of couples are choosing to engage in some or all of the customs which can precede the wedding: an *aufruf* (that is, an *aliyah*) to the Torah on the Shabbat preceding the wedding, but now often with the bride as well as the groom participating and sometimes with one or both of them giving a *d'var Torah* as well; fasting from sunrise on the day of the wedding; a groom's table (*hatan's tisch*), in which the groom (and sometimes now also the bride) gives a *d'var Torah* interrupted by joyful singing; *bedecken*, that is veiling of the bride and blessing her; and, after the procession to the *huppah* (wedding canopy), the bride sometimes walks around the groom three or seven times, and sometimes the groom walks around the bride as well and/or they both walk around the *huppah* together, symbolizing that each now becomes the center of the other's world and they are about to create a new home, symbolized by the *huppah*. None of these ceremonies is necessary to make the wedding legal and binding, and few, if any, of them were in common practice in mid-century, but more and more weddings include at least some of these features in order to involve the couple and their friends more intimately in the way they will mark their wedding day.

Finally, funerals remain, of course, a difficult time of life for everyone concerned, but even here the increasing trend toward more participation is in evidence. A number of synagogues have created a *hevra kaddisha*, one consisting of men to prepare male bodies for burial and another consisting of women for female bodies. In addition to the rabbi's eulogy, close family members of the deceased often offer remembrances of their own during the funeral. The closer and more serious community which now makes up many of our synagogues are then likely to provide the *minyanim* for services during the week of *shivah* (the seven days of mourning) together with the emotional support and the simple services (like meals) which the family needs at that time.

In all of these cases, the trend among those who care enough to join a synagogue is toward taking Jewish ritual life more seriously, making it a meaningful part of their lives.

Questions:

1) As people participate more actively in leading worship and in shaping their life cycle events, what is the role of the rabbi? the cantor?

2) Are there any limits to the innovations now being tried in life cycle ceremonies? Consider halakhic parameters and the practical considerations of time, the patience of those attending, the skill and taste of the planners, etc.

10. Moral Issues Facing the Conservative Movement

The Jewish tradition, of course, consists not only of faith in God, membership in the Jewish people, study of Jewish sources, and Jewish ritual life, but of moral thought and action as well. We are called upon to "do the right and the good in the eyes of God" (Devarim 6:18), and a large number of the Torah's commandments require that we be respectful, honest, and caring in our interactions with others and that we seek to alleviate the pain and suffering in this world.

Even when we want to do the right thing, sometimes it is not clear as to what that is. Should, for example, we support government efforts to get poor people off of welfare and into jobs, in line with the highest form of charity described by Maimonides (namely, helping people to support themselves), or should we provide a safety net to the poor even when they do not or cannot work, in line with the Torah's apparently unconditional commands to help the poor? Should we support abortion legislation which limits abortion, as the Jewish tradition does, to cases in which the mother's or child's life or health is at stake, or should we opt for no governmental interference at all in the woman's right to choose on the grounds of religious freedom? What should our stance be toward gays and lesbians? When the right path is not clear, as in these cases, we are duty-bound to try to discern God's will in our day so that we can know how to "do the right and the good in God's eyes."

Questions:

1)   The Conservative Movement's Committee on Jewish Law and Standards has recently ruled on such issues as family violence, privacy in cyberspace, and a variety of questions in medical ethics. What is the status of such rulings for you as a Conservative Jew? What would make such rulings more meaningful for you in guiding your moral decisions?

2)   The Rabbinical Assembly's Commission on Human Sexuality recently published its *Rabbinic Letter on Human Intimacy*, intended to be studied widely as the springboard for discussions among teenagers and adults on matters of sex and family relations. Is that a better format than legal rulings (teshuvot) for bringing the Jewish tradition to bear on moral issues of our time for Conservative Jews? When do you think a *teshuvah* is appropriate, and when is a rabbinic letter a better format? (Consider the difference between those cases where the Jewish tradition is clear about what is moral and what is not, as against those situations in which it is not clear as to what Judaism would have us think and do.)

B. Envisioning the Future of Conservative Judaism

Each of the issues above is important in itself, and much can and should be done in each area to resolve the problems involved and to maximize the opportunities. At some point, though, Conservative leaders of today and tomorrow must turn their attention to an even broader picture. They must ask themselves what the Jewish and non-Jewish world of the future is likely to be like and how Conservative Judaism can function productively in that world.

This level of discussion is important for several reasons. First, if the world of the future will most likely be significantly different from present circumstances in specific ways, reasonable planning for the future of the movement must take that into account. After all, to contribute effectively and meaningfully to that world, and to attract people because the movement is doing that, requires that Conservative Judaism understand the new realities and prepare for them so that it can respond appropriately.

Moreover, thinking about the future may help us with our present planning. It may be, for example, that one of the issues which bothers us tremendously today (like one of those on the list above) simply will not be an issue tomorrow, and so maybe our time and effort is better spent elsewhere. On the other hand, it may be that resolving an issue today, or taking advantage of an opportunity today, is absolutely critical in our being able to function effectively as Conservative Jews tomorrow, and so we should concentrate as much of our time and resources on this as we can. We can only choose intelligently among our present problems and opportunities, then, if we think about the long-term.

The problem with this kind of thinking, though, is that it is very speculative. After all, how can we really know what tomorrow will bring? We can guess, and we can even guess intelligently if we consult a variety of experts to advise us about demographic, social, economic, and cultural trends in the future. In the end, though, this kind of thinking requires us to predict what may well be beyond our capability to imagine. Moreover, how can the most imaginative among us know which of our dreams are realistic and which are only pipe-dreams?

With these cautions in mind, then, but with the rationales for doing this kind of thinking also in mind, discuss in your group questions such as the ones below. In each area, there is one question asking about the general world and another asking about Jews. If you think of other areas which should be considered in our vision for the future, please add them! *After you discuss one area, ask what the implications for Conservative Judaism are for that area before you move on to the next.*

Population.

a) How do you think the world's overpopulation problem will be resolved in the future? By mass starvation? By mass war? By enforced birth control measures? By improved economic and social circumstances? (Now, at any rate, the higher the economic level of a society, the lower its reproductive rate.) Will the world be able to feed the human population on it? If so, how? Will other resources – clean air and water, energy, etc. – be available to all or most of the world's people?

b) How will the Jews' contrary problem of a diminishing population be resolved? Will we simply be even fewer than we are now? If so, will we be able to survive as a people with half or a quarter of our present numbers? Will we retain our ranks or grow more numerous through education? through conversion? in response to anti-Semitism?

Economics.

a) What are the prospects for economic stability or even growth in the future? Will increased population ultimately mean that the gap between rich and poor will widen yet further? Will the middle class hold? What do these factors mean for the stability of nations and of world peace in general?

b) How will Jews fare in the economic world of the future? Will the fact that Jews are increasingly becoming doctors and lawyers rather than businesspeople mean that Jews as a whole will have less money and that Jewish institutions will gain less in charitable contributions? How will Jewish families and the Jewish community as a whole afford to pay for the social services they need and for the Jewish education of their members?

Family Patterns.

a) In what kind of family settings will most people be living? What implications will that have for the stability of society and for the place of religion in it?

b) Will changing family patterns make a family-oriented religion like Judaism obsolete? Will Jews instead develop new Jewish rituals, or new forms of doing the old ones, to make Jewish home rituals meaningful? Will Jewish moral norms, currently based on the assumption of heterosexual families living with children, change to accept and guide Jews living in the new family patterns, or will they simply condemn them? If the former, how will that happen?

Living Arrangements.

a) In response to increasing population and therefore increasing scarcity and rising prices for land, will people in North America live in more densely populated arrangements -- that is, apartment buildings rather than single-family homes? Will they instead spread out even further from urban centers and commute long distances to work -- or do their work at home by computer linkup? What will this mean for the feelings of people about their relations to others?

b) Jewish life depends on Jewish community. As living arrangements change for everyone, will Jews live in areas nearby to each other so that they can continue Jewish communal life, or will they instead spread out and thus make Jewish communal life hard to make happen? What will their living arrangements mean for the placing and function of synagogues? schools? How will the Jewish community be organized?

Transportation and Communication.

a) How close will our "global village" actually become in the future? What will this mean in terms of national and regional loyalties? What will it mean for our knowledge of other cultures and peoples?

b) As Jews interact ever more constantly with non-Jews, will Jews be ever more tempted to question the importance of their specific Jewish identity and to assimilate? Will they instead gain an appreciation for their own culture and religion when they learn about those of others?

Education.

a) Will the new forms of technology radically change the way and the settings in which people learn? Are both the urban ghetto school and the rural schoolhouse things of the past as people do all their learning at home? Will the goals as well as the forms of education change?

b) How can Jewish education benefit from the new technology? Will the goals of Jewish education change as Jews plumb their tradition for guidance in living in a significantly new world?

These kinds of questions can literally drive you crazy! They are, clearly, unanswerable with any degree of certainty until the future is actually here. They are, moreover, so speculative that one quickly loses any sense of how to judge what is a correct answer and what is not. And yet anyone planning seriously for the future must consider them. Are there yet other areas which good planning for the future should include?

A Faith for Moderns

Conservative Judaism involves a combination of Jewish commitment, flexibility, tolerance, intellectual vigor, moral sensitivity, and spirituality that has characterized Judaism historically and that has made it the wise tradition that it is. To practice it requires maturity and responsibility in both action and thought. Consequently, it is not easy to identify seriously as a Conservative Jew, but it is an especially authentic and meaningful way of being Jewish.

Endnotes

Chapter Two

1.   Cited in Mordecai Waxman, ed., *Tradition and Change* (New York: The Burning Bush Press, 1958), p. 9.

2.   Arthur Hertzberg, "Conservative Judaism," *Encyclopedia Judaica*, Vol. 5, col. 902.

3.   John J. Appel, "The *Trefa* Banquet," *Commentary*, February, 1966, pp. 75-78; cf. also *American Jewish Archives* of Hebrew Union College - Jewish Institute of Religion, November, 1974, pp. 128-133. I would like to thank Rabbis Stuart Kelman and Stanley Chyet for these references.

4.   Oscar I. Janowsky, *The JWB Survey* (New York: The Dial Press, 1948), p. 239.

5.   *American Hebrew*, XXIX (November 16, 1886), p. 34, cited in Moshe Davis, *The Emergence of Conservative Judaism* (Philadelphia: The Jewish Publication Society of America, 1963) p. 239.

6.   Solomon Schechter, *Report of the First Annual Meeting of the United Synagogue* (New York: United Synagogue, 1913), pp. 16-19; reprinted in Waxman, *Tradition and Change*, pp. 163-172.

7.   Solomon Schechter, *Report of the Second Annual Meeting of the United Synagogue*, p. 26.

8.   Norman Bentwich, *Solomon Schechter: A Biography* (Philadelphia: The Jewish Publication Society of America, 1938), pp. 191, 195, 190.

9.   *American Hebrew*, XXIX (January 7, 1887), p. 136; cited in Davis, *Emergence*, p. 239.

10.   *American Hebrew*, XXV (February 5, 1886), pp. 194-195; cited in Davis, *Emergence*, p. 235.

11.   Alexander Kohut, *The Ethics of the Fathers* (New York: 1920), pp. 3, 14-17; cited in Davis, *Emergence*, pp. 222-223.

12.   Alexander Kohut, "Science and Judaism," *Jewish Messenger*, LIX (May 7, 1886), p. 4; cited in Davis, *Emergence*, pp. 289-290.

13.   Kohut, *Ethics*, p. 48; cited in Davis, *Emergence*, pp. 223-224.

14.   The phrase occurs only in the Jerusalem Talmud (P. T. Bava Metzia 7:1 [11b] and Yevamot 12:1 [12c]), but the principle is used in the Babylonian Talmud and the later codes as well: cf. Menachem Elon, "Minhag." in the *Encyclopedia Judaica*, Vol. 12, cols. 5-26, esp. cols. 13-19. As Elon points out, custom could add to Jewish law in many areas, and change it in monetary matters, but it could not permit that which had been forbidden in ritual areas. Only a formal takkanah (revision) by the rabbis could do that.

15.   Solomon Schechter, *Studies in Judaism* (New York: Meridian Books and Philadelphia: The Jewish Publication Society of America, 1958 [paperback]), pp. 16-17, 15.

16.   Robert Gordis, "Authority in Jewish Law," *Proceedings of the Rabbinical Assembly*, 1941-1944 (New York: The Rabbinical Assembly, 1944), pp. 64-93; reprinted in Seymour Siegel, ed., *Conservative Judaism and Jewish Law* (New York: The Rabbinical Assembly, 1977), pp. 47-78.

17.   Schechter, *Studies*, p. 15.

18. The Rabbis of the Talmud also distinguished between *peshat* and *derash*, but for them *peshat* signified the accepted interpretation of the text; cf. *Shabbat 63a*, where what passes as *peshat* is clearly not that, and cf. R. Loewe, "The Plain Meaning of Scripture in Early Jewish Exegesis, " *Papers of the Institute of Jewish Studies* (London: Institute of Jewish Studies, 1964), Vol. 1, pp. 140-185, and Bacher, *Arkhai Midrash* (Jerusalem: Carmiel, 1923, 1960), Vol. II, p. 269, n. 3. It was only when the medieval Jewish grammarians had done their work that *peshat* came to denote the meaning of the text itself as distinct from any of its later rabbinic interpretations. I would like to thank my friend, colleague, and teacher, Dr. Elieser Slomovic, for directing me to these sources.

19. For example, cf. the papers reprinted in Part II of Waxman, *Tradition and Change*, the earliest of which is by Louis Finkelstein, entitled "The Things that Unite Us," from the *Proceedings of the Rabbinical Assembly*, 1927.

20. E. g., Arthur J. Levine, "Needed--A Definition," *Judaism*, Vol. 26, No. 3 (Summer, 1977), pp. 292-295. Cf. Chapter V of this sourcebook.

21. Solomon Schechter, "The Work of Heaven," in Waxman, *Tradition and Change*, pp. 163-172.

Chapter Three

1. Mordecai Waxman, *Tradition and Change*, p. 20.

2. For example, compare Deuteronomy 16:3 with Deuteronomy 16:8. A good summary of the evidence for the historical approach is in the article "Biblical Criticism" by Isaac Landman in *The Universal Jewish Encyclopedia*, Vol. II, pp. 284-293.

3. Except for *Massekhet Berakhot*, there is no Babylonian Talmud on *Seder Zeraim* (perhaps because the agricultural laws applied only to Israel), and there is no Babylonian Talmud on *Seder Tohorot* either, except for *Massekhet Niddah*, probably because all other forms of impurity could no longer be dissolved since, according to the Torah, that required sprinkling with the ashes of the red heifer which had been slaughtered in the Temple, which became impossible after the destruction of the Temple. The Babylonian Talmud also lacks *Massekhtot Eduyyot, Avot, Middot,* and *Kinnim*. The Jerusalem Gemara is missing all of *Seder Kodashim* and *Seder Tohorot* (except for a brief section on *Massekhet Niddah*) as well as *Massekhtot Eduyyot* and *Avot*. Most of these omissions deal with laws dependent upon the Temple, and so the lack of these sections of Talmud may be because those laws could no longer be followed and therefore were not discussed, or it may be that they were discussed but that the record of those discussions got lost over time, as more and more generations lived without the Temple and therefore paid little attention to the laws concerning it.

4. B. *Shabbat* 87a, B. *Yoma* 75a, B. *Haggigah* 14a.

5. This theme is considered in Max Kadushin, *The Rabbinic Mind* (New York: The Jewish Theological Seminary of America, 1952), Chapters, III - IV, esp. on the "indeterminacy of belief," pp. 131-142.

6. I would like to thank my friend and colleague, Dr. Joel Rembaum, for his advice on Section (B) of this chapter.

7. Others suggest a nice, alternative interpretation of the last words of this Midrash, "*Nitzhuni banai, nitzhuni banai.*" Instead of "My children have overcome Me, they have overcome Me," translate (on the basis of the root *netzah*) "My children have given Me eternal life, they have given Me eternal life."

8. The Hebrew phrase, תורה מסיני, literally means "(Torah) from Sinai," although here -- and often -- it is translated "on Sinai." Prof. Jose Faur, formerly of the Jewish Theological Seminary of America, suggests

another interpretation based on time rather than space: "Torah from (the time of) Sinai," i.e., beginning at Sinai and continuing through history.

9. For further discussion of this doctrine of tacit consent to bind future generations, as well as an alternative line of explanation following the philosophy of the French Jewish philosopher, Emmanuel Levinas, see my *Mitzvah Means Commandment*, (New York: United Synagogue of America, 1989), pp. 81-96.

10. It is, of course, the case that this is a book on Conservative Judaism and not on our sister movements, but that is not the only reason why this book describes multiple theories of revelation within the Conservative Movement and only one in each of the Orthodox and Reform movements. The primary reason for that is because, for all of their variations, all elements of the Orthodox movement subscribe to the theory I am describing as Orthodox, and the same is true for the theory of revelation that I am describing as Reform. Remember that, for the Orthodox, I quote Rabbis Lamm and Berkovits, who are among the most modern within the Orthodox world. If they affirm verbal revelation a copy of which we have in hand in the written Torah, how much more so do those to their right, who assume that view to such an extent that few of them even bother to justify it. Any Chabad tract will demonstrate this, and the program of Aish Ha-Torah which pretends to prove the divinity of the Torah through computer programs is based on this view with a vengeance. On the Reform side, I am citing no less than the official statements of the movement. I also cite in the material that follows two of their major theologians, Rabbis Borowitz and Petuchowski. The former is the rabbi who defines more than any other the ideological center of the movement; the latter was on the right end of the movement, and even he affirms individual autonomy. Therefore, if anything, my disclaimer of "Despite some variations" is too strong!

11. The Editors of *Commentary* Magazine, *The Condition of Jewish Belief* (New York: The American Jewish Committee, 1966), p. 24.

12. *Ibid.*, p. 124.

13. *Ibid.*, pp. 124-125.

14. *Ibid.*, p. 25.

15. David Singer, in "What Do American Jews Believe? A Symposium," *Commentary* 102:2 (August, 1996), p. 83.

16. One clear exception to this is Rabbi Emanuel Rackman, formerly of New York and now President of Bar Ilan University in Israel, who wrote an article in the 1960s in which he pleaded with his Orthodox confreres openly to recognize the variations in Jewish belief and practice which have characterized Judaism over the centuries; see Emanuel Rackman, "A Challenge to Orthodoxy," in his *One Man's Judaism* (New York: Philosophical Library, 1970), pp. 262-283 (an article printed earlier in *Tradition* magazine). Rabbi Rackman says there (p. 263):

> It is not difficult to demonstrate that the giants of the Tradition held widely divergent views on the nature of God, the character of historic revelation, and the uniqueness of the Jewish faith. Not all of these views could possibly be true, and yet not one of them may be deemed heretical, since one respected authority or another has clung to it. The only heresy is the denial that God gave the Written and Oral Law to His people, who are to fulfill its mandates and develop their birthright in accordance with its own built-in methodology and authentic exegesis.

Subsequently, Rabbi David Hartman (*A Living Covenant: The Innovative Spirit in Traditional Judaism* (New York: Free Press, 1985), esp. ch. 4, and Rabbi Eliezer Berkovits himself in his book, *Not In Heaven: The Nature and Function of Halakha* (New York: Ktav, 1983), both argue for flexibility in Jewish law, Rabbi Hartman going so far as to say (pp. 89-90) that "the surrender of human rationality and the sacrifice of one's human ethical sense are not required by Judaic faith." These, though, are rare voices within contemporary Orthodoxy, for during the last ten years Orthodoxy in both North America and Israel has shifted sharply to the right in both belief and practice. Moreover, it is not even clear that Rabbis Rackman, Hartman, or Berkovits would endorse an historical understanding of the Torah, and even they might say (and possibly mean quite literally) that any changes which occurred in history were already revealed at Sinai. It is one thing to acknowledge changes; it is another to explain them in historical terms.

17. *Occident II* (April, 1884), p. 4; cited in Davis, *Emergence*, p. 285.

18. Isaac Lesser, *Bible View of Slavery*, p. 22; cited in Davis, *Emergence*, p. 293.

19. *American Hebrew*, LI (July 1,1892), pp. 279-280; cited in Davis, *Emergence*, p. 296.

20. As far as I can demonstrate, the first Rabbinical School course in which the historical method was used on a book of the Torah was Professor Moshe Greenberg's course on Exodus, taught in 1967-1968, a class which I had the privilege of taking — and even that was more of a course on four medieval commentators to Exodus than on the text of Exodus itself. When I mentioned this to Professor Robert Gordis, z"l, though, he told me that while that may have been the first official course given on a book of the Torah in the Rabbinical School, that was because the Seminary assumed that students knew the Torah already upon entrance, as demonstrated by entrance examinations. Moreover, from at least the 1940s on, Professor Gordis told me, he and other Seminary instructors taught other books of the Bible assuming, and referring to, historical biblical scholarship on the Torah.

21. Schechter, *Studies*, p. 15.

22. *Ibid.*, pp. 12-13, 17-18.

23. Solomon Schechter, "Higher Criticism — Higher Anti-Semitism," in his *Seminary Addresses and Other Papers* (Cincinnati: Ark Publishing Company, 1915), pp. 35-40; Joseph H. Hertz, *Pentateuch and Haftorahs* (London: Soncino Press, 1936), pp. 198-200, 397-399, 403-406, 554-559, 937-942.

24. Joel Roth, *The Halakhic Process: A Systematic Analysis* (New York: The Jewish Theological Seminary of America, 1986), pp. 5-7 (his italics).

25. *Ibid.*, p. 9 (my italics).

26. *Ibid.* (his italics).

27. *Ibid.*, p. 10 (my italics).

28. He affirms that one could still believe in the authority of Jewish law without any reference to God at all, framing the *grundnorm* as follows: "The document called the Torah embodies the constitution promulgated by J, E, P, and D, which it behooves man to obey, and is, therefore, authoritative" (p. 10). One would then, though, have to provide a reason why one should obey a document written by J, E, P, and D to motivate the "leap of faith" which one must take in accepting the Torah as authoritative. Moreover, although Rabbi Roth does not say this, one then encounters the problem of why one should pray and, in general, how one should understand the norms in Jewish law directed to God. Conservative IV will encounter this problem, but its adherents then provide an elaborate restructuring of the concept of God and prayer, which Rabbi Roth does not. I take it then, both from his silence on this issue and from the way he lives his life, that his own "leap of faith" affirms the Torah as "the word and will of God."

29. In the first, 1977 edition of this book, I cited another modern exponent of this view of the authority of Jewish law, namely, Rabbi David Novak, who is now a professor at the University of Toronto. In the intervening years, however, he has left the Conservative movement, not because he no longer believes

in historical study of the Torah and other Jewish texts, but rather because of some of the decisions which have been made within the Movement, in particular the one to authorize ordaining women as rabbis. His theory, though, remains another good example of Conservative I. Specifically, he shares the belief that revelation is God's verbal communication with mankind:

> A theory of revelation must account for the fact that in classical Jewish teaching there is content in revelation, that is, not only do the people experience a Presence wherein God makes Himself manifest, they also hear the word. The denotation of the word is initially intelligible, and thus the word can become a matter of discourse in the community.
>
> "And these words which I command you this day shall be on your heart. And you shall repeat them to your children and speak of them..." (Deut. 6:6-7). "For the word is very near to you in your mouth and in your heart to do it" (Deut. 30:14).
>
> Law as content presupposes discursibility and normativity. That which is by definition wordless can neither be communicated nor commanded. Of course, there is both preverbal and nonverbal communication. Surely a child communicates with his mother long before he can speak. Surely lovers communicate in more than words. But preverbal communication eventually gives birth to words; indeed it evokes words, as any sensitive parent can testify. Nonverbal or extraverbal communication also evokes words; a totally silent lover would be inhuman. In other words, discourse and law, and personal relationship and encounter, are not necessarily mutually exclusive in our ordinary experience. Why must they be so in the religious life? (David Novak, *Law and Theology in Judaism* [New York: Ktav Publishing House, Inc. 1976], Series II, pp. 10, 13-14.)

But he is considerably more comfortable with modern biblical scholarship than the Orthodox are. In the following, he even shows why such scholarship does not pose a threat to belief in revelation:

> Revelation denotes a communication from God accepted by man. Such an event cannot be either proved or disproved by any critical discipline, whether physics or history, because it is posited as something *sui generis*, something without any empirical analogue. Therefore, one could hold a strictly fundamentalist attitude towards the Pentateuch – assuming that every word was written down by Moses himself -- and still not believe in revelation. Assumptions about the Pentateuch are empirical models; beliefs about revelation are faith assertions. The former can well be challenged by biblical criticism; the latter cannot be, because they are outside the purview of empirical evidence....
>
> "Higher" biblical criticism is concerned with the dating and composition of the biblical text. Even if one accepts the assumption common to all the biblical critics -- namely that the Pentateuch in particular is made up of various documents (J,E,P,D, etc.) which were written at different times by different authors -- one can still view it as a unity because of the way it was accepted in subsequent Jewish history. Once the official text was finally agreed upon during the time of Ezra, the Jewish people had an indisputable point of reference for both law and theology. Thus, the theory which accepts both a possibly diverse origin along with a definite subsequent unity enables one to be a traditionalist without being a fundamentalist. (David Novak, "A Response to 'Towards an Aggadic Judaism,'" *Conservative Judaism*, Vol. XXX, No. 1 (Fall, 1975) pp. 58-59).

Another contemporary Conservative exponent of this view is Rabbi Harlan Wechsler, rabbi of Congregation Or Zarua in New York and a professor at the Jewish Theological Seminary of America. See his contribution to the 1996 *Commentary* symposium, *Commentary* 102:2 (August, 1996), pp. 89-91, where he says (p. 90), "Revelation is more than divine presence; it yields divine commandments, all of which are binding," although "God's word is subject to human hearing, hearing that is frustrated by the inherent limits of language."

30.   Ben Zion Bokser, *Judaism: Profile of a Faith* (New York: The Burning Bush Press, 1963), pp. 273-274.

31.   *Ibid.*, pp. 268-270.

32.   Maimonides, *Guide for the Perplexed*, Part II, Ch. 36; Heschel, *The Prophets*, pp. 358-9, 443.

33.   Bokser, *Profile*, pp. 270-271.

34.   *Ibid.*, p. 269.

35.   *Condition of Jewish Belief*, p. 186.

36.   Robert Gordis, *A Faith for Moderns* (New York: Bloch Publishing Company, 1960), p. 155.

37.   Abraham J. Heschel, *God in Search of Man* (New York: Farrar, Straus & Giroux, Inc., 1955), p. 198.

38.   *Ibid.*, p. 230.

39.   *Condition of Jewish Belief*, pp. 52-53.

40.   Franz Rosenzweig, "The Builders," in *On Jewish Learning*, Nahum N. Glatzer, ed. (New York: Schocken Books, 1955), pp. 72-92; substantially reprinted in E. Dorff, *Jewish Law and Modern Ideology* (New York: United Synagogue Commission on Jewish Education, 1970) pp. 112-120.

41.   Louis Jacobs, *A Jewish Theology* (New York: Behrman House, Inc. Publishers, 1973), pp. 202-206, 208-210.

42.   Ismar Schorsch, in "What Do American Jews Believe? A Symposium," *Commentary* 102:2 (August, 1996), p. 82.

43.   Readers of the first edition of this book will know that there I classified his thought as an example of Conservative I. Truthfully, he does not make his position nearly as clear as one would hope, and my interpretation of his thought then was influenced primarily by passages such as those I cite here, that, for example, "`God spoke' is not a symbol" and that it would diminish the concept of God to presume that God could not do what human beings can do, namely, speak. Moreover, Heschel says that there was "a mysterious voice coming through the clouds" at Sinai (*God in Search of Man*, p. 219; cf. also pp. 225, 228, 245, and 247), that we should care "for what God has to say" (p. 222) and that God spoke "while Moses heard" (p. 241). Similarly, in *The Prophets* (Philadelphia: The Jewish Publication Society of America, 1962), he speaks about the "word" of God (pp. 12, 25, etc.) and His "Voice" (p. 358), and he points out "The prophets asserted that many of their experiences were not moments of passive receptivity, mere listening to a voice or mere beholding a Presence, but dialogues with God. By response, pleading, and counterspeech, the prophet reacts to the word he perceives" (p. 366). Cf. also *ibid.*, pp. 221-223, 430, and 432. Rabbis Neil Gillman and Lawrence Pearlman, however, have subsequently convinced me that Heschel's position is rightfully placed in Conservative III, and so I have presented him here. See Lawrence Perlman, *Abraham Heschel's Idea of Revelation* (Altanta: Scholars Press, 1989), esp. pp. 109-113.

44.   Abraham Joshua Heschel, *God in Search of Man*, pp. 180-181, 244-245.

45.   Heschel, *The Prophets*, pp. 388-389 and 364. Note also the rest of Chapter 22 and Chapters 24 and 25.

46. Heschel, *God in Search of Man*, pp. 185-186, 183.

47. *Ibid.*, p. 187 (my italics). Heschel's citations of these two thinkers are on p. 188. Their sources: Rabbi Solomon ibn Adret, *Ma'amar Al Ishmael*, in J. Perles, *R. Salomo b. Abraham b. Aderath*, Breslau, 1863 (Hebrew), p. 12; and Rabbi Loew of Prague, *Tiferet Israel*, ch. 43.

48. Heschel, *God in Search of Man*, p. 187.

49. *Ibid.*, p. 265.

50. *Ibid.*, pp. 178-179.

51. *Ibid.*, p. 275.

52. Neil Gillman, in "What Do American Jews Believe? A Symposium," *Commentary* 102:2 (August, 1996), p. 39.

53. Jacob J. Petuchowski, *Ever Since Sinai* (New York: Scribe Publications Inc., 1961), pp. 108-110, 112-113.

54. Eugene Borowitz, *How Can a Jew Speak of Faith Today?* (Philadelphia: The Westminster Press, 1968), p. 68.

55. Eugene Borowitz, *A New Jewish Theology in the Making* (Philadelphia: The Westminster Press, 1968), p. 213.

56. Eugene B. Borowitz, *Renewing the Covenant: A Theology for the Postmodern Jew* (Philadelphia: Jewish Publication Society, 1991), p. 288 (his italics).

57. See *ibid.*, pp. 286-287.

58. Jacobs, *A Jewish Theology*, p. 224.

59. Neil Gillman, in "What Do American Jews Believe? A Symposium," *Commentary* 102:2 (August, 1996), p. 39.

60. I talk about this distinction at somewhat greater length in my review essay of Borowitz' book, *Renewing the Covenant*, entitled, "Autonomy vs. Community: The Ongoing Reform/Conservative Difference," *Conservative Judaism* 48:2 (Winter, 1996), pp. 64-68.

61. David Lieber, in "What Do American Jews Believe? A Symposium," *Commentary* 102:2 (August, 1996), p. 68.

62. *Ibid.*, pp. 140, 141, 143-144.

63. Emil Fackenheim, *God's Presence in History* (New York: Harper and Row, 1970), Ch. 3.

64. Elliot N. Dorff, "God and the Holocaust," *Judaism*, Vol. 26, No. 1 (Winter, 1977), pp. 27-34.

65. This is a composite formulation of what I wrote in my article, "Revelation," *Conservative Judaism*, Vol. XXXI, Nos. 1-2 (Fall-Winter, 1976-77), pp. 64-65, 68; and later, in a different articulation within an expanded context, in my book, <u>Knowing God: Jewish Journeys to the Unknowable</u> (Northvale, NJ: Jason Aronson, 1992), pp. 99-113, and see ch. 4 generally; with a few sentences added to bridge the two.

66.   Elliot Dorff, "Two Ways to Approach God," *Conservative Judaism*, Vol. XXX, No. 2, (Winter, 1976), pp. 58-67; reprinted in *God in the Teachings of Conservative Judaism*, Seymour Siegel and Elliot Gertel, eds. (New York: Rabbinical Assembly, 1985), pp. 30-41; and see my *Knowing God: Jewish Journeys to the Unknowable*, pp. 113-127 ("Experiencing Revelation," in contrast to the first part of that chapter, "Understanding Revelation") and, more broadly, see chs. 1 and 2 there.

       See also how another exponent of this objectivist approach, namely, Rabbi Jacob Agus, z"l, formerly rabbi of Beth El Congregation in Baltimore, a member of the Committee on Jewish Law and Standards, and an important philosopher of Jewish law, interweaves the personal with the objective: Jacob Agus, *Guideposts in Modern Judaism* (New York: Bloch Publishing Company, 1954), Part II, Section 2.

67.   As indicated in Chapter Two, some who identify as Reconstructionist Jews do not see themselves also as Conservative Jews, but some do. In particular, the five rabbis whom I will cite in this section either were ordained by the Jewish Theological Seminary of America or belong to the Rabbinical Assembly, or both, and so I have continued to categorize Reconstructionism as a tendency within Conservative Judaism even though it is also an independent movement.

68.   *Condition of Jewish Belief*, p. 120.

69.   Mordecai M. Kaplan, *Questions Jews Ask: Reconstructionist Answers* (New Yok: Reconstructionist Press, 1956), pp. 265, 266.

70.   *Conditions of Jewish Belief*, pp. 45-46.

71.   Arthur Green, "What Do American Jews Believe? A Symposium," in *Commentary* 102:2 (August, 1996), pp. 42-43.

72.   David A. Teutsch, in "What Do American Jews Believe? A Symposium," *Commentary* 102:2 (August, 1996), p. 88.

73.   *Ibid.*, pp. 216-219.

74.   "The Columbus Guiding Principles," cited in W. Gunther Plaut, *The Growth of Reform Judaism* (New York: World Union for Progressive Judaism, Ltd., 1965), pp. 96-99.

75.   *Ibid.*, p. 99.

76.   "Reform Judaism: A Centenary Perspective," Central Conference of American Rabbis, June, 1976, pp. 2-3.

77.   Some years ago, I noted that the English name "Conservative" invites misinterpretation, for English speakers hearing our name might well think that we are the most conservative (with a small "c") in both religion and politics. I therefore proposed that we change our name in English to match our name in Hebrew -- that is, that we call ourselves "Traditional Judaism." That name would not only have the advantage of avoiding such misinterpretations; it would also announce to people within the movement and outside it much more effectively what our agenda is. See Elliot N. Dorff, "Traditional Judaism," *Conservative Judaism*, 34:2 (November/December, 1980), pp. 34-38.

78.   See David Weiss Halivni, "The Role of the Mara D'atra in Jewish Law," *Proceedings of the Rabbinical Assembly 1976* (New York: Rabbinical Assembly, 1977), vol. 38, pp. 124-129.

79.   See Louis Finkelstein, *Jewish Self-Government in the Middle Ages* (New York: Jewish Theological Seminary of America, 1924; second ed., New York: Feldheim, 1964).

80. See *Summary Index Supplement, 5756* of the *Summary Index: The Committe on Jewish Law and Standards*, p. 9:2. In the case of the second one of these, the one demanding a *get*, another exception to that demand which is obviously assumed, although not stated in the standard, is if the former spouse has died in the interim between the time of divorce and now, the time when the surviving spouse wants to remarry. Under those circumstances, the status of the surviving spouse changes from that of a person still married in Jewish law (despite being divorced in civil law) to that of a widowed person, and no *get* is possible or required. On the last of these standards, see *Proceedings of the Committee on Jewish Law and Standards of the Rabbinical Assembly, 1980-1985* (New York: Rabbinical Assembly, 1988), pp. 177-178.

81. Elliot N. Dorff, "Artificial Insemination, Egg Donation, and Adoption," approved March, 1994, to be published in the Fall, 1996 issue of the journal, *Conservative Judaism*. Aaron Mackler, "In Vitro Fertilization," approved December, 1995. Both of these *teshuvot* will also be published in a volume, to be edited by Rabbi Mackler, of the Law Committee's responsa on issues in bioethics. That volume is expected to be published in 1997 or 1998.

82. *Summary Index: The Committee on Jewish Law and Standards* (New York: Rabbinical Assembly, 1994), p. 9:14.

83. In an article I have written for the journal *Conservative Judaism*, I suggest that custom may be the root of our response to the question of women serving as witnesses, especially since the legal texts seem closed to that possibility. See Elliot N. Dorff, "Custom Drives Jewish Law on Women," scheduled to be published in 1997.

84. On these topics generally, including communal forums for making Jewish law, the role of custom in the law, and the Conservative movement's approach to Jewish law in contrast to that of the Orthodox and Reform movements, see Elliot N. Dorff and Arthur Rosett, *A Living Tree: The Roots and Growth of Jewish Law* (Albany, NY: State University of New York Press and New York: Jewish Theological Seminary of America, 1988), pp. 337-363, 402-434, 523-545.

85. *Emet Ve-Emunah: Statement of Principles of Conservative Judaism* (New York: The Jewish Theological Seminary of America, The Rabbinical Assembly, United Synagogue of America, Women's League for Conservative Judaism, Federation of Jewish Men's Clubs, 1988), pp. 23-24.

86. *Emet Ve-Emunah*, p. 24. For one view of the Conservative use of ethics in making moral decision, see Seymour Siegel, "Ethics and the Halakhah," *Conservative Judaism*, Vol. XXV, No. 3 (Spring, 1971), pp. 33-40 (reprinted in Siegel, ed., *Conservative Judaism and Jewish Law* [New York: Rabbinical Assembly, 1977], pp. 123-132), an article which also includes some examples of how the Rabbis of the Talmud used ethics in their legal decisions. The latter point is developed more fully in Elliot N. Dorff, "The Interaction of Jewish Law with Morality," *Judaism*, Vol. 26, No. 4 (Fall, 1977), pp. 455-466. Cf. also David Novak, *Law and Theology in Judaism*, Series I (New York: Ktav, 1976), Chapter 1; and Abraham Heschel, *God in Search of Man* (New York: Farrar, Straus, and Giroux, 1955), Chap. 33. For a variety of views on the relationship between morality, on the one hand, and Jewish belief and practice, on the other, including some by authors affiliated with the Conservative Movement, see Elliot N. Dorff and Louis E. Newman, eds., *Contemporary Jewish Ethics and Morality: A Reader* (New York: Oxford, 1995), chs. 1-15.

87. For the command to sanctify God's name (reputation), see Leviticus 20:7-8 and M.T. *Laws of the Foundations of the Torah* 5:11.

88. All of these shortened lists are in B. *Makkot* 24a, where the original number of 613 commandments also appears.

89.   B. *Shabbat* 31a. Hillel's principle is probably his paraphrase of Leviticus 19:18, "Love your neighbor as yourself," although when one analyzes Hillel's maxim and that Torah verse, one finds differences (perhaps significant ones) between Hillel's negative formulation of the Golden Rule and the Torah's positive version of it.

Chapter Four

1.   Robert Gordis points out that, שאור, "leaven," is probably an error. It is not applicable to Torah, since its metaphoric use refers to sinfulness. The reading should probably be מאור, "light."

2.   See Joshua Trachtenberg, *Jewish Magic and Superstition: A Study in Folk Religion* (Philadelphia: Jewish Publication Society, 1939, 1961).

3.   Abraham J. Heschel, *God in Search of Man*, Ch. 32 (pp. 320-335).

4.   Schechter, *Studies*, p. 15.

5.   *Ibid.*, pp. 19-20.

6.   Quoted in Davis, *Emergence*, p. 283.

7.   **Books on Conservative Judaism's beliefs appearing before 1988:**
All but the first book on the above list were published by either the Rabbinical Assembly or the United Synagogue: Robert Gordis, *Conservative Judaism: An American Philosophy* (New York: Bloch, 1945); Simon Greenberg, *The Conservative Movement in Judaism: An Introduction* (New York, 1955); Mordecai Waxman, ed., *Tradition and Change* (New York, 1958); Seymour Siegel, *Conservative Judaism and Jewish Law* (New York, 1977); Robert Gordis, *Understanding Conservative Judaism* (New York, 1978); Seymour Siegel and Elliot Gertel, eds., *God in the Teachings of Conservative Judaism* (New York, 1985); and, of course, the first edition of this book, Elliot N. Dorff, *Conservative Judaism: Our Ancestors to Our Descendants* (New York, 1977).

In addition, sections of books written by Conservative rabbis sought to articulate the beliefs of Conservative Judaism. See, for example, Gilbert S. Rosenthal, *Four Paths to One God: Today's Jew and His Religion* (New York, 1973), pp. 148-212; and Jacob Neusner, *Understanding American Judaism*, 2 vols. (New York, 1975), vol. II, pp. 195-299.

Articles on Conservative Judaism's beliefs appearing before 1988 (obviously, a partial list)**:**
a) In the journal, *Conservative Judaism*: Louis Finkelstein, "The Underlying Concepts of Conservative Judaism," 26:4 (Summer, 1972), 2-12; the articles of Jordan Ofseyer, Stuart E. Rosenberg, Gilbert S. Rosenthal, Morton Siegel, and Mordecai Waxman, 27:1 (Fall, 1972), 12-26; Elliot N. Dorff, "Towards a Legal Theory of the Conservative Movement," 27:3 (Spring, 1973), 68-77; the articles written by Samuel Morell, Alan J. Yuter, and Elliot N. Dorff in discussion of the last article, appearing in 28:2 (Winter, 1974), 68-78; Neil Gillman, "Toward a Theology for Conservative Judaism," 37:1 (Fall, 1983).

b) In the magazine, *United Synagogue Review*: Benjamin Z. Kreitman, "Reform Judaism: A Conservative Point of View," 28:3 (Spring-Summer, 1976), 8ff; Elliot N. Dorff, "What It Means to Be a Conservative Jew," 31:2 (Winter, 1979), 1ff.

c) The entire Summer, 1977 issue of the journal, *Judaism*, was devoted to Conservative Judaism, including some articles on its beliefs.

8. A partial list of the books on theology before 1977 by Conservative writers (in alphabetical order) includes:

Jacob Agus, *Guideposts in Modern Judaism* (1954); *The Vision and the Way: An Interpretation of Jewish Ethics* (1966)..

Ben Zion Bokser, *Judaism: Profile of a Faith* (1963).

Robert Gordis, *Judaism for the Modern Age* (1955); *A Faith for Moderns* (1960).

Simon Greenberg, *Foundations of a Faith* (1967).

Abraham Joshua Heschel, *Man Is Not Alone: A Philosophy of Religion* (1951) and *God in Search of Man* (1955).

Louis Jacobs, *Jewish Prayer* (1955); *We Have Reason to Believe* (1957); *Principles of the Jewish Faith* (1964); *Faith* (1968); *A Jewish Theology* (1973).

Mordecai M. Kaplan, *Judaism as a Civilization* (1934), *The Meaning of God in Modern Jewish Religion* (1936), *Questions Jews Ask: Reconstructionist Answers* (1956; 1966, revised), *Judaism Without Supernaturalism* (1958); *The Religion of Ethical Nationhood* (1970).

Jacob Kohn, *Evolution as Revelation* (1963).

Harold Kushner, *When Children Ask About God* (1971).

David Novak, *Law and Theology in Judaism*, 2 vols. (1974, 1976).

Richard Rubenstein, *After Auschwitz* (1966; second edition, 1992); *The Religious Imagination: A Study in Psychoanalysis and Jewish Theology* (1968); *Morality and Eros* (1970).

Milton Steinberg, *A Believing Jew* (1951); *Anatomy of Faith* (1960).

9. Here is a partial list in alphabetical order of the books on theological issues written by Conservative thinkers since 1977. The list is restricted to publications of people writing from their own perspective (in contrast, for example, to historical or philosophical analyses of other people's thinking), but it includes treatments not only of God, but also how one's view of God influences Jewish morals and rituals, and vice-versa:

Jacob Agus, *Jewish Identity in an Age of Ideologies* (1978); *The Jewish Quest: Essays on Basic Concepts of Jewish Theology* (1983).

David Blumenthal, *God at the Center: Meditations on Jewish Spirituality* (1988); *Facing the Abusing God: A Theology of Protest* (1993).

Elliot Dorff, *Knowing God: Jewish Journeys to the Unknowable* (1992).

Elliot Dorff and Louis Newman, eds., *Contemporary Jewish Ethics and Morality* (1995).

Ze'ev Falk, *Law and Religion: The Jewish Experience* (1981).

Edward Feld, *The Spirit of Renewal: Finding Faith after the Holocaust* (1994).

Richard Freund, *Understanding Jewish Ethics* (1990).

Neil Gillman, *Sacred Fragments: Recovering Jewish Theology for the Modern Jew* (1990).

Michael Goldberg, *Theology and Narrative* (1981); *Jews and Christians: Getting Our Stories Straight* (1985); *Why Should Jews Survive? Looking Past the Holocaust Toward a Jewish Future* (1995).

Daniel Gordis, *God Was Not in the Fire* (1995).

Robert Gordis, *Jewish Ethics for a Lawless World* (1986); *The Dynamics of Judaism: A Study in Jewish Law* (1990).

Arthur Green, *Seek My Face, Speak My Name: A Contemporary Jewish Theology* (1992).

Simon Greenberg, *A Jewish Philosophy and Pattern of Life* (1981).

Susan Grossman and Rivka Haut, *Daughters of the King: Women and the Synagogue* (1992).

Louis Jacobs, *God, Torah, and Israel: Traditionalism without Fundamentalism* (1990); *Religion and the Individual: A Jewish Perspective* (1992).

Harold Kushner, *When Bad Things Happen to Good People* (1981); *Who Needs God?* (1989).

Debra Orenstein, *Lifecycles: Jewish Women on Life Passages and Personal Milestones* (1994).

Harold Schulweis, *Evil and the Morality of God* (1984); *In God's Mirror* (1990); *For Those Who Can't Believe: Overcoming Obstacles to Faith* (1994).

Byron Sherwin, *In Partnership with God* (1990); *Toward A Jewish Theology* (1991).

Ira Stone, *Seeking the Path to Life: Theological Meditations on God and the Nature of People, Love, Life, and Death* (1992).

David Wolpe, *The Healer of Shattered Hearts: A Jewish View of God* (1990); *In Speech and in Silence: The Jewish Quest for God* (1992).

An anthology of articles until 1985 on theological issues by thinkers affiliated with Conservative Judaism (with articles from before and after 1977) is: Seymour Siegel and Elliot Gertel, eds., *God In the Teachings of Conservative Judaism* (1985).

10. *Zohar* following 73a.

11. Moshe Davis, *The Emergence of Conservative Judaism*, pp. 283-284.

12. Simon Greenberg, *Foundations of a Faith* (1967); *A Jewish Philosophy and Pattern of Life* (1981); Louis Jacobs, *We Have Reason to Believe* (1957), chs. 3-5; *Principles of the Jewish Faith* (1964), ch. 2; *Faith* (1968), entire; *A Jewish Theology* (1973), entire.

13. Mordecai Kaplan, *Judaism as a Civilization* (1934, 1957), Part Five; *The Meaning of God in Modern Jewish Religion* (1937, 1962), entire; Eugene Kohn, *Religious Humanism: A Jewish Interpretation* (1953), chs. 1-3; Harold Kushner, *When Bad Things Happen to Good People* (1981); Harold Schulweis, "From God to Godliness: Proposal for a Predicate Theology," *Reconstructionist*, Vol. 40, No. 1 (February, 1975); *Evil and the Morality of God* (1984); *For Those Who Can't Believe* (1994).

14. Jacob Kohn, *Evolution as Revelation* (1963), entire.

15. Jacob Agus, *Guideposts in Modern Judaism* (1954), Part II, Section 2; Ben Zion Bokser, *Judaism: Profile of a Faith* (1963), chs. 3-4; Robert Gordis, *A Faith for Moderns* (1960), chs. 1, 6-9; Elliot N. Dorff, *Knowing God: Jewish Journeys to the Unknowable* (1992), entire, but esp. chs. 1-2.

16. Milton Steinberg, *A Believing Jew* (1951), ch. 1. Steinberg's stance changed several times during his life, but in this essay he openly characterizes his position as an adaptation of Hegel (and others).

17. Max Kadushin, *Organic Thinking: A Study in Rabbinic Thought* (1938) and *The Rabbinic Mind* (1952). I am not sure how to place Byron Sherwin's work in these categories, but since he emphasizes the polarity of Jewish thinking, my guess is that he rightly belongs here. See Byron Sherwin, *Toward A Jewish Theology: Methods, Problems, and Possibilities* (1991); his commitment to polarity: pp. 3-4, 17-18.

18. Richard Rubenstein, *After Auschwitz* (1966, 1992); *Morality and Eros* (1970), ch. 11. In the latter book Rubenstein associates himself with Western and Oriental mysticism in that he is affirming belief in God as "the ground and source of all existence" (p. 185; this is the mystic *Ein Sof*), but Western mystics also affirm belief in the God who acts in history (the *Shekhinah*), as he is not willing to do. Since his approach in *After Auschwitz* is heavily influenced by the psychological needs of the individual, I have preferred to characterize him as an existentialist, a description which he himself adopts in the title of Chapter 6 of *After Auschwitz*.

19. Cf. Herschel Matt and Seymour Siegel in *The Condition of Jewish Belief* (the *Commentary* symposium of 1966) and Arnold J. Wolf, *Rediscovering Judaism* (1965), Introduction. Rosenzweig had considerable influence on a number of my colleagues when I was at the Seminary in the late 1960s, and I am frankly disappointed that more of the many in our Movement who follow the existentialist approach have not stated their views in writing.

20. See Abraham Joshua Heschel's many works, especially *God in Search of Man* (1955) and *Man Is Not Alone* (1951). Dr. Heschel indicated his preference for associating his theology with the phenomenological approach in a conversation with Dr. David Lieber, and see Lawrence Perlman, *Abraham Heschel's Idea of Revelation* (1989), esp. pp. 109-113. Heschel specifically rejected the description of "mystic," but some of his disciples have written in a mystic or neo-Hassidic vein (e.g., Samuel Dresner, Arthur Green).

21. Arthur Green, *Seek My Face, Speak My Name* (1992).

22. Michael Goldberg, *Narrative Theology: An Introduction* (1981); *Jews and Christians Getting Our Stories Straight* (1985); Neil Gillman, *Sacred Fragments: Recovering Jewish Theology for the Modern Jew* (1990).

23. This is not a school of thought, *per se*, but it is an approach to questions of God which addresses the emotional, or spiritual, quests for God and evidences of God in our lives -- what Byron Sherwin has called "descriptive theology" in contrast to "philosophic theology" (see his *Toward A Jewish Theology* (1991), p. 23). Examples include David Blumenthal, *God at the Center: Meditations on Jewish Spirituality* (1988); *Facing the Abusing God: A Theology of Protest* (1993); Edward Feld, *The Spirit of Renewal: Finding Faith after the Holocaust* (1994); Daniel Gordis, *God Was Not in the Fire: The Search for a Spiritual Judaism* (1995); Debra Orenstein, *Lifecycles: Jewish Women on Life Passages and Personal Milestones* (1994); Ira Stone, *Seeking the Path to Life: Theological Meditations on God and the Nature of People, Love, Life, and Death* (1992); David Wolpe, *The Healer of Shattered Hearts* (1990); *In Speech and in Silence: The Jewish Quest for God* (1992). Although my own approach is primarily rooted in rationalism, it asserts the limits of finding God through reason alone and appeals to the evidences of God in the experiences of our lives, which, as Sherwin says, must be the case if philosophic theologies are not to be "a roof hanging in air, destined to collapse for lack of a foundation" (*ibid.*, pp. 19, 23). On the other hand, as Sherwin also notes, descriptive theologies are primary, lacking and waiting for the philosophic clarity which second-level thinking brings, and, as Louis Jacobs has written (*A Jewish Theology*, p. 5), "Holy nonsense is still nonsense." For my own attempt to integrate descriptive and philosophic theology, then, see Elliot N. Dorff, *Knowing God: Jewish Journeys to the Unknowable* (1992), chs. 3-6.

24. Davis, *Emergence*, p. 321; cf. note 8 there.

25. A.J. Heschel, *The Insecurity of Freedom* (New York: Farrar, Straus & Giroux, Inc., 1972), p. 283.

26. Reprinted in Waxman, *Tradition and Change*, pp. 457-466.

27. Preface to *Seminary Addresses*; reprinted in Waxman, *Tradition and Change*, p. 100.

28. Cf. Moshe Davis, *Emergence*, pp. 268-274; David Dalin, "Cyrus Adler, Non- Zionism, and the Zionist Movement: A Study in Contradictions," *AJS Review* [of the Association of Jewish Studies] 10:1 (Spring, 1985), pp. 55-87. See also David Dalin, "Cyrus Adler and the Rescue of Jewish Refugee Scholars," *American Jewish History* 78:3 (March, 1989), pp. 351-362.

29. Robert Gordis, *Conservative Judaism* (New York: The National Academy for Adult Jewish Studies, The United Synagogue of America, 1956), p. 22.

30. *Proceedings of the Rabbinical Assembly*, 1927, p. 33.

31. Kaplan first proposes the curriculum of "A University of Judaism" in the last chapter of his book, *The Future of the American Jew* (New York: Reconstructionist Foundation, 1948), a chapter with that as its title. The chapter is a commencement address which Kaplan gave at the Seminary in 1945, and the University of Judaism was founded in 1947. For more on the history of the University of Judaism and the way in which Kaplan's vision found concrete expression in it, see Arthur Hoffnung, *The University of Judaism at Forty* (Los Angeles: University of Judaism, 1991).

32.   Zechariah Frankel, cited in W. Gunther Plaut, *The Rise of Reform Judaism* (New York: World Union for Progressive Judaism, Ltd., 1963), pp. 87-88.

33.   Solomon Schechter, *Seminary Addresses and Other Papers* (New York: The Burning Bush Press, 1959), pp. 88-89.

34.   Quoted by Louis Finkelstein in Waxman, *Tradition and Change*, p. 323.

35.   This has led to many discussions in Jewish communal institutions of late as to what the word "Jewish" means in the title of their organization, and that has produced much clearer mission statements about the connections of those organizations to Jews and the values of Judaism. As a Vice President of Jewish Family Service in Los Angeles, I can attest to multiple conversations about what the "J" means in "JFS," and similar conversations have taken place on boards of the Jewish Community Centers and the Jewish Federation itself, especially since most of these agencies use government funds and therefore must be open to non-Jewish clients. Interestingly, one of the ways in which the question has been answered in Los Angeles has been through insistence on kosher food in the meals-on-wheels programs for the elderly and in all Los Angeles Federation functions.

Chapter Five

1.   Barry A. Kosmin, Sidney Goldstein, Joseph Waksberg, Nava Lerer, Ariella Keysar, and Jeffrey Scheckner, *Highlights of the CJF 1990 National Jewish Population Survey* (New York: Council of Jewish Federations, 1991), p. 37, according to which only 41% of core Jews belong to synagogues.

2.   *Ibid.*, p. 6; see definitions on p. 3 and Chart 1 on p. 4.

3.   I am including in this the 1.1 million which report Jewish identity but no Jewish religion, the 415,000 adults who have Jewish parentage but were raised in another religion and practice it, the 210,000 who were born and raised Jewish but who converted to another religion, and the 700,000 children under 18 who were born to a Jewish parent but who are being raised in another religion, for a total of 2,425,000 Jews. This must be compared to the 4,200,000 who were born Jewish and report Judaism as their religion (whether they affiliate with a synagogue or not), and the 185,000 Jews by Choice, for a total of 4,385,000. Roughly, then, of the total of 6,810,000 people with Jewish parentage, a third (2,424,000) have assimilated, at least to the extent of denying that Judaism is their religion.

4.   Over 50% of marriages involving Jews were to non-Jews, but that figure is a little misleading because each in-marriage, by definition, involves two Jews, while each intermarriage involves only one, and so the percentage of Jews involved in intermarriage is much smaller than the percentages of marriages involving Jews which are intermarriages. Still, 28% of Jews intermarrying is not something we can ignore if we have hope for the Jewish future. The figures of 28% of Jews married to non-Jews and over 50% of marriages involving Jews being intermarriages: Kosmin, Goldstein, etc., *Highlights of the CJF 1990 National Jewish Population Survey*, pp. 13, 14.

5.   Bruce A. Philipps, *Intermarriage, Assimilation, and Social Structure: Findings from the 1990 National Jewish Population Survey*, to be published in 1997 by the Wilstein Institute for Jewish Policy Studies.

6.   For more on the issues involved in intermarriage, see Alan Silverstein, *It All Begins with a Date: Jewish Concerns about Intermarriage* (Northvale, NJ: Jason Aronson, 1995), for a full-length treatment of the many sides of this issue. For a summary, see his booklets, *Interdating: A Jewish Parents Guide: 10 Questions and Answers* (New York: Women's League for Conservative Judaism, 1994), and *Intermarriage: Our Grounds for Concern -- 14 Questions, 14 Answers* (New York: United Synagogue of Conservative Judaism, 1992).

7. For more on developments in American synagogue structures, see Jack Wertheimer, ed., *The American Synagogue: A Sanctuary Transformed* (Cambridge: Harvard University Press, 1987), esp. pp. 1-34.

8. The clause did not address the other circumstances in which women become *agunot* (literally, "chained women" – that is, legally chained to their first husbands and therefore unable to marry someone else) -- namely, when the husband has disappeared or has become mentally incompetent to issue a divorce.

9. Those interested in a more philosophical treatment of how pluralism can be justified in Jewish sources should see my article, "Pluralism: Models for the Conservative Movement," *Conservative Judaism* 48:1 (Fall, 1995), pp. 21-35.

10. See my article, "Catholic/Jewish Dialogue: A Jewish Perspective on Vatican Documents," *Ecumenical Trends* (September 1988), pp. 116-120: reprinted in *Three Score and Ten: Essays in Honor of Rabbi Seymour J. Cohen* (Hoboken, N.J.: KTAV, 1991), pp. 283-291.

11. The *Journal of Ecumenical Studies* is devoted almost entirely to such matters, and a number of books have been written on the subject from Jewish, Christian, and Muslim points of view. See, for example [in alphabetical order by author], David M. Gordis, George Grose, and Muzammil Siddiqi, *The Abraham Connection: A Jew, Christian, and Muslim in Dialogue* (Notre Dame, IN: Cross Roads Books, 1994); John Hick, *God and the Universe of Faiths: Essays in the Philosophy of Religion* (London: Macmillan, 1973, 1988); John Hick and Hasan Askari, eds., *The Experience of Religious Diversity* (Brookfield, VT: Gower, 1985); Jacob Neusner, ed., *Judaism and Christianity: The New Relationship* (New York: Garland, 1993); Jakob J. Petuchowski, ed., *When Jews and Christians Meet* (Albany, NY: State University of New York Press, 1988); and Joseph P. Schultz, *Judaism and the Gentile Faiths: Comparative Studies in Religion* (Rutherford, NJ: Fairleigh Dickenson Press, 1981). For my own contributions to this discussion, see my articles, "The Covenant as the Key: A Jewish Theology of Christian-Jewish Relations," in *Toward A Theological Encounter: Jewish Understandings of Christianity*, Leon Klenicki, ed. (New York: Paulist Press [A Stimulus Book], 1991), pp. 43-66; and "A Jewish Theology of Jewish Relations to Other People," in *People of God, Peoples of God: A Jewish-Christian Conversation in Asia*, Hans Ucko, ed. (Geneva: World Council of Churches, 1996), pp. 46-66.

12. A thorough, yet clear and interesting treatment of this issue from biblical times to our own is the book by Benjamin J. Segal, *Returning: The Land of Israel as Focus in Jewish History* (Jerusalem: Department of Education and Culture of the World Zionist Organization, 1987). See also the following USY sourcebooks: Jules Gutin, *Rejoice With Jerusalem* (1983); and Simcha Kling, *Am Yisrael Ve-Eretz Yisrael: The People and Its Land* (1988).

13. Harold M. Schulweis, "Restructuring the Synagogue," *Conservative Judaism* 27:4 (Summer, 1973), pp. 13-23. See also note 7 above.

APPENDIX I
The "Trefah Banquet"

Here is a copy of the menu that symbolized issues that ultimately led to the birth of Conservative Judaism (with translations of some of the French terms) as it appeared in the Cincinnati Enquirer for July 12, 1883:[*]

MENU
Little Neck Clams (half shell)

Amontillado Sherry

Potages (soup)
Consomme (soup) Royal

Sauternes (wines)

Poissons (fish)
Fillet de Boef, aux Champignons (beef with mushrooms)
Soft-shell Crabs
Salade de Shrimps (shrimp salad)

St. Julien (a brand of liquor)

Entree [Main Course]
Sweet Breads a la Monglas
Petits Pois (peas) a la Francais

Diedescheimer (liquor)

Revelee [To reawaken the appetite]
Poulets (chicken) a la Viennoise,
Asperges Sauce
Vinaigrette Pommes Pate (potato pie)

Roman Punch

Grenouiles (frogs' legs) a la Creme
and Cauliflower Roti (roast)
Vol aux Vents de Pigeons a la Tryolienne
Salade de Laitue

G.H. Mumm Extra Dry

Hors D'Oeuvres
Bouchies de Volaille a la Regeurs
Olives Caviv
Sardeiles (sardines) de Hollands
Brissotins au Supreme Tomatoe
Mayonaise
[Dessert]
Sucres (candies)
Ice Cream
Assorted and Ornamented Cakes
Entremets (during the entertainment)
Fromages Varies (various cheeses)
Fruits Varies (various fruits)
Cafe Noir (black coffee)
Martell Cognac

---

[*] John J. Appel, "The Trefa Banquet," Commentary, Feb., 1966, pp. 75-78.

APPENDIX II
The Pittsburgh Platform
(1885) -- Reform

The following points were agreed upon and became known as the Pittsburgh Platform.

First. We recognize in every religion an attempt to grasp the Infinite, and in every mode, source, or book or revelation held sacred in any religious system, the consciousness of the in-dwelling of God in man. We hold that Judaism presents the highest conception of the God idea as taught in our holy Scriptures and developed and spiritualized by the Jewish teachers, in accordance with the moral and philosophical progress of their respective ages. We maintain that Judaism preserved and defended, midst continual struggles and trials and under enforced isolation, this God idea as the central religious truth for the human race.

Second. We recognize in the Bible the record of the consecration of the Jewish people to its mission as priest of the one God, and value it as the most potent instrument of religious and moral instruction. We hold that the modern discoveries of scientific researches in the domains of nature and history are not antagonistic to the doctrines of Judaism, the Bible reflecting the primitive ideas of its own age, and at times clothing its conception of Divine Providence and justice, dealing with man in miraculous narratives.

Third. We recognize in the Mosaic legislation a system of training the Jewish people for its mission during its national life in Palestine, and to-day we accept as binding only the moral laws, and maintain only such ceremonies as elevate and sanctify our lives, but reject all such as are not adapted to the views and habits of modern civilization.

Fourth. We hold that all such Mosaic and rabbinical laws as regulate diet, priestly purity, and dress, originated in ages and under the influence of ideas altogether foreign to our present mental and spiritual state. They fail to impress the modern Jew with a spirit of priestly holiness; their observance in our days is apt rather to obstruct than to further modern spiritual elevation.

Fifth. We recognize, in the modern era of universal culture of heart and intellect, the approaching of the realization of Israel's great messianic hope for the establishment of the kingdom of truth, justice, and peace among all men. We consider ourselves no longer a nation, but a religious community, and therefore expect neither a return to Palestine, nor a sacrificial worship under the sons of Aaron, nor the restoration of any of the laws concerning the Jewish state.

270

Sixth. We recognize in Judaism a progressive religion, ever striving to be in accord with the postulates of reason. We are convinced of the utmost necessity of preserving the historical identity with our great past. Christianity and Islam being daughter religions of Judaism, we appreciate their providential mission to aid in the spreading of monotheistic and moral truth. We acknowledge that the spirit of broad humanity of our age is our ally in the fulfillment of our mission, and therefore, we extend the hand of fellowship to all who operate with us in the establishment of the reign of truth and righteousness among men.

Seventh. We reassert the doctrine of Judaism, that the soul of man is immortal, grounding this belief on the divine nature of the human spirit, which forever finds bliss in righteousness and misery in wickedness. We reject as ideas not rooted in Judaism the beliefs both in bodily resurrection and in Gehenna and Eden (Hell and Paradise) as abodes for everlasting punishment or reward.

Eighth. In full accordance with the spirit of Mosaic legislation, which strives to regulate the relation between rich and poor, we deem it our duty to participate in the great task of modern times, to solve on the basis of justice and righteousness, the problems presented by the contrasts and evils of the present organization of society.

At its founding in 1889, the Central Conference of American Rabbis (CCAR), the Reform rabbinical organization, adopted the platform in toto, and it remained the major statement of the basic tenets of Reform Judaism until its extensive revision by the CCAR in Columbus, Ohio, in 1937.

APPENDIX III
Charter of The Jewish Theological Seminary of America

The Jewish Theological Seminary of America was incorporated through an act of the legislature of the State of New York, being Chapter 56 of the Laws of 1902, which became law on February 20, 1902, with the approval of the Governor. The new corporation was the successor to the Jewish Theological Seminary Association, which had been operating the school since 1886. Over the years, the original charter has been amended several times. Selected paragraphs of the present charter and the dates on which they became operative follow.

Sec. 1. (As amended in 1951)

Jacob H. Schiff, Leonard Lewisoba, Daniel Guggenheim, Mayer Sulzberger, Cyrus Adler, Simon Guggenheim, Adolphus S. Solomons, Felix M. Warburg, Philip S. Henry and Louis Marshall and their associates and successors, are hereby constituted a body corporate by the name of The Jewish Theological Seminary of America, in perpetuity, to be located in the City of New York, for the purpose of establishing and maintaining a theological seminary for the perpetuation of the tenets of the Jewish religion; the cultivation of Hebrew literature; the pursuit of biblical, rabbinic, theological and archaeological research; the integration of Jewish and general philosophy and learning; the advancement of Jewish scholarship; the establishment of a library; the fostering of the study of Jewish sacred music; the education and training of Jewish Rabbis and teachers; the ordination of rabbis; the promotion of better understanding among people of different religious and ethnic backgrounds and the fostering of deeper insights into the philosophy and thought of religion; establishing and maintaining a college of liberal arts. Such corporation shall possess the general powers prescribed by the General Corporation Law of the State of New York except as the same are inconsistent herewith...

Sec. 3. (As amended in 1958)

The directors shall have power to confer the degrees of bachelor of divinity (B.D.), bachelor of Hebrew literature (B.H.L.), master of Hebrew literature (M.H.L.). doctor of Hebrew literature (D.H.L.), bachelor of sacred music (S.M.B.), master of sacred music (S.M.M.), doctor of sacred music (S.M.D.), bachelor of religious education (B.R.E.), master of religious education (M.R.E.), doctor of religious education (D.R.E.), master of comparative religion (M.C.R.), doctor of comparative religion (D.C.R.), master of theology (M.Th.), doctor of theology (D.Th.), bachelor of arts (B.A.), master of arts (M.A.), and doctor of philosophy (Ph.D.), in course, and the honorary degrees of doctor of divinity (D.D.), doctor of Jewish theology (D.J.T.), doctor of sacred theology (S.T.D.), doctor of humane letters (L.H.D.), doctor of laws (LL.D.), doctor of Hebrew letters (Litt. H.D.), and doctor of letters (Litt. D.), in conformity with the rules of the Regents of the University and the regulations of the Commissioner of Education for registration of institutions of higher education, and, in testimony thereof, to award suitable diplomas, and also to award certificates of proficiency to persons qualified to act as Hazanim...

Sec. 6. (As enacted in 1902) This act shall take effect immediately.

APPENDIX IV
Preamble to the Constitution of The United Synagogue
(adopted in 1913)

The purpose of this organization is as follows:

The advancement of the cause of Judaism in America and the maintenance of Jewish tradition in its historical continuity,

To assert and establish loyalty to the Torah and its historical exposition,

To further the observance of the Sabbath and the dietary laws,

To preserve in the service the reference to Israel's past and the hopes for Israel's restoration,

To maintain the traditional character of the liturgy with Hebrew as the language of prayer,

To foster Jewish religious life in the home, as expressed in traditional observances,

To encourage the establishment of Jewish religious schools, in the curricula of which the study of the Hebrew language and literature shall be given a prominent place, both as the key to the true understanding of Judaism, and as a bond holding together the scattered communities of Israel throughout the world.

It shall be the aim of the United Synagogue of America, while not endorsing the innovations introduced by any of its constituent bodies, to embrace all elements essentially loyal to traditional Judaism and in sympathy with the purposes outlined above.

APPENDIX V
The Structure of the Mishnah

Title   **Subject**

A) *Seder Zeraim* (Agricultural Law)

    1) Berakhot   Blessings
    2) Pe'ah   Gleanings from the harvest (Vayikra 19:9-10)
    3) Demai   Doubtfully tithed produce
    4) Kilayim   Diverse kinds (Devarim 22:9-11)
    5) Shevi'it   The Sabbatical Year (Shemot 23:10-11)
    6) Terumot   Heave offering (Vayikra 22:10-14)
    7) Ma'aserot   Tithes (Bamidbar 18:21)
    8) Ma'aser Sheni   Second Tithe (Devarim 14: 22ff.)
    9) Hallah   Dough offering (Bamidbar 15:17-21)
    10) Orlah   The fruit of young trees (Vayikra 19:23-25)
    11) Bikkurim   First fruits (Vayikra 26:1-11)

B) *Seder Mo'ed* (Special Days)

    1) Shabbat   The Sabbath
    2) Eruvin   Sabbath limits
    3) Pesahim   Passover
    4) Shekalim   The Shekel dues (Shemot 30:11-16)
    5) Yoma   The Day of Atonement
    6) Sukkah   The Feast of Tabernacles
    7) Betzah   Festival laws
    8) Rosh Hashanah   Rosh Hashanah and other new years
    9) Ta'anit   Fast days
    10) Megillah   Purim
    11) Mo'ed Katan   The intermediate days of Festivals
    12) Hagigah   The Festival offering (Devarim16:16-17)

C) *Seder Nashim* ("Women" – i.e., Family Law)

    1) Yevamot   Levirate marriage (Devarim 25:5-10)
    2) Ketubbot   Marriage contracts
    3) Nedarim   Vows (Bamidbar 30)
    4) Nazir   The Nazirite (Bamidbar 6)
    5) Sotah   The suspected adulteress (Bamidbar 5:11 ff.)
    6) Gittin   Divorce
    7) Kiddushin   Betrothal, marriage

D) *Seder Nezikin* ("Damages" – i.e., Civil and Criminal Law)

    1) Bava Kamma   Torts (e.g.. personal injury, property damage)
    2) Bava Metzia   Civil law (e.g., questions of ownership, renting, etc.)
    3) Bava Batra   Property law
    4) Sanhedrin   Courts (procedures, jurisdiction, remedies)

5)	Makkot	Whipping (Devarim 25:2), cities of refuge (Bamidbar 35:9ff.)
6)	Shevu'ot	Oaths
7)	Eduyyot	Testimonies, hierarchy of courts
8)	Avodah Zarah	Idolatry, wine, milk and meat
9)	Avot	Moral maxims
10)	Horayot	Erroneous rulings of the court (Vayikra 4:22ff.)

E) *Seder Kodashim* (Sacrifices)

1)	Zevahim	Animal offerings
2)	Menahot	Meal offerings
3)	Hullin	Animals slaughtered for food
4)	Bekhorot	Offering of first-born animals (Devarim 15:19ff.)
5)	Arakhin	Vows of valuation (Vayikra 27:1-8)
6)	Temurah	Substitution of offerings (Vayikra 27:10)
7)	Keritot	Extirpation (Vayikra 18:29)
8)	Me'ilah	Sacrileges (Vayikra 5:15-16)
9)	Tamid	The daily sacrifices (Bamidbar 28:3-4)
10)	Middot	Measurements of the Temple
11)	Kinnim	The bird offering (Vayikra 5:7ff.)

F) *Seder Tohorot* (Purity)

1)	Kelim	Impurity of articles
2)	Oholot	Impurity through overshadowing (Bamidbar 19:14-15)
3)	Nega'im	Leprosy (Vayikra 13-14)
4)	Parah	Red heifer (Bamidbar 19)
5)	Tohorot	Ritual purity
6)	Mikva'ot	The ritual pool of water for purification
7)	Niddah	The menstruant woman
8)	Makhshirin	Liquid that predisposes food to become impure (Vayikra 11:37-38)
9)	Zavim	Emissions (Vayikra 15)
10)	Tevul Yom	Impurity between immersion and sunset (Vayikra 22:6-7)
11)	Yadayim	The impurity of hands
12)	Uktzin	Parts of plants susceptible to impurity

THE WORLD OF HALAKHAH -- הֲלָכָה (JEWISH LAW)

How do *we* as Conservative Jews get answers to questions involving Jewish Law? Below is a typical example.

> A person has a question about Jewish Law

> They ask their rabbi for a decision. Most often the rabbi can give them an answer to their question, and the process ends here. If not...

> If the rabbi cannot answer the question, or if the rabbi thinks the question needs to be discussed on a Movement wide level s/he asks the Committee on Law and standards of the Conservative Movement. The Committee is comprised of rabbis and scholars from throughout the Movement. Different positions on a topic are presented, discussed and voted upon.

How does Jewish law get determined? Below are some of the major sources from which Jewish Law has been determined and is determined in our time (with approximate dates for when the source was compiled). The arrows from one source to another mean the source had some influence on the later source. For example the Torah directly affects all works of Jewish Law, so the arrows go out from the Torah to all of the sources. Since the Torah is the *first* source in Jewish Law, no arrows go to the Torah.

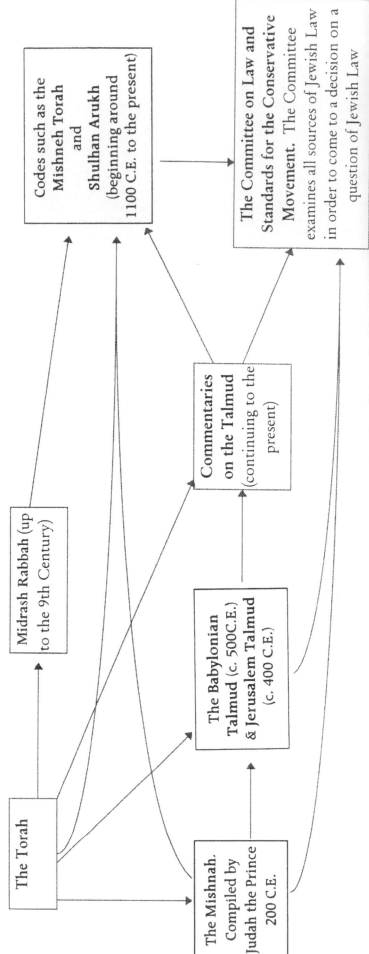

Codes such as the **Mishneh Torah** and **Shulhan Arukh** (beginning around 1100 C.E. to the present)

The Committee on Law and Standards for the Conservative Movement. The Committee examines all sources of Jewish Law in order to come to a decision on a question of Jewish Law

Midrash Rabbah (up to the 9th Century)

Commentaries on the Talmud (continuing to the present)

The Babylonian Talmud (c. 500C.E.) & Jerusalem Talmud (c. 400 C.E.)

The Torah

The Mishnah. Compiled by Judah the Prince 200 C.E.

FOR FURTHER READING

Conservative Jews and others interested in Conservative Judaism should definitely read the new, official statement of the philosophy of the Conservative Movement:

> *Emet Ve-Emunah: Statement of the Principles of Conservative Judaism* (New York: Jewish Theological Seminary of America, The Rabbinical Assembly, United Synagogue of America, Women's League for Conservative Judaism, and Federation of Jewish Men's Clubs, 1988).

To help people study that document seriously, the Conservative Movement has published two study guides, one for adults and one for teenagers:

> *Willing, Learning and Striving: A Course Guide for Teaching Jewish Youth Based on Emet Ve-Emunah*, by Steven M. Brown.

> *Willing, Learning and Striving: A Course Guide to Emet Ve-Emunah -- Sources and Approaches for Teaching Adults*, by Elliot Dorff and Sheldon Dorph.

Emet Ve-Emunah and its two study guides are both available through the United Synagogue Book Service.

Among the best sources for further reading on Conservative Judaism are one general book on the movement and three books which include a number of essays by various people in the Movement:

> Robert Gordis, *Understanding Conservative Judaism* (New York: Rabbinical Assembly, 1978).

> Seymour Siegel, ed., *Conservative Judaism and Jewish Law* (New York: The Rabbinical Assembly, 1977).

> Seymour Siegel and Elliot Gertel, eds. *God in the Teachings of Conservative Judaism* (New York: Rabbinical Assembly, 1985).

> Mordecai Waxman, ed., *Tradition and Change* (New York: The Rabbinical Assembly, 1958).

The other ongoing sources of thought, discussions, decisions, and programs in the Conservative Movement are the journals of its various arms, including:

Conservative Judaism (The Rabbinical Assembly and The Jewish Theological Seminary of America)

Proceedings of the Rabbinical Assembly

The Torchlight (Federation of Jewish Men's Clubs)

The United Synagogue Review

Women's League Outlook

Beyond that, students interested in Conservative approaches to **theological** issues should consult one or more of the books listed in endnotes 7-9 and 12-23 of Chapter IV.

Those interested in further reading of **halakhic decisions** made by the Conservative Movement's Committee on Jewish Law and Standards should consult the ongoing reports of committee's Chair in *The United Synagogue Review*, the fuller reports in the annual *Rabbinical Assembly Proceedings*, and, for the years 1980-1985, the book entitled *Proceedings of the Committee on Jewish Law and Standards of the Conservative Movement, 1980-1985* (New York: Rabbinical Assembly, 1988). The Committee plans on publishing all of its approved responsa for subsequent years as well in book form, and the book covering the ones approved between 1985-1990 is due out soon. In addition, the Israeli Conservative rabbinate has a Committee on Jewish Law (*Va'ad Halakhah*), and it has published its decisions in Hebrew, with English summaries, in (to date) five volumes, entitled *Responsa of the Va'ad Halakhah of the Rabbinical Assembly of Israel*. A very good collection of Conservative theories of Jewish law and some responsa that appeared by its publication date of 1977 is *Conservative Judaism and Jewish Law*, edited by Seymour Siegel and Elliot Gertel (New York: Rabbinical Assembly, 1977); although as of this date it is unfortunately out of print, it is undoubtedly available in many synagogue and university libraries. For a comprehensive listing of decisions and articles written on specific issues of Jewish law by Conservative authors, see David Golinkin, *An Index of Conservative Responsa and Practical Halakhic Studies: 1917-1990* (New York: Rabbinical Assembly, 1992). See also *Summary Index: The Committee on Jewish Law and Standards* (New York: Rabbinical Assembly, 1994, with annual supplements).

Books on **Jewish legal history and thought** by individual Conservative rabbis include the following:

Boaz Cohen, *Law and Tradition in Judaism* (1959).

Elliot Dorff and Arthur Rosett, *A Living Tree: The Roots and Growth of Jewish Law* (1988).

Elliot N. Dorff, *Mitzvah Means Commandment* (1989 – a USY sourcebook).

David Golinkin, *Halakhah For Our Time: A Conservative Approach to Jewish Law* (1991).

Robert Gordis, *The Dynamics of Judaism: A Study in Jewish Law* (1990).

Louis Jacobs, *A Tree of Life: Diversity, Flexibility, and Creativity in Jewish Law* (1984).

David Novak, *Law and Theology in Judaism*, Series I (1974) and Series II (1976).

Joel Roth, *The Halakhic Process: A Systematic Analysis* (1986).

Philip Sigal, *New Dimensions in Judaism* (1972).

For books on **Jewish rituals** from a Conservative perspective, consider the following *USY sourcebooks*:

Stephen Garfinkel, ed., *Slow Down and Live: A Guide to Shabbat Observance and Enjoyment* (1981).

Stephen Garfinkel, ed., *The Symbols of Judaism: The Challenge to Learn and to Create* (1975).

Isaac Klein, *A Time to Be Born, A Time to Die* (1976).

Sam Kieffer, *The Jewish Life Cycle: Rituals and Concepts* (date unknown).

James Lebeau, *Ma'alin Bakodesh – The Jewish Dietary Laws* (1982).

Additional books by Conservative authors on Jewish religious practice (with some chapters on Jewish ethics, in some of the books below), again too many to enumerate, include the following:

Bradley Shavit Artson, *It's A Mitzvah: Step-By-Step to Jewish Living* West Orange, NJ: Behrman House, and New York: Rabbinical Assembly, 1995).

Samuel H. Dresner, *The Sabbath* (New York: United Synagogue of America,1970).

Samuel H. Dresner and Seymour Siegel, *The Jewish Dietary Laws: Their Meaning for Our Time and A Guide to Observance* (New York: Rabbinical Assembly and United Synagogue Commission on Jewish Education, 1959, 1982).

Samuel H. Dresner and Byron Sherwin, *Judaism: The Way of Sanctification* (New York: United Synagogue of America, 1978).

Susan Grossman and Rivka Haut, eds., *Daughters of the King: Women and the Synagogue* (Philadelphia: Jewish Publication Society, 1992).

Susannah Heschel, *On Being a Jewish Feminist: A Reader* (New York: Schocken, 1983).

Louis Jacobs, *The Book of Jewish Practice* (West Orange, NJ: Behrman House, 1987).

Isaac Klein, *Guide to Jewish Religious Practice* (New York: Jewish Theological Seminary of America, 1979).

Isaac Klein, *Responsa and Halakhic Studies* (New York: Ktav, 1975).

Debra Orenstein, ed., *Lifecycles: Jewish Women on Life Passages and Personal Milestones* (Woodstock, VT: Jewish Lights Publishing, 1994).

Leo Trepp, *The Complete Book of Jewish Observance* (New York: Behrman House and Summit Books, 1980).

Ron Wolfson, *A Time to Mourn, A Time to Comfort* (New York: Federation of Jewish Men's Clubs and Los Angeles: University of Judaism, 1993).

Ron Wolfson, *The Passover Seder* (New York: Federation of Jewish Men's Clubs and Los Angeles: University of Judaism, 1993).

Ron Wolfson, *Seder Hanukkah* (New York: Federation of Jewish Men's Clubs and Los Angeles: University of Judaism, 1990).

Ron Wolfson, *The Shabbat Seder* (New York: Federation of Jewish Men's Clubs and Los Angeles: University of Judaism, 1985).

For books on various **moral theories and issues** by writers affiliated with the Conservative movement, review *the list of USY sourcebooks* on the back cover of this book, for many of them deal with Jewish moral issues from a Conservative perspective, as, for example, the following:

Carl Astor, *...Who Makes People Different: Jewish Perspectives on the Disabled* (1984).

Barry Cytron and Earl Schwartz, *When Life is in the Balance; Life and Death Decisions in Light of the Jewish Tradition* (1986).

Barry Cytron and Earl Schwartz, *Who Renews Creation* (1993).

David M. Feldman, *The Jewish Family Relationship* (1975).

Bernard, Novick, *In God's Image: Making Jewish Decisions About the Body* (1994).

Barbara Fortgang Summers, *Community and Responsibility in the Jewish Tradition* (1979).

In addition, books and articles by Conservative authors on Jewish ethical theories and on moral issues from a Jewish perspective – which, frankly, are far too many to enumerate – include the following:

Bradley Artson, *Love Peace and Pursue Peace: A Jewish Response to War and Nuclear Annihilation* (New York: United Synagogue of America,1988).

Elliot N. Dorff, *"This Is My Beloved, This Is My Friend": A Rabbinic Letter on Intimate Relations* (New York: Rabbinical Assembly, 1996).

Elliot N. Dorff and Louis E. Newman, eds., *Contemporary Jewish Ethics and Morality: A Reader* (New York: Oxford University Press,1995).

Wayne Dosick, *The Business Bible: Ten New Commandments for Creating an Ethical Workplace* (New York: William Morrow, 1993).

David M. Feldman, *Birth Control in Jewish Law* (New York: New York University Press, 1968; republished in 1974 by Schocken as *Marital Relations, Birth Control, and Abortion in Jewish Law*).

David M. Feldman, *Health and Medicine in the Jewish Tradition* (New York: Crossroad, 1986).

Richard Freund, *Understanding Jewish Ethics* (San Francisco: EMText, 1990).

Michael Gold, *And Hannah Wept: Infertility, Adoption, and the Jewish Couple* (Philadelphia: Jewish Publication Society, 1988).

Michael Gold, *Does God Belong in the Bedroom?* (Philadelphia: Jewish Publication Society, 1992).

Robert Gordis, *Judaic Ethics for a Lawless World* (1986).

Byron Sherwin, *In Partnership with God: Contemporary Jewish Law and Ethics* (Syracuse, NY: Syracuse University Press, 1990).

On **the practice and theory of prayer** within the Conservative movement, see, first, the following pages in the two prayer books most widely used in the movement, namely,

Jules Harlow, *Siddur Sim Shalom* (New York: Rabbinical Assembly and United Synagogue of America, 1985), pp. xi-xxxi.

Morris Silverman, Sabbath and Festival Prayer Book (New York: Rabbinical Assembly of America and United Synagogue of America, 1946), pp. iv-xiii, 379-383.

In addition, see the following works by Conservative authors on the **liturgy** (with special recommendation of the new book by Reuven Hammer):

Evelyn Garfiel, *Service of the Heart: A Guide to the Jewish Prayer Book* (New York: Thomas Yoseloff, 1958).

Rose Goldstein, A Time to Pray: A Personal Approach to the Jewish Prayer Book (Bridgeport, CT: Media Judaica, 1972 [a publication of the Women's League for Conservative Judaism]).

Reuven Hammer, *Entering Jewish Prayer: A Guide to Personal Devotion and the Worship Service* (New York: Schocken, 1994).

Abraham Millgram, *Jewish Worship* (Philadelphia: Jewish Publication Society, 1971).

For **understandings of the act of prayer** (that is, discussions about the nature and goals of prayer), see, first, the USY sourcebook on the subject, namely,

Steven M. Brown, *Higher and Higher: Making Jewish Prayer Part of Us* (1980).

The following discussions of prayer by Conservative authors will also be helpful:

Elliot N. Dorff, *Knowing God: Jewish Journeys to the Unknowable* (Northvale, NJ: Jason Aronson, 1992), pp. 149-208.

Abraham Joshua Heschel, *Man's Quest for God: Studies in Prayer and Symbolism* (New York: Charles Scribner's Sons, 1954).

Max Kadushin, *Worship and Ethics* (Evanston, IL: Northwestern University Press, 1963).

In addition, the section of this bibliography devoted to books on Conservative theologies (see above) include a number of books which contain theories of prayer.

The most comprehensive **history** of the early years of the Conservative Movement is Moshe Davis' *The Emergence of Conservative Judaism* (Philadelphia: The Jewish Publication Society of America, 1963). The continuing history of the movement, with emphasis on the halakhic and ideological developments in the last several decades, is treated comprehensively and insightfully by Neil Gillman in his *Conservative Judaism: The New Century* (West Orange, NJ: Behrman House, 1993). A comprehensive collection of biographical sketches of Conservative leaders ordained, in the case of rabbis, before 1962, appears in Pamela S. Nadell, *Conservative Judaism in America: A Biographical Dictionary and Sourcebook* (New York: Greenwood Press, 1988). Those interested in the history of the Movement would also find these books and articles interesting:

Cyrus Adler, *I Have Considered the Days* (Philadelphia: The Jewish Publication Society of America, 1941). The autobiography of Schechter's successor.

Cyrus Adler, "Jacob Schiff," *American Jewish Yearbook*, Vol.23 (1921).

Cyrus Adler, *Lectures, Selected Papers and Addresses* (Philadelphia: Priv. print., 1933).

Cyrus Adler, "Solomon Schechter," *American Jewish Yearbook,* Vol.18 (1916).

John Appel, "The *Trefa* Banquet," *Commentary,* Vol.41, No. 2 (February,1966), 75-78.

Max Artz, "The Legacy of Solomon Schechter," *Conservative Judaism,* Vol. XI, No. 2 (Winter, 1957), 5-12.

Norman Bentwich, *Solomon Schechter: A Biography* (New York: The Burning Bush Press, 1940).

Israel Friedlaender, *Past and Present* (New York: The Burning Bush Press. [1919], 1961).

Eli Ginzberg, *Students, Scholars and Saints* (New York: Meridian Books, 1928, 1958).

Abraham Karp, ed., *The Jewish experience in America* (New York: Ktav Publishing House., Inc., 1969), Vol. 5, "Solomon Schechter comes to America."

Bertram Wallace Korn, *German-Jewish Intellectual Influences on American Jewish Life 1824-1972* (Syracuse University, 1972).

Bernard Mandelbaum, *Tales of the Fathers of the Conservative Movement* (New York: Shengold, 1989).

Herbert Parzen, *Architects of Conservative Judaism* (New York: Jonathan David, 1964).

Herbert Rosenblum, *Conservative Judaism: A Contemporary History* (New York: United Synagogue of America, 1983).

David Rudavsky, *Modern Jewish Religious Movements* (New York: Behrman House, Inc., Publishers, 1967). Good background material on 19th and 20th century Jewish thought.

Solomon Schechter, *Studies in Judaism* (Philadelphia: The Jewish Publication Society of America, 1958).

And finally, those interested in **sociological** analyses of the Conservative Movement should consult Marshall Sklare, *Conservative Judaism: An American Religious Movement* (New York: Schocken Books, 1955, 1972); and Charles S. Leibman, *The Ambivalent American Jew* (Philadelphia: The Jewish Publication Society of America, 1973), Chapters 3 and 5.

ABOUT THE AUTHOR

ELLIOT N. DORFF is currently Rector and Professor of Philosophy at the University of Judaism in Los Angeles. After receiving his A.B. *summa cum laude* from Columbia College in 1965, he was ordained as a rabbi by the Jewish Theological Seminary of America in 1970. In 1971 he received his Ph.D. in Philosophy from Columbia University.

Rabbi Dorff's publications include over one hundred articles on Jewish ethics, law, and theology, as well as five books besides this one: *Jewish Law and Modern Ideology* (1970); *A Living Tree: The Roots and Growth of Jewish Law* (with Arthur Rosett) (1988); *Mitzvah Means Commandment* (1989); *Knowing God: Jewish Journeys to the Unknowable* (1992); and, as co-editor with Louis Newman, *Contemporary Jewish Ethics and Morality* (1995). He has also written a number of *teshuvot* for the Conservative Movement's Committee on Jewish Law and Standards, and he wrote, for and with the Rabbinical Assembly's Commission on Human Sexuality, *"This Is My Beloved, This Is My Friend": A Rabbinic Letter on Intimate Relations*. He is currently working on a book on Jewish medical ethics.

Rabbi Dorff is a member of several national commissions of the Conservative Movement, including the Commission on the Philosophy of the Conservative Movement, the Editorial Committee for the new Conservative Torah commentary, and the Committee on Jewish Law and Standards and its Subcommittee on Bioethics. In Spring, 1993, he served on the Ethics Committee of President Clinton's Health Care Task Force. He is also a past chairman of the Jewish Hospice Commission of Los Angeles, a vice-president of Jewish Family Service of Los Angeles and chair of its Ethics Committee, co-chair of the Priest-Rabbi Dialogue sponsored by the Board of Rabbis of Southern California and the Los Angeles Archdiocese, and a member of the Ethics Committee of U.C.L.A. Medical Center.

Elliot Dorff and his wife, Marlynn, have four children. He is a member of the United Synagogue National Youth Commission and led a USY Pilgrimage group to Israel in 1969. He has served as Rabbi-in-Residence at Camp Ramah in California for fifteen years, has taught in the Los Angeles Hebrew High School for eleven years, and has long been active in other aspects of the youth activities of the Conservative Movement.